The Ecology of Food

The Ecology of Food

Sustainable Food Systems and Diets

Edited by

Nicolas Bricas, Damien Conaré and Marie Walser

BLOOMSBURY ACADEMIC
LONDON • NEW YORK • OXFORD • NEW DELHI • SYDNEY

BLOOMSBURY ACADEMIC
Bloomsbury Publishing Plc, 50 Bedford Square, London, WC1B 3DP, UK
Bloomsbury Publishing Inc, 1359 Broadway, New York, NY 10018, USA
Bloomsbury Publishing Ireland, 29 Earlsfort Terrace, Dublin 2, D02 AY28, Ireland

BLOOMSBURY, BLOOMSBURY ACADEMIC and the Diana logo are trademarks of
Bloomsbury Publishing Plc

First published in Great Britain 2026

Cover design: Grace Ridge

A catalogue record for this book is available from the British Library.

Library of Congress Cataloging-in-Publication Data available

ISBN: HB: 978-1-350-54494-9
PB: 978-1-350-54495-6
ePDF: 978-1-350-54493-2
eBook: 978-1-350-54496-3

Typeset by Amnet
Printed and bound in Great Britain

For product safety related questions contact productsafety@bloomsbury.com.

To find out more about our authors and books visit www.bloomsbury.com
and sign up for our newsletters.

Contents

Illustrations

Authors, contributors and proofreaders

Arlène Alpha is a researcher in political economy at CIRAD, UMR MoISA (Montpellier Interdisciplinary center on Sustainable Agri-food systems), Montpellier, France.

Sylvie Avallone is a researcher in food science and nutrition at L'Institut Agro Montpellier, UMR MoISA (Montpellier Interdisciplinary center on Sustainable Agri-food systems), Montpellier, France.

Nicolas Bricas is a researcher in socio-economy at CIRAD, UMR MoISA (Montpellier Interdisciplinary center on Sustainable Agri-food systems) and Head of the UNESCO Chair in World Food Systems, Montpellier, France.

Damien Conaré is Secretary-General of the UNESCO Chair in World Food Systems at L'Institut Agro Montpellier, France.

Mathilde Coudray is a project manager at RENETA, Montpellier, France.

Nicole Darmon is Honorary Research Director in nutrition at INRAE, UMR MoISA (Montpellier Interdisciplinary center on Sustainable Agri-food systems), Montpellier, France.

Anindita Dasgupta is Associate Professor and Director of the School of Liberal Arts and Sciences and Associate Director of the Centre for Asian Modernisation Studies, Taylor's University, Kuala Lumpur, Malaysia.

Benoît Daviron is a retired researcher in political economy at CIRAD, UMR MoISA (Montpellier Interdisciplinary center on Sustainable Agri-food systems), Montpellier, France.

Vincent Devictor is a researcher in ecology at the CNRS, Isem (Institut des sciences de l'évolution), Montpellier, France.

Mathilde Douillet is an economist and former Head of the Sustainable Food Program at the Daniel and Nina Carasso Foundation, Paris, France.

Anne Dupuy is a researcher in sociology at Toulouse Jean Jaurès University, UMR Certop (Centre d'étude et de recherche Travail Organisation Pouvoir), Toulouse, France.

Muriel Figuié is a researcher in sociology at CIRAD, UMR MoISA (Montpellier Interdisciplinary center on Sustainable Agri-food systems), Montpellier, France.

Claude Fischler is a social scientist and Emeritus Research Director at the CNRS, UMR IIAC (Institut interdisciplinaire d'anthropologie du contemporain, EHESS), Paris, France.

Estelle Fourat is a social scientist and research coordinator at MSH-SUD, Montpellier, France.

Stéphane Fournier is a researcher in economics at L'Institut Agro Montpellier, UMR Innovation (Innovation et développement dans l'agriculture et l'alimentation), Montpellier, France.

Tristan Fournier is a researcher in sociology at CNRS, IRIS (Institut de recherche interdisciplinaire sur les enjeux sociaux), Paris, France.

Michelle Holdsworth is a researcher in nutrition at IRD, UMR MoISA (Montpellier Interdisciplinary center on Sustainable Agri-food systems), Montpellier, France.

Bernard Hubert is an emeritus researcher in ecology at INRAE and Director of Studies at EHESS, UR Ecodevelopment and Norbert Elias Centre, Avignon, France.

Aurélie Javelle is a researcher in anthropology at L'Institut Agro Montpellier, UMR Innovation (Innovation et développement dans l'agriculture et l'alimentation), Montpellier, France.

Myriam Kessari is a researcher in economics at Ciheam-IAMM, UMR MoISA (Montpellier Interdisciplinary center on Sustainable Agri-food systems), Montpellier, France.

Olivier Lepiller is a researcher in sociology at CIRAD, UMR MoISA (Montpellier Interdisciplinary center on Sustainable Agri-food systems), Montpellier, France.

Ronan Le Velly is a researcher in sociology at L'Institut Agro Montpellier, UMR Innovation (Innovation et développement dans l'agriculture et l'alimentation), Montpellier, France.

Jean-Marc Louvin is a campaign coordinator at ICLEI Europe.

Danièle Magda is a researcher in ecology at INRAE, UMR AGIR (Agroécologie, innovations et territoires), Toulouse, France.

Éric Malézieux is a researcher in agronomy at CIRAD, UR Hortsys (Fonctionnement agroécologique et performances des systèmes de culture horticoles), Montpellier, France.

Magalie Marais is a researcher in management science at Montpellier Business School, MRM (Montpellier Research in Management), Montpellier, France.

Maryline Meyer is a researcher in management science at Montpellier Business School, MRM (Montpellier Research in Management), Montpellier, France.

Claire Mouquet-Rivier is a researcher in nutrition at IRD, UMR QUALISUD (Démarche intégrée pour l'obtention d'aliments de qualité), Montpellier, France.

Marie Mourad is a sociologist and independent consultant, New York, United States.

Paule Moustier is a researcher in economics at CIRAD, UMR MoISA (Montpellier Interdisciplinary center on Sustainable Agri-food systems), Montpellier, France.

Florence Palpacuer is a researcher in management science at Montpellier University, MRM (Montpellier Research in Management), Montpellier, France.

Véronique Pardo is an anthropologist at OCHA (Observatoire Cniel des habitudes alimentaires), Pôle Prospective, Cniel, Paris, France.

Dominique Paturel is a researcher in management science at INRAE, UMR Innovation (Innovation et développement dans l'agriculture et l'alimentation), Montpellier, France.

Coline Perrin is a researcher in geography at INRAE, UMR Innovation (Innovation et développement dans l'agriculture et l'alimentation), Montpellier, France.

Jean-Louis Rastoin is an honorary professor of management sciences at L'Institut Agro Montpellier, founder and former holder of the UNESCO Chair in World Food Systems, Montpellier, France.

Pauline Scherer is a sociologist, Vrac & Cocinas association (Coopérations citoyennes pour l'alimentation et la solidarité), Montpellier, France.

Audrey Soula is an anthropologist at Institut Lyfe, Lyon, France.

Jacques Tassin is a researcher in ecology at CIRAD, UPR Forêts et Sociétés, Montpellier, France.

Leïla Temri is a researcher in management sciences at L'Institut Agro Montpellier, UMR MoISA (Montpellier Interdisciplinary center on Sustainable Agri-food systems), Montpellier, France.

Laurence Tibère is a researcher in sociology at Toulouse Jean Jaurès University, CNRS, UMR Certop (Centre d'étude et de recherche Travail Organisation Pouvoir), Toulouse, France.

Gilles Trystram is a researcher in process engineering at AgroParisTech, UMR SayFood (Paris-Saclay Food & Bioproduct Engineering), Paris, France.

Élodie Valette is a researcher in geography at CIRAD, UMR ART-Dev (Acteurs, ressources et territoires dans le développement), Montpellier, France.

Marie Walser is a project manager at the UNESCO Chair in World Food Systems, L'Institut Agro Montpellier, France.

Hayat Zirari is a researcher in anthropology at Hassan II University, Communication, Society and Organisations Laboratory, Casablanca, Morocco.

The authors, contributors and proofreaders from the research organizations CIRAD, INRAE, L'Institut Agro Montpellier, IRD and Ciheam-IAMM, whose research units are in Montpellier, are part of the University of Montpellier consortium (France).

Preface

The phagic dimension

Claude Fischler

From blade of grass to earthworm

Imagine a blade of grass grazed by a ruminant such as a buffalo or gazelle. The gazelle is eaten by its predator – say, a lion. The lion leaves the remains of its meal to vultures, hyenas and other scavengers, and then to detritus feeders such as earthworms. Bacteria and other decomposing microorganisms subsequently intervene and further contribute to the humus enrichment process, but they may themselves be preyed upon by protozoa.

In 1866, Ernst Haeckel coined the term 'ecology' to refer to the study of interactions between species and their environment. Ecologists subsequently realized that the environment (or biotope) interacts in a complex way with the species living in it (biocenosis), modifying these inhabitants while in turn being modified by them – together, this constitutes an ecosystem.

The ecosystem can thus be described in 'phagic' terms – that is, according to who eats whom. Researchers have designed and measured the so-called trophic index, which helps determine the position of species in the food chain – that of *Homo sapiens* is around 2.2, which is close to that of, say, anchovies or pigs (Bonhommeau et al., 2013).[1] *H. sapiens*' position in the trophic chain, therefore in the ecosystem, can be measured precisely because this species is part of what is commonly called 'nature', which means we should have second thoughts about the nature–culture dichotomy or any other way of opposing 'human' and 'natural'.

---

[1] The trophic index represents the number of intermediaries between primary producers and their predators. *Homo sapiens* would therefore not be the top predator it is commonly thought to be, unless one considers the species in non-food terms. The trophic index markedly varies depending on the diet of human groups.

The trophic (nutritional) dimension is essential to ecosystems and to our planet's ecosphere. The topic of food therefore obviously raises questions pertaining to the fundamental mechanisms of life. But it also relates to society – to the distribution of edible resources gathered or produced and therefore to social organization and the economy, to daily life and history, to solidarity and inequality, to sharing and competition and so on. Inevitably, food studies must be ecological and multi-, inter- and transdisciplinary, encompassing a diverse range of disciplines, including the social sciences and biology. Yet – and perhaps because of this – social scientists have long had little to say about food.

For almost fifteen years, the UNESCO Chair has disproved this latter statement. With food as the central issue, it has been relentlessly presenting research from multiple disciplines, fieldwork as well as reflections and 'real-life experiments' from around the world. The watchword of 'decompartmentalizing knowledge' echoes the call of the French sociologist and philosopher Edgar Morin – further relayed by UNESCO – to 'close the knowledge gap' by breaking down the 'Great Wall of China between spheres of knowledge'. As Morin once remarked, 'brain and body are studied in biology departments while the mind and social life are studied in psychology and sociology departments'. The present book wraps up a decade-long streak of relentless, painstaking research gathering knowledge on the phagic dimension of *H. sapiens*.

This preface does not aim to outline the history of food research. Instead, based on a few examples – though at the risk of overlooking some key authors – it illustrates how food can be investigated from an ecological perspective, while highlighting the project that underpins this book and reflecting on the future and the looming issues that may arise over the next decade.

We first see that food research in the social sciences has lagged, marked by indifference, prejudice or mere inertia. We then observe that food has sometimes been treated as an ancillary topic rather than a specific focus of research. Finally, we briefly review the time period during which food became a flourishing and even prolific research theme, while pondering the potential emergence of social demand.

'Below the belt'

Quite plainly, it seems that there has been a kind of food blindness in the social sciences. Some pioneering researchers may well have been adversely affected by this indifference, with their research lacking support or attracting little attention.

Many disciplines have long resisted exchange, communication, the free and unhampered transgression of the divide between disciplines, and even any form of mixing and merging.

Hence, in the 1930s, the British anthropologist Audrey Richards, a student of Bronislaw Malinowski and pioneer of an interdisciplinary approach to food and nutrition, was astounded that food, being the most basic biological need, received so little interest in the social sciences – unlike sexuality, which she believed psychoanalysis showcased excessively. According to Richards's so-called functionalist perspective, the 'primary biological function' – in other words, nutritional needs – underpinned much of the organization and institutions of the groups she studied. Yet at the same time, 'the biological facts of appetite and diet are themselves shaped by human relationships and traditional activities'. This was in some ways an ecosystemic vision ahead of its time, while also demonstrating that the organizational process of gathering and exploiting resources before distributing them raises issues of hierarchy, justice, solidarity, legitimacy and division of labour – all of which constitute the building blocks of social organization.

For anthropologists, the reason for the lack of interest in food lay precisely in its primary and basic nature, which these specialists considered self-evident and even trivial. Some of the 'founding fathers' of anthropology and the social sciences before Audrey Richards (as she herself pointed out) had in fact shown an interest in food, but had focused on aspects that were 'naturally' perceived as being of key importance to their discipline – that is, sacred, ritualistic, symbolic, festive, Dionysian or, in a nutshell, extraordinary events. The ordinary features all but fell to the wayside. Émile Durkheim (1982 [1895]), the fervent founder of French sociology who was always keen to delineate, appropriate and legitimize the academic scope of his discipline, sternly stated: 'Each individual drinks, sleeps, eats and reasons, and society has a vital interest in ensuring that these functions are regularly fulfilled. If such matters were social, sociology would have no purpose on its own, and its sphere of activity would overlap that of biology and psychology'. This staunch defence of an academic turf that had only recently been conquered was rooted in an archaic and fairly universal view of food as a 'lowly' and trifling function, which relegates the human condition to the realm of animality – the same stance that sees fasting as a pathway to enlightenment and spirituality.

As the biblical maxim goes, 'Man does not feed on bread alone' but also needs the word of God (Deut. 8:3; Mt. 4:4). Is it therefore any wonder that food has long been literally regarded as a 'below-the-belt' research topic?

An ecology of social bonds

It took an atypical researcher – renowned in his time (somewhat belatedly) yet not as well regarded within as outside academia and keen to stress the fundamental sociological importance of intimate and everyday life – to try to reinstate the ordinary meal as a major sociological and anthropological focus. Georg Simmel (1992 [1910]) wrote an essay on 'The Sociology of the Meal' (Soziologie der Mahlzeit). He showed in particular that the daily meal inextricably combines a highly individual act (what is ingested by one individual cannot be ingested by anyone else) and an event of far-reaching social and collective significance – namely the sharing of a substance and an experience that is repeated, codified and ritualized, while engendering a sense of belonging. In France, Simmel was only slowly and belatedly (re)discovered (around the 1980s). Much later, the sociologist Philippe Joron (2017) noted that Simmel had actually heralded ecosystemic thinking. He wrote that, according to Simmel, 'the social bond is thus situated at the interface between individuals and society, which are embedded in the natural environment. It is in this all-encompassing system – what Edgar Morin later called "an ecology" and Augustin Berque referred to as mesology – that social bonds are forged'.

Half a century after Audrey Richards and six to seven decades after Simmel, the humanities were in a state of flux, caught up in debates and discussions around Marxism, psychoanalysis and structuralism, as well as the events of May 1968 and their aftermath in the case of France. Claude Lévi-Strauss and Mary Douglas had sought to grasp cultural structures – and even culture as a whole – through the prism of cooking and table manners. In his book *Mythologies*, Roland Barthes (1972) had delved into the semiology of steak and chips, wine and milk, culinary photographs in Elle magazine and – with morose delight – displays of 'petty bourgeois ideology' with regard to food. In this context, the topic of food began acquiring an inkling of legitimacy, though more as a gateway than as a subject per se.

A little later, in the 1970s, Pierre Bourdieu (1984 [1979]), in *La Distinction: Critique Sociale du Jugement* (Distinction: A Social Critique of the Judgement of Taste), approached culinary tastes and table manners in the same way and on the same terms as artistic tastes or political preferences, aiming to show that the same class logic applies to social criteria of taste and disgust in these different domains: judgements of taste reflect social position and involve the corresponding habitus. In other words, once again, food is used rather than considered as a specific object. It carries a theoretical challenge that either goes beyond it or reduces it, but it is not envisaged as a scientific object in its own right.

The role of history

The discipline of history specifically devoted attention to food quite early on. The subject was at first treated as a 'minor anecdotal history',[2] flourishing in an indifferent or even condescending vacuum and disregarded by legitimate academic authorities (Toussaint-Samat, 1992). It was also sometimes regarded as a form of highly specialized or marginal history. For instance, in 1932, the Swiss doctor of Polish origin Adam Maurizio (2019 [1932]) published a book on the history of plant food in German, later translated into French as *Histoire de l'alimentation végétale de la préhistoire à nos jours* (History of Plant-Based Food, from Prehistory to Present Days) and reprinted several times.

With the French École des Annales and its successive historical currents ('quantitative history', 'history of mentalities', 'new history' etc.), the discipline initially focused on the material history of food, particularly the provisioning and management of castles, monasteries and other institutions, and, when sources were available, on the food of 'common people'. With Fernand Braudel, then later Jacques Le Goff and Michel Foucault, and subsequently Georges Vigarello, Alain Corbin and many others, history began opening up to new topics (the body, senses and sensibility etc.) and above all to other disciplines in the social sciences. History – perhaps because it is a time-honoured discipline with a sound sense of legitimacy and capable of assimilating and incorporating contributions without feeling overly threatened by them – has embraced anthropo- and socio-historical approaches. Roland Barthes (1961), for instance, published *Pour une psycho-sociologie de l'alimentation* (For a Psychosociology of Food) in a special issue of Annales.

In the book *L'invention du quotidien* (The Practice of Everyday Life [1998]), Michel de Certeau helped legitimize the study of everyday cooking. Somewhat of a maverick, Jean-Paul Aron (1976) then proposed a history of food sensitivities in *Histoire de la sensibilité alimentaire (Le Mangeur du XIXe siècle)* (History of Food Sensibility [The Eater of the Nineteenth Century]), and a little later Jean-Louis Flandrin began focusing his research on a history of taste, the scope of which eluded many of his colleagues (see in particular Flandrin, 1992, 2007).

---

[2] About which the leading historian of food and taste Jean-Louis Flandrin (pers.com) often expressed some degree of annoyance.

Growth and its limits

In 1972, the Club of Rome published the Meadows Report on *The Limits to Growth*. In the same year, Edgar Morin and Nobel Prize–winning biologist Jacques Monod convened a transdisciplinary conference titled *Unity of Man*. Morin later expanded his paper into a book, *Le Paradigme perdu: la nature humaine* (Paradigm Lost: Human Nature), in which he gathered the threads he had been weaving for several years between biology and the social sciences, ecosystems, information and self-organization. The topic of food was only touched upon occasionally, but it seemed apt for an approach similar to that applied in the book, articulating biology and the social sciences. This is how it appeared to this author – still a novice researcher at the time – and it was largely guided by these influences that food became the subject of his PhD thesis and further research (Fischler, 1979, 1990). Other researchers adopting a similar stance on food had to contend with mocking condescension in academic circles regarding the subject of their dissertations, thereby forcing them to assert their legitimacy through the rigorous application of sociological and anthropological tenets (Poulain, 2017b).

Food studies and social trends

In the following years and decades, research on food in the social sciences and humanities grew steadily, to the extent that between 1990 and 2000 a new academic field, food studies, emerged in the United States and Europe. In 2015, thirty-nine universities in nineteen countries worldwide were offering master's degrees on food with a humanities and social sciences (HSS) focus, while eight were titled food studies, most retained the name of a core discipline (Poulain, 2017a).

Many of these programmes are still quite a-theoretical, sometimes leaning towards minor anecdotal history. Food as an object of study nevertheless seems to have gained a certain legitimacy. This could be explained by the ongoing twofold process of individualization and problematization of food.

After 'giving' people the freedom to choose their career, spouse or romantic partner, and in the wake of the legitimization of self-esteem, the historical process of individual empowerment has now reached food, with impacts on consumption patterns, table manners and their transmission to children, relationships between eaters and forms of commensality.

In hunter-gatherer societies – as in the past memories of baby boomers and their parents – what was eaten was clearly considered to be a share, that is, a part of a shared or shareable whole for which the eater was essentially accountable. There was no question of eating more than one's share, loudly voicing a preference or aversion, or expressing disgust (except to forewarn others of a danger), and especially of declaring an intention to shun a particular food or food category. Eating alone was to be avoided and was even viewed with suspicion or repressed in many cultures.

In our individualized world, however, the main driver is freedom of choice rather than the obligation to share. A form of individualist–utilitarian utopia is unfolding in which choosing is paramount, yet choices must be responsible. In this utopia, food would be just another consumer product, if not simply a commodity. Food consumers would then have the freedom to make choices – assuming that they are good, responsible choices – while being supported and protected by public authorities. In a book published in 2010, we mentioned this utopia of the perfect food consumer but may have underestimated its reality:

> In a world of perfect eaters (as understood in this implicit worldview), consumers would walk through the supermarket aisles reading labels, noting the nutritional information and composition of products, comparing their nutrient and calorie contents to recommended nutrient intake levels or to guidelines issued by relevant official bodies, consumer organizations and scientific publications. A pocket computer would clearly be an indispensable shopping accessory for this task. (Fischler and Masson, 2010)

Our mention of a pocket computer shows that we underestimated the potential of the nascent smartphone and did not foresee the advent of the Nutri-Score system,[3] though we did anticipate the emergence of what are now widespread apps.

The truth, however, is that food does not readily fit the consumer product mould, especially as the growing trend towards industrial food processing has led to increasing wariness and even active distrust of processed foods, often marked by outbursts of anger and disgust. A call for standards has been mounting for decades, with people asking: What and how should we eat, how do we choose and how and whom should we trust?

Moreover, this free-choice environment has given rise to issues in dealing with the array of choices, a situation which the psychologist Barry Schwartz (2005) refers to as the paradox or even tyranny of choice and which he contends to be a recipe for disarray, anxiety and even depression. All this begs

[3] The Nutri-score is a five-level French nutritional labeling system, ranging from A to E and from green to red, placed on the front of food packaging, based on the nutritional value of a food product.

the question: Will it ever be possible to create a new status for food as another consumer product – based on total transparency of product information, from farm to fork? This is a complex challenge, given the deluge of innovations emerging worldwide – cellular agriculture, plant-based meat, in vitro meat (also known as 'cellular meat') and so on. Yet this world is in the throes of an ecological transition, with the development of agroecology, the rise of organic farming and nutritional education campaigns. Meanwhile, industrial processing is being challenged with growing fury. This world will most likely be very wary of new products which, despite being plant based, seem to fall into the ultra-processed category.

A profoundly changing world

We are living in a time of global transition. Major civilizational changes are unfolding at an accelerated pace. IT, digitization and now AI are reshaping the world, lifestyles, lives, knowledge and understanding. A gender revolution is also underway, with an increasingly radical contestation of gender relations Another no-less radical challenge has also emerged as the question of humans relationships with animals has been explicitly placed on the global agenda, with major implications for food and potentially for ecosystems in general.

The current pandemic crisis has put the brakes on some aspects of globalization, prompting border closures and curbing trade and travel. But it may also have heightened awareness of the importance of global unity in dealing with health issues as well as environmental threats and their climate impacts.

We are witnessing a dizzying watershed moment for biology, neo-Darwinism. heredity, the key concepts that shape them and their relationship with the social sciences. Let us now look at recent developments in two areas and consider their implications for food.

Biological revolutions

In the early twentieth century, Elie Metchnikoff, vice-director of the Pasteur Institute in Paris and winner of the 1908 Nobel Prize for his seminal work on immunity (phagocytosis), was convinced that the apparent and remarkable number of centenarians in the Balkans could be explained by their traditionally high consumption of fermented dairy products – he believed certain lactic acid bacteria found in such products could play a role in protecting the digestive tract (he practised what he preached by consuming a lot of yoghurt and other fermented dairy products). More than a century later, although there now seems to be greater interest in the Japanese centenarians of Okinawa than in those of the Balkans, Metchnikoff's obsessive whim almost seems like early intuition: what was then called 'intestinal flora' has now come to be known as the 'gut microbiome'.

While Metchnikoff had envisioned a linear and univocal determinism based on a category of foods, discoveries over the last decade or so have shown that the gut microbiota consists of 50–100 billion bacteria and other microorganisms (the genes of which are known as the microbiome) and is involved in a complex way in shaping our immunity, in the functioning of our central nervous system, with which it communicates, and in regulating our moods and mental states. Moreover, dysbiosis (an imbalance or depletion of the gut microbiota) is associated with conditions ranging from obesity to type 2 diabetes and depression, and the microbiome may also play a role in autism and even schizophrenia.

The community of bacteria, yeasts and other microbes that reside in our digestive tract is now regarded as both an organ and an internal ecosystem. In addition to inhabiting the digestive tract, the microbiome is an integral part of the body: it interacts with it, communicates with its cells, co-produces metabolites (which in turn communicate with other organs), informs and is informed, regulates and is regulated. Food is the vehicle of communication with the external ecosystem that informs – or distorts – its composition and functioning.

We live on and in a global ecosystem that is itself a collection of ecosystems. Each of us consists of or harbours one or more diverse ecosystems – the skin, the respiratory system, the mouth and the vagina all host microbiota. The microbiome interacts with our brain – the organ within which representations and beliefs emerge, thrive and spread – which drives our individual and social behaviours while being influenced by collective norms, rules, traditions and practices. We can begin to picture how a continuum from microorganisms to the social and macrosocial might look like.

The biological revolution was ushered in by growing insight into the microbiome, yet another, even more fundamental, sea change is also unfolding with the rise of epigenetics. The natural selection-based genetic evolution paradigm is being forced to change or, at the very least, one might say, to add a touch of Lamarckism to its Darwinism – or rather, neo-Darwinism.

Epigenetics is the study of the set of mechanisms that fine-tune gene expression. Various environmental mechanisms may activate or inactivate (i.e. silence) the expression of certain genes, particularly through food. It is now recognized that some traits acquired through food can be passed on for several generations. Obesity is a typical example. This condition has a strong social dimension. It is linked to a poor diet and an overly sedentary lifestyle and may also lead to type 2, adult-onset diabetes. Young men who develop this condition because of poor diet and lack of physical activity could produce offspring who may in turn be overweight and diabetic regardless of their lifestyle (see, for instance, Danchin, 2021, p. 72). These findings come after the discovery of prions during the mad cow crisis, when research into Creutzfeldt-Jakob disease revealed that misfolded proteins are the cause of the disease and that this defect can be transmitted to other proteins with which they come into contact. This illustrates the joint hereditary and dietary transmission of a disease through the ingestion of contaminated tissues.

The medium and the message

Food plays a pivotal role in these closely related scientific revolutions or revelations. It can be considered in terms of not only the provision of energy (calories) and biochemicals (nutrients, micronutrients) but also information. Food is both medium and message, vector and content, information and informed. This understanding calls into question – or complexifies – reductionist and linear models of causality. Our internal ecosystems communicate with external ecosystems through our food. Moreover, heredity is now approached less as being exclusively genetic and more from the perspective of its cultural, environmental and epigenetic dimensions. Conclusions warrant the utmost caution, as they are sometimes drawn too hastily and could lead to the kinds of stigmatization seen in the past – for instance, regarding the hereditary nature of the pathogenic impacts of inequalities.

Still, it is now absolutely essential to contemplate the world and food from an ecological and ecosystemic perspective. History, anthropology, sociology and social psychology initially showed little interest in one another and progressed separately before attempts were made to forge closer links, marked by the late emergence of food studies. Throughout this process, the HSS were initially sidelined or overlooked by the medical discipline of nutrition, even though the latter was itself in its infancy and lacked recognition among the other established fields of medicine. At first, only modest attempts were made to bridge the disciplinary divide on specific issues such as obesity and eating disorders.

But the rise of the environmental question – slow at first but increasingly inexorable since the turn of the millennium, and now reaching the point of critical urgency – has brought to light the striking need to link approaches, points of view, research questions, acquired knowledge and emerging issues: to grasp food not only in terms of an emerging 'bio-social nutrition' but also within those of a generalized ecosystemic thinking.

References

Aron J.-P., 1976. *The art of eating in France: manners and menus in the nineteenth century*, New York, Harper & Row, 249 p. Translation of 'Le mangeur du XIXe siècle' (1973).

Barthes R., 1961. Pour une psychosociologie de l'alimentation. *Annales*, 16(5): 977–986.

Barthes R., 1972. *Mythologies*, New York, Farrar, Straus and Giroux, 158 p. Translation of 'Mythologies' (1957).

Bonhommeau S., Dubroca L., Le Pape O., Barde J., Kaplan D.M., Chassot E., Nieblas A.-E., 2013. Eating up the world's food web and the human trophic level. *Proceedings of the National Academy of Sciences*, 110(51): 20617–20620.

Bourdieu P., 1984. *Distinction: a social critique of the judgement of taste*, Cambridge, MA, Harvard University Press, 613 p. Translation of 'La distinction: critique sociale du jugement' (1979).

Certeau M. de, Giard L., Mayol P., 1998. *The practice of everyday life*. Vol. 2: Living and cooking, Minneapolis/London, University of Minnesota Press, 292 p. Translation of 'L'invention du quotidien. 2. Habiter, cuisiner' (1994).

Danchin E., 2021. *L'hérédité comme on ne vous l'a jamais racontée*, Paris, Humensis.

Durkheim É., 1982 (1895). *The rules of sociological method*, New York, Free Press, 264 p. Translation of 'Les règles de la méthode sociologique' (1894).

Fischler C., 1979. Gastro-nomie et gastro-anomie. *Communications*, 31(1): 189–210.

Fischler C., 1990. *L'Homme et la table*, thèse de doctorat en sociologie, Paris, EHESS.

Fischler C., Masson E., 2008. *Manger: Français, Européens et Américains face à l'alimentation*, Paris, Odile Jacob.

Flandrin J.-L., 1992. *Chronique de Platine: pour une gastronomie historique*, Paris, Odile Jacob.

Flandrin, J.-L., 2007. *Arranging the meal: a history of table service in France*, Berkeley, University of California Press, 209 p. Translation of 'L'ordre des mets' (2002).

Joron P., 2017. Georg Simmel et la sociologie du futile. Dans les anfractuosités du social et de l'intime . . . *Revista Memorare*, 4(2-II): 106–121.

Maurizio A., 2019 (1932). *Histoire de l'alimentation végétale – depuis la préhistoire jusqu'à nos jours*, Paris, Payot.

Poulain J.-P., 2017a. Socio-anthropologie du fait alimentaire ou Food Studies. Les deux chemins d'une thématisation scientifique. *L'Année sociologique*, 67(1): 23–46.

Poulain J.-P., 2017b. *The sociology of food: eating and the place of food in society*, London/New York, Bloomsbury Academic, 288 p. Translation of 'Sociologies de l'alimentation' (2002).

Schwartz B., 2005. *The paradox of choice: why more is less*, New York, ECCO.

Simmel G., 1992 (1910). Sociologie du repas. *Sociétés*, 37: 211–216.

Toussaint-Samat M., 1992. *A history of food*, Oxford/Cambridge, MA: Blackwell Reference. Translation of 'Histoire naturelle et morale de la nourriture' (1992).

Acknowledgements

The long adventure of this book was made possible thanks to the support and inspiration of many people who have worked with the UNESCO Chair in World Food Systems since 2011.

Special thanks to the members of our steering committee, our scientific council and our evaluation committees, to the representatives of our hosting institutions, L'Institut Agro Montpellier and CIRAD, who in one way or another have encouraged us and shared their advice and constructive criticism, and to the Daniel & Nina Carasso Foundation, faithful and inspiring supporters of our Chair: Marie-Josèphe Amiot-Carlin, Sylvie Avallone, Khalid Belarbi, Clément Cheissoux, Benoît Daviron, Mathilde Douillet, Jalila El Hati, Claude Fischler, Ève Fouilleux, Stéphane Fournier, Harriet Friedmann, Étienne Hainzelin, Michelle Holdsworth, Magali Jeannoyer, Myriam Kessari, Carole Lambert, Yves Le Bars, Olivier Lepiller, Ronan Le Velly, Éléonore Loiseau, Sélim Louafi, Éric Malézieux, Marie-Stéphane Maradeix, Sarah Marniesse, Yves Martin-Prével, Paule Moustier, Dominique Paturel, Sylvain Perret, Coline Perrin, Véronique Planchot, Jean-Louis Rastoin, Carole Sinfort, Lucie Sirieix, Guilhem Soutou, Leïla Temri, Laurence Tibère, Jean-Marc Touzard and Anne-Lucie Wack.

We would also like to thank all the people who have presented at our various events, particularly at our symposia and as part of our Advanced M.Sc® in 'Innovation and Policies for Sustainable Food'. Each of these talks inspired us with new ideas.

Many thanks to Denis Delebecque (CIRAD), who helped us with the graphic design of this book.

We of course thank all the contributors to this book, both authors and reviewers, who kindly accepted our invitations, often at very short notice.

A special mention goes to the executive team of the UNESCO Chair in World Food Systems, which contributed greatly to the conception and structuring of this book: Géraldine Chaboud, Hélène Lançon and particularly Mathilde Coudray, whose meticulous and thorough copy-editing of the entire book was extremely valuable. Thank you to all current members of the team and to the past members who built our Chair.

Finally, thank you, dear readers, whom we spent so much time thinking about as we tried to answer the one question we were endlessly asked during the writing process: 'Who is your book for?' For you, it would appear . . .

Abbreviations

Ciheam-IAMM   Mediterranean Agronomic Institute of Montpellier
              (Centre international de hautes études agronomiques
              méditerranéennes – Institut agronomique méditerranéen
              de Montpellier)

CIRAD   French Agricultural Research Centre for International
              Development *(Centre de coopération internationale en*
              recherche agronomique pour le développement)

Cniel   National Interprofessional Centre for the Dairy Economy
              (Centre national interprofessionnel de l'économie laitière)

CNRS   French National Centre for Scientific Research *(Centre*
              national de la recherche scientifique)

INRAE   French National Research Institute for Agriculture, Food
              and Environment *(Institut national de recherche pour*
              l'agriculture l'alimentation et l'environnement)

IRD   French National Research Institute for Sustainable
              Development *(Institut de recherche pour le développement)*

Introduction

Food and all its dimensions

Nicolas Bricas, Damien Conaré and Marie Walser

This book marks (and celebrates) the first chapter of activity for the UNESCO Chair in World Food Systems, created in 2011 by Professor Jean-Louis Rastoin (L'Institut Agro Montpellier), together with a multidisciplinary group of teachers and researchers from different institutions[1] at the Agropolis Campus in Montpellier, France. In this sense, this book is an important step: writing it helped us reflect on our own work, taking stock of the ground we had already covered and thinking about our future commitments.

Since its creation, the UNESCO Chair in World Food Systems has dedicated itself to decompartmentalizing knowledge on food systems and to supporting the different actors driving change to promote sustainable food systems. The Chair fulfils its mandate of bringing science and society together through training, action research and knowledge dissemination activities, with a view to addressing all the dimensions of food systems (environmental, socio-cultural, health, economic, political etc.).

A unique approach

Over the years, and aided by external evaluations of its work, the Chair has arrived at a number of clearly identified pillars, including the following:

– Developing an approach focused on fieldwork and its challenges by building bridges between researchers, stakeholders and citizens through the creation of tools and spaces for reflection and discussion, including publications, talks, engagement with the media, participation in networks of committed actors, meetings with local authorities, participation in expert commissions and so

[1] L'Institut Agro Montpellier, Cirad, IRD, IAMM, Irstea, Inrae, University of Montpellier.

on. In this respect, the Chair plays a political role (in the sense of involvement in the affairs of the polity) which it intends to continue developing in the years to come.

- Disseminating knowledge by articulating different perspectives and points of view and by drawing on different types of knowledge from academia (across different disciplines) and the professional world, as well as from artistic fields for a sensitive approach.
- Adopting a broad definition of food systems, spanning the full range of activities and actors involved in food production, processing, distribution, consumption and waste management as well as the institutions that support and regulate them, striving not for the advent of a sustainable food system but rather for a sustainable articulation of different food systems.
- Adopting an international perspective to be able to approach situations in their context, with a particular focus on bridging the 'North/South divide'.
- Finally, considering all the dimensions of food systems – health, social, environmental, cultural, economic or hedonic dimensions – and giving them all equal importance.

This book reflects the unique approach that the Chair has followed over the past years. It is intended as a source of inspiration for agents of change and strives to articulate different perspectives on food and the associated contemporary issues. As they have developed, food systems – most often described as 'industrialized' – raise a number of global challenges such as climate change, biodiversity loss, soil depletion and health crises, the effects of which are felt throughout our societies. These challenges call for the transformation of food systems.

To therefore take all aspects of food systems into account in its reflection on this transformation, the book weaves an 'ecology of food' so as to better address the sustainability issues surrounding food systems. The analogy we draw between food and ecology is rooted in the double meaning of ecology, as a science of relationships (between the different elements of the biosphere) and as a political commitment (political ecology). We consider food as a vehicle for both relationships and societal engagement: this is the core premise of our work.

On the menu

Food is a 'total social fact': as previously mentioned, it is essential (not to say fundamental, which could be interpreted as self-important) to the construction of our different relationships in the world (Part 1). This starts with our relationship with ourselves, as our nourished bodies raise questions relating to health, emotions, pleasure and the construction of our identities – in other words, to the affirmation of the 'self' through food. Next, there are our relationships with others (our companions and fellow diners) through the conviviality (or animosity) of shared meals, the transmission of table etiquette and culinary know-how, the mixing of food cultures, the economic exchanges that take place between actors in food systems and so on. Sharing a meal is a way of connecting with others: eating the same flesh creates collective relationships, since literally incorporating this collective sustenance is, symbolically, to incorporate ourselves into the collective. Food also plays a key role in our spiritual relationships with invisible worlds, for instance, through offerings. Finally, food informs our relationships with the biosphere, with other non-human living beings, from the worlds of animals and plants but also across the entire microbial universe, which both forms part of us (our intestinal microbiota) and plays a role in the transformation and preservation of our food (through fermentation, for example).

After exploring these relationships, we take a long-term historical perspective to discuss the major issues facing contemporary food systems (Part 2). We first look at the industrialization of agriculture following the transition from a socio-metabolism based on energy from the sun to a fossil fuel–dependent socio-metabolism (relying first on coal and then on oil), which saw the establishment of increasingly specialized production sectors and the development of international trade. We then consider the history of the industrialization of the food supply (food processing industries, the globalization of trade, the concentration of players in food supply chains, the challenges associated with digital technology etc.) and the evolution of our eating habits in connection with these societal changes. This historical perspective helps shed light on how we reached the present situation, where the limitations of industrialized food systems are plain to see in the light of sustainability issues, with adverse effects on the environment, health, crops and social inequalities, among others.

We then describe our proposal for an ecology of food (Part 3), which calls for both articulating the different dimensions of food through which the bonds between the living are woven and reflecting on forms of political commitment to bring about sustainable food systems. Such transformation will contribute to individual health, justice and cohesion, as well as co-viability with non-humans. This highlights the importance of situating ourselves as being part of the living and of appreciating its diversity in order to develop forms of co-viability between environmental and social systems.

This multidimensional and political approach to food leads us to revisit a number of common food tenets or dictates (Part 4) surrounding sustainable food systems, namely the emphasis on increasing production to feed the planet, the use of fortified foods to fight malnutrition, the transition from animal to vegetable protein consumption, the fight against food waste, food aid, the promotion of homemade food, the relocalization of our food supply and the power of 'active consumers'.

Finally, this book aims to instil enthusiasm in the actors striving for the transformation of food systems (Part 5). To this end, we analyse the role of existing alternatives: the 'world after tomorrow' is already being experimented with today; this must be recognized and made known. This points to the challenge of scaling up these initiatives and raises the question of the roles that the private sector, academia and training actors, as well as public authorities, can play in order to stimulate, support and promote these transformations.

A progress report

It is important to consider this book as a work in progress and not as an end result. As stated in the preface, it is our attempt at articulating several years of discussions, papers, training sessions, symposia, research project outputs, publications and the like. It thus developed over the course of numerous encounters, whether fortuitous or sought out. This openness to diverse and disparate works relating to food obviously entails the risk of incompleteness in each of these areas. This is inevitable. The present book is not intended as a scientific work in the sense of advancing a particular disciplinary field of research. Its aim, first and foremost, is to offer readers a broad overview of the current challenges surrounding food systems in order to grasp their full complexity and be able to articulate seemingly unrelated issues. The authors we called upon for this book, and with whom we developed the different chapters, all have in common their involvement with themes long central to the Chair's mandate.

Another bias that we openly acknowledge is our geographical prism. This book was written in France, which has a relatively singular relationship with food compared to other countries or regions that may have their own ways of understanding the world through the prism of their own food systems. Although we attempt to refer to these different understandings, the overall perspective of this book is certainly Eurocentric. We are well aware of this limitation and in no way wish to universalize our idiosyncrasies.

We wish you a delicious read and hope you will consume, share and disseminate this work without moderation.

Part One

Food as relationships

Food is at once universal and unique: all humans must eat in order to live, and at the same time, there are many ways to eat. Food is also both biological and cultural. It is material and symbolic but also rational and emotional, personal and collective, internal and external to our bodies. It is a vehicle for expression, an object of daily life and a subject of scientific study. Food is at once a condition of individual life, a cement of human groups and an anchoring in the biosphere. It is a cornerstone of existence that pervades it, structures it and is transformed by it.

'In the secluded space of domestic life', to use the words of Michel de Certeau, everyday food consumption is what it has always been: a matter of course, marked by habit and experienced as self-evident. Nevertheless, the following pages argue that it is underpinned by fundamental questions. Every day, our food connects us to the world.

> Food shapes our lives [. . .]. We may not be aware of its influence, but it is everywhere: even in the parts of our brain that can't stop wondering about the meaning of life. Food's effects are so ubiquitous that they can be hard to spot, which is why learning to see through the lens of food can be so revelatory. One perceives a remarkable connectivity: an energy that flows through our bodies and world, linking and animating everything as it goes.

Echoing Carolyn Steel's concept of 'connectivity' from *Sitopia – How Food Can Save the World* (2020), we therefore approach food as a vector of connection that fully contributes to building our relationships with ourselves (Chapter 1), with others (Chapter 2) and with the biosphere (Chapter 3). This first part explores the multiple relationships woven by food, and by recognizing its biological, social, hedonic, cultural, economic and environmental roles, it reveals its multidimensional nature.

1

Food as a link with ourselves

Marie Walser, Tristan Fournier and Nicolas Bricas

Food, beyond its biological and health functions, connects us with ourselves. It is a source of sensory experience and pleasure, provides the building blocks for our individual and collective identities, and is a vehicle for self-optimization. What we eat today shapes the fate of our bodies and minds and, thus, our futures.

Food is not just any consumer commodity. Despite its commonplace nature, eaters face a fundamental paradox every day: eating is vitally essential, yet it involves taking risks (Fischler, 1990). Apart from drugs, food is one of the very few things that, once ingested, is processed to facilitate its assimilation. It thus transits from the outer world to the individual's interior – from the outside to the inside – transcending personal barriers. The mouth could therefore be likened to a chamber with a safety valve that allows food to be swallowed or not. The subsequent journey of food within the body reshapes the most intimate aspects of the individual on biological, emotional, identity and moral levels. Hence, food intake is not only objective but also symbolic: it influences the eater's well-being as well as their overall sense of self and self-affirmation. This chapter explores this connection to the self through food.

A health component

The first thought that springs to mind when contemplating the role of food is often: 'it's essential for life!' Definitively ceasing to eat would rapidly result in death. Apart from extreme situations of total deprivation or intoxication, eating 'well' is widely regarded as key to good health.

Awareness of the nexus between food and health is certainly not new. This connection has been recognized in dietetic principles since ancient times. According to Hippocrates, as well as traditional Chinese medicine and Indian Ayurvedic medicine practitioners, some foods may serve as medicine to maintain a healthy individual's state or to restore the sick to health. Foodstuffs such as garlic and ginger in China or asparagus and barley in Europe are thus often used together in daily cooking and for therapeutic purposes, sometimes in combination with pharmaceutical remedies (Ausécache, 2006; Marie, 2015). Dietary advice on food was long underpinned by empirical evidence due to a lack of knowledge of the pathophysiological mechanisms underlying the relationship between food and health. Ancient European medicine, for instance, maintained that diet improved health when the four fundamental elements that make up the body – water, earth, air and fire – were in balance. Some of these dietary tenets were nevertheless effective. For instance, since ancient times, endemic goitre (an increase in the volume of the thyroid gland due to iodine deficiency) had been treated by prescribing marine-derived remedies, even though no one was aware of the existence of iodine or of the thyroid gland (Jaffiol, 2011). Since the seventeenth century, in Western societies, dietetics has gradually given rise to the nutritional sciences, with research shedding light on the microconstituents of food (macro- and micronutrients, bacteria etc.) and their cellular and molecular mechanisms of action on the human body (Chapter 9).

The food diet is certainly only one of several components of health – alongside physical activity, lifestyle, sleep and genetics, for example – yet its effects on bodily functions are so profound that it perpetually redefines human beings on a biological level. Food quality affects parameters as diverse as a person's height, life expectancy, and physical and intellectual abilities. Malnutrition, when it affects young children or their parents prior to conception, can have lifelong ramifications for individuals. A child's 'first 1,000 days of life' (from conception to two years of age) are thus seen as a critical window of opportunity during which dietary practices (in utero, breastfeeding, diet diversification etc.) may influence the risk of developing diseases in adulthood. Even before birth, there is evidence of fetal programming of obesity and metabolic diseases (Barker, 1998).

Beyond malnutrition, micronutrient deficiencies (vitamins, minerals) can impair certain physiological functions such as eyesight and immunity, while overeating may lead to overweight, obesity and certain non-communicable diseases (cardiovascular diseases, type 2 diabetes and some forms of cancer). Moreover, a person's health can be affected by substandard food quality, with adverse effects ranging from vomiting to death in the most acute cases. In industrialized societies, the medium-term health effects of certain chemical compounds contained in food, such as microplastics, pesticides and additives, are also starting to be identified (Tandel, 2011; Bouwmeester et al., 2015; Kim et al., 2017).

Recent advances in nutrition, which have highlighted the critical roles of intestinal microbiota and epigenetics, have provided a more detailed understanding of the link between diet and health. Food, far from being merely one of many determinants of health, exerts a lasting effect on our bodies.

A sensory and emotional experience

Foods all have in common that they trigger a taste sensation when placed in the mouth. The sense of taste, like those of sight, touch and smell, transmits information to the nervous system, thereby enabling the eater to determine the nature and quality of the food. Yet it also has the particularity of causing an 'affective resonance of information' (Chiva, 1983): the taste of food triggers a clear and immediate emotional response associated with a hedonic dimension (Chiva, 1979; Le Magnen, 1984). These emotions are primarily innate – newborns subjected to taste stimulations systematically show a mimicry response that differs depending on the sapid quality of the stimulus (Steiner, 1974). This reaction is unintentional in the first months of life (Chiva, 1983); it is an affective reflex rather than the result of cognitive processing of sensory information. Cognitive processes subsequently take precedence in shaping food choices. Yet the pleasure – or displeasure – induced by the taste sensation remains a fundamental driver of food intake (Le Magnen, 1951) and a powerful regulator of eating behaviour through its ability to change based on a person's physiological state (Cabanac, 2010; Dupuy, 2013).

Throughout life (and as early as pregnancy, when the child's eating patterns begin to develop), biological and socio-cultural processes are interwoven to shape the unique tastes of each individual. The food neophobia phase, which usually occurs during childhood between the ages of three and seven, is an anthropological landmark in which children experiment and build their own food choices (Fischler, 1990; Rochedy and Poulain, 2015). At first, the child often refuses foods that are unfamiliar or prepared in new ways (Rigal, 2006). Their taste palette will subsequently broaden to a varying extent, depending on the child's socio-cultural and emotional background. The taste of food, along with its associated representations and the circumstances in which it is consumed, shapes the complex configuration of food pleasure through which a person asserts their status as a plural eater (Corbeau, 1997; Dupuy, 2013). On a more general level, psychologically, food plays a role in structuring the individual's relationship with pleasure. The oral phase, which is characterized by the pleasure induced by sucking when the infant nurses and the satisfaction of the biological tension caused by hunger, is a key stage in the development of their personality (Freud, 1905).

The act of eating is sometimes driven solely by the quest for pleasure. Moreover, even prior to eating, simply thinking about a food may trigger a specific emotion linked to individual appetites and histories, creating a desire to concretely relive this emotion through the experience of eating. From the food-preparation stage, one may derive sensory pleasure from the smells, the combination of tastes and textures, and the presentation of food on the plate. The prospect of pleasure is itself a source of satisfaction, which can also contribute to promoting a healthier diet when it involves reducing the amount of food consumed (Chandon and Jouvent, 2017). Like Proust's madeleine, food is thus a vector of well-being and even of fulfilment and comfort. We should note that the affective dimension of food is also involved in the broad range of eating disorders (EDs) that can develop as a way to control negative emotions (Bourdier, 2017). Food hedonism – through both its organoleptic and contextual dimensions – therefore contributes to eaters' emotional balance.

A medium of individual identity

Eating means accepting to be transformed by food through the ingestion of all or part of its properties. Humans feed on nutrients, yet they are also nourished by meaning. Food intake occurs on a biological level but also on an imaginary one, where the symbolic, moral and intellectual qualities of foods, particularly those of the animals consumed, are transferred to the eater (Fischler, 1990) (Chapter 3). Depending on the socio-cultural context, some foods are specifically prized for their real and imagined benefits. Meat is regarded as a food that conveys strength (Chapter 13). The people of northeast India whom Lucien Lévy-Bruhl interviewed more than a century ago claimed that they liked eating owls to improve their night vision (Lévy-Bruhl, 1926). In the Bulu community of southern Cameroon, some foods are considered remedies for both physiological and so-called supernatural diseases (Otye Elom, 2018).

Conversely, eating a food deemed to have bad symbolic qualities poses a threat to the eater's identity. For example, warriors in some communities studied by James George Frazer in 1890 avoided eating hare or hedgehog 'for fear of losing their courage or shrinking away from danger' (Frazer, 1894). Moreover, the symbolic impurity of a food implies a risk of contamination (Douglas, 1969), which may lead to cognitive revulsion and inhibit consumption. This is the case of foods that are labelled as forbidden in certain religions or cultures. Hence even food that may be considered 'good to eat' (*bon à manger*), as it is safe for the body, is not always 'good to think about' (*bon à penser*) (Lévi-Strauss, 2021). Since we become what we eat, each mouthful represents an opportunity or a risk (Fischler, 1990).

'Tell me what you eat and I'll tell you who you are'. Two centuries ago, in his book *The Physiology of Taste* (first published in French in 1825), Jean Anthelme Brillat-Savarin (1971) described food as a kind of 'mirror of the self'. By reflecting our identities as eaters, forged from our personal histories, socio-cultural roots and shared values and beliefs, it is revealing of our person and our interactions with the collective. In this regard, the concept of incorporation provides a framework for exploring the relationship between the individual and the collective, for to eat is to embed oneself in a community and incorporate its rules (Fischler, 1990) (Chapter 2). From a constructivist perspective, identity is a dynamic and reflexive process that is continually reshaped by the individual's various structuring experiences of socialization across different spheres of activity (Dubar, 1991). By eating, individuals adopt the values and codes of the group to which they belong. At the same time, they assert their individuality, sometimes through adaptation or opposition and often by influencing the group in return. Meals thus appear to constitute a key site of socialization from the earliest age (Larson et al., 2006; Dupuy, 2013; Comoretto, 2015). A child, through contact with their close circle, gradually adopts the family's range of preferred foods (Watiez, 1994) while asserting their position as an individual within the collective identity (Chapter 2). In many other situations, eaters use food to assert their position in a specific social context, engaging in processes of compliance, identification, distinction, provocation or transgression. The consumption of alcohol among adolescents and young adults clearly exemplifies this identity-assertion process (Palierne et al., 2015).

The way in which each eater relates to their food is therefore shaped by their own experiences. Food practices – particularly cooking and the possibilities it offers for creativity and self-distinction – reflect the eater's individual history. This may involve a recipe inherited from one's grandmother and adapted to suit the person's current mood, an exotic food discovered during a trip and bought from a gourmet shop, a striking dish recreated after a dinner at a restaurant, a food supplement consumed as part of a medical treatment and so on. Food choices reveal a symbolic and social construction of the 'self', conveying a person's mindset, constraints and preferences.

A form of self-optimization

Food can also be a vehicle for presenting oneself to the world. In his book *The Presentation of Self in Everyday Life*, Erving Goffman (1959) approaches the social world as a theatre: actors (us) have roles that are prepared backstage (where rehearsals take place) and performed in plays (social interactions) before an audience (the others). The restaurant is a typical example of a venue where people stage themselves in a relatively explicit and codified way and where food may serve as a social foil. The dishes selected and openly savoured, as well as those prepared privately in the kitchen for a spouse, family or friends or to bring to work, reveal a whole part of a person. This process is far from trivial: it reflects our tastes, values, living standards, commitments and degree of receptiveness to nutritional recommendations or ethical debates. This self-staging mechanism has become all the more pronounced with the current growth of the self-help market and the widespread use of social media and mobile apps, which allow the public sharing of pictures of one's dishes and meals. One's diet can thus become a narcissistic and selfish endeavour, an ordinary everyday self-narration tool (Hassoun, 2010) geared towards publicly flaunting oneself in the best light. Food consumption is therefore constantly articulating the individual and the collective, while also being the outcome of the convergence of 'centrifugal' and 'centripetal' forces (Corbeau, 1992).

But what do we actually stage when we invite friends to a barbecue evening or share a picture online of the cake we made for our child's birthday? This process of promoting part of oneself may relate to the idea of (dietary) performance: we perform what others expect of us, or rather what we think they expect of us, or what we would like them to think of us. This performance is closely dependent on the moral injunctions that permeate our society, the degree of appropriation of which varies based on the prevailing social-attachment criteria such as class, age and gender (Parsons, 2015). If one belongs to the upper-middle class, it might be a matter – in the case of a barbecue with friends – of showing that one has assimilated the nutritional norm but is also able to deviate from it on social and festive occasions. If one is a man, it may – in the case of the birthday cake – involve showing one's commitment to the egalitarian gender norm by presenting oneself as a so-called modern man who knows how to cook and care for his children.

These moral injunctions – that is, healthy eating (Adamiec, 2016) and sharing domestic chores (Fidolini and Fournier, 2022) – trigger reactions ranging from enthusiastic support to outright rejection, with more implicit or negotiated positions in between. The question of interest here is, above all, how individuals appropriate these injunctions to optimize their diet. What do they make of them in practice? The everyday act of eating could be likened to the bed of a river that always flows in the same direction but meanders according to the roughness of the landscape. The moral injunctions mentioned above, as well as the biographical events and the interaction settings in which food is consumed, constitute these rough features. They challenge eaters and foster their reflexivity; that is, they drive them to gain perspective on themselves and the ability to (self-)critique. This also sometimes enables eaters to do things differently, which can lead them to consume new categories of food products (food supplements, organic food etc.) or to adopt new practices (veganism, 'free-from' diets etc.).

This reflexivity may therefore be enacted on a daily basis through cooking and eating. Moreover, it may be conducive to wandering (deliberately strolling through a market or allowing oneself to 'waste time' making a dish from scratch) and even lead to individual experimentation (monotrophic diets, intermittent fasting etc.). All of this improvisation, which may be both discreet and instructive, has a transformative potential that ranges from seeking a more relaxed relationship with oneself to individual and collective forms of politicization of food (Lepiller and Yount-André, 2020). In this sense, food can be grasped as a form of self-optimization (Dalgalarrondo and Fournier, 2019), that is, as a social space, a technique or yet a practice that provides a means of seeking and sometimes achieving a satisfactory compromise between norms and possibilities, between moral injunctions and individual preferences.

Conclusion

To eat is to satisfy hunger, treat oneself and reveal oneself to others in the moment. A nourished body will almost instantly emit messages of satisfaction, more or less pleasant emotions and regulatory signals, particularly satiety. Yet eating is also a long-term self-construction process. Food shapes our bodies and minds through its biological, hedonic, social and identity dimensions. We become what we eat, consciously or subconsciously, voluntarily or not.

Becoming aware of this relationship with ourselves, woven through food consumption, enables us to gain some perspective on this essential component of our lives, while contemplating the question – beyond who we are – of who we want to be. Eaters, through their food and the ways they improvise it, find ways to 'optimize' their lives so as to fulfil their own expectations or those of others, while also navigating the constraints placed upon them. However, the configuration of certain forms of food consumption is now changing the situation. In light of the range of products available on the market, people can tailor their own special diet and optimize it according to their genetic profile, preferences and lifestyle. These new options broaden the scope of opportunities while also raising questions about the reshaping of the relationship between eaters and their tablemates, food retailers and, more generally, their food culture. Food is clearly a vehicle for connecting with others.

This chapter partly draws on the input of contributors at two conferences organized by the UNESCO Chair in World Food Systems, *I Am What I Eat?* (2016) and *Pleasures in Food* (2017).

The authors would like to thank Mathilde Coudray, Anne Dupuy and Michelle Holdsworth for proofreading this chapter and for their suggested improvements.

References

Adamiec C., 2016. *Devenir sain: des morales alimentaires aux écologies de soi*, Rennes/Tours, PUR, Presses universitaires François-Rabelais de Tours, 202 p.

Ausécache M., 2006. Des aliments et des médicaments. Les plantes dans la médecine médiévale. Cahiers de recherches médiévales et humanistes. *Journal of Medieval and Humanistic Studies*, 13 spécial: 249–258. https://doi.org/10.4000/crm.866

Barker D.J.P., 1998. *Mothers, babies, and health in later life*, Edinburgh, Churchill Livingstone, 232 p.

Bourdier L., 2017. *Affectivité et alimentation: étude de leurs liens au travers des concepts d'alimentation émotionnelle et d'addiction à l'alimentation*, thèse de doctorat, spécialité Psychologie, Université Paris Nanterre, Nanterre, 235 p.

Bouwmeester H., Hollman P.C.H., Peters R.J.B., 2015. Potential health impact of environmentally released micro- and nanoplastics in the human food production chain: experiences from nanotoxicology. *Environmental Science & Technology*, 49(15): 8932–8947. https://doi.org/10.1021/acs.est.5b01090

Brillat-Savarin J.A., 1971. *The physiology of taste; or, Meditations on transcendental gastronomy*, New York, Knopf, 443 p. Translation of 'Physiologie du goût' (1825).

Cabanac M., 2010. *The fifth influence or the dialectics of pleasure*, Bloomington, iUniverse, 284 p. Translation of 'La cinquième influence ou la dialectique du plaisir' (2003).

Chandon P., Jouvent R., 2017. Sensory pleasure and mindfulness, allies of a healthier diet. *So What? A collection of the Unesco Chair in World Food Systems*, (6): 4 p.

Chiva M., 1979. Comment la personne se construit en mangeant. *Communications*, 31(1): 107–118. https://doi.org/10.3406/comm.1979.1472

Chiva M., 1983. Goût et communication non verbale chez le jeune enfant. *Enfance*, 36(1): 53–64. https://doi.org/10.3406/enfan.1983.2802

Comoretto G., 2015. *Manger entre pairs à l'école: synchronisme et complémentarité des processus de socialisation*, thèse de doctorat, spécialité Sociologie, Université de Versailles Saint-Quentin-en-Yvelines, Guyancourt, 596 p.

Corbeau J.-P., 1992. Rituels alimentaires et mutations sociales, *Cahiers internationaux de sociologie*, 92: 101–120.

Corbeau J.-P., 1997. Socialité, sociabilité et sauce toujours, in Duvignaud J., Khaznadar C. (éd.), *Cultures, nourritures*, Arles, Babel/Actes Sud, 69–81.

Dalgalarrondo S., Fournier T. 2019. "Introduction. Optimization as morality, or the routes of the self", *Ethnologie française*, 176(4): 639-651. https://doi.org/10.3917/ethn.194.0639

Douglas M., 1969. *Purity and danger, an analysis of the concepts of pollution and taboo*, London, Routledge/Kegan Paul, 179 p.

Dubar C., 1991. *La socialisation. Construction des identités sociales et professionnelles*, Paris, Armand Colin, 278 p.

Dupuy A., 2013. *Plaisirs alimentaires. Socialisation des enfants et des adolescents*, Rennes, PUR, 510 p.

Fidolini V., Fournier T., 2022. À la table des stéréotypes. Dialogue fictif entre un homme et une femme au restaurant. *Anthropology of Food*, S17. https://doi.org/10.4000/aof.13234

Fischler C., 1990. *L'homnivore*, Paris, Odile Jacob, 448 p.

Frazer J.G., 1894. *The golden bough, a study in comparative religion* (Vols. 1 and 2), New York/London, Macmillan.

Freud S., 1905. *Drei Abhandlungen zur Sexualtheorie*, Leipzig-Wien, Franz Deuticke.

Goffman E., 1959. *The presentation of self in everyday life*, Garden City, NY, Doubleday.

Hassoun J.-P., 2010. Deux restaurants à New York: l'un franco-maghrébin, l'autre africain. *Anthropology of Food*, 7. https://doi.org/10.4000/aof.6730

Jaffiol C., 2011. *Alimentation et santé dans l'histoire humaine: paradoxes et incertitudes de notre siècle*, Montpellier, Académie des sciences et lettres de Montpellier.

Kim K.-H., Kabir E., Jahan S.A., 2017. Exposure to pesticides and the associated human health effects. *Science of the Total Environment*, 575: 525–535. https://doi.org/10.1016/j.scitotenv.2016.09.009

Larson R.W., Wiley A.R., Branscomb K.R., 2006. *Family mealtime as a context of development and socialization*, New York, Jossey-Bass, 120 p.

Le Magnen J., 1951. *Le goût et les saveurs*, Paris, PUF, 128 p.

Le Magnen J., 1984. Bases neurobiologiques des comportements alimentaires, in Delacour J. (éd.), *Neurobiologie des comportements*, Paris, Hermann, 1–54.

Lepiller O., Yount-André C., 2020. Quand la défiance frémit. Une assiette qui se politise à petit feu ?, in Fouilleux E., Michel L. (éd.), *Quand l'alimentation se fait politique(s)*, Rennes, PUR, 49–64.

Lévi-Strauss C., 2021. *Wild thought*, Chicago, University of Chicago Press, 379 p. Translation of 'La pensée sauvage' (1962).

Lévy-Bruhl L., 1926. *How natives think*, New York, Knopf. Translation of 'Les fonctions mentales dans les sociétés inférieures' (1910).

Marie É., 2015. Se nourrir des souffles et des saveurs: la diététique de la médecine chinoise. Transtext(e)s Transcultures 跨文本跨文化. *Journal of Global Cultural Studies*, 10. https://doi.org/10.4000/transtexts.602

Otye Elom P.U., 2018. *Alimentation et santé en négro-culture; contribution à une ethno-anthropologie de l'aliment-remède chez les Bulu du Sud-Cameroun*, Sarrebruck, Éditions universitaires européennes, 564 p.

Palierne N., Gaussot L., Le Minor L., 2015. Le genre de l'ivresse. *Journal des anthropologues*, 140–141(1–2): 153–172. https://doi.org/10.4000/jda.6079

Parsons J.M., 2015. *Gender, class and food: families, bodies and health*, London, Palgrave Macmillan, 195 p.

Rigal N., 2006. *Winning the food fight: how to introduce variety into your child's diet*, Rochester, Healing Arts Press, 160 p. Translation of 'La naissance du goût: comment donner aux enfants le plaisir de manger' (2000).

Rochedy A., Poulain J.-P., 2015. Approche sociologique des néophobies alimentaires chez l'enfant. *Dialogue*, 3(209): 55–68. https://doi.org/10.3917/dia.209.0055

Steiner J.E., 1974. Discussion paper: innate, discriminative human facial expressions to taste and smell stimulation. *Annals of the New York Academy of Sciences*, 237(1): 229–233. https://doi.org/10.1111/j.1749-6632.1974.tb49858.x

Tandel K.R., 2011. Sugar substitutes: health controversy over perceived benefits. *Journal of Pharmacology & Pharmacotherapeutics*, 2(4): 236–243. https://doi.org/10.4103/0976 -500X.85936

Watiez M., 1994. Psychologie et nutrition: contribution à l'étude du processus de socialisation alimentaire. *Médecine et Nutrition*, 30(4): 171–177.

2

Food as a link with others

Marie Walser and Nicolas Bricas

Food is a vehicle to anchor oneself in the collective and connect with others, whether by sharing food with others at the dinner table, through the social interactions involved in grocery shopping practices, when travelling and embracing food as a gateway to local cultures and related experiences.

Beyond the question of our relationship with ourselves (Chapter 1), food is a fundamentally collective matter that has connected humans for thousands of years. Social behaviour associated with food flourished with the domestication of fire some four hundred thousand years ago (de Lumley, 2006). The collective dimension of food emerged as social organization became more complex (Perlès, 1999), first in terms of the eating process and later through the development of activities such as agriculture and cooking. Food is thus a key means of connecting with others on a social, economic, identity and even spiritual level.

A social institution

Eating meals with others is a pivotal part of community life in many societies. This is referred to as 'commensality', a term derived from the Latin word *commensalis* (combining *cum*, meaning 'with', and *mensa*, meaning 'table' or 'food'), which essentially denotes the act of 'eating together'.

Sharing a meal involves being together in the same 'commensal circle' (Sobal, 2000). While this seemingly ordinary setting may appear to revolve around the performance of a series of movements all geared towards food intake, in reality it is far more complex. Mealtimes are structured by a set of codes that may define the daily time slots of meals and the order in which dishes are served, for instance, as well as the composition of the meals, the way the food is prepared and eaten, and table manners (Poulain, 2002). These codes are naturally expressed differently depending on the socio-cultural context. For example, meals may have a so-called synchronic structure, with all dishes served at once, as in Vietnam or China, or a 'diachronic' structure, with dishes served one after the other, as in France since the introduction of 'Russian-style service' in the nineteenth century (previously, the grand service à la française was synchronic!) (Aron, 1976; Poulain, 2002). Depending on the occasion, it is also common to use cutlery, chopsticks or fingers to channel food into one's mouth.

Not everything is allowed or deemed appropriate at meals, and diners' behaviour (in terms of consumption and interaction with one another) is governed by what sociologists call 'social norms'. Jean-Pierre Poulain stresses (2006) the composite origin of these norms, describing them as a 'cluster of injunctions rooted in cultural, social and family traditions'. These norms are often underpinned by strong values such as sharing, social hierarchy, respect for elders, control of overindulgence and concern for hygiene, which are not to be violated or tensions could arise (Poulain, 2002). Meals are also a special time for adults to pass on these values and rules of social life to children – a process referred to as 'food socialization' (Larson et al., 2006). However, commensal meals do not bear the same importance in all societies and are gradually becoming less structured in some places, particularly as a result of the individualization of food practices (Fischler and Masson, 2008).

On a symbolic level, eating together also implies 'food communion' with others (Chombart de Lauwe, 1956). According to Claude Fischler (2015), 'the process of eating together is considered to bring people together – eating the same thing means producing the same flesh and blood, and symbolically constructing or reconstructing a common destiny'. Similarly, Émile Durkheim (1965) spoke of 'artificial kinship' achieved through food sharing. Symbolically, sharing the same flesh provides a sense of belonging while strengthening bonds within the community. The term 'companion' (one who shares our bread) reflects this connection. In Cameroon, a young child truly becomes part of the community only once they have eaten from the family food pot (Kouokam Magne, 2021). Another example concerns meals at funeral wakes, where the deceased person's living relatives come together and the grieving process begins (Biotti-Mache, 2019). Sharing the same food is also a sign of trust, providing a basis for forging alliances (marriages, trade agreements, peace agreements). Refusing to share food offered to one is also a symbolic denigration of a relationship and may be perceived as offensive (Fischler, 2015). In this regard, poor people dependent on food aid are often unable to engage in food sharing, thereby deepening their social isolation (Abi Samra and Hachem, 1997; Caillavet et al., 2006).

In some cultures, 'eating well' necessarily involves the pleasure of sharing a meal with family or friends (Fischler and Masson, 2008). It is important to note, however, that the bonds formed during a collective meal can also be negative, and thus feared or even shunned (Corbeau and Poulain, 2002). A meal may in fact be a backdrop for power dynamics or conflicts that raise tensions (Wilk, 2010). For instance, drawing on fieldwork conducted in a French medicalized elderly care home, Laura Guérin (2018) demonstrated that some residents' behaviour – such as falling asleep at the table, shouting repeatedly or moving around the space instead of remaining seated – was not welcomed by others and often disrupted the collective eating routine. Finally, although conviviality may be associated with temporary excesses, such as during festive events or restaurant outings (Fournier and Poulain, 2008), other interpretations suggest that commensality helps regulate eating behaviours while preventing obesity and other eating disorders (Fischler, 2012). Commensality, by exposing eaters to the social dictates of togetherness, tends to reduce the scope of individualistic eating behaviours and related excesses (e.g. heavy snacking). Either way, close friends and relatives – often unknowingly – influence our eating habits: We do not always eat in the same way or eat the same things depending on our tablemates.

A socio-economic interaction

Food is a field of activity spanning both the domestic and economic spheres and involves several stages, including agricultural production, food processing, distribution, cooking and consumption. These stages underpin the functioning of food systems, defined by Louis Malassis (1994) as 'the way in which people organize themselves in space and time to acquire and consume their food'. These activities are rooted in interactions between actors, intertwining economic dynamics – relating to time or financial management – and social ones.

On a domestic level, the household is a preferred space for the organization of daily food activities. In many societies, women shoulder most of the practical responsibility for food and the associated mental load, from farming to cooking (Allen and Sachs, 2007). This division of food labour raises the issue of gender relations (Chapter 16). While these relations are partially shaped by forms of male domination (Counihan and Kaplan, 1998), food is also a means of rebalancing them when it is embraced by women as a vehicle for creation, resistance (Avakian and Haber, 2005) or empowerment (Robson, 2006).

Besides cooking, grocery shopping is also a key socio-economic activity (Perrot, 2009). Going to a market or a shop is not just a matter of buying food; it is a way of meeting neighbours or, alternatively, of blending into and thus feeling part of an anonymous crowd. Some consumers consider that the supermarket is the ultimate place for social mixing, where one may meet a diverse range of people. Moreover, the market is a space where people can catch up on life in the neighbourhood and where everyone may simultaneously experience the same events. Strolling through shop aisles or gazing at market stalls is also a way to find out what is on offer, what is new and the prices of products. It is an opportunity for shoppers to fully immerse themselves in their food environment with all of their senses (Bricas, 2010).

Farmers selling directly to consumers at markets sustain the local economy and foster urban–rural relations, as well as interactions between locals and visitors (Bessière and Annes, 2018). Through haggling, buyers and sellers develop a bargaining relationship that serves economic interests while enhancing mutual understanding. Likewise, restaurants are both sites of economic activity and meeting places. A range of different social relations unfold in these spaces, such as neighbourly relations at the *warung makan* (street restaurants) of the *kampung* (slums) in Jakarta (Arciniegas, 2021), friendships at *garbadromes* (outlets selling garba, a highly popular cassava- and fish-based dish) in Abidjan (Egnankou, 2020), and even ties between ethnic groups at food courts in Malaysia (Tibère et al., 2019). Informality often seems to help strengthen the social ties associated with food provision.

Upstream of the economic sphere, seed producers, farmers, processors and distributors are all links in the same food chain, connected through a trade network. According to Ronan Le Velly (2002), these commercial dealings 'take place in an intricate context of interpersonal relations, formal rules, tools and collective representations'. This perspective suggests that economic action is embedded within its social context (Granovetter, 1985). Economic activity can be regulated: actors trading comply with standards set by external regulatory bodies that settle disputes. Yet the existence of regulation does not preclude power asymmetries. Economic actors may also strive to build trust, particularly on small scales that foster tacit compliance with social norms. The collective dimension of trading may be instrumental in building this trust. Emmanuelle Cheyns (2004) has shown that consumers in Ouagadougou more readily trust women's groups than individual women in the preparation of quality soumbala (a fermented condiment made from West African locust beans). The groups convey social values, while their mode of functioning, including the self-monitoring of group members, minimizes the risks of opportunistic neglect of the soumbala preparation procedures.

Yet market trade is also a realm of power relations, subjugation and violence. Montesquieu's claim that 'trade mollifies morals and leads to peace' is far from always being true. Long-distance trade has historically been developed through the use of violence, whether through land-grabbing for farming purposes, securing trade monopolies (e.g. the spice trade monopolies of the Dutch and English East India companies) or relying on slave labour to ensure the low-cost production of commodities such as cane sugar. Until the nineteenth century, economic powers and hegemonies were forged on the basis of countries' ability to harness energy and materials from (food and non-food) biomass, particularly from remote sources (Daviron, 2020). Unequal power relations are not specific to international trade; they are also apparent in local trade, where wholesalers, processors and supermarkets are accused of abusing their dominant positions to drive down farmers' prices (Chapter 7).

In response to these power asymmetries, fair trade and short supply chains have emerged as platforms for the integration of marginalized producers, rebuilding ties with peers, institutions in the agricultural sector and society at large (Chiffoleau, 2012). Social ties can thus help promote economic activity.

Food as a form of anchorage in the collective identity

Food, like language, is a powerful vehicle for mediation between people. Through its intake, food shapes individual identities (Chapter 1), yet at the same time it also transforms individuals in terms of their attachment to a collective cultural, social, religious or generational identity (Fischler, 1990): our food practices enable us to signal our belonging (or differences) within different collectives. Food is a means of symbolically linking ourselves to an imaginary 'Other' with whom we identify by seeking to share beliefs and practices – sometimes simply over the course of a meal.

Food is not just a random combination of commodities; it is a consistent and unified system of social practices, values and representations (Stano and Boutaud, 2015). Food is a mooring for cultural specificities and for strengthening links between individuals who share the same collective identity. So-called totem or ritual dishes are thus prime vectors of family memory (Calvo, 1982), while also contributing to people's self-identification (Douglas, 1984). All the material elements of food cultures (food, recipes, tools etc.) as well as their immaterial elements (table manners, rituals, values etc.) constitute a shared heritage (Bessière et al., 2010). This heritage is both an object of transmission, perpetuating a portion of the collective identity, and a space for invention and recomposition (Bessière et al., 2010). This is exemplified by *bâbenda*, a traditional dish of the Mossi ethnic group in Burkina Faso, the recipe for which is in the process of being 'modernized' to satisfy city dwellers' tastes (Héron, 2021). Food heritages, which remain firmly rooted in a regional rural identity and may be attached to a place through the concept of terroir, benefit from diverse enrichments – intergenerational, intercultural and other enrichments – and are thus in constant flux. Hence 'tradition' is embedded in an unceasing process of legitimization of new activities, resulting from the improvisation of individual culinary practices that blend, pick from or deviate from family or regional practices (Warde, 1997).

Through cooking, eaters can therefore both reconnect with their origins and open up (or not) to otherness, that is, to people who eat differently. In societies with high cultural diversity, food enhances the sense of 'living together'. It encompasses both that which is 'in common' – through hybrid cuisines or those commonly regarded as 'national', such as *nasi lemak* in Malaysia (Dasgupta et al., 2021) – and differences (Tibère, 2013; Tibère et al., 2019). In cities, through culinary innovations, food provides a medium for building a specific identity that transcends city dwellers' rural regions of origin (Soula et al., 2021). *Ceebu jën* (a rice and fish dish) was invented in Senegalese cities in the nineteenth century using broken Asian rice, groundnut oil from Central America, vegetables introduced by the Portuguese and later the French, vegetables of African origin and fish caught off the coasts of these cities. It has become a dish emblematic of urban areas, and like Senegalese cuisine, it is currently spreading throughout the continent (Tibère and Leport, 2018). Likewise, garba was invented in Abidjan by Nigerian immigrants and has followed the same trend, becoming a cuisine embraced by a new urban culture (Sédia et al., 2021).

Eating with people who have different tastes and prohibitions may require some adjustments, but it helps build cultural bridges between groups (van den Berghe, 1984). Travelling eaters may also assume several positions with regard to foreign cuisine. They may be 'neophilic' and seek to sample the food of the location visited as a symbolic incorporation of part of the local identity. Yet they might also be 'neophobic' and opt to eat familiar foods that are reminiscent of their own food culture to feel safe and comfortable (Cohen and Avieli, 2004). In situations of migration or exile, food choices are central to fostering a sense of belonging and integration. They thus constitute a resource for finding a place between one's home country and the host society (Étien and Tibère, 2013). Within the same country, food practices allow for navigating different collective identities. In South Africa, for instance, people make different food choices depending on whether they are at home or in the workplace. At work, in order to fit in, a person may deliberately refrain from following their own personal food-consumption habits and embrace those of the 'Other' (Zembe, 2017).

In France, the example of the 'new millionaires' (people who have recently become wealthy) discussed by Pinçon and Pinçon-Charlot (2010) highlights the dynamics surrounding changes in social class: new codes must be acquired, particularly regarding food, for instance, in terms of the behaviour to adopt at a luxury restaurant. Hence, food is in many ways a tremendous vector of collective bonding but also a space of distinction reflecting the lines between groups, senses of belonging and assigned identities (Stano and Boutaud, 2015).

A relationship with spiritual entities

Diverse beliefs have permeated humanity since its origins, based on which humans envisage the existence of supernatural beings or invisible entities, gods, spirits or ancestors to whom they attribute properties (Boyer, 2001). Guided by these beliefs, people are driven to interact with these supernatural agents, gifted with intellect and willpower (Albert, 2009), through ritual acts that may involve offerings of food or meals. Without trying to be exhaustive or drawing general conclusions, we here offer a few examples to explore the ways in which food may foster ties between human beings, their deceased kin and deities.

The question of life after death is a major concern in all human societies. Funeral rites strive to facilitate the passage of the deceased from the world of the living to that of the dead – a process that may possibly include a food sequence. According to Mesopotamian popular belief between the second and first millennia BCE, when they passed away, the dead would begin a long journey to the Western edge of the world, to 'the place where the sun sets', by the Great Gate of the Netherworld. Provisions for the journey of the deceased, including water, beer, cereals (oatmeal, barley, bread) and honey, were placed in dishes near the tomb. When the deceased reached the Netherworld at the end of their journey, their only source of sustenance was the food offerings, without which they would be unable to rest, at the risk of becoming errant and a danger to the living (Da Silva, 1998). In Romania, the living eat to nourish the dead. They consume *colivă* – a cake prepared by the oldest woman in the house of the one who has died – which symbolizes the body of the deceased (Vassas, 2001). Beyond the offerings, funeral meals are a celebration of the passage of the dead into the afterlife, while these feasts may also play an atoning and liberating role for the living 'who remain', as is the case in Japan (Giraud, 2015).

Yet food-based interactions with the deceased are not solely limited to the immediate post-death period. For the Mixe people of Mexico, food offerings in cemeteries are an everyday means of seeking permission from the dead (Pitrou, 2014), while ancestors may be worshipped through commensal activities, with their essence preserved in the form of food (Rowlands and Fuller, 2009). In West Africa, when opening a bottle of beer, even commercial beer, it is customary to pour the first drops on the ground as a libationary tribute to the memory of the ancestors. In Bali, the spirits of the dead are offered the foods and other items they loved during their lifetimes such that sweets, fruit and cigarettes are commonly seen on altars.

Food is also sometimes believed to be a vehicle for interaction with spirits or gods. Food rites – meals or offerings – may, for instance, serve to appease the gods (Rowlands and Fuller, 2009), to ask for the help of nature's entities when a human undertaking is deemed uncertain (Pitrou, 2014) or to ward off evil spirits (Charlier-Zeineddine, 2014).

Conclusion

People meet and interact through food in many ways, whether through commensality, sociability in the marketplace, the discovery and transmission of food heritage and related cultural practices. A closer look reveals that these food-driven interactions shape human societies – days are organized according to mealtimes, the vibrancy of a place can be gauged by that of its food supply, solidarity often begins by helping a hungry person in need, and exceptional food makes events special. Finally, our modes of food production and consumption shape the ways in which we live in society. They bring us together but also prompt us to work together to invent new alternatives (Chapter 19). In studying a field as profoundly rooted in the living world as food, this social cooperation cannot be grasped without reflecting on our links, as humans, within the biosphere (Chapter 3).

This chapter partly draws on the input of contributors at several conferences organized by the UNESCO Chair in World Food Systems: *Sustainable Food: A Common Good?* (2012), *What Did We Eat Yesterday? What Will We*

Eat Tomorrow? (2015), *Pleasures in Food* (2017), *Food Journeys* (2018), *Life Abounds in Food* (2019) and *Being Together* (2021).

The authors would like to thank Mathilde Coudray, Paule Moustier and Laurence Tibère for proofreading this chapter and for their suggested improvements.

References

Abi Samra M., Hachem F., 1997. *Manger, se nourrir dans la précarité – Dossier annuel 1997*, Rhône-Alpes, Lyon, Mission régionale d'information sur l'exclusion, 59–71.

Albert J.-P., 2009. Le surnaturel: un concept pour les sciences sociales ? *Archives de sciences sociales des religions*, 145: 147–159. https://doi.org/10.4000/assr.21076

Allen P., Sachs C., 2007. Women and food chains: the gendered politics of food. *International Journal of the Sociology of Agriculture and Food*, 15(1): 1–23. https://doi.org/10.48416/ijsaf.v15i1.424

Arciniegas L., 2021. Warung makan – public kitchens at the epicentre of informality in Jakarta, in Soula A., Yount-André C., Lepiller O., Bricas N. (ed.), *Eating in the city: socio-anthropological perspectives from Africa, Latin America and Asia*, Versailles, Quae, 78–88. Translation of 'Le warung makan: une cuisine publique au cœur de l'informalité à Jakarta' (2020).

Aron J.-P., 1976. *The art of eating in France: manners and menus in the nineteenth century*, New York, Harper & Row, 249 p. Translation of 'Le mangeur du XIXe siècle' (1973).

Avakian A.V., Haber B., 2005. *From Betty Crocker to feminist food studies: critical perspectives on women and food*, Amherst, University of Massachusetts Press, 299 p.

Bessière J., Annes A., 2018. L'alimentation au cœur des sociabilités ville-campagne, *Anthropology of Food*, 13. https://doi.org/10.4000/aof.8297

Bessière J., Barthe L., Mognard E., Pilleboue J., Rayssac S., Soulenq E., Tibère L., 2010. Patrimoine alimentaire et innovations, essai d'analyse typologique sur trois territoires de la Région Midi-Pyrénées, in *ISDA 2010*, Montpellier, Cirad, Inra, SupAgro, 12.

Biotti-Mache F., 2019. Banquets funéraires et derniers repas de quelques aspects historiques. *Études sur la mort*, 152(2): 13–38. https://doi.org/10.3917/eslm.152.0013

Boyer P., 2001. *Religion explained: the evolutionary origins of religious thought*, New York, Basic Books, 375 p.

Bricas N., 2010. Sentir et goûter. Écouter. Voir. Toucher, in Baisse V. (ed.), *Quelques pas en marchés africains*, Chamonix, éditions Véronique Baisse, 16, 28, 97, 104.

Caillavet F., Darmon N., Lhuissier A., Régnier F., 2006. L'alimentation des populations défavorisées en France. Synthèse des travaux dans les domaines économique, sociologique et nutritionnel, in *Les Travaux de l'Observatoire national de la pauvreté et de l'exclusion sociale 2005-2006*, Paris, La Documentation française, 279–322.

Calvo M., 1982. Migration et alimentation. *Information sur les sciences sociales*, 31(3): 383–446. https://doi.org/10.1177/053901882021003003

Charlier-Zeineddine L., 2014. Manger pour ne pas être mangé. Anthropologie de l'alimentation dans les Andes boliviennes. *Anthropology of Food*, S8. https://doi.org/10.4000/aof.7371

Cheyns E., 2004. Qualification des produits alimentaires artisanaux dans l'espace marchand: vers des dispositifs civiques ? Le cas des groupements féminins au Burkina Faso. *Économie et Société*, 38(3): 591–610.

Chiffoleau Y., 2012. Circuits courts alimentaires, dynamiques relationnelles et lutte contre l'exclusion en agriculture. *Économie rurale. Agricultures, alimentations, territoires*, 332: 88–101. https://doi.org/10.4000/economierurale.3694

Chombart de Lauwe P.-H., 1956. *La vie quotidienne des familles ouvrières*, Paris, CNRS, 308 p.

Cohen E., Avieli N., 2004. Food in tourism: attraction and impediment. *Annals of Tourism Research*, 31: 755–778. https://doi.org/10.1016/j.annals.2004.02.003

Corbeau J.-P., Poulain J.-P., 2002. *Penser l'alimentation. Entre imaginaire et rationalité*, Toulouse, Privat, 209 p.

Counihan C.M., Kaplan S.L., 1998. *Food and gender. Identity and power*, Amsterdam, Harwood Academic Publishers, 168 p.

Dasgupta A., Selvadurai S., Ponniah L.G., 2021. 'Home and away' – narratives of food and identity in the context of urbanization in Malaysia, in Soula A., Yount-André C., Lepiller O., Bricas N. (ed.), *Eating in the city: socio-anthropological perspectives from Africa, Latin America and Asia*, Versailles, Quae, 89–96. Translation of 'Chez soi et ailleurs. Alimentation, identité et urbanisation en Malaisie' (2020).

Da Silva A., 1998. Offrandes alimentaires aux morts en Mésopotamie. *Religiologiques*, 17: 5–8.

Daviron B., 2020. *Biomasse. Une histoire de richesse et de puissance*, Versailles, Quæ, 392 p.

Douglas M., 1984. *Food in the social order: studies of food and festivities in three American communities*, New York, Russell Sage Foundation, 303 p.

Durkheim É., 1965. *The elementary forms of the religious life*, New York, Free Press, 507 p. Translation of 'Les forms élémentaires de la vie religieuse' (1912).

Egnankou A.P., 2020. *Femmes-mâles et jeux de pouvoir par l'alimentation à Abidjan*, presented at Symposium international « Manger dans les villes d'Afrique, d'Amérique latine et d'Asie », 3e édition « Genre et alimentation à l'épreuve de la vie urbaine », 30/09 et 01/10/2020, Paris, Cirad, MoISA/Chaire Unesco Alimentations du monde.

Étien M.-P., Tibère L., 2013. Alimentation et identité entre deux rives. *Hommes & Migrations*, 1303: 57–64. https://doi.org/10.4000/hommesmigrations.2552

Fischler C., 1990. *L'homnivore*, Paris, Odile Jacob, 448 p.

Fischler C., 2012. Commensalité, in Poulain J.-P. (ed.), *Dictionnaire des cultures alimentaires* (1st edition), Paris, PUF, 271–286.

Fischler C. (ed.), 2015. *Selective eating: the rise, the meaning and sense of 'personal dietary requirements'*, Paris, Odile Jacob, 272 p. Translation of 'Les alimentations particulières. Mangerons-nous encore ensemble demain ?' (2013).

Fischler C., Masson E., 2008. *Manger: Français, Européens et Américains face à l'alimentation*, Paris, Odile Jacob, 336 p.

Fournier T., Poulain J.-P., 2008. Les déterminants sociaux du non-suivi des régimes alimentaires. Le cas des patients hypercholestérolémiques. *Cahiers de nutrition et de diététique*, 43(2): 97–104. https://doi.org/10.1016/S0007-9960(08)71428-7

Giraud J.-P., 2015. Dieux et défunts au Japon: la Grande Bouffe. Transtext(e)s Transcultures 跨 文本跨文化. *Journal of Global Cultural Studies*, 10. https://doi.org/10.4000/trans texts.601

Granovetter M., 1985. Economic action and social structure: the problem of embeddedness. *American Journal of Sociology*, 91(3): 481–510.

Guérin L., 2018. Façonner les émotions en Ehpad: du rôle dédié au repas dans la lutte contre la solitude des personnes âgées. *Sociologie et sociétés*, 50(1): 91–111. https://doi .org/10.7202/1063692ar

Héron R., 2021. Bâbenda – a modernized traditional dish: Urban trajectory of a Burkinabe culinary specialty, in Soula A., Yount-André C., Lepiller O., Bricas N. (ed.), *Eating in the city: socio-anthropological perspectives from Africa, Latin America and Asia*, Versailles, Quæ, 109–120. Translation of 'Le bâbenda, un « mets traditionnel modernisé ». Trajectoire d'une spécialité culinaire burkinabè en ville' (2020).

Kouokam Magne E., 2021. 'Food from the pot': Child nutrition and socialization in two Cameroonian cities, in Soula A., Yount-André C., Lepiller O., Bricas N. (ed.), *Eating in the city: socio-anthropological perspectives from Africa, Latin America and Asia*, Versailles, Quæ, 131–141. Translation of 'La nourriture de la marmite: alimentation et socialisation de l'enfant dans deux villes camerounaises' (2020).

Larson R.W., Wiley A.R., Branscomb K.R., 2006. *Family mealtime as a context of development and socialization*, New York, Jossey-Bass, 120 p.

Le Velly R., 2002. La notion d'encastrement: une sociologie des échanges marchands. *Sociologie du travail*, 44(1): 37–53. https://doi.org/10.1016/S0038-0296(01)01199-2

Lumley H. de, 2006. Il y a 400 000 ans: la domestication du feu, un formidable moteur d'hominisation. *Comptes Rendus Palevol*, 5(1–2): 149–154. https://doi.org/10.1016/j .crpv.2005.11.014

Malassis L., 1994. *Nourrir les Hommes: un exposé pour comprendre, un essai pour réfléchir*, Paris, Flammarion, 126 p.

Perlès C., 1999. Feeding strategies in prehistoric times, in Flandrin J.-L., Montanari M. (ed.), *Food: a culinary history*, New York, Columbia University Press, 21–31. Translation of 'Les stratégies alimentaires dans les temps préhistoriques' (1996).

Perrot M., 2009. *Faire ses courses*, Paris, Stock, 190 p.

Pinçon M., Pinçon-Charlot M., 2010 *Les millionnaires de la chance. Rêve et réalité*, Paris, Payot, 271 p.

Pitrou P., 2014. Nourrir les morts ou « Celui qui fait vivre », les différents régimes de commensalité rituelle chez les Mixe (Oaxaca, Mexique). *Journal de la Société des américanistes*, 100(2): 45–71. https://doi.org/10.4000/jsa.14008

Poulain J.-P., 2002. *Manger aujourd'hui: attitudes, normes et pratiques*, Toulouse, Privat, 235 p.

Poulain J.-P., 2006. Combien de repas par jour ? Normes culturelles et normes médicales en Polynésie française. *Journal des anthropologues*, 106–107(3–4): 245–268. https://doi.org/10.4000/jda.1351

Robson E., 2006. The 'kitchen' as women's space in rural hausaland, Northern Nigeria. *Gender, Place & Culture*, 13(6): 669–676. https://doi.org/10.1080/09663690601019869

Rowlands M., Fuller D.Q., 2009. Moudre ou faire bouillir ? Nourrir les corps et les esprits dans les traditions culinaires et sacrificielles en Asie de l'Ouest, de l'Est et du Sud. *Techniques et Culture*, 52–53(2–3): 120–147. https://doi.org/10.4000/tc.4855

Sédia N.A.G., Konan A.G., Akindès F., 2021. Attiéké-garba – good to eat and think about. Social distinction and challenging hygiene standards in the Ivorian urban context, in Soula A., Yount-André C., Lepiller O., Bricas N. (ed.), *Eating in the city: socio-anthropological perspectives from Africa, Latin America and Asia*, Versailles, Quæ, 121–130. Translation of 'L'attiéké-garba, « bon » à manger et à penser. Contestation des normes d'hygiène et distinction sociale en contexte urbain ivoirien' (2020).

Sobal J., 2000. Sociability at meals: facilitation, commensality, and interaction, in Meiselman H. (ed.), *Dimensions of the meal: the science, culture, business, and art of eating*, Gaithersburg, Aspen Publishers, 119–133.

Soula A., Yount-André C., Lepiller O., Bricas N. (ed.), 2021. *Eating in the city: socio-anthropological perspectives from Africa, Latin America and Asia*, Versailles, Quæ, 158 p. Translation of 'Manger en ville: Regards socioanthropologiques d'Afrique, d'Amérique latine et d'Asie' (2020).

Stano S., Boutaud J.-J., 2015. L'alimentation entre identité et altérité: le Soi et l'Autre sous différents régimes. *Lexia*, 19–20: 99–115. https://doi.org/10.4399/97888548857147

Tibère L., 2013. Alimentation et vivre-ensemble: le cas de la créolisation. *Anthropologie et Sociétés*, 37(2): 27–43. https://doi.org/10.7202/1017904ar

Tibère L., Laporte C., Poulain J.-P., Mognard E., Aloysius M., 2019. Staging a national dish: the social relevance of nasi lemak in Malaysia. *Asia-Pacific Journal of Innovation in Hospitality and Tourism*, 8(1): 51–66.

Tibère L., Leport J., 2018. Ceebujën, in Poulain J.-P. (ed.), *Dictionnaire des cultures alimentaires* (2nd edition), Paris, PUF, 278–282.

van den Berghe P.L., 1984. Ethnic cuisine: culture in nature. *Ethnic and Racial Studies*, 7(3): 387–397. https://doi.org/10.1080/01419870.1984.9993452

Vassas C., 2001. En Roumanie, l'autre moitié du rite: les cuisinières des morts. *Clio. Femmes, Genre, Histoire*, 14: 119–153. https://doi.org/10.4000/clio.105

Warde A., 1997. *Consumption, food, and taste: culinary antinomies and commodity culture*, London, Sage Publications, 231 p.

Wilk R., 2010. Power at the table: food fights and happy meals. *Cultural Studies-Critical Methodologies*, 10(6): 428–436. https://doi.org/10.1177/1532708610372764

Zembe Y., 2017. *Food choices at the intersections of race, class and gender struggles in postapartheid South Africa*, presented at Manger en ville: les styles alimentaires urbains en Afrique, Amérique latine et Asie, Paris.

3

Food as a link with the biosphere

Marie Walser, Nicolas Bricas and Damien Conaré

Humankind is an integral part of nature and even a complex ecosystem in itself. In many ways, food connects us to our immediate surroundings and to the living organisms we encounter and ingest.

Our food, derived from the living world, embeds us in what Western thinking refers to as nature. Through the diverse activities that enable us to feed ourselves – farming, processing, cooking and digesting – we encounter non-human living organisms (plants, animals, microorganisms) and the tangible world inhabited by the living, on both physical and imaginary levels. This raises questions about the essence of our relationship with a biosphere that this chapter broadly outlines and explores from different angles: the landscape, the productive biosphere and the concept of nature or the living world. Through our food, we shape a biosphere that in turn shapes us and to which we relate on a landscape, sensory, imaginary and biological level.

Landscape development

Activities geared towards generating food, such as crop and livestock farming, fishing, hunting and gathering, transform the ecosystems in which they occur. Production activities involving practices as diverse as deforestation, planting, plant breeding, grazing, irrigation, fertilization, pest control and plot management may 'artificialize' the environment (Mazoyer and Roudart, 2006). These practices induce ecological changes within the biosphere, and over time, they have shaped many rural landscapes worldwide. Forests have been replaced by fields, moorlands by hedgerows, swamps by rice paddies and deserts by oases through ingenious management methods that have made it possible to articulate the needs of plants and animals, the potential of the natural environment and the imperatives of social organization (Mollard and Walter, 2008; Marshall, 2009).

Some forms of production-oriented agriculture, however, geared towards meeting the growing food demand and keeping food prices low, undermine the maintenance of ecological functions within agroecosystems, for instance, by causing biodiversity loss or soil fertility depletion. These practices can also have adverse impacts on natural environments, such as wetland drainage, pesticide pollution of waterways and seabed degradation through intensive bottom trawling (Chapter 7). Finally, beyond the prevailing farming methods, 'what food we eat, and why we eat the food the way we do, [also] shapes "the landscape"' (Wessell, 2010). From this perspective, the landscape is therefore not a separate entity but the result of the interaction between humans, their food choices (across varying distances) and the environment (Brulotte and Di Giovine, 2014).

This suggests a constructed dimension of landscape that is both identity-based and subjective (Périgord and Donadieu, 2007), which Roland Barthes (1985) defines as 'the cultural sign of Nature'. With the concept of 'tastescape', Adele Wessell (2010) approaches the landscape as 'a gastronomic text that records cultural dynamics and change over time'. By connecting time and space, as well as production and consumption, this concept of tastescape allows for understanding the ways in which we produce our food through the physical landscape, while also accounting for the experiences, imagination, beliefs and ideas associated with it. The concept of 'terroir', which underpins many collective cultural identities, stems from this very relationship with the landscape, at once objective and subjective (Chapter 2). Some landscapes transformed by our food activities are cultural landscapes recognized as UNESCO World Heritage: the Alto Douro Wine Region in Portugal, the Honghe Hani Rice Terraces in China, the Fray Bentos Cultural-Industrial Landscape where meat is processed in Uruguay and the Wachau Cultural Landscape where vineyards flourish in Austria (Roe, 2016). The layouts of these landscapes, as well as of more ordinary agricultural landscapes, reveal visual configurations (shapes, colours) that have developed at the crossroads of farmers' practices, values and sensitivities (Busck, 2002). They often reflect an aesthetic that is sometimes visible only from the air (e.g. the layout of agricultural lowlands and hedgerows).

The link between food and landscape, however, is not limited to farming and the rural environment. Our food contributes to structuring cities and to the way in which they articulate with food production areas. In the Middle Ages, so-called organic cities were structured according to the food flows that transited through them – streets were designed to channel food products to the central marketplace, which was the very heart of the city (Steel, 2008). These urban spaces are forged by food habits, with food shaping the sense of place and meaning in urban areas. Large cities have developed on fertile plains, thereby enabling food production, or near rivers and seas, where ports are built to facilitate the transportation of goods, including food (Steel, 2008).

On land, food is supplied to cities through networks of roads used by farmers to transport their products, including livestock. In pre-industrial societies, although physical food supply constraints may have imposed a certain degree of compactness (Steel, 2008), cities operated in interaction with their breadbasket hinterlands. According to the model developed by Von Thünen in 1826, the agricultural belt around a city was to be structured in concentric circles – first the market gardens and dairies, then the fuel wood–production area, and finally the arable land for wheat cultivation and livestock grazing. Following a so-called urban metabolism cycle, cities were long fed by peri-urban farmland harvests, which they in turn fed with the waste they produced and processed into fertilizer (Barles, 2002). Agricultural industrialization (Chapter 4) disrupted this circular economy, with waste accumulating in cities and only marginally being used to supplement fertility cycles.

It is nevertheless important to note that not all cities – far from it – have relied solely on shaping a peri-urban agricultural landscape. As Fernand Braudel (1992) has clearly shown, since ancient times, many cities have been fed with products from afar, often without consideration for the socio-economic conditions of this remote production. Cities thus shape landscapes far beyond their sight. Today, for instance, urban consumers of palm oil products are contributing to the destruction of Asian forests. In cities, urban agriculture helps rethink spaces and landscapes and restore the human–nature nexus through activities such as gardening (Alarcon and Hochedez, 2018).

A collaboration with the living world

As an omnivorous species, humans are able to live in a range of environments and experiment with a wide variety of relationships with the biosphere. These human–nature links are reflected in the ways in which food is procured and produced. Since the beginning of sedentarization around 10,000 years ago, most human communities have shifted from a predatory to a production economy to meet their food, material and energy needs. In such an economy, producers engage in a process of collaboration with the living world. Rather than being human creations, agro-systems are actually co-productions by humans and nature – that is, a combination of natural processes and human-made disruptions (Larrère, 2002) leading to a voluntary structuring of the living world (Renaud, 2016).

Agriculture, livestock farming and fishing are not merely professional fields but also 'life-worlds' in their own right (von Bonsdorff, 2005). These activities go beyond the command of theoretical knowledge and practical know-how; they are underpinned by a sensitive understanding of living things, rooted in the body and experience. It is a matter of taming: farmers know their land, adapt to the climatic conditions, monitor their plants and form a bond with their livestock, which they perceive as emotional, communicative and intelligent beings (Porcher, 2004). These farmers rely on their senses to determine whether their crops are ready for harvest – by looking at the colour of a field, taking an ear of grain in their hand and testing its hardness, or biting into the kernels (von Bonsdorff, 2005). From experience, they know where and when to sow, which varieties to select and combine, and what conditions are affecting their animals. The complex and contextual nature of crop and livestock farming, as well as fishing, hinges on an ongoing interplay between knowledge and the senses and between knowledge and perceptions of the environment: this is the basis of farming expertise. The body is also involved in the effort to produce, rear or fish. Pulling up a net, helping a cow give birth and bending down to harvest crops are all ways of being an actor in the biosphere. This special link can be a key part of farmers' identity, as is the case for the Peul people of Niger, a nomadic group whose identity is not attached to a territory but rather to their cattle herds (Sow, 2001), and for the Vezo people of Madagascar, who live off fishing and whose name means 'paddling' in Malagasy (Grenier, 2013).

The relationship with the productive biosphere is just as complex and should therefore not be romanticized. First, some production systems tend to reduce living organisms to an instrumental value, which raises ethical questions. This has been noted, for instance, with the development of genetically modified organisms used in agriculture (where an external gene is inserted into a plant's genome by transgenesis) and with novel breeding techniques (where an existing gene in a plant is modified by mutagenesis). Second, working with the living world means recognizing the forces that are beyond our control: the climate, fires, the spread of pathogens, wild animals that threaten livestock and crops (e.g. wolves and elephants), and even the 'wild' side of plants (Javelle, 2020). Finally, the relationship with the biosphere, like that between humans, involves intuition, adaptation and harmony, but also violence and opposition. Moreover, the notion of nature is non-existent in some communities: interactions with the non-human world are subject-to-subject relationships (Descola, 1986).

Collaboration with the living is also at play in food processing, especially during the fermentation process, which is undoubtedly one of our oldest food technologies. Fermentation is driven by microorganisms (bacteria, fungi, yeast) that feed on food. This process involves the physicochemical and biological transformation of foods, thus preserving and detoxifying them, while also boosting their nutritional virtues and changing their rheological and flavour qualities (Selosse, 2017). Regarding this latter point, fermentation enhances flavours, thereby enabling people, in some circumstances, to vary their otherwise monotonous diet. People living in Arctic regions, for example, who have no spices or condiments in their natural environment, are particularly fond of the taste of fermented fish (Robert-Lamblin, 1999). Historically, this process marked the agricultural transition to the Neolithic period, when it became essential to manage food stocks (Selosse, 2017). Fermentation then developed in many cultures, involving a variety of raw materials and preparations (milk, fish, meat, cereals, fruit and vegetables, seeds, cocoa etc.) that gave rise to a wide range of fermented products: yoghurt, cured meat, beer, wine and so on.

Fermentation involves a set of sometimes very complex techniques based on empirical knowledge and the careful monitoring of phenomena (Bérard and Marchenay, 2005). The gradual control of processing conditions went hand in hand with the 'steering' (Larrère, 2002) of the microbial communities involved in the fermentation process, even before humans were aware of the existence of these microorganisms. Fermentation was thus often considered a 'magical' process – it partly eluded eaters, who made sense of it through different interpretations, for instance, by imagining that gods were involved in the process. People thus had to surrender to this transformation process in spite of its inherent invisible dangers and unpredictable results: not everything can be controlled, but it is sometimes possible to adapt to microorganisms' activities, for instance, by mixing wine casks after fermentation to achieve the right aromatic balance.

The growing focus on hygiene in industrialized societies nevertheless reflects a fear of microbes, which in turn informs production practices (e.g. the massive use of antibiotics in livestock farming) as well as consumption practices (e.g. the ideal of aseptization) that can give rise to various issues such as bioresistance and waste. Breaking away from the Pasteurian vision of the invisible living world seems to be a step in the right direction towards envisaging harmonious cohabitation with microbes, which are in fact part of our history, biological heritage and culture (Figuié, 2019).

Incorporating the living

What should we eat among the infinite food opportunities offered by the living world? The edible food space is fundamentally cultural (Chapter 2), determined by society's perception of the status of human beings within the living world. Eating involves giving meaning to food, with a magical dimension to its representation. This recalls the incorporation principle (Chapter 1) – 'you are what you eat' – on a nutritional, social and imaginary level. The qualities projected onto the food ingested become those of the eater. For instance, in his research, the philosopher and anthropologist Lucien Lévi-Bruhl (1926) reported that in New Zealand, children destined to become chiefs were fed *korimako* (a very melodious songbird) so that they would become eloquent and good orators.

This magical thinking regarding food is also prevalent in industrialized societies and shapes many of our representations of food (Rozin, 1994; Lahlou, 1998). For example, water and green vegetables are seen as having cleansing properties for the body (Fournier, 2012). Laurence Ossipow (1994) conducted an ethnographic survey of vegetarians in French-speaking Switzerland between 1983 and 1990 and found that they viewed plants as living entities, especially those that can be eaten raw, such as sprouts. Plants were said to contain positive vibrations from Mother Earth, so eating them would enhance health and prolong life. Many cultures also see fermented foods as a source of vitality: fermentation is perceived as a process whereby inert and perishable material is transformed into living, preservable matter (Bérard and Marchenay, 2005).

Meat is another highly symbolic product that is often associated with vigour and strength, yet it may also represent a danger, as it did for the vegetarians interviewed by Laurence Ossipow (1994) who claimed that by eating meat one risked being exposed to 'the animals' moods' or 'being morally contaminated', such that it was in some ways tantamount to 'absorbing death'. The consumption of animal products raises questions about the animal–human continuum (Fischler, 1990) and, depending on the culture, may lead to various forms of 'food murder' management: sacred rituals, giving thanks to the animal, euphemization and dissociation of the meat from the animal (Cazes-Valette, 2012). The consumption of animal products is also part of a biologically and culturally defined repertoire: the only animals that can be eaten are those which, in a given situation, are neither too familiar (pets) nor too remote (wild animals that are not hunted). Some animals are deliberately avoided because of their symbolic status, such as the 'Universal Mother' cows, respected in India, and pigs, associated with impurity in Islam.

In terms of practices, the contents of our plates and the way in which they are presented are also telling of our link to the biosphere. Japanese cuisine, for instance, reflects its connection to the natural world through its attachment to the seasons, freshness, natural tastes and rawness. In the Inuit tradition, this link to the biosphere – and to culture – is reflected in the fact that food is eaten raw: beluga whale or caribou meat is eaten frozen and raw, as the elders did. In Nordic cuisine, the dishes are astute compositions through which cooks and eaters replicate the colours of the environment in which they live. The somewhat cold and metallic colours of seafood are 'warmed up' with bread, cheese and berries (Fumey, 2008). Gastronomy is no exception, with chefs inventing new ways of connecting with the biosphere. The French chef Michel Bras, for example, created a dish called Gargouillou, almost entirely composed of a variety of plants from his countryside in the Aubrac region – vegetables, young shoots, leaves, flowers, seeds and roots – which he described as 'a dish that breathes life' and 'a tribute to nature'.

Symbiosis or the 'extended' individual

As we have just seen, food gives us many opportunities to connect with the biosphere. Yet ultimately the strongest, closest and most tangible relationship with the living world is the one of which we are likely least aware. This world is within us, in our mouth and intestinal tract, colonized by microorganism communities that transform and protect us (Selosse, 2017). In the digestive system, these microorganisms form the so-called gut microbiome, which uses the food we ingest as a substrate to fuel its own metabolism. We host about 160 different bacterial species in our gut, representing a mass of 1–2 kg (Insem, 2016). This microbiome in turn contributes to the proper physiological functioning of our body and health. These microbes not only break down food in the intestine but also produce essential amino acids, vitamins and vital molecules that humans do not otherwise synthesize, while detoxifying food and providing a barrier to the growth of pathogenic bacteria (Selosse, 2017).

This interdependence constitutes a perfect symbiotic relationship. Humans are not in fact autonomous entities, for their survival is dependent on other organisms, such as the flora that make up their microbiome, which has come to be regarded as a fully fledged organ (Pradeu, 2008). Finally, the act of eating brings non-human living organisms into the human realm (Trubek, 2005). The composition of the microbiome depends not only on biological factors but also on eating habits. For instance, Asian eaters host a bacterium in their microbiome that is capable of digesting algae, whereas European eaters lack this organism. This is an example of the co-evolution of diets and the microbiome, the array of microbes in which are gradually selected based on a person's diet. The microbiome is thus an essential component of human beings' biological and cultural identity; this raises questions about their individuality and calls for rethinking humans as 'extended' individuals (Rees et al., 2018).

Conclusion

Eating is about connecting with oneself, with others and, as we have just seen, with the biosphere, which is also inside us after all. How then can we consider ourselves as external to what Westerners call 'nature' if nature is in fact lurking deep within our bodies and interacting with us in a genuinely symbiotic manner?

Our food, by making us aware of the diverse relationships in which we engage daily through it, enables us to close the loop in our relationship with the world. This perspective invalidates the anthropocentric idea of the environment as external to us and prompts reflection on the conditions of co-viability between social and ecological systems in the ways in which we produce (Javelle, 2016), process, distribute and consume our food (Chapter 8). We transform our world by organizing and negotiating the way we eat with other living organisms and physical elements (Parts 2 and 5).

This chapter partly draws on the input of contributors at several conferences organized by the UNESCO Chair in World Food Systems: *What Resources to Feed Cities?* (2013), *What Did We Eat Yesterday? What Will We Eat Tomorrow?* (2015), *I Am What I Eat?* (2016), *Life Abounds in Food* (2019) and *Food and Biodiversity* (2020).

The authors would like to thank Mathilde Coudray, Muriel Figuié and Aurélie Javelle for proofreading this chapter and for their suggested improvements.

References

Alarcon M., Hochedez C., 2018. L'agriculture urbaine dans les quartiers défavorisés de Malmö: un outil de recomposition des relations homme-nature, in *Actes du colloque Nature des villes, nature des champs. Synergies et controverses*, Valenciennes, Presses universitaires de Valenciennes, 93–120.

Barles S., 2002. Le métabolisme urbain et la question écologique. *Les Annales de la recherche urbaine*, 92(1): 143–150. https://doi.org/10.3406/aru.2002.2469

Barthes R., 1985. *L'aventure sémiologique*, Paris, Seuil, 368 p.

Bérard L., Marchenay P., 2005. Les dimensions culturelles de la fermentation, in Montel M.-C., Béranger C., Bonnemaire J. (ed.), *Les fermentations au service des produits de terroir*, Paris, Inra éditions, 13–28.

Braudel F., 1992. *Civilization and capitalism, 15th–18th century*. Vol. III: The perspective of the world, Berkeley/Los Angeles, University of California Press, 704 p. Translation of 'Civilisation, économie et capitalisme, XVe–XVIIIe siècles, tome 3: Le temps du monde' (1979).

Brulotte R.L., Di Giovine M.A., 2014. *Edible identities: food as cultural heritage*, Burlington, Ashgate, 237 p.

Busck A.G., 2002. Farmers' landscape decisions: relationships between farmers values and landscape practices. *Sociologia Ruralis*, 42(3): 233–249. https://doi.org/10.1111/1467-9523.00213

Cazes-Valette G., 2012. Viande, in Poulain J.-P. (ed.), *Dictionnaire des cultures alimentaires* (1st edition), Paris, PUF, 1391–1403.

Descola P., 1986. *La Nature domestique. Symbolisme et praxis dans l'écologie des Achuar*, Paris, éditions de la Maison des sciences de l'homme, 457 p.

Figuié M., 2019. *Conclusion de la journée*, presented at Colloque annuel de la Chaire Unesco Alimentations du monde « Manger le vivant », Montpellier.

Fischler C., 1990. *L'Homnivore*, Paris, Odile Jacob, 448 p.

Fournier T., 2012. Pensée magique, in Poulain J.-P. (ed.), *Dictionnaire des cultures alimentaires* (1st edition), Paris, PUF, 996–1002.

Fumey G., 2008. Manger au Nord. Les couleurs de la cuisine scandinave, in Chartier D., Walecka-Garbalinska M. (ed.), *Couleurs et lumières du Nord. Actes du colloque international en littérature, cinéma, arts plastiques et visuels*. Stockholm 20–23 avril 2006, Stockholm, Acta Universitatis Stockholmiensis, 43–49.

Grenier C., 2013. Genre de vie vezo, pêche « traditionnelle » et mondialisation sur le littoral sud-ouest de Madagascar. *Annales de géographie*, 693(5): 549–571. https://doi.org/10.3917/ag.693.0549

Inserm, 2016. *Microbiote intestinal (flore intestinale)*, Paris, Inserm.

Javelle A. (éd.), 2016. *Les relations homme-nature dans la transition agroécologique*, Paris, L'Harmattan, 234 p.

Javelle A., 2020. L'acceptation de la part « sauvage » des plantes pour développer des systèmes maraîchers « diplomatiques ». *La pensée écologique*, 6: 16–26. https://doi.org/10.3917/lpe.006.0016

Lahlou S., 1998. *Penser Manger. Les représentations sociales de l'alimentation*, Paris, Presses universitaires de France, 256 p.

Larrère R., 2002. Agriculture: artificialisation ou manipulation de la nature ? *Cosmopolitiques*, 1: 158–173.

Lévy-Bruhl L., 1926. *How natives think*, New York, Knopf. Translation of 'Les fonctions mentales dans les sociétés inférieures' (1910).

Marshall A., 2009. *S'approprier le désert. Agriculture mondialisée et dynamiques socioenvironnementales sur le piémont côtier du Pérou*, thèse de doctorat, spécialité Géographie, Université Paris I Panthéon-Sorbonne, Paris, 496 p.

Mazoyer M., Roudart L., 2006. *A history of world agriculture: from the neolithic age to the current crisis*, London, Earthscan, 528 p. Translation of 'Histoire des agricultures du monde. Du néolithique à la crise contemporaine' (1997).

Mollard É., Walter A., 2008. *Agricultures singulières*, Paris, IRD éditions, 343 p.

Ossipow L., 1994. Aliments morts, aliments vivants, in Fischler C. (ed.), *Manger magique, Aliments sorciers, Croyances comestibles*, Paris, Autrement, 127–135.

Périgord M., Donadieu P., 2007. *Le paysage. Entre natures et cultures*, Paris, Armand Colin, 128 p.

Porcher J., 2004. L'animal d'élevage n'est pas si bête. *Ruralia*, 14: 159–170.

Pradeu T., 2008. Qu'est-ce qu'un individu biologique ?, in Ludwig P., Pradeu T. (ed.), *L'Individu: perspectives contemporaines*, Paris, Vrin, 97–125.

Rees T., Bosch T., Douglas A.E., 2018. How the microbiome challenges our concept of self. *PLoS Biology*, 16(2): e2005358. https://doi.org/10.1371/journal.pbio.2005358

Renaud R., 2016. Pourquoi l'apparition de la domestication ? Les interprétations du néolithique, in Javelle A. (ed.), *Les relations homme-nature dans la transition agroécologique*, Paris, L'Harmattan, 29–44.

Robert-Lamblin J., 1999. Saveurs recherchées dans le grand Nord, in Stäuble N., Raboud-Schüle I. (ed.), *Ferments en folie*, Vevey, Fondation Alimentarium, 79–83.

Roe M., 2016. Editorial: food and landscape. *Landscape Research*, 41(7): 709–713. https://doi.org/10.1080/01426397.2016.1226016

Rozin P., 1994. Manger sympathique, in Fischler C. (ed.), *Manger magique, aliments sorciers, Croyances comestibles*, Paris, Autrement, 22–37.

Selosse M.-A., 2017. *Jamais seul. Ces microbes qui construisent les plantes, les animaux et les civilisations*, Arles, Actes Sud, 368 p.

Sow S., 2001. Les noms sociaux en fulfulde. Essai de description de la construction des noms sociaux chez les Peuls. *Cahiers d'études africaines*, 41(163–164): 557–564. https://doi.org/10.4000/etudesafricaines.109

Steel C., 2008. *Hungry city: how food shapes our lives*, London, Chatto and Windus, 383 p.

Trubek A.B., 2005. Place matters, in Korsmeyer C. (ed.), *The taste culture reader*, Oxford, Berg, 260–270.

von Bonsdorff P., 2005. Agriculture, aesthetic, appreciation and the worlds of nature. *Contemporary Aesthetics*, 3: 17.

Wessell A., 2010. We are what we grow: reading a tastescape as a text of cultural history. *Text*, S14 (special issue 9): 1–14.

Part Two

Dynamics of the contemporary food systems

Throughout the ages and across all societies, the ways of producing and consuming food have continuously evolved over the course of the slow or sudden transformations that have punctuated the history of each region of the world. Exploration and long-distance trade, as well as human migration, have facilitated the spread of plants and animals and generated real food revolutions since Antiquity. In Western societies, the Industrial Revolution that began in the late eighteenth century brought about profound technical, social and economic changes. These upheavals, which affected all sectors of society, had a major impact on farming methods and food-consumption practices and led to the emergence of an 'industrialized' food system.

We here explore the dynamics observed in the evolution of food systems over a more or less extended period of time, and particularly the way in which the industrialization of societies has reconfigured agricultural production (Chapter 4), food processing and distribution (Chapter 5) and consumption habits (Chapter 6). Although these different stages are addressed individually, the developments described for each one are informed by a shared dynamic.

In these early years of the twenty-first century, the industrialization of food systems is still at work. As it gains ground, intensifies and gradually locks in the potential for change, the sustainability problems it raises – on environmental, health, social and economic levels – are becoming increasingly apparent (Chapter 7).

4

The origins of industrial farming

Benoît Daviron

Agriculture has a long history. Starting at a time when its main source of energy was the sun and it provided food, energy, materials and fertilizers, it reached the current age of industrial agriculture, founded on the widespread use of non-renewable resources and chemicals, and largely reduced to food production.

Over the last two and a half centuries, human societies have undergone a series of profound changes in the name of modernization. These transitions, although extraneous, have revolutionized agriculture. As a result, agriculture has become embedded in what is often called the 'industrial food system'. These changes can be traced back to three major interconnected transitions[1]:

- The socioecological metabolism: It refers to the nature and scale of the energy and matter flows that permeate societies to sustain them in the long term. This socioecological metabolism transition involves a metabolic regime shift from the energy of the sun to fossil fuel use (Fischer-Kowalski and Haberl, 2007; Haberl et al., 2016). This major event in human history was triggered by the Industrial Revolution, which began in England in the mid-eighteenth century.

---

[1] The specific factors that underlie these three major transitions are beyond the scope of this chapter. The literature on food regimes – very popular in the English-speaking world and now also in the French-speaking world – tends to systematically attribute them to capitalism, itself seen as 'always already in crisis'. The history of the twentieth century, spectacularly marked by the experience of real socialism, negates this interpretation. Real socialism was perfectly comfortable with the mining-dependent socio-metabolic regime and the division of labour. Instead of solely referring to capitalism, I therefore prefer to draw on richer perspectives, such as that of Ernest Gellner (1983, 1989), with his interpretation of industrialism, or that of Anthony Giddens (1990) and his four institutional dimensions of modernity – capitalism, of course, but also surveillance, industrialism and military power.

– The deepening division of labour: It spread within human communities and over large areas, with each individual becoming specialized in a particular activity and their existence depending on exchanges with others (Durkheim, 1933). As Adam Smith (1776) pointed out, the state of the division of labour – the driver of the 'wealth of nations' – is informed by the spatial and functional scope of the market. The way in which, over time, market transactions have spread to an increasing number of areas, activities and regions worldwide must be taken into account when analysing the deepening of the division of labour.

– 'The Americanization of the world': This refers to the series of political, economic and military events that turned the United States into the unrivalled hegemonic leader of the 'concert of nations' over the course of the twentieth century. It became the country that set the technical standards for production and consumption, and the locus for the emergence of a number of private and public institutions and bureaucratic frameworks that supported or superseded trade.

This chapter outlines the evolution of agriculture over the nineteenth and twentieth centuries, based on these three major simultaneous transition processes.

The mining-dependent socio-metabolic regime and agriculture

The socio-metabolic regime that was common to all societies prior to the Industrial Revolution of the eighteenth century was based on the energy of the sun and was characterized by material dependence on biomass (organic matter of plant, animal, bacterial or fungal origin). Biomass is a source of food and energy (Wrigley, 1988, 2004, 2010) and also a virtually unique source of raw materials. Within a socio-metabolic regime reliant on energy from the sun, agriculture (which produces biomass) generates more than just food. It also provides households with fuel for heating and lighting, fibres and hides for clothing, and much of the materials needed for housing and, through animals, most of the mechanical energy available to these households. Moreover, it plays an essential role in maintaining soil fertility, particularly through livestock farming.

Conversely, the mining-dependent socio-metabolic regime is characterized by the essential role of fossil resources. Coal, oil and natural gas (and to a lesser extent uranium) virtually became the sole sources of mechanical and thermal energy from the Industrial Revolution onwards. The sourcing of materials was also profoundly altered by the use of ores (which could be mined and processed using the abundance of energy available) and by the replacement of biomass-derived products with synthetic ones. The development of organic chemistry played a key role in this regard. From the mid-nineteenth century, it facilitated the production of synthetic dyes, which in turn gave rise to the powerful chemical industry and its giant corporations (Bayer, BASF[2] etc.). This industry – always with a view to replacing natural resources deemed too expensive or with an unreliable supply – then started producing plastics, textile fibres, rubber and so on.

Within the mining-dependent socio-metabolic regime, the demand for agricultural products was no longer driven by a need for energy or materials, and food became the main outlet for agriculture. The emergence of the 'agri-food' and 'food system' concepts, which became self-evident in the twentieth century, clearly reflects this exceptional situation in the history of humankind. Our relationship with animals, especially cattle, is certainly the most illustrative example of this transformation. This livestock – once a source of horns and bones for making widely diverse objects, of fibres and hides for making garments, of tallow for lighting, of mechanical power for ploughing and transport, and of manure to fertilize fields – was then only reared for meat and milk, thus being reduced to a source of protein and lipids.

At the same time, the switch to the mining-dependent socio-metabolic regime led to far-reaching changes in agricultural production, food processing and distribution methods (see Chapter 5). These changes occurred in two distinct stages. First, the agricultural supply process was mainly transformed by the sharp drop in transport costs – for both maritime and, especially, inland transport. Steam engines' fundamental role in this respect cannot be overstated. For the first time in human history, this invention made it possible to convert thermal energy into mechanical energy, thereby completely redefining the question of transport and overcoming the so-called tyranny of distance. This was especially the case for inland transport as it had previously wholly relied on energy from humans and animals. Hinterlands could now be systematically tapped to supply faraway markets. The drop in transport costs also led to massive human migrations, enabling millions of Europeans, as well as Asians (mainly Chinese and Indians), to leave their homelands and 'colonize' distant lands. The steam engine thus helped link previously empty areas (or, more accurately,

---

[2] Abbreviation for the German industrial corporation Badische Anilin und Soda-Fabrik, a world leader in the chemical industry.

areas 'emptied' of their indigenous populations) to Europe, even when they were located thousands of kilometres away. A host of pioneer fronts sprang up in temperate and tropical regions during the second half of the nineteenth century and into the 1920s: the steppes north of the Black Sea, the Manchurian plains, the North American prairies, the Argentinian Pampas, the South African veldt, Brazil's Mata Atlantica, the Sumatran forest and so on.

The second stage in the agricultural industrialization process began after the First World War and was characterized by the direct use of fossil fuels in agricultural production. Three innovations – hallmarks of industrial agriculture and directly linked to fossil fuel use – formed a 'technical package' that was first adopted in the United States before spreading to the rest of the world:[3]

– Tractors: Tractors became accessible from 1917, following the launch of the
   Fordson tractor in the United States, and replaced draught animals (oxen,
   horses and mules) within just a few decades, thereby prompting the widespread
   mechanization of agricultural tasks, a process that had been underway in the
   United States since the early nineteenth century. The tractor emerged as the
   symbol of the agricultural modernization project (Fitzgerald, 2003) and
   became central to the formatting of farm work, which it revolutionized.
– Synthetic nitrogen fertilizers: With the synthesis of ammonia through the
   Haber-Bosch process,[4] fossil fuel use in agriculture took on an entirely
   new dimension. A milestone was reached in 1908 when Haber (working
   for BASF) perfected the process in the laboratory (Smil, 2001). The first
   manufacturing plant became operational in September 1913, a little less
   than a year before the First World War broke out. Ammonia synthesis
   using the Haber-Bosch process accounted for 16 per cent of the world's
   nitrogen fertilizer production (in nitrogen equivalent) by 1920, 62 per cent
   by 1935 and 99 per cent by 1980. At the same time, the total quantity of
   nitrogen used for fertilizer increased tenfold.
– Pesticides: The chemical industry again played a key role in the development
   and dissemination of this new type of input. As Edmund Russell (2001) has
   shown, the first pesticides were a direct by-product of the First World War,
   for which the chemical industry was heavily mobilized.

[3] One specific feature of hegemons is their ability to shape ideas and convince people that the general
    interest is the same as their own (Arrighi, 1994). This is how the United States has broadly set the
    stage for how problems and their solutions are understood, as also relayed by René Dumont, an
    agronomy professor renowned as a leading figure in ecology, in his book *Les leçons de l'agriculture
    américaine* (Dumont, 1949).
[4] A chemical process for fixing atmospheric nitrogen gas into ammonia, used in particular to
    manufacture synthetic nitrogen fertilizers.

Phosphate mining began in the mid-nineteenth century, followed by potash mining in the early twentieth century. The use of these fossil resources offset the need to use recycled sludge and waste to fertilize soils depleted of these two minerals as a result of plant production.

The influence of the chemical industry has more recently extended to a crucial agricultural resource: seeds. Between 1996 and 2013, 200 seed companies were bought up by large chemical corporations (Howard, 2015). This massive chemical industry penetration into the seed business has led to enormous market concentration. The market share of the top five seed companies grew from 10 per cent in 1985 to 47 per cent in 2015, when four of these five leaders were chemical corporations (Monsanto, DuPont, Syngenta and Dow Chemical), with Limagrain being the only exception (Bonny, 2017).

These technical innovations have boosted crop production, with yields soaring as a result of the massive use of inputs and varietal selection geared towards producing varieties that perform well with these chemical inputs. Under the mining-dependent socio-metabolic regime, chemistry – both as a discipline and as an industrial sector – has thus gained a dominant role in dictating agricultural practices through the supply of inputs. From this point of view, so-called conventional agriculture should really be called 'chemical agriculture'.

Agriculturalization, 'sectorization' and the division of labour

Local 'traditional' farming communities, which in France subsisted until the late nineteenth century (Weber, 1979), were involved in a broad range of activities on their farms that enabled them to produce most of the materials required for their agricultural work and for their daily lives. This system did not preclude a division of labour and specialization within farming households, based on the age and gender of individuals. These smallholders were sometimes also involved in various manufacturing activities (weaving, glove making, embroidery, nail making etc.), supplying regional industries.

In Europe, as in the United States, today's farmers are a striking illustration of the division-of-labour approach. Working alone on their farms, these farmers specialize in growing a few crops or rearing a particular livestock species (Nicourt, 2013). They buy fertilizers, seeds, machinery and pesticides from specialist companies and sell raw materials. Meanwhile, their spouses work in neighbouring towns, and their cash earnings serve to buy virtually all of the goods consumed by the household from a nearby supermarket. This situation can be seen as the result of a dual farm-specialization dynamic driven by a vertical (agriculturalization) and horizontal (sectorization) division of labour.

The agriculturalization of the peasant economy (Shanin, 1974), in other words the increased specialization of peasants in agricultural activities, was the first stage in the process of division of labour. The Industrial Revolution triggered this trend by reducing the price of manufactured goods and concentrating their production in urban areas. This led to the emergence of food processing industries, which performed (increasingly standardized) agricultural product–processing operations that had previously been carried out on farms at a low cost and on a more regular basis (albeit using a great deal of fossil fuel). For example, wine growers became wine producers, cheese makers became milk producers and so on. It is worth noting that the food industry also began taking on a growing number of tasks previously handled by households, right up to actual cooking, with the development, in the twentieth century, of ready-made canned, frozen or tray meals that could be reheated at home. The rise of agriculturalization also stemmed from the fact that it enabled farmers to gain income by engaging in the long-distance national and international trade of agricultural products (facilitated by the development of transport). The creation of standards and futures markets, which underpinned the status of primary commodities and, later, price stabilization policies, transformed the trading profession. Once protected from price risks, traders were able to step beyond their delivery or brokering role – never owning the product but merely organizing its circulation – and source the products directly in rural areas (Daviron, 2002).

At the same time, farms were specializing in a limited number of products. In Europe, one of the most visible signs of this was the demise of mixed farming and the separation of crop and livestock production. Synthetic chemical fertilizer treatments enabled farmers to grow crops year after year without manure. Moreover, as animal feed became readily available, farmers could rear livestock without land, or with the bare minimum of land necessary to spread the farm manure and slurry generated on the farm, which had become burdensome waste products. Mechanization was also a major driving force of specialization, forcing farmers to produce large quantities of a particular crop or livestock product in order to cushion the cost of specialized equipment. This also prevented, or severely restricted, the growing of mixed crops on the same plot of land.

A division of labour also emerged at national and international levels, as a result of the reduction in transport costs and the advent of new food preservation techniques (refrigeration, freezing). Some regions specialized in growing a certain crop or raising a particular type of livestock. Entire countries followed suit in the late nineteenth and early twentieth centuries, with Argentina specializing in wheat, corn, beef and flax; Burma in rice; Brazil in coffee; and New Zealand in dairy products. Today, this trend is once again witnessed as part of the so-called second globalization, for instance, with soybeans being produced in Latin America and wheat and maize in Ukraine.

Industrial farming is thus now specialized and integrated, with upstream multinational chemical corporations supplying pesticides, fertilizers and seeds; feed mills supplying animal feed; banks providing credit; and specialized companies providing agricultural machinery. Likewise, large-scale cooperatives, traders and a handful of food companies and supermarkets prevail downstream. To complete the picture, it is also worth mentioning the host of organizations – cooperatives, whether private or public – offering services as well as technical and economic advice. Farmers are now just cogs in what has become the 'industrial food system', dependent on many other actors. Little is left of farming communities' relative autonomy – understood here as their ability to set their own rules.

Americanization, liberalization and bureaucratization

Although the hegemony of the United States has repeatedly been proclaimed to be declining or dead, it never ceased to assert itself over the course of the twentieth century. However, it did not follow a linear trend; two defining moments stand out: the victory over Germany and Japan in 1945 and the victory over the USSR in 1989. Throughout the period in between, despite a sharp drop in its share of global wealth and radical shifts in economic policy, the United States has provided a model for the rest of the world, disseminating new ways of organizing production and trade.

The United States has played a pioneering role in the fields of agriculture and food since the nineteenth century. A diverse range of agricultural machines were invented in that country, which heralded the advent of motorization in the following century as well as the standardization of agricultural products and the invention of futures markets (Cronon, 1991) – almost perfect markets according to economics textbooks, with pure and perfect competition, perfect information, no uncertainty over the quality of the traded commodities and so on. It was also in the United States that the 'visible hand of managers' (Chandler, 1977) first took hold, with the rise of giant corporations (General Foods, Procter and Gamble, Massey Ferguson, Cargill etc.). These corporations could only prosper through bureaucratic abundance, with an army of white-collar workers responsible for planning, controlling, advising, negotiating and influencing, in addition to many other functions in the so-called management domain – a process which Michel Foucault referred to as the 'conduct of conduct' of individuals (Dreyfus and Rabinow, 1982).

In the mid-twentieth century, in the wake of two world wars and an equally global economic crisis, the United States became the national economy par excellence, capable of producing everything it consumed and consuming everything it produced. It became a model, which six Western European countries sought to replicate by uniting within a community. Under the banner of 'development', this model also fascinated the rulers of Latin American countries and recently decolonized African and Asian countries. In the agricultural sector, the focus on the national market was largely underpinned by generalized state intervention. Franklin D. Roosevelt's presidency had implemented this intervention strategy to tackle overproduction, which free market forces had not seemed capable of curbing. Surpluses built up again at the end of the Second World War and the Korean War (1951–3). Set-aside land, public stockpiling, support for the promotion of meat consumption, food aid, the opening up of oilseed and protein crop markets elsewhere in the world, and the subsequent support for biofuels were instruments deployed by US authorities to reduce these surpluses. In Europe, the Common Agricultural Policy (CAP) also introduced a wide range of instruments to regulate agricultural markets. French dreams of imperial self-sufficiency were abandoned in favour of a new dream: food self-sufficiency. Now so-called developing countries also embraced this slogan, even though agricultural taxation prevailed in the name of accelerated industrialization (Daviron, 2020).

In the late 1970s, neoliberalism emerged. State intervention in the market, though previously praised, became reviled. Margaret Thatcher was the first to negotiate this turn in the United Kingdom. Ronald Reagan soon followed suit in the United States, using resources on an entirely different scale (including the dollar) to offer the world a new economic policy standard. Compared to the liberalism of the eighteenth and nineteenth centuries, neoliberalism was marked by a vision of the market as an instrument of competition rather than cooperation. Liberalization became the watchword in agricultural markets. International negotiations under the General Agreement on Tariffs and Trade (GATT) – the forerunner of the World Trade Organization – and the structural adjustment programmes of the International Monetary Fund and the World Bank forced the dismantling of public market regulation systems at a pace and on a scale inversely proportional 'to the wealth (and power) of nations'. In countries of the Organisation for Economic Co-operation and Development

(OECD), decoupled payments – direct aid paid to farmers irrespective of the volumes produced – were widely adopted. In African countries, the impacts of liberalization were tempered by their reduced participation in international trade. In China and India, countries with both a population and soon an amount of US Treasury bonds (loans issued by the US government) that have passed the billion mark, state intervention held firm.

True, honest and effective competition, however, cannot be achieved simply through the withdrawal of the state; it is also essential to monitor, control and accredit respect for this competition. Hence the new wave of bureaucracy on the horizon (Hibou, 2015): after being chased away together with the administrative machinery implemented to regulate agricultural market prices, bureaucracy is back in a new guise. Farmers now have to demonstrate the merits of their practices in order to benefit from certain types of support in the form of targeted public aid (second pillar of the CAP) or higher prices (organic products). These practices must therefore be monitored. Certification – like auditing in the world of joint-stock companies – is the preferred instrument to do so. Industrial agriculture has thus acquired a new component that is far from being conducive to farmers' autonomy.

Conclusion

This chapter has presented a brief history of industrial agriculture, up to and including recent developments. This is just a basic outline: although the different processes discussed above occurred almost worldwide, this does not imply uniformization or the emergence of a 'global food system'. The distinction between 'states' and 'trends' (Kautsky, 1988) is key here. Trends may potentially influence all countries, but their effects (the resulting states) may radically differ between areas due to the diverse range of baseline situations at stake and the different degrees of resistance and opposition encountered. Diversity prevails despite hegemony.

Finally, although industrialization has been the target of substantial well-founded social and environmental criticism (Chapter 7), it is important to keep in mind that this system has helped feed a global population whose numbers soared over the course of the twentieth century. Despite the downturn in agricultural commodity prices, this trend has also led to a very significant increase in farmers' incomes as a result of labour productivity increasing even faster than crop yields. I point this out not to defend industrial agriculture on the grounds of its productive performance, but rather to highlight the challenges facing the different widely advocated agricultural and food alternatives (as described in other chapters of this book).

This chapter largely draws on the author's book *Biomasse – Une histoire de richesse et de puissance* (2020) and his contributions at the 2019 Master's training seminar organized by the UNESCO Chair in World Food Systems titled 'From solar energy to fossil fuels, a history of the role of agriculture in development'.

The author would like to thank Nicolas Bricas, Damien Conaré, Mathilde Coudray and Marie Walser for proofreading this chapter and for their suggested improvements.

References

Arrighi G., 1994. *The long twentieth century: money, power, and the origins of our times*, London, Verso, 400 p.

Bonny S., 2017. Corporate concentration and technological change in the global seed industry. *Sustainability*, 9: 1632. https://doi.org/10.3390/su9091632

Chandler A.D., 1977. *The visible hand: the managerial revolution in American business*, Cambridge, MA, Belknap Press, 608 p.

Cronon W., 1991. *Nature's metropolis. Chicago and the Great West*, New York, W. W. Norton & Company, 530 p.

Daviron B., 2002. Small farm production and the standardization of tropical products. *Journal of Agrarian Change*, 2: 162–184. https://doi.org/10.1111/1471-0366.00029

Daviron B., 2020. *Biomasse. Une histoire de richesse et de puissance*, Versailles, Quæ, 392 p.

Dreyfus H., Rabinow P., 1982. *Michel Foucault: beyond structuralism and hermeneutics*, Brighton, Harvester Press, 231 p.

Dumont R., 1949. *Les leçons de l'agriculture américaine*, Paris, Flammarion, 368 p.

Durkheim É., 1933. *The division of labor in society*, New York, Free Press, 439 p. Translation of 'De la division du travail social' (1893).

Fischer-Kowalski M., Haberl H., 2007. *Socioecological transitions and global change: trajectories of social metabolism and land use*, Cheltenham/Northampton, Edward Elgar Publishing, 288 p.

Fitzgerald D., 2003. *Every farm a factory: the industrial ideal in American agriculture*, New Haven, Yale University Press, 242 p.

Gellner E., 1983. *Nations and nationalism*, Ithaca, Cornell University Press, 150 p.

Gellner E., 1989. *Plough, sword, and book: the structure of human history*, Chicago, University of Chicago Press, 288 p.

Giddens A., 1990. *The consequences of modernity*, Cambridge, Polity Press, 186 p.

Haberl H., Fischer-Kowalski M., Krausmann F., Winiwarter V., 2016. *Social Ecology – Society-nature relations across time and space*, New York, Springer International Publishing, 610 p.

Hibou B., 2015. *The bureaucratization of the world in the neoliberal era*, New York, Palgrave Macmillan, 260 p. Translation of 'La bureaucratisation du monde à l'ère néolibérale' (2012).

Howard P.H., 2015. Intellectual property and consolidation in the seed industry. *Crop Science*, 55(6): 2489–2495. https://doi.org/10.2135/cropsci2014.09.0669

Kautsky K., 1988. *The agrarian question* (2 vols.), London, Zwan Publications, 459 p.

Nicourt C., 2013. *Être agriculteur aujourd'hui. L'individualisation du travail des agriculteurs*, Versailles, Quæ, 288 p.

Russell E., 2001. *War and nature: fighting humans and insects with chemicals from World War I to Silent Spring*, Cambridge/New York, Cambridge University Press, 332 p.

Shanin T., 1974. The nature and logic of the peasant economy II & III. *Journal of Peasant Studies*, 1(2): 186–206. https://doi.org/10.1080/03066157408437883

Smil V., 2001. *Enriching the Earth: Fritz Haber, Carl Bosch, and the transformation of world food production*, Cambridge, MA/London, MIT Press, 338 p.

Smith A., 1776. *The wealth of nations*, New York, The Modern Library.

Weber E., 1979. *Peasants into Frenchmen: the modernization of rural France, 1870–1914*, London, Chatto and Windus, 615 p.

Wrigley E.A., 1988. *Continuity, chance and change: the character of the industrial revolution in England*, Cambridge, Cambridge University Press, 154 p.

Wrigley E.A., 2004. *Poverty, progress, and population*, Cambridge, Cambridge University Press, 478 p.

Wrigley E.A., 2010. *Energy and the English industrial revolution*, Cambridge, Cambridge University Press, 288 p.

5

The industrialization of the food supply

Nicolas Bricas, Damien Conaré and Marie Walser

A far-reaching transformation of the food supply is underway, fuelled by technical and economic developments that are not specific to the food sector. An industrial food model is emerging and spreading. This model, however, should not be understood as a natural outcome of the way we organize our food supply.

The configuration of any food system[1] is determined by the articulation of different forms of agricultural production (Chapter 4), the processing and distribution of the food supply (the focus of this chapter), and food demand (Chapter 6). It is closely linked to the technical, social and economic dynamics that permeate societies.

The history of food supply has been shaped by technological and economic developments that have influenced the ways in which food is produced and distributed, as well as its nature, origin and the ways of accessing it. This chapter looks at four major trends with a more or less long history: the intensification and juxtaposition of these trends over the nineteenth and twentieth centuries led to the emergence and dissemination of an industrial agri-food model.[2] We focus specifically on technological changes in the way our food is processed, the globalization of trade, the concentration of stakeholders in the agri-food industry and the boom in digital technology. Ultimately, this chapter seeks to nuance the widely held belief that the contemporary food system was built in stages – linearly

---

[1] As defined by Louis Malassis (1994), this refers to 'the way in which people organize themselves in space and time to obtain and consume their food'.

[2] Rastoin and Ghersi (2010) refer to the 'agro-industrial model', with the prefix 'agro' referring more to agriculture and the production of agricultural raw material than to food processing, marketing and distribution operations and actors further downstream, which the term 'agri-food' is deemed to denote more accurately.

over time – and that it is converging towards its final stage, founded on an industrial model.

Technological developments in food processing

For hundreds of thousands of years, humans have implemented a range of methods to process all or part of their food resources for the purpose of extracting their edible components, slowing down or controlling their degradation, ensuring their safety or digestibility and improving their organoleptic properties. The first food processing operations date back to prehistoric times, which were already characterized by the use of processing tools (stone or wooden), the cooking of food in connection with the domestication of fire and the application of fermentation methods (Hutkins, 2018; Sinsheimer, 2018). For instance, as early as the seventh millennium BCE in China, there is evidence of the production – in clay jars – of a fermented beverage made from rice, honey and fruit (hawthorn and grapes), which had a social, religious and medicinal function (McGovern et al., 2004).

Food processing was long a manual domestic activity handled mainly by women. The first processing operations – cereal threshing, seed grinding and pressing – served to separate edible from inedible components and to prepare products for storage. With the advent of water and animal power, the first mechanized processing operations appeared, leading to the emergence – at different times around the world – of specialized craft activities, often carried out by men who became millers, pressers, dryers, slaughterers and other food processors (Sigault, 1993). During Antiquity, in parallel with domestic cooking, 'secondary processing' (from flour to bread and pasta, from crude to refined oils, from carcass meat to cut pieces etc.) became more professionalized. There is evidence that specialized staff – brewers, bakers, butchers, pastry makers and other culinary professionals – worked in ancient Egyptian palaces (Bresciani, 1999).

With the Industrial Revolution came significant developments in technical food processing systems, particularly as a result of advances outside the food industry (Birlouez, 2019). Progress in various scientific disciplines (thermodynamics, biology, chemistry, physics, mechanics and materials science), the development of process engineering, as well as the rise of computer science and electronics from the twentieth century all contributed to the emergence of the agri-food industry. The discovery of appertization (canning) in 1795 and the invention of the ammonia refrigeration machine in 1858 heralded a major revolution in food preservation. Building on the scientific advances of the nineteenth century, the following century was marked by the invention of a host of new technologies: food irradiation (1905), freeze-drying (1906), high-pressure processing (1910), rapid freezing (1929), microwaves (1947), milk ultrafiltration (1969) and others.

In processing plants, step by step, the use of low-cost fossil fuels, the development of automation and the rationalization of work helped boost production rates while reducing post-harvest losses. This revolutionized food processing, preservation and traceability – the mass, standardized production of industrial food began, driven by economies of scale and long-distance transportation, which in turn enhanced food hygiene and shelf life.

At the same time, the food industry was also changing in step with advances in food science, especially with the implementation of a two-stage food processing approach (Soler et al., 2013). Raw materials – which were becoming increasingly standardized and more competitive in the upstream agricultural sector – were processed to extract simple ingredients such as sugar, flour, fats, fruit purées, milk proteins, starch, carrageenan and so on. These ingredients, derived from different processing operations, were then used to make finished products with new organoleptic, nutritional or preservative properties. This food reconstitution process sometimes required the use of additives, including texture, colour and taste enhancers, which could be natural – for example, soya lecithin, turmeric or starch – or chemical – for example, aspartame. This approach was pushed to the limit with the manufacture of so-called ultra-processed foods, which now dominate the food supply in high-income countries[3] (Monteiro et al., 2013).

This approach is illustrated by the hourglass in Figure 5.1. Working with a certain range of agricultural raw materials, a handful of intermediate products and new processes can be used to manufacture a multitude of novel processed end products (Soler et al., 2013) to meet ever-changing consumer expectations (Chapter 6).

Food supply diversification is not limited to opportunities afforded by technical developments in processing methods. Industrial products are linked with a growing number of tangible and intangible services: increasingly sophisticated packaging designed for new uses, information and advice shared by brands on their digital platforms, games and competitions and similar digital activities. These features help differentiate products and target ever more refined consumer segments (children, seniors, sports fans, sick people etc.), thereby giving rise to personal nutrition opportunities and thus new potential sources of added value. Hence, the raw materials in industrially produced food products account for

---

[3] Yet these foods are also becoming widely available in low-income countries, particularly in Southeast and East Asia.

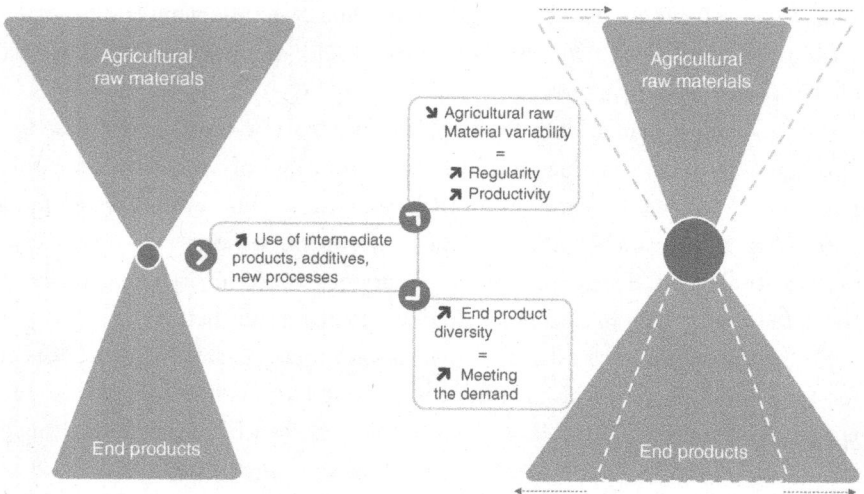

Figure 5.1 The shift of the diversification of the agroindustrial food supply further downstream through the use of intermediate goods and new processes.

Diagram adapted from Gilles Trystram's presentation 'What food technology innovations?' (UNESCO Chair in World Food Systems, 2014).

an ever smaller share of the final product value. Coffee exemplifies this trend: when a person buys a coffee, they first pay for the beans, then for the fact that it is ground, freeze-dried and packaged in pods and capsules. Paradoxically, this means that although food product prices are rising, producers are not being paid more (Daviron and Ponte, 2005).

In addition, the industrialization of food processing has coincided with advances in logistics. The internal combustion engine and oil-based technologies revolutionized transport, speeding up its development and reducing its cost. Agricultural raw materials upstream and finished products downstream can now be transported far beyond their production areas. The development of cold-chain processes has also enhanced the transportation of fresh produce. These advances have been essential to long-distance trade, mass distribution and out-of-home catering. The domestic use of certain technologies, such as refrigerators (from the 1930s) and microwaves (from the 1970s), created new opportunities for innovation in the food processing industry. Together, these technological developments in food processing and preservation have fostered growth in production volume, greater food availability across space and time, cost savings through economies of scale and, above all, the diversification of the food supply.

Finally, the food supply influences consumption patterns while also being responsive to changing lifestyles. Food innovations do not suddenly emerge, nor do they affect everyone – the dynamics of the prevailing gastronomic value system may dictate how slowly or quickly they are adopted (Flandrin, 1989) (Chapter 6).

Trade globalization

While trade globalization has intensified since the nineteenth century (Marnot, 2012), it dates back to much earlier times. Recent studies have shown that Asian foods were already being imported into the Mediterranean Basin as far back as the Bronze Age, 4,000 years ago (Scott et al., 2021). More recently, in the sixteenth century, potatoes, tomatoes and maize were brought to Europe from Latin America, gradually expanding the variety of foods eaten by Europeans as well as by Asians and Africans (Mendes Ferrão, 2005; Fumey and Raffard, 2013). Food products were sometimes the drivers of exploration voyages to discover novel ingredients such as spices and stimulants. Breakfast – which in Europe is a combination of tea, coffee, chocolate and sugar – is a clear illustration of the fact that 'the world [has long been] in our cups' (Mintz, 1986; Grataloup, 2017). In Europe, in the fourteenth and fifteenth centuries, around three quarters of bourgeois and noble cuisine dishes featured large quantities of more than fifteen spices. The French subsequently came to neglect spices from the sixteenth century, with the exception of pepper, cloves and nutmeg (Flandrin, 1989). It was not just food that travelled; culinary techniques were also exchanged and enriched (Gassie, 2017). For instance, in the sixteenth century, cassava was introduced to the Gulf of Guinea region of Africa, along with the Brazilian technique for processing it into fermented semolina. The Beninese dish gari was thus inspired by the Brazilian dish farinha (Muchnik and Vinck, 1984).

This trade is also driven by the urbanization of our planet. Historically, with the exception of fresh produce grown in the vicinity of suburban areas and cities with a flourishing breadbasket hinterland (e.g. Paris and the Île-de-France region in France), urban areas were supplied in part through long-distance trade. In the fifteenth century, cities such as Venice and Genoa, located by the sea or inland waterways, imported wheat from Egypt. Amsterdam did the same with imports from Ukraine. But as Fernand Braudel points out:

> It matters little to them who produces [the food] and the archaic or modern way it is produced [. . .]. Most, if not all, of the primary sector necessary to ensure their subsistence and even luxury standards are mainly outside [the cities], and work for them without them having to contend with the economic or social difficulties surrounding production.
>
> —Braudel, 1992

A few major cities, such as Angkor and Alexandria, were outliers in this regard: it was not the food there that came from afar, but rather the fertilizers. These cities were located close to agricultural areas enriched by fertilizing alluvial deposits percolating from distant upstream watersheds (Evans et al., 2007; Viollet, 2007). This highly productive land produced surplus crops that could feed city dwellers employed in the construction of temples.

From the second half of the nineteenth century, long-distance trade accelerated. The steady increase in fossil fuel use reduced the cost and time of sea and road transport, while the introduction of quality standards enabled people to obtain goods through long-distance purchases without having to actually see them. This latter mechanism in turn facilitated the development of futures markets for agricultural raw materials (Chapter 4). As part of the market expansion process, standardization embeds companies in global value chains comprising networks of international private or private–public actors. Moreover, standardization helps companies meet multiple objectives, such as compliance with hygiene and health safety regulations (with the development of standard methods like the HACCP[4] standards system, for instance) or the implementation of commercial differentiation strategies through the creation of labels for products meeting precise specifications – registered designations of origin, protected geographical indications, private brands and so on (Lamanthe, 2007).

This food standardization process is intensifying competition within agricultural sectors, as products such as cereals, oilseeds, coffee, milk powder and sugar can all be traded on the same market irrespective of their origin. A growing number of countries are able to take part in this trade depending on their comparative advantages. This expansion is helping to stabilize agricultural prices, which are inherently volatile due to irregular crop harvests – the inevitable risk of an exporter defaulting after a poor harvest may be offset by the performance of another, better-off exporter. Yet futures markets and their speculative contracts have also heralded the arrival of financial players in the food trade, with the risk of generating speculative bubbles such as the one that fuelled the surge in food prices in 2008. Speculation by merchants has always been rife in agricultural markets whenever stockpiling was possible, but the scale and scope of this phenomenon changed markedly with the advent of economic globalization and financialization.

---

[4] Acronym for 'Hazard Analysis Critical Control Points', an analytical system for monitoring food hazards.

A concentration of actors

This dual trend of replacing human labour with machines and growing market financialization is contributing to the reconfiguration of food system actors. What started as a decentralized patchwork of small-scale commercial activities – initially rural and then increasingly urban – is giving way to larger and more concentrated companies, with the rise of the giant multinational corporations that prevail today: Nestlé, PepsiCo, Unilever, Coca-Cola, Mars, Mondelez, Danone, General Mills, Kellogg's, Associated British Food and so on. It is thus estimated that the top ten food and beverage companies account for 37.5 per cent of the market share of the world's hundred leading food companies (IPES-Food, 2017). However, these companies account for only a quarter of total sales across the entire industry. Concentration is far higher in agricultural supply sectors – particularly for pesticides – where the top ten companies have captured 80 per cent of the market (Rastoin and Ghersi, 2010).

As the sector becomes more concentrated, its market structure is moving towards an oligopoly-fringe model (Rastoin, 2012) – a few leading firms dominate, with smaller operators (micro-, small- and medium-sized enterprises. on-farm processors etc.) filling the market gaps. Power is concentrated among a handful of giant companies that use their massive influence to shape and implement public policy in their favour.

Yet we should not limit ourselves to an 'evolutionary' typology of the actors involved, going from 'rural and traditional' actors to large 'consolidated industrial' companies (HLPE, 2017; Johns Hopkins University and GAIN, 2021), which would imply that small businesses are doomed to disappear and make way for larger ones. More often than not, interactions between micro-, small-, medium- and large-sized companies are competitive or complementary (Gasselin et al., 2023). Moreover, new business forms are emerging in response to purely capitalist dynamics, for instance, within the social solidarity economy (Chapter 20). They are also prompting conventional companies to innovate to meet social sustainability challenges (Boltanski and Chiapello, 2005).

In the late twentieth century, a new actor emerged and became increasingly powerful: mass retailers. This sector, which initially focused on retail (supermarkets and hypermarkets), has expanded into a range of areas – logistics (platforms), competing with wholesale markets; processing, with the development of private labels; and the banking sector, with consumer credit offers. Supermarkets and hypermarkets are springing up almost everywhere worldwide, in step with the rise of the middle class (Reardon et al., 2003). Competition between suppliers and upstream producers in this sector has increased as a result of operator concentration and globalization.

With the advent of mass conventional and digital retail, competition between products displayed on the same shelf or web page is intensifying. Marketing and communication are now crucial to business strategies. Brands have become virtual substitutes for products – in other words, the symbolic prestige of the brand transcends the actual tangible features of the product. Merchandising, packaging and advertising are all ways to make a product stand out from the competition (Cochoy, 2002). A product's reputation thus precedes its use. On supermarket shelves, consumers now find product information on the packaging, which has superseded interpersonal relationships with shopkeepers. Hence, major agri-food groups are seeking to gain knowledge of their customers and get closer to them by enlisting marketing professionals. Meanwhile, the concentration of mass-market retailers is increasing the power imbalance within the food industry. These retailers' payment terms enable them to invest the cash flow generated by consumer sales, which in turn allows them to operate with relatively narrow commercial margins and thus to offer highly competitive prices.

Finally, there are more and more intermediaries, and the chain between producers and eaters is lengthening. The food system is no longer confined to the actors directly working with food products. The role of suppliers of equipment and intermediate inputs and services (energy, packaging, digital solutions) is also steadily growing. An entire economic sector now indirectly supports companies that produce and market food products (research, studies, consultancy, insurance, finance, communication etc.). As these facilitation services professionalize, they are also increasingly engaging with a diverse range of food and non-food sectors.

The rise of digital technology

Since the late twentieth century, food systems have increasingly been incorporating digital economy tools and operators. Digital technology is transforming all stages of the food system – from agricultural production to meal ordering – in terms of both the way they operate and the configuration of the networks of actors involved.

On a global scale, digital technology has been bolstered by the development of satellite and airborne imagery (via drones), delivering increasingly precise geographical information that enables users to calculate the size of a population, its movements and living conditions, and even to estimate the extent of poverty

(Jean et al., 2016). In the agricultural sector, satellite imagery is used on more localized scales to map agro-climatic indicators that may be useful to farmers. These maps enable farmers to fine-tune the management of their farming operations. Pesticide suppliers, for instance, propose digital applications in combination with agricultural machinery to optimize the use of inputs (GRAIN, 2021). These tools also serve to record farming practices and thus report on production conditions. This facilitates the certification of compliance with specifications without the need for costly visits from an agency to monitor a farmer's practices – provided the farmer is able to invest in this new digital equipment. This monitoring also extends to workers. It is now possible to precisely track, and therefore control, these workers' movements and activities through smartphone location tracking – a process that is already implemented in online retailers' warehouses.

Blockchain – a shared database that allows for any transaction to be recorded without the risk of falsification – a technology initially developed for the Bitcoin cryptocurrency, is now being used for land titles and product traceability (Tian, 2016). Its high level of tamper resistance removes the need for central control agencies. This trend is paving the way for greater traceability of product origin and routing, though it is of course contingent on the standardization of product quality.

The greatest impact of the rise of digital technology is likely to be on distribution and consumption. First, it is shaping online food product ordering practices. The recording of food references in databases used to fill the virtual shelves of online ordering sites makes it considerably easier to compare products within the same category, thus paving the way for comparative rating systems that offer better consumer advice. The composition of food products and the conditions under which they are produced are now more easily identifiable, thus making them key areas of competition for businesses. Online shopping is also giving rise to new purchasing practices. It provides access to online ratings or comments, which shoppers can use to assess the reputation of different products or manufacturers. However, the lack of oversight of these participatory systems means that this information can be adulterated. For instance, companies can purchase pseudo-user reviews to promote their products or undermine the reputation of competitors (Casilli, 2019).

The growing use of computers, tablets and smartphones for online information, shopping and payment has facilitated the collection of information on consumers' interests, purchases, movements and sometimes health, and – through nanotechnology – perhaps soon even their live physiological state (blood sugar, blood alcohol content etc.). The arrival of smart food processors and fridges in households is also enabling the collection of data on domestic practices. These data can be analysed to draw up consumer profiles – so-called profiling, which is valuable to businesses – and to advise consumers directly, offering them suggested products or personalized recommendations.

Messaging applications and video chats on social networks are used in various ways in the food industry, including the sharing of advice, testimonials (e.g. so-called grocery haul posts on online video sites), information and tutorials on products, shops, cooking, nutrition and religious and ethical practices. This has led to the emergence on social networks of 'food influencers' (Zirari, 2017) whose videos are widely viewed. Social networks are also used to advertise, sell and order products or ready-made meals within a customer network (Chapter 16). This commercial avenue allows people to buy food directly from farmers or ready-made meals from semi-professional, work-from-home chefs.

The rise of digital technology seems to be a continuation of the ever-increasing standardization of products and a means of streamlining and saving time, thus furthering the food system industrialization process. At the same time, private individuals are mobilizing this technology to share knowledge, practices and innovations via potentially copyright-free processes (IPES-Food, 2017; Hérault et al., 2019) (Chapter 18). Such sharing takes place outside, and sometimes even in opposition to, capitalist markets while generating new forms of social ties.

Conclusion

All of the trends described in this chapter have contributed to the industrialization of the food supply and the commodification of food. First, the social perception of food is changing: in our collective imaginary, it is gradually being stripped down to its commercial market attributes (price, convenience, image), to the detriment of its cultural, health, environmental and ethical dimensions, which are regarded as externalities at best. Second, the management of food systems has been entrusted to a hybrid form of governance by public authorities and the private sector, ultimately excluding citizens (Vivero Pol et al., 2020) (Chapters 18 and 22). However, contrary to the idea of a 'triumph of mass consumption and the capitalized and internationalized agro-industrial system' suggested by Louis Malassis (1997), the rise of this kind of food system does not preclude other forms of food organization – it combines with, shapes and draws inspiration from these forms of organization rather than replacing them. While digital technology is gaining ground and offering new opportunities for industrial actors, it is also a counterbalancing force used in alternative initiatives. Despite trade globalization, the food system industrialization process is far from being a reality everywhere. In all regions of the world, food-consumption patterns combine local and distant production, as well as raw produce and industrially processed food (Chapter 6).

The authors would like to thank Mathilde Coudray, Jean-Louis Rastoin and Gilles Trystram for proofreading this chapter and for their suggested improvements.

References

Birlouez E., 2019. L'évolution de la perception de la qualité alimentaire au cours des âges. *INRAE Productions Animales*, 32(1): 25–36. https://doi.org/10.20870/productions-animales.2019.32.1.2419

Boltanski L., Chiapello È., 2005. *The new spirit of capitalism*, London/New York, Verso, 601 p. Translation of 'Le nouvel esprit du capitalisme' (1999).

Braudel F., 1992. *Civilization and Capitalism, 15th–18th century*, Vol. III: The perspective of the world, Berkeley/Los Angeles, University of California Press, 704 p. Translation of 'Civilisation, économie et capitalisme, XVe–XVIIIe siècles, tome 3: Le temps du monde' (1979).

Bresciani E., 1999. Food culture in Ancient Egypt, in Flandrin J.-L., Montanari M. (ed.), *Food: a culinary history*, New York, Columbia University Press, 38–45. Translation of 'Nourritures et boissons de l'Égypte ancienne' (1996).

Casilli A.A., 2019. *En attendant les robots. Enquête sur le travail du clic*, Paris, Seuil, 394 p.

Cochoy F., 2002. *Sociologie du packaging ou l'âne de Buridan face au marché*, Paris, PUF, 232 p.

Daviron B., Ponte S., 2005. *The coffee paradox: global markets, commodity trade and the elusive promise of development*, London/New York, Zed Books, 320 p.

Evans D., Pottier C., Fletcher R., Hensley S., Tapley I., Milne A., Barbetti M., 2007. A comprehensive archaeological map of the world's largest preindustrial settlement complex at Angkor, Cambodia, *Proceedings of the National Academy of Sciences*, 104(36): 14277–14282. https://doi.org/10.1073/pnas.0702525104

Flandrin J.-L., 1989. Le goût a son histoire. *Autrement*, 108: 56–65.

Fumey G., Raffard P., 2018. *Atlas de l'alimentation*, Paris, CNRS, 290 p.

Gasselin P., Lardon S., Cerdan C., Loudiyi S., Sautier D. (ed.), 2023. *Coexistence and confrontation of agricultural and food models: a new paradigm of territorial development?*, Versailles/Dordrecht, Quæ/Springer, 315 p. https://doi.org/10.1007/978-94-024-2178-1

Gassie J., 2017. Les conduites alimentaires, in Claquin P., Martin A., Deram C., Delgoulet E., Gassie J., Hérault B. (ed.), *MOND'Alim 2030, panorama prospectif de la mondialisation des systèmes alimentaires*, Paris, La Documentation française, 23–47.

GRAIN, 2021. *Contrôle numérique: comment les Big Tech se tournent vers l'alimentation et l'agriculture (et ce que cela signifie)*, Barcelona, GRAIN, 18 p.

Grataloup C., 2017. *Le monde dans nos tasses. Trois siècles de petit-déjeuner*, Paris, Armand Colin, 272 p.

Hérault B., Gassie J., Lamy A., 2019. *Transformations sociétales et grandes tendances alimentaires*, document de travail, Paris, Ministère de l'Agriculture et de l'Alimentation, Centre d'études et de prospective, 43 p.

HLPE, 2017. *Nutrition and food systems. A report by the High Level Panel of Experts on Food Security and Nutrition of the Committee on World Food Security*, Rome, Committee on World Food Security, 151 p.

Hutkins R.W., 2018. *Microbiology and technology of fermented foods* (2nd edition), Oxford, Wiley-Blackwell, 624 p.

IPES-Food, 2017. *Too big to feed. Exploring the impacts of mega-mergers, consolidation and concentration of power in the agri-food sector*, Brussels, IPES-Food, 108 p.

Jean N., Burke M., Xie M., Davis W.M., Lobell D.B., Ermon S., 2016. Combining satellite imagery and machine learning to predict poverty. *Science*, 353(6301): 790–794. https://doi.org/10.1126/science.aaf7894

Johns Hopkins University, GAIN, 2021. *Food systems dashboard/food systems types*, Baltimore, Johns Hopkins University, GAIN.

Lamanthe A., 2007. Extension des marchés et normalisation: les systèmes agroalimentaires dans la mondialisation. *Géographie, économie, société*, 9(3): 257–270. https://doi.org/10.3166/ges.9.257-270

Malassis L., 1994. *Nourrir les hommes: un exposé pour comprendre, un essai pour réfléchir*, Paris, Flammarion, 126 p.

Malassis L., 1997. *Les trois âges de l'alimentaire. Tome II: L'âge agro-industriel*, Paris, éditions Cujas, 376 p.

Marnot B., 2012. *La mondialisation au XIXe siècle*, Paris, Armand Colin, 288 p.

McGovern P.E., Zhang J., Tang J., Zhang Z., Hall G.R., Moreau R.A. et al., 2004. Fermented beverages of pre- and proto-historic China. *Proceedings of the National Academy of Sciences*, 51(101): 17593–17598. https://doi.org/10.1073/pnas.0407921102

Mendes Ferrão J., 2005. *A aventura das plantas e os descobrimentos portugueses*, Lisboa, Institute of Tropical Scientific Research, 288 p.

Mintz S.-W., 1986. *Sweetness and power: the place of sugar in modern history*, New York, Elisabeth Sifton Books, 274 p.

Monteiro C.A., Moubarac J.-C., Cannon G., Ng S.W., Popkin B., 2013. Ultra-processed products are becoming dominant in the global food system. *Obesity Reviews*, 14(S2): 21–28. https://doi.org/10.1111/obr.12107

Muchnik J., Vinck D., 1984. *La transformation du manioc. Technologies autochtones*, Paris, Agence de coopération culturelle et technique, Conseil international de la langue française, PUF, 172 p.

Rastoin J.-L., 2012. The agri-food industry at the heart of the global food system, in Jacquet P., Pachauri K., Tubiana L. (ed.), *Development, the environment and food: towards agricultural change?*, New Delhi, Teri Press, 183–194.

Rastoin J.-L., Ghersi G., 2010. *Le système alimentaire mondial. Concepts et méthodes, analyses et dynamiques*, Versailles, Quæ, 586 p.

Reardon T., Timmer C., Barrett C., Berdegué J., 2003. The rise of supermarkets in Africa, Asia, and Latin America. *American Journal of Agricultural Economics*, 85: 1140–1146. https://doi.org/10.1111/j.0092-5853.2003.00520.x

Scott A., Power R.C., Altmann-Wendling V., Artzy M., Martin M.A.S., Eisenmann S. et al., 2021. Exotic foods reveal contact between South Asia and the Near East during the second millennium BCE. *Proceedings of the National Academy of Sciences*, 118(2): e2014956117. https://doi.org/10.1073/pnas.2014956117

Sigault F., 1993. Le pain, histoire alimentaire, histoire technique, in Muchnik J. (ed.), *Alimentation, techniques et innovations dans les régions tropicales*, Paris, L'Harmattan, 31–51.

Sinsheimer M., 2018. *Microbe farmers: how fermentation artisans are bringing peace to the war on microbes* (project submitted in partial fulfilment of the requirements for the degree of Master of Arts in the Graduate Liberal Studies Program in the Graduate School of Duke University), Max Sinsheimer.

Soler L.G., Requillart V., Trystram G., 2013. Industrial organisation and sustainability, in Esnouf C., Russel M., Bricas N. (ed.), *Food system sustainability: Insights from duALIne*, Cambridge, Cambridge University Press, 101–114.

Tian F., 2016. An agri-food supply chain traceability system for China based on RFID blockchain technology, in *2016 13th International Conference on Service Systems and Service Management (ICSSSM)*, Piscataway, Institute of Electrical and Electronics Engineers, 1–6. https://doi.org/10.1109/ICSSSM.2016.7538424

Viollet P.-L., 2007. *Water engineering in ancient civilizations: 5,000 years of history*, Boca Raton, CRC Press, 334 p. Translation of 'L'hydraulique dans les civilisations anciennes: 5 000 ans d'histoire' (2004).

Vivero Pol J., Ferrando T., De Schutter O., Mattei U. (ed.), 2020. *Routledge handbook of food as a commons*, London, Routledge, 424 p.

Zirari H., 2017. *De ces nouveaux « prédicateurs de l'alimentaire »*, presented at Symposium international Manger en ville: une défiance durable ? Paris, Unesco, 6 décembre 2017.

6

Changing food habits

Nicolas Bricas and Marie Walser

Major contemporary societal changes are reshaping our relationship with food. Nevertheless, it is important to nuance the hypothesis of food-style standardization. Moreover, changes in the way eaters relate to their food can be interpreted as a result of various forms of distancing.

What we eat, how we prepare to eat – shopping, cooking, serving meals and managing waste – and how we think about it – our representations, values and concerns – constitute what are called 'food styles'. As these styles are relatively constant over the short to medium term, they are more commonly referred to as 'food habits'. They can however change over longer periods of time, either slowly or suddenly. For instance, there were no potatoes in France, no tomatoes in Italy, and no cassava or maize in Africa before the sixteenth century. In France, foods such as swans, peacocks, cranes, herons, whales and porpoises were highly esteemed socially in the seventeenth and eighteenth centuries but then completely vanished from the realm of what was considered edible (Flandrin, 1989). Changes in food habits correlate with agricultural (Chapter 4) and food supply (Chapter 5) transitions, but they also reflect societal changes that transform food consumers' lifestyles and values.

The effects of societal change

Developments in agriculture and food systems are clearly instrumental in changing the world, prompting demographic growth and shaping landscapes. But human societies are also marked by major trends external to the food sector that contribute to transforming the way we think about and organize food. We offer a few examples here.

Urbanization, made possible by the production of surplus food to feed 'non-farmers', has transformed people's ways of life and food practices. In urban areas, purchasing power has become the main factor determining access to food. These areas are home to populations of diverse origins with distinct food cultures, who have arrived over the waves of migration that have populated towns and cities. The food offer in urban areas is therefore more diverse than in rural areas. Moreover, city dwellers' connection to the agricultural world is waning. People now often work far from their homes in an increasingly fast-paced world (Rosa, 2010), where time saving and convenience largely inform food practices. In Morocco, for instance, urban mothers' social roles are diversifying, so they often seek to lighten their meal-planning load by outsourcing some meal preparation tasks or by patching together meals from leftovers or prepared takeaway products (Zirari, 2020). Finally, city dwellers often live in denser housing, where some food processing tasks are harder to carry out (drying, smoking, fermenting, pounding).

The increase in salaried employment, with the development of industry and services, has led to more regular and less fragmented incomes. Purchasing power is increasing in all countries with the emergence of a middle class. It is estimated that there were 3.2 billion middle-class people worldwide in 2020, a figure set to increase to 4.9 billion by 2030, with two-thirds of these people concentrated in Asia (Kharas, 2010). This middle class represents a market for processed foods that reduce some of the burden of housework. Yet, despite this economic growth, there are still people living in poverty, particularly in low-income countries, where over 200 million of the nearly 350 million existing jobs are filled by people considered to be moderately (95 million) or very (125 million) poor (Bendjebbar and Bricas, 2019). From the eighteenth century to the 1970s, inequality in living standards increased between countries but decreased within individual countries. Thereafter, the trend totally reversed (Giraud, 2019), with inequality declining between countries but rising within them, even in the richest countries.

Human migration is not solely the result of an exodus of rural people flocking to cities. It also involves inverse or even pendular movements that are conducive to the circulation of food styles between these rural and urban worlds (Odéyé and Bricas, 1985). It is also international and enriches food styles with new products, cuisines and consumer practices. The cuisines of North Africa, Southeast Asia, Japan and Lebanon, for instance, have spread to many countries. These cuisines are tailored and transformed in the host countries and can in turn be re-exported following this initial reappropriation (Herskovits, 1945), as in the case of Italian pizza (Sanchez, 2008) and Tex-Mex cuisine (Pilcher, 2001) following a North American detour. Cuisines must therefore be viewed in light of 'the cultural mixes that permeate, structure, maintain and transform them' (De Lima and Do Paço, 2012). Catering plays a key role in the spread of foreign cuisines and in the cultural mixing process.

The individualization of lifestyles since the nineteenth century is considered to be a major trend in Western and, more broadly, urban societies (Étienne et al., 1994, e.g. in Africa). This is reflected in the reduction of household sizes and the growing number of people living alone (15 per cent of the French population in 2013). It is also reflected in the rise of more individualistic values and attitudes. Community catering is becoming a way of putting together a communal meal consisting of portions of different dishes that are chosen according to individual preferences. Commensality (i.e. eating together) is changing shape – the same moment is shared but not always the same food (Fischler, 2015). In terms of food, and especially nutrition, this individualization trend has been compounded by the drive to personalize the food supply in order to better meet the specific biological needs of individuals according to their height, weight, age, genetic traits, place of residence or level of physical activity (Fournier and Poulain, 2017).

Identity diversification is the counterpart of individualization. With urbanization and population mixing, communities of individuals are being reconstituted, becoming more complex and multiplying. Alongside the major traditional institutions (family, religion, profession) – which are becoming weaker in some countries and stronger in others – new social structures are emerging, such as affinity-based tribes (Maffesoli, 1996). This diversification is reflected in individuals' belonging to multiple social groups (Kaufmann, 2004; de Singly, 2016). One may simultaneously feel attached to their parents' region of origin, be an ardent supporter of a football club in the town where they live and be a great fan of a particular music genre. With this multifaceted identity, behaviours – especially eating behaviours – may shift depending on the situation and the group involved (Ascher, 2005). This trend has led to recognition of the diversity of acculturation processes, far beyond the linear notion of a transition from a 'traditional' to a 'modern' model. Deculturation refers to the loss of traditional food bearings, which can in turn trigger food anxiety among eaters (Fischler, 1990). Hyperculturation refers to a defensive overvaluing of one's heritage culture, pendulism to an alternation between one's culture of origin and host culture, mixing to the blending of cultures and innovation to the creation of a new culture.

While the feminization of society is taking place at very different paces across different societies, it is facilitated by urbanization and the influence of external models. This enables women to access salaried employment where they acquire new skills and responsibilities, in turn affording them a more independent income, even though they are often paid substantially less than men for the same qualifications and responsibilities. This feminization trend is also transforming (though generally very slowly) the gendered division of household food–related tasks: shopping, cooking, washing up and so on.

Trends towards the 'medicalization' (Foucault, 1988) and 'healthification' (Poliquin, 2015) of society can also be observed. Medicalization refers to the growing influence of scientific knowledge produced by health professionals as a substitute for religious precepts, while healthification denotes the trend towards individuals striving to enhance their state of health through a range of practices to control their body and environment. Nutritionalization (Chapter 9), which reduces food to its biological function, fits within this movement. These trends reflect the development of scientific knowledge in biology, medicine and epidemiology, which on a daily basis reveal new risk factors that receive wide media coverage. They also translate into growing concern for health issues, with food emerging as a key vector of health. However, against a backdrop of dietary confusion marked by the proliferation of competing standards (Fischler, 2019) and distrust of scientists, choosing food that is good for one's health is not always an easy feat.

Environmental degradation in the form of pollution, deforestation, resource depletion and climate change is scientifically documented. This degradation is increasingly publicized in the media and perceived tangibly by people, which has heightened ethical concerns, especially for the environment, while also boosting awareness of livestock living conditions. This is in line with the more long-standing quest to maintain a relationship with an idealized 'nature', which many societies perceive as being external to humankind (Chapters 3 and 10). Rural and natural areas are valued as 'wellness' spaces, a perception that fuels efforts to reintroduce such areas within city centres through urban forests, ecological corridors, urban agriculture and related ecological projects. Naturalness is now considered a quality attribute (Lepiller, 2012) for both the environment and food products.

These changes in the environment, lifestyles and societal concerns are shaping food behaviour and demand. Agri-food companies are also taking them into account, turning them into opportunities for innovation (Chapter 5). This has accentuated the trends outlined above, which are spreading worldwide, particularly through the globalization of information and the penetration of multinational corporations into markets in emerging countries. But does this mean that food habits are converging towards a unified model?

Towards standardized food styles?

Throughout the world, food consumption is gradually converging towards a new average calorie intake structure: while the initial carbohydrate-lipid-protein ratio was around 75-15-10 (in per cent), all countries are heading towards a ratio of around 50-40-10 (Combris and Soler, 2011). The protein intake structure is also changing, with a reduced intake of plant proteins in favour of animal proteins. This trend is presented as a food transition driven by the increased food supply, the commodification of access to food, rising living standards and urbanization (Popkin, 2014). This nexus of trends is also reflected in the overall increase in processed products and the global spread of certain foods (bread, pasta, chicken, onions, tomatoes, sugar, beer, soft drinks) and even dishes (pizza, hamburgers, sushi, kebab). For some authors, this trend indicates the 'Westernization' (Popkin, 2014) or even 'Coca-colonization' (Ritzer, 1992) of global food. However, there is a lack of consensus in the analysis of these trends. Figure 6.1 below illustrates two perspectives on the evolution of total caloric intake (x-axis) and animal caloric intake (y-axis) between 1961 and 2005 in major countries around the world (representing more than 5.3 billion people).

The graph on the left highlights the overall trend, which appears to be structurally inescapable, whereas the graph on the right shows the disparity between situations for the same total caloric intake level and focuses more on what differentiates them. These two perspectives point to two approaches in the strategies adopted by multinational food corporations – the first is geared towards disregarding the historical and cultural backdrop to focus on spreading a unified model, while the second, conversely, calls for taking these differences into account.

If we consider the more granular scale of products consumed rather than large agro-nutritional aggregates, the convergences are less apparent. Although wheat, rice and maize are staple foods for half the global population, communities in entire regions of the world still rely on cassava, yams, millet, sorghum or potatoes as their main staples. China and India, whose economic trajectories are marked by a high increase in purchasing power, differ in that meat consumption has risen sharply in China and dairy consumption in India. At an even more granular scale, even though some dishes are now becoming globalized, culinary specificities still prevail. Lebanon is a prime example. With a large global diaspora exposed to a wide range of influences, and with imports accounting for 70–80 per cent of its food (Bessaoud, 2020), the country is a perfect symbol of globalization. Yet Lebanese cuisine itself is still very much alive within the country and is exported all over the world. The dissemination of

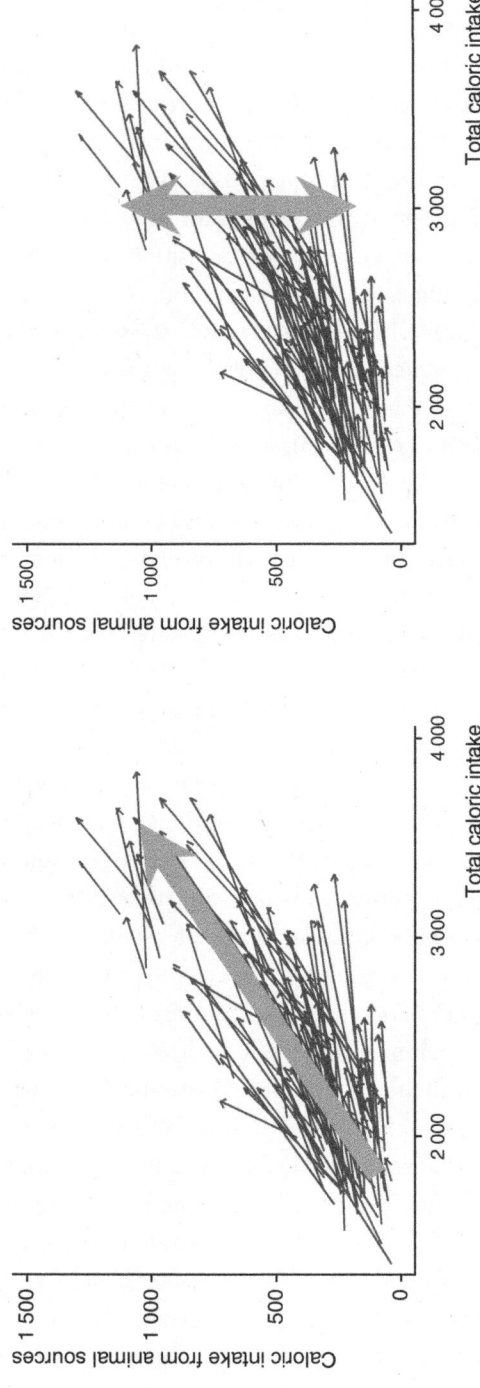

Figure 6.1 Two perspectives on the evolution of food calorie intake worldwide in kilocalories per person per day.

(source: Combris and Soler, 2011)

food models from dominant countries can trigger a hyperculturation response (Juvin and Lipovetsky, 2010) – that is, an assertion and over-appreciation of models perceived as being threatened (Barber, 2010).

Global cuisines do more than simply resist outside influences. They are constantly developing, adapting, mixing and innovating by borrowing from a host of different sources. Foreign products are reclaimed in different ways depending on culture, habits and lifestyles (Gassie, 2017). *Ceebu jën* (rice with fish) was invented in the late nineteenth century by cooks in Saint-Louis (Senegal) using broken rice imported from Indochina, vegetables introduced by Europeans, African vegetables, peanut oil from Central America introduced during French colonial rule, and the abundant fish caught along the Senegalese coast. Its preparation method differed markedly from that of Senegalese dishes at the time: the rice and sauce were cooked in a single pot (*ben cin*), whereas 'traditional' dishes were cooked in two separate pots (*niari cin*) – one for the cereal base and the other for the sauce (Sankale et al., 1980). This dish – initially an urban invention from Saint-Louis and then Dakar – is now a hallmark of Senegalese cuisine and has been exported throughout the rest of West Africa, along with a meat variant, *riz au gras* or *riz wolof* (named after the dominant ethnic group and language in Dakar). Cities are therefore major hotbeds of innovation, in terms of both cuisine and the ways in which food is sourced and meals are organized, as the African, Latin American and Asian contributors to the 'Eating in the city'[1] symposia highlighted (Soula et al., 2021).

Soaring food prices in 2008 and then 2011, along with the riots they triggered worldwide, have raised a recurring question in the media: what will we be eating in the future? Prospective future food products – insects, in vitro meat, textured soy, nutritional beverages, algae, pills and so on – are attracting as much attention as the discovery of the unique features of 'exotic' peoples' food. They evoke a mixture of curiosity and fear, even disgust, much to the delight of the media. Yet, looking back over the last fifty years, food habits have remained relatively stable. The pills, powders and food tablets that science fiction characters have been eating for decades have been slow to catch on, despite some companies regularly launching them on the market (e.g. Soylent) or developing them in laboratories

---

[1] These symposia were organized by CIRAD and the UNESCO Chair in World Food Systems in Paris in 2017 and 2020 and in Porto Alegre in 2018 on the topic of street food (https://www.chaireunesco-adm.com/2018-Comer-en-la-calle-Eating-in-the-Cities). They led to the publication of a book (Soula et al., 2021) and, in 2020, a special issue of the journal *Anthropology of Food* on the theme of 'Gender and foodways under the urban life'.

(Monbiot, 2020). Changes in the food sector are relatively slow compared with trends in other consumer sectors such as communication technology.

Out-of-home eating habits are also diverse. While catering has existed since markets and fairs first emerged and since the advent of urbanization with street food and inns, in France, restaurants really began to develop in the nineteenth century (Pitte, 1999). Compared to home cooking, out-of-home catering is still more of a complementary service that people rely on for convenience or enjoyment on special occasions. Yet there are major differences between countries. For instance, eating out is very popular in Indonesia (Tinker and Cohen, 1985), but far less so in India, where home cooking is still the norm, although this often involves sending home-cooked meals to the other end of the city, as in Bombay, with its incredible system of *dabbawalas* – delivery persons who work as a network to dispatch food throughout the city (Roncaglia, 2013). Street food and small-scale catering prevail worldwide (Abrahale et al., 2019) despite the proliferation of food industries and supermarkets run by global corporations. However, it will be important to keep an eye on the online ordering and delivery revolution that is now extending to processed convenience food, with the growing involvement of both small- and industrial-scale caterers (Chapter 16).

An increasingly distant relationship with food

The growing distance in eaters' relationship to food can be observed on several levels (Figure 6.2). Different forms of distancing may occur simultaneously:

- Geographical: not all areas, especially cities, can produce their own food; those that cannot are therefore forced to source it from increasingly distant areas. Urban sprawl, which encroaches on fertile land and production areas, along with the low cost of maritime shipping that makes long-distance trade very inexpensive, contributes to this geographical distance. Food consumers thus no longer know the exact origins of the food they buy and consume.
- Economic: this is the result of the growing number of food processing, transportation, storage and distribution intermediaries between farmers and food consumers. The price paid by the consumer is shared proportionally among a growing number of actors, while the share left to producers is shrinking.
- Cognitive: the proportion of farmers is declining against a backdrop of low generational transition and the lack of appeal of farming professions. At the same time, city dwellers are increasingly disconnected from rural communities.

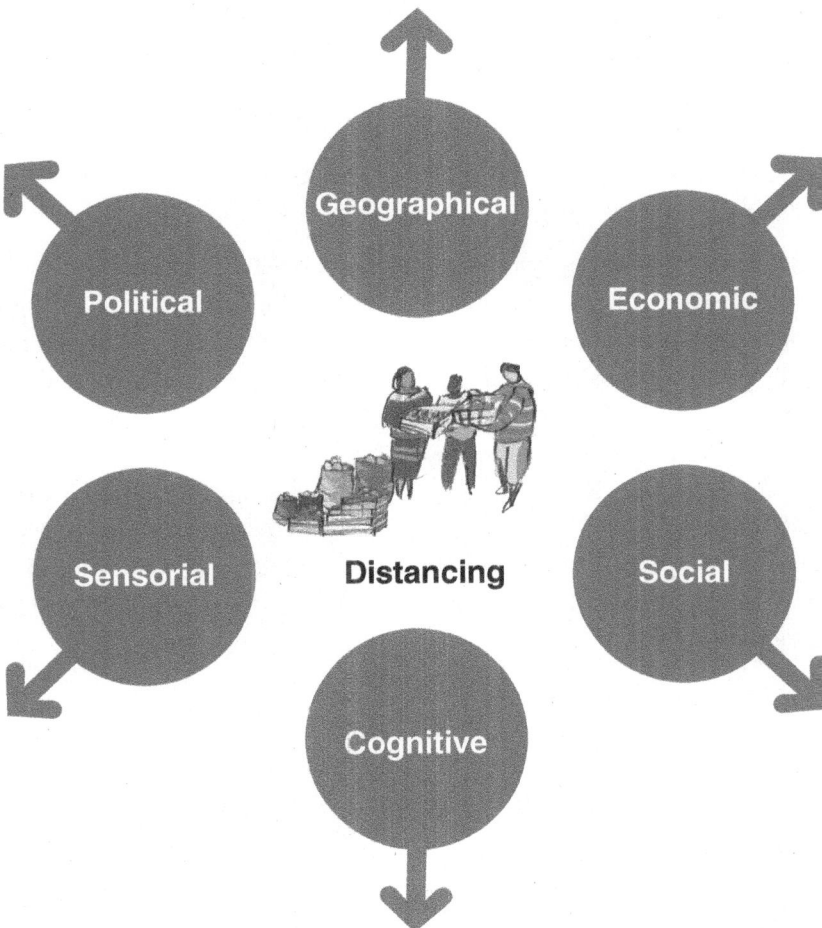

Figure 6.2 The forms of growing distance between consumers and their food.

There is also less first-hand knowledge of the farming and food sectors. Some city dwellers no longer know where milk or cheese comes from, how to identify certain fruits and vegetables, or what the additives listed in the ingredients of processed products actually are.

-   Sensorial: whereas food quality used to be assessed by tasting, smelling or touching an item, nowadays this is increasingly done by reading the information on packaging labels. The prehensile senses (taste and touch) are being superseded by the perceptive sense – sight, for instance, to read labels (Figuié and Bricas, 2014).
-   Social: the individualization of eating behaviour is undermining the social standards that once made food a 'no-brainer' (Poulain, 2017). People are

becoming increasingly responsible for their individual food choices and – under growing pressure – must personally decide what is and is not healthy to eat.

– Political: citizens' control over their food system has been reduced to the choice of places to shop and products to buy, while their influence on food policy – for instance, in relation to pesticides – is limited.

These forms of distancing generate worry and anxiety (Fischler, 1990), which can even trigger a crisis of consumer trust (Masson, 2011) and a feeling of abandonment. In response, people are seeking proximity: geographical proximity (local), economic proximity (direct sales and short supply chains), cognitive proximity (gardening, fooding), sensory proximity (taste schools), social proximity (food influencers) and political proximity (food democracy). This response could be regarded as a grassroots movement – a pendulum swing towards a widespread return to local proximity (Chapter 17). It could also be viewed as intermittent or partial practices, which companies sometimes take advantage of to allay eaters' concerns without actually calling into question the blind frenzy of excessive consumption.

Conclusion

Food styles are a reflection of society and are shaped by the food supply, lifestyles and values, but they also shape society. Food consumers send signals to companies that cater to their needs; these companies may also in turn stimulate or surpass these needs by creating substitute foods that may or may not leave a mark on people's eating habits. The consumption of these foods – whether responsible or not – may have impacts on the environment, social equity, consumer and animal health and the biosphere. Food-style dynamics are reflected in this interaction between food consumers and their environment. Hence the importance of research on food environments or foodscapes, transcending the idea that only people's specific characteristics are relevant to understanding their behaviour. Recognizing that supply matches the demand while also shaping it shifts the responsibility from the sovereign consumers to the actors (NGOs, non-profit organizations, institutions, politicians etc.) who build the foodscape (Part 5).

Diversification indeed appears to be a general trend in the evolution of food styles: this highlights the need to take into account the diversity and combination of eaters' food preferences, eating practices and representations. Food styles should be approached through the prism of the diverse range of food products and places of procurement, production and processing, as well as the ways in which products are arranged in dishes, dishes in meals, and meals in food weeks, months or years. This can help avoid simplistic representations that pigeonhole food consumers into boxes, categories or typologies.

This chapter draws on the research carried out by a working group on foodways involving Nicolas Bricas, Claude Fischler, Pierre Combris and Julia Gassie as part of the MOND'Alim 2030 foresight initiative – as outlined in the chapter by Julia Gassie (2017) – on a summary supplementing this foodways foresight initiative (Hérault et al., 2019), on the annual symposia of the UNESCO Chair in World Food Systems from 2014 to 2017 and on three symposia on the topic of 'Eating in the city' organized by CIRAD and the UNESCO Chair in World Food Systems from 2014 to 2017.

The authors would like to thank Mathilde Coudray and Véronique Pardo for proofreading this chapter and for their suggested improvements.

References

Abrahale K., Sousa S., Albuquerque G., Padrão P., Lunet N., 2019. Street food research worldwide: a scoping review. *Journal of Human Nutrition and Dietetics*, 32(2): 152–174 https://doi.org/10.1111/jhn.12604

Ascher F., 2005. *Le mangeur hypermoderne*, Paris, Odile Jacob, 337 p.

Barber B.R., 2010. *Jihad Vs McWorld*, New York, Random House, 432 p.

Bendjebbar P., Bricas N., 2019. Major trends in food systems drivers, in Dury S., Bendjebbar P., Hainzelin E., Giordano T., Bricas N. (ed.), *Food systems at risk. New trends and challenges*, Rome/Montpellier/Brussels, FAO/Cirad/European Commission, 25–32.

Bessaoud O., 2020. *Une lecture politique de la sécurité alimentaire de l'Algérie et du Liban*, Tunis, Observatoire de la Souveraineté Alimentaire et de l'Environnement, 8 p.

Combris P., Soler L.G., 2011. Consommation alimentaire: tendances de long terme et questions sur leur durabilité. *Innovations agronomiques*, 13: 149–160.

De Lima D., Do Paço D., 2012. Le métissage, dynamique des gastronomies. *Hypothèse*, 15(1): 289–301. https://doi.org/10.3917/hyp.111.0289

Étienne G., Leimdorfer F., Marie A., Vuarin R., 1994. *Processus d'individualisation dans les villes ouest-africaines*, Paris, Institut d'études du développement économique et social, 442 p.

Figuié M., Bricas N., 2014. Faire ses courses au Vietnam aujourd'hui: quand les supermarchés touchent aux sens. *Anthropology of Food*. https://doi.org/10.4000 /aof.7445

Fischler C., 1990. *L'homnivore*, Paris, Odile Jacob, 448 p.

Fischler C. (ed.), 2015. *Selective eating: the rise, the meaning and sense of 'personal dietary requirements'*, Paris, Odile Jacob, 272 p. Translation of 'Les alimentations particulières. Mangerons-nous encore ensemble demain ?' (2013).

Fischler C., 2019. L'alimentation: de la méfiance à la défiance. *Après-demain*, 50(2): 26–28. https://doi.org/10.3917/apdem.050.0026

Flandrin, J.L. (1989), Le lent cheminement de l'innovation alimentaire. *Nourritures. Plaisirs et angoisses de la fourchette, Autrement, Paris*, (108): 68–74.

Foucault M., 1988. Histoire de la médicalisation. *Hermès, La Revue*, 2(2): 11–29.

Fournier T., Poulain J.-P., 2017. La génomique nutritionnelle: (re)penser les liens alimentation-santé à l'articulation des sciences sociales, biomédicales et de la vie. *Natures Sciences Sociétés*, 25(2): 111–121. https://doi.org/10.1051/nss/2017023

Gassie J., 2017. Les conduites alimentaires, in Claquin P., Martin A., Deram C., Delgoulet E., Gassie J., Hérault B. (ed.), *MOND'Alim 2030, panorama prospectif de la mondialisation des systèmes alimentaires*, Paris, La Documentation française, 23–47.

Giraud P.-N., 2019. *L'inégalité du monde. Économie du monde contemporain*, Paris, Gallimard, 495 p.

Hérault B., Gassie J., Lamy A., 2019. *Transformations sociétales et grandes tendances alimentaires, document de travail*, Paris, Ministère de l'Agriculture et de l'Alimentation, Centre d'études et de prospective, 43 p.

Herskovits M., 1945. The processes of cultural change, in Linton R. (ed.), *The science of man in the world crisis*, New York, Columbia University Press, 143–170.

Juvin H., Lipovetsky G., 2010. *L'Occident mondialisé. Controverse sur la culture planétaire*, Paris, Grasset, 332 p.

Kaufmann J.-C., 2004. *L'invention de soi. Une théorie de l'identité*, Paris, Armand Colin, 352 p.

Kharas H., 2010. *The emerging middle class in developing countries*, document de travail du Centre de développement de l'OCDE, Paris, Éditions OCDE, 61 p.

Lepiller O., 2012. *Critiques de l'alimentation industrielle et valorisations du naturel: sociologie historique d'une « digestion » difficile (1968–2010)*, thèse de doctorat, spécialité Sociologie, Université de Toulouse II-Le Mirail, Toulouse, 713 p.

Maffesoli M., 1996. *The time of the tribes: the decline of Individualism in mass society*, London, Sage Publications, 192 p. Translation of 'Le temps des tribus. Le déclin de l'individualisme dans les sociétés de masse' (1988).

Masson E., 2011. Représentations de l'alimentation: crise de la confiance et crises alimentaires. *Bulletin de psychologie*, 514(4): 307–314. https://doi.org/10.3917/bupsy .514.0307

Monbiot G., 2020. Lab-grown food will soon destroy farming – and save the planet. *Guardian*, 8 janvier 2020.

Odéyé M., Bricas N., 1985. À propos de l'évolution des styles alimentaires à Dakar, in Bricas N., Courade G., Coussy J., Hugon P., Muchnik J. (ed.), *Nourrir les villes en Afrique sub-saharienne*, Paris, L'Harmattan, 179–195.

Pilcher J.M., 2001. Tex-Mex, Cal-Mex, New Mex, or Whose Mex? Notes on the historical geography of southwestern cuisine. *Journal of the Southwest*, 43(4): 659–679.

Pitte J.-R. 1999. The rise of the restaurant, in Flandrin J.-L., Montanari M. (ed.), *Food: a culinary history*, New York, Columbia University Press, 471–480. Translation of 'Naissance et expansion des restaurants' (1996).

Poliquin H., 2015. Analyse critique et dimensionnelle du concept de santéisation. *Aporia*, 7(1): 17–29. https://doi.org/10.18192/aporia.v7i1.2819

Popkin B.M., 2014. Nutrition, agriculture and the global food system in low and middle income countries. *Food Policy*, 47: 91–96. https://doi.org/10.1016/j.foodpol.2014.05.001

Poulain J.-P., 2017. *The sociology of food: eating and the place of food in society*, London/ New York, Bloomsbury Academic, 288 p. Translation of 'Sociologies de l'alimentation' (2002).

Ritzer G., 1992. *The McDonaldization of society*, Newbury Park, Pine Forge Press, 221 p.

Roncaglia S., 2013. *Feeding the city: work and food culture of the Mumbai dabbawalas*, Cambridge, Open Book Publishers, 234 p.

Rosa H., 2010. *Alienation and acceleration: towards a critical theory of late-modern temporality*, Malmö/Aarhus, NSU Press, 111 p.

Sanchez S., 2008. Frontières alimentaires et mets transfrontaliers: la pizza, questionnement d'un paradoxe. *Anthropologie et Sociétés*, 31(1): 197–212. https://doi.org/10.7202/029724AR

Sankale M., Wone I., Morosov T., Morosov S., de Lauture H., 1980. La place du « ceebu-jën » dans l'alimentation des populations suburbaines de Dakar. *Présence africaine*, 11: 39–44. https://doi.org/10.3917/presa.113.0009

Singly F. de, 2016. *Libres ensemble. L'individualisme dans la vie commune* (2nd edition), Paris, Armand Colin, 320 p.

Soula A., Yount-André C., Lepiller O., Bricas N. (ed.), 2021. *Eating in the city: socio-anthropological perspectives from Africa, Latin America and Asia*, Versailles, Quæ, 158 p. Translation of 'Manger en ville: Regards socioanthropologiques d'Afrique, d'Amérique latine et d'Asie' (2020).

Tinker I., Cohen M., 1985. Street foods as a source of income for women. *Ekistics*, 52(310): 83–89.

Zirari H., 2020. Entre alimentation (*makla*) et nutrition (*taghdia*): Arbitrages et réinvention au quotidien des pratiques alimentaires en contexte urbain. *Hespéris-Tamuda*, 55(4): 385–407.

7

The limits of industrialized food systems

Nicolas Bricas

Industrialized food systems generate a number of negative environmental, health, socio-economic and political externalities. Identifying these sustainability issues sheds light on the fact that food systems not only play a role in feeding the planet, but they are also instrumental in enhancing the viability of the biosphere while fostering inclusive and resilient socio-economic development.

There is no real consensus on the definition of 'sustainable food' or 'sustainable food systems' (Béné et al., 2019). Nevertheless, there is agreement on the reasons why currently widespread industrialized food systems are problematic. First, in areas where they prevail, these systems have irreversible impacts that will be very hard or even impossible for future generations to manage. Second, their generalization (should it occur) is not feasible within the limits of our planet's resources. The term 'sustainable food' currently tends to encompass demands and objectives relating to a host of challenges associated with the limitations of industrialized food systems and more general societal changes. There is also debate as to the legitimacy or relevance of pigeonholing some of these as being sustainability concerns, since they do not necessarily pertain to issues of irreversibility or to the impossibility of generalizing industrialized food systems, as, for instance, in the case of animal welfare or consumer anxiety (Chapter 6).

At any rate, industrialized food systems are now widely criticized, despite the fact that they have quantitatively and qualitatively enhanced the food supply to an extraordinary extent. Population growth, urbanization and the rising living standards of most of the world's population are partly the result of food system industrialization. Yet the many long-overlooked negative externalities of this industrialization and its intensification can no longer be swept aside. This chapter outlines, in turn, the environmental, health, social, economic and governance issues raised by the growing industrialization of food worldwide (Figure 7.1).

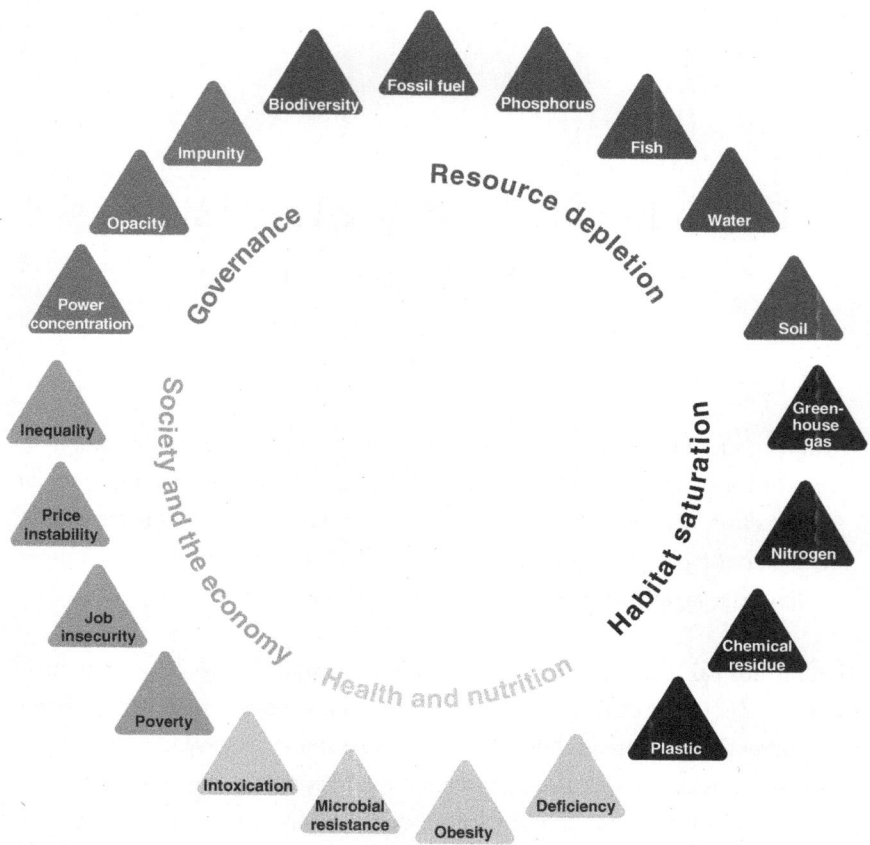

Figure 7.1 The limits of industrialized food systems.

Natural resources overexploitation and depletion

Industrialized food systems' heavy reliance on an economy based on non-renewable fossil resources (Chapter 4) – primarily fossil fuels (coal, oil and gas) – is precipitating the depletion of these resources. In France, fossil fuel energy is used at all levels of the food system for the production of agricultural raw materials (27 per cent of energy consumption in the food system), transport (31 per cent), processing (15 per cent), refrigeration and household cooking (14 per cent) and distribution and catering (13 per cent) (Barbier et al., 2019). Other sources of energy (especially renewable energy) could be adopted in the future to offset fossil fuel depletion. But such substitution is not an option for phosphorus, which is essential to plant fertilization. This precious element is present in finite quantities in the soil, and its partial recycling – which was common practice until the nineteenth century – has given way to the growing use of mined phosphate, which is contributing to its depletion. Despite some controversy, there is broad consensus that rock phosphate resources will be depleted before 2150 (Peñuelas et al., 2013). Nitrogen, another fertilizer element, can be synthesized by legume plants (soybeans, groundnuts, peas, beans, alfalfa, clover, broad beans etc.), and there are abundant potassium mines, meaning that there is less risk of depletion for these two minerals.

Other resources, although renewable, are threatened by overexploitation. This includes forests – a carbon sink and biodiversity reservoir – the surface area of which is steadily being eroded by farmland encroachment, particularly in tropical regions (Congo Basin, Malaysia, Indonesia, Brazil), mainly as a result of the development of livestock farming and industrial crops such as oil palm. It should be noted that agriculture accounts for almost 40 per cent of the land area on earth, two-thirds of which is used for livestock grazing and feed production (FAO, 2020c). While the rate of global forest cover loss has slowed in recent decades, it is still estimated to have amounted to approximately 10 million ha per year since 2015 (FAO, 2020b). Recent assessments indicate that 17 per cent of tropical forests have disappeared since 1990 (Vancutsem et al., 2021). Moreover, stocks of fish and other marine resources are being harvested at a rate that exceeds their renewal, which is in turn threatened by the ongoing pollution of marine and continental waters by algae, waste, plastics and chemicals. The proportion of fish stocks harvested at a biologically sustainable level worldwide fell from 90 per cent in 1974 to 65.8 per cent in 2017 (FAO, 2020d). In some regions, water grabbing to irrigate crops and meet the needs of certain agri-food companies has had a direct impact on natural habitats and their functioning.

Finally, industrial agriculture and agri-food processing are largely responsible for the erosion of domesticated biodiversity – a process that is occurring much faster than the regeneration rate (IPBES, 2019). According to the FAO, just fifteen plants[1] provide 80 per cent of plant-derived food energy, with wheat, rice and maize alone accounting for more than half. The diversity of cultivated plant varieties is also being eroded by the market dominance of a few large seed companies. According to FAO estimates (2010), three-quarters of cultivated plant varieties were wiped out during the twentieth century. This loss of diversity, particularly genetic diversity, undermines the resilience of agricultural systems to threats such as pests, pathogens and climate change; it therefore poses a risk to food security

---

[1] Rice, wheat, sugarcane, maize, soybean, potato, oil palm, cassava, sunflower, rapeseed, sorghum, millet, groundnut, beans and sweet potato.

(IPBES, 2019). Biodiversity loss also affects plants and animals that are not edible but are vital for pollinating and fertilizing plants or preventing disease. Moreover, this loss threatens agricultural production in the medium term (Hainzelin, 2019).

Natural habitat saturation

The massive use of relatively inexpensive chemical fertilizers in farming has resulted in the pollution of groundwater, rivers and coastal waters, and the eutrophication (algal blooms leading to oxygen depletion) of aquatic environments. This phenomenon is compounded by sewage sludge discharge – human excrement that is nitrogen- and phosphorus-rich but no longer recycled. In 2010, it was estimated that around 250,000 km^2 of aquatic environments worldwide – equivalent to the surface area of the United Kingdom – were eutrophic (Pinay et al., 2018). This has caused major disruptions in the aquatic ecosystem, thereby endangering biodiversity, posing health risks for local residents and creating economic risks for activities linked to these environments. Chemical (especially nitrogen) fertilizers also cause airborne pollution. Ammonia emitted during the application of chemical nitrogen fertilizers combines in the air with nitrogen oxide produced by combustion engines and with sulphur dioxide from industrial sources, forming fine particles that are extremely harmful to health (Aubert, 2021). In the European Union (EU), it is estimated that agriculture is responsible for 90 per cent of ammonia emissions, which are a major contributor to air pollution and claim the lives of four hundred thousand Europeans every year (IPES-Food, 2019).

The use and discharge of chemical and petroleum industry products, namely pesticide and drug residues, is a secondary source of pollution. This pollution affects not only human health and the environment but also agricultural production capacity due to the disappearance of crop pollinators and the reduced fertility of soils as a result of overuse. Nearly two-thirds (64 per cent) of farmland worldwide exhibits chemical pesticide levels above the predicted no-effect concentration, while 31 per cent is considered to be at high risk of pollution, especially in Europe and Asia (Tang et al., 2021). Meanwhile, pollution from plastics, which are widely used in agriculture and food packaging, has been increasing very rapidly (half of the plastic manufactured since 1950 has been produced since 2000) without the faintest hint of a slowdown (Dalberg Advisors, 2019). Of the nearly 400,000 tonnes of plastic produced worldwide in 2016, a quarter of it ended up polluting land, rivers and oceans (Kaza et al., 2018). Marine fauna are hit particularly hard by easily ingested plastic micro- and nanoparticles. These particles travel very long distances and contain (or have absorbed) various chemical substances (Hermabessiere et al., 2017) that are likely to have serious impacts on human health (Azoulay et al., 2019).

Finally, greenhouse gas (GHG) emissions represent a third major form of pollution. The most recent estimates indicate that in 2015 the agri-food system was responsible for a third of all global anthropogenic emissions (Crippa et al., 2021), a quarter of which (27 per cent) originated from industrialized countries that host only 15 per cent of the world's population. The remaining emissions (73 per cent) were generated by countries of the Global South, including China, which account for 85 per cent of the world's population. These figures should not mask the fact that households in industrialized countries have a higher carbon footprint due to their reliance on imported foods produced in developing countries – a production that is also a source of GHG emissions. These are referred to as 'imported emissions' and are often overlooked in carbon footprint calculations. Emission sources differ markedly between industrialized and developing countries (Figure 7.2). In developing countries, 71 per cent of food system-derived GHG emissions are linked to land use, agricultural production and livestock farming, compared with 57 per cent in industrialized countries. In the latter, post-harvest activities (transport, processing, packaging, distribution, consumption and waste management) account for a major share (43 per cent) of emissions. Interestingly, transport – which food supply redistribution efforts often aim to minimize (Chapter 17) – accounts for only 10 per cent of emissions (Crippa et al., 2021).

Nutrition and health risks

Global food shortages and famines have been scarce over the past half century. A large share of the global population has been lifted out of dire poverty, and food safety has significantly improved (Stanziani, 2005). Yet the industrialization of food systems has failed to eradicate malnutrition and has generated new individual health risk factors.

Undernutrition has declined overall in both absolute and relative terms since the 1960s, but in 2019 it still affected nearly 700 million people worldwide, with an uptick since 2014 (FAO and WHO, 2020). This recent historic reversal is not due to a shortage of food supplies, as the planet loses and wastes around 30 per cent of what it produces (Gustavsson et al., 2011). Instead, it is due to persistent poverty and, above all, to the fact that climate crises and conflicts

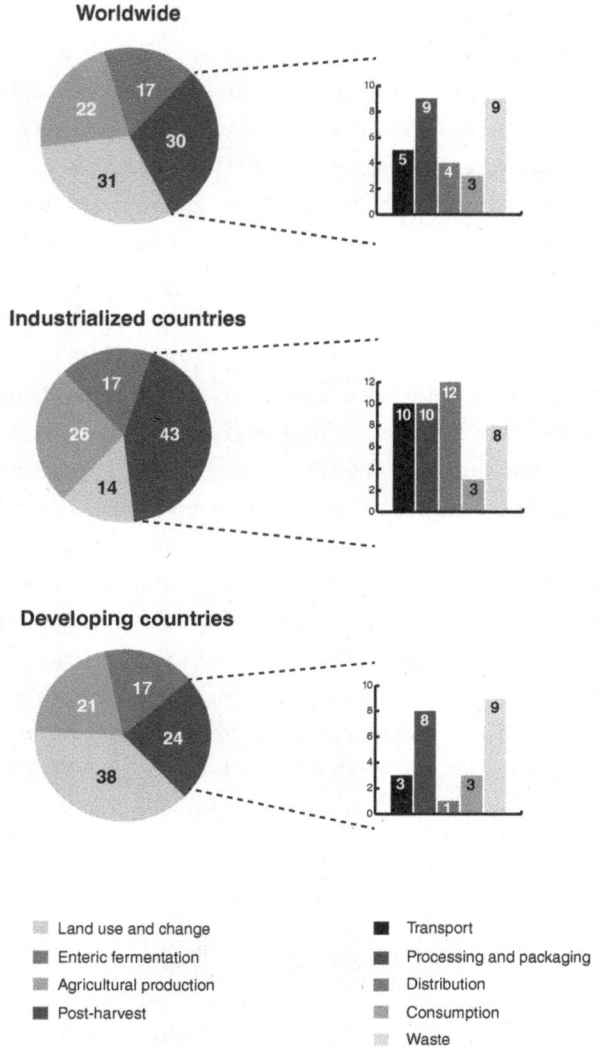

Figure 7.2 Greenhouse gas emissions (per cent) of food systems.
(source: Crippa et al., 2021)

are on the rise, which in turn has led to an increase in the number of displaced people who no longer have access to healthy, high-quality food. In 2019, the Internal Displacement Monitoring Centre (2020) recorded 24 million new climate refugees and 8.5 million people displaced by conflicts worldwide. The number of displaced people doubled from 24 million to more than 50 million between 2009 and 2019.

Micronutrient deficiencies (vitamins and minerals) – or 'hidden hunger' – stunt individuals' physical and intellectual growth and weaken their immune defences. These deficiencies have irreversible health impacts and reduce people's working capacity, thereby representing a major economic handicap. In von Grebmer et al. (2014), it was estimated that they still affected 2 billion people worldwide. Meanwhile, the rise in calorie consumption associated with increased intake of high-fat and sweet products, combined with a reduction in physical activity, has led to an increase in overweight and obesity, which are risk factors for illnesses such as type 2 diabetes, cardiovascular disease and certain cancers. One in three people worldwide was affected by this trend in 2020 (Global Nutrition Report, 2020).

Protein-energy undernutrition, micronutrient deficiency and overnutrition may coexist in the same country and even within the same family or the same person. This so-called triple burden (Labadarios, 2005) primarily affects developing countries, complicating the implementation of nutritional policy. Food safety risks could be considered as a fourth burden. According to the World Health Organization (WHO, 2015), every year 600 million people around the world fall ill from eating contaminated food, and 420,000 die from this foodborne contamination. The focus was long on the microbiological risks (Griffith, 2006) that contribute to malnutrition. Diarrhoea is a major risk factor for childhood malnutrition. But a new, as yet poorly documented, twofold risk is emerging throughout the world: chemical contamination and microbial resistance. First, this affects farm workers exposed to the chemicals they use. The WHO estimated that every year a million farmers were poisoned by pesticides worldwide in 1990, compared with 385 million in 2020 – 44 per cent of the overall farming population (Boedeker et al., 2020). Second, this toxicant poisoning also affects consumers, as ingested foodborne chemicals gradually accumulate in the body. The health effects are now being documented, especially those caused by endocrine disruptors, which may not be present in sufficient amounts to cause problems on their own but can be dangerous in combination ('cocktail effect') (Gaudriault et al., 2017; Muncke et al., 2020).

Environmental and health risks do not necessarily affect all people in the same way. For instance, climate change is having a major impact on the intertropical convergence zone, where very poor communities are concentrated, despite the fact that their GHG emissions are low. Moreover, obesity is more prevalent among poor populations residing in food deserts, where the supply of fatty, sweet and salty products is particularly high. Finally, food poisoning is often caused by eating very low-cost foods from the informal food sector that is generally predominant in the poorest neighbourhoods of towns and cities.

Socio-economic issues

Industrialization has been a driver of economic development, creating jobs and increasing consumer purchasing power, yet it has not eliminated poverty or reduced inequalities, including those that prevail in food systems. There is even a looming risk that poverty will grow in the years ahead as a result of climate change (+ 68 to 135 million people by 2030, according to the World Bank, 2021) and the COVID-19 pandemic (+ 88 to 115 million) (Lakner et al., 2021). These figures add to the 690 million people currently living in extreme poverty (with less than $1.9 per capita per day). These two combined phenomena could explain the anticipated worsening of food insecurity in these countries and the risk of massive outmigration, which would in turn generate new food crises.

Given that population growth is still high in many countries of the Global South – particularly in Africa – creating millions of decent-paying jobs, especially in rural areas, is a major challenge for food systems, which constitute the leading economic sector in these countries. According to the World Bank (2021 data), in 2018 four out of five people living under the international poverty line ($1.9 per capita per day) resided in rural areas. The poverty rate in these areas is estimated to be three times higher than that in urban centres. This disparity suggests that farmers in developing countries are underpaid, which, combined with the fact that living conditions in rural areas are generally worse than in cities, partially accounts for the trend of rural outmigration and the resulting mass urban unemployment. Inequality in the distribution of added value within commodity chains is especially acute in the agricultural sector and even more so in sectors exporting agricultural products from the Global South to rich countries. Moreover, a study by the Bureau for the Appraisal of Social Impacts for Citizen information (Basic, 2018) revealed that coffee producers earn only around 5.5 per cent of the sale price of ground coffee packets sold in supermarkets (7.8 per cent under fair-trade labels) and less than 1 per cent of the price of coffee sold in individual pods.

In the EU, it is estimated that the agricultural sector's value share in the food chain dropped from 31 per cent in 1995 to 21 per cent in 2018, while farmers had to contend with a 40 per cent increase in input prices between 2000 and 2010 (IPES-Food, 2019). In addition, soaring food prices on international markets in 2008 and 2011 sounded the end of a roughly thirty-year period of relatively stable prices. The decline in buffer and/or security stocks, the tighter functioning of just-in-time markets and the increasingly close links between food, energy and financial markets suggest that the world could be entering a phase of greater price volatility (Galtier, 2019), thereby making farmers even more vulnerable.

Markets for farm products have, admittedly, always been relatively unstable, given their dependence on climatic conditions. But this situation is now likely to be compounded by the growing number of climate crises (IPCC, 2013), epidemics (Tollefson, 2020) and conflicts affecting production and trade.

Finally, the highly disparate range of businesses (in terms of size, investment capacity, market share, financial strength etc.) competing for markets or resources – especially land – often accelerates the marginalization of smallholder farmers (Soulier et al., 2019). Competition between family farming and industrial farms or plantations is prevalent. The same competitive situation also exists further down the supply chain between industrial and small-scale processors and between supermarkets and street vendors. In countries undergoing demographic transition, such as those in sub-Saharan Africa, which will have to cope with an influx of 730 million new workers between 2020 and 2050, employment is therefore a major issue (Giordano et al., 2019). The rapid growth of low-labour industrialization potentially carries a very high risk. Moreover, the food system employs a huge number of low-paid workers: in farming (using migrant labour), in agri-food companies (assembly-line workers, e.g. in slaughterhouses where the work pace can sometimes lead to animal abuse), in the transport and retail sectors (drivers, handlers, cashiers), in the catering industry (cooks) and, in recent years, in meal delivery (the uberization of work) (Barthélémy and Cette, 2017).

All of these environmental, health and socio-economic risks overlap and combine (Bricas et al., 2019). While the compounding effects of these risks are still poorly documented, they raise fears of serious future crises and highlight the need for further research into the vulnerability and resilience of food systems.

Governance issues

Market concentration through mergers and acquisitions in the food system concerns suppliers of intermediate products (seeds, chemical fertilizers, pesticides and pharmaceutical products, agricultural machinery etc.) as well as companies involved in international trade, food processing and distribution. For instance, 70 per cent of the international agrochemical industry is now in the hands of just three companies and up to 90 per cent of global grain trade is controlled by four multinationals (IPES-Food, 2019). This concentration has several problematic consequences. It weakens the independence and bargaining power of farmers, who become dependent on upstream companies for their inputs and downstream companies for their market outlets, which dictate prices or force farmers to comply with very strict production specifications. This concentration trend steers technical innovation policies towards the most profitable solutions for companies, which do not necessarily take sustainability issues into account. Through oligopolies and agreements between competing firms, big business gains the power to sway public policy in favour of its own interests. These companies are highly opaque. They can manipulate information (and even scientists) to their benefit (Foucart et al., 2020) and act with relative impunity in relation to their impacts on the health of humans and the global environment, which they can contribute to deteriorating (Rastoin, 2016).

The digital technology boom is generating new opportunities (Chapter 5) but at the cost of increased governance risks. First, there are fears that the digital tech giants, namely the GAFAMs (Google, Apple, Facebook, Amazon, Microsoft), will increasingly gain control over these systems (GRAIN, 2021; IPES-Food and ETC Group, 2021). The deployment of personalized advice systems to help consumers make better food choices, based on the compiled history of their practices and interests, is showcased as a tool for strengthening consumer power. The FAO (2020a) director-general signed an agreement with CropLife International – a trade association representing the interests of the major agrochemical players – stating that 'digital technologies can remodel agri-food systems so that production and trade would be driven by consumers'. We can rightfully wonder whether the development of big data is not in fact creating a major new challenge for society, namely the monitoring and control of individual behaviour and therefore of freedom, at a time when it seems vital for this behaviour to change in order to tackle sustainability challenges.

Conclusion

Development models designed in highly industrialized countries and disseminated worldwide through private investment and partly within the framework of international cooperation are now being challenged. In 2015, aware of the new risks raised by these development models, the 193 UN Member States drew up seventeen so-called sustainable development goals (SDGs). Unlike the millennium development goals (MDGs) of the preceding fifteen years, which applied only to developing countries, the SDGs concern all countries on earth, including the richest and most industrialized ones. Food systems, irrespective of whether or not they underlie the issues identified, are relevant and can contribute to achieving most of these goals (Figure 7.3). Food systems can therefore no longer be geared towards

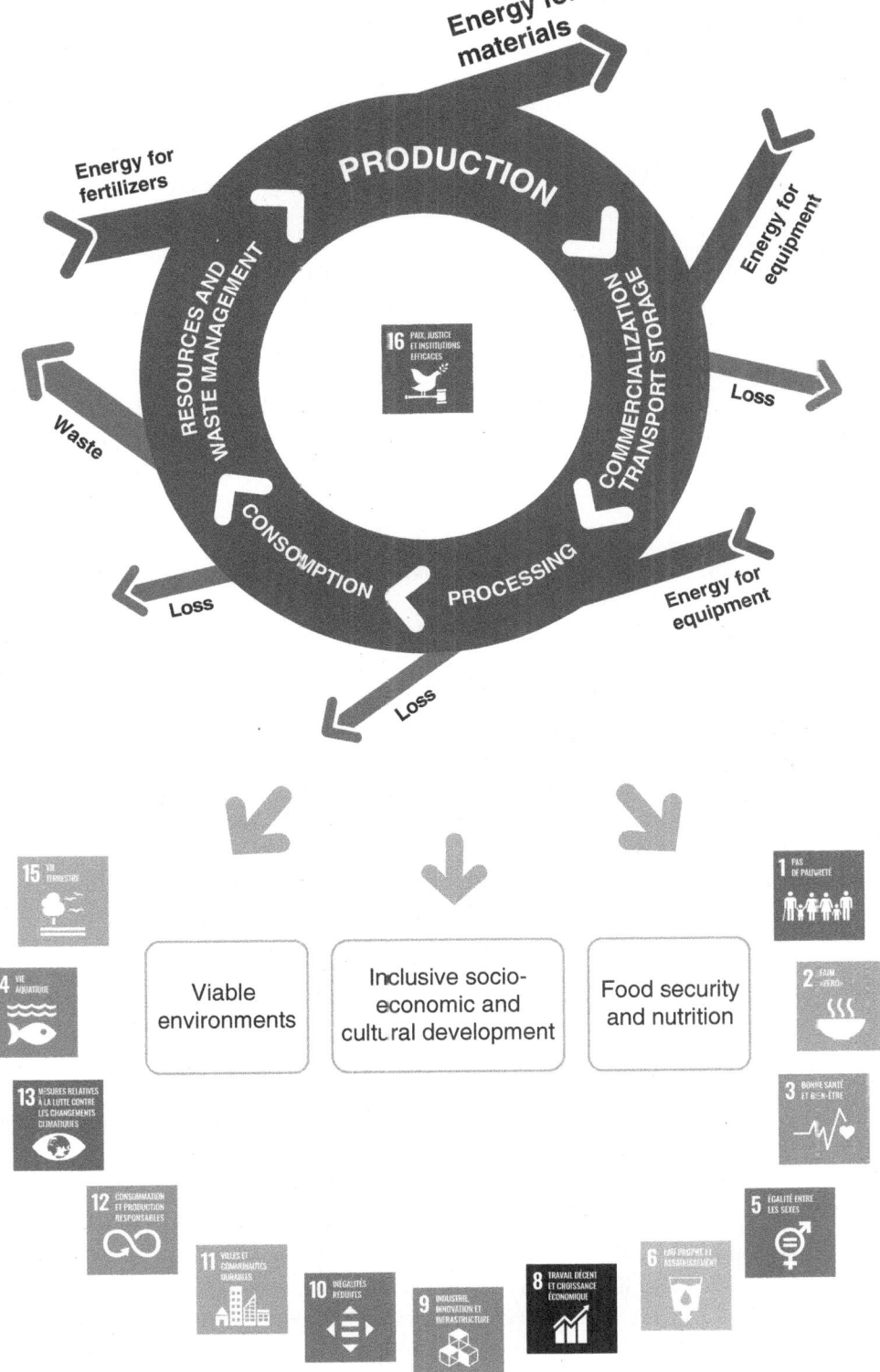

Figure 7.3 Food systems are impacted by other sectors and contribute to many sustainable development goals.

feeding humans, which they do by maximizing food production with a high degree of success, as is well known. They must now be guided by at least two other ambitions: actively contributing to ensuring the viability of the biosphere while also contributing to inclusive and equitable socio-economic and cultural development.

This chapter largely draws on Bricas (2019) and the report Food Systems at Risk: New Trends and Challenges (Dury et al., 2019).

The author would like to thank Mathilde Coudray for proofreading this chapter and her suggested improvements.

References

Aubert C., 2021. *Les apprentis sorciers de l'azote. La face cachée des engrais chimiques*, Mens, éditions Terre Vivante, 144 p.

Azoulay D., Villa P., Arellano Y., Gordon M., Moon D., Miller K., Thompson K., 2019. *Plastic & health: the hidden costs of a plastic planet*, Washington, DC, Center for International Environmental Law, 74 p.

Barbier C., Couturier C., Pourouchottamin P., Cayla J.-M., Silvestre M., Pharabod I., 2019. *L'empreinte énergétique et carbone de l'alimentation en France*, Paris, Club Ingénierie Prospective Énergie et Environnement, 24 p.

Barthélémy J., Cette G., 2017. *Travailler au XXIe siècle: l'ubérisation de l'économie ?*, Paris, Odile Jacob, 127 p.

Basic, 2018. *Café: la success story qui cache la crise. Étude sur la durabilité de la filière du café*, rapport de recherche, Paris, Max Havelaar France, Commerce équitable France, Collectif « Repenser les filières », Basic, 165 p.

Béné C., Oosterveer P., Lamotte L., Brouwer I.D., de Haan S., Prager S.D. et al., 2019. When food systems meet sustainability. Current narratives and implications for actions. *World Development*, 113: 116–130. https://doi.org/10.1016/j.worlddev.2018.08.011

Boedeker W., Watts M., Clausing P., Marquez E., 2020. The global distribution of acute unintentional pesticide poisoning: estimations based on a systematic review. *BMC Public Health*, 20(1): 1875. https://doi.org/10.1186/s12889-020-09939-0

Bricas N., 2019. Urbanization issues affecting food system sustainability, in Brand C., Bricas N., Conaré D., Daviron B., Debru J., Michel L., Soulard C.-T. (ed.), *Designing urban food policies, concepts and approaches*, Cham, Springer, 1–25. Translation of 'Les enjeux de l'urbanisation pour la durabilité des systèmes alimentaires' (2017).

Bricas N., Bendjebbar P., Hainzelin E., Dury S., Giordano T., 2019. General conclusion, in Dury S., Bendjebbar P., Hainzelin E., Giordano T., Bricas N. (ed.), *Food systems at risk. New trends and challenges*, Rome/Montpellier/Brussels, FAO/Cirad/European Commission, 123–126.

Crippa M., Solazzo E., Guizzardi D., Monforti-Ferrario F., Tubiello F.N., Leip A., 2021. Food systems are responsible for a third of global anthropogenic GHG emissions. *Nature Food*, 2(3): 198–209. https://doi.org/10.1038/s43016-021-00225-9

Dalberg Advisors, 2019. *Pollution plastique: à qui la faute? Identification des défaillances systémiques et présentation du scénario zéro plastique dans la nature en 2030*, Gland, WWF, 46 p.

Dury S., Bendjebbar P., Hainzelin E., Giordano T., Bricas N. (ed.), 2019. *Food systems at risk. New trends and challenges*, Rome/Montpellier/Brussels, FAO/Cirad/European Commission, 128 p.

FAO, 2010. *The second report on the state of the world's plant genetic resources for food and agriculture*, Rome, FAO, 370 p.

FAO, 2020a. FAO and CropLife International strengthen commitment to promote agri-food systems transformation, https://www.fao.org/newsroom/detail/FAO-and -CropLife-International-strengthen-commitment-to-promote-agri-food-systems -transformation/ [online].

FAO, 2020b. *Global forest resources assessment 2020: Key findings*, Rome, FAO, 13 p.

FAO, 2020c. *Land statistics. Global, regional and country trends 1990–2018*, Rome, FAO, 19 p.

FAO, 2020d. *The state of world fisheries and aquaculture 2020*, Rome, FAO, 206 p.

FAO, WHO, 2020. *The future of food safety: Transforming knowledge into action for people, economies and the environment*, Rome, FAO/WHO, 99 p.

Foucart S., Horel S., Laurens S., 2020. *Les gardiens de la raison. Enquête sur la désinformation scientifique*, Paris, La Découverte, 368 p.

Galtier F., 2019. Why food prices are likely to become more unstable, in Dury S., Bendjebbar P., Hainzelin E., Giordano T., Bricas N. (ed.), *Food systems at risk. New trends and challenges*, Rome/Montpellier/Brussels, FAO/Cirad/European Commission, 107–110.

Gaudriault P., Mazaud-Guittot S., Lavoué V., Coiffec I., Lesné L., Dejucq-Rainsford N. et al., 2017. Endocrine disruption in human fetal testis explants by individual and combined exposures to selected pharmaceuticals, pesticides, and environmental pollutants. *Environmental Health Perspectives*, 125(8): 087004. https://doi.org/10.1289 /EHP1014

Giordano T., Losch B., Sourisseau J.-M., Girard P., 2019. Risks of mass employment and worsening of working conditions, in Dury S., Bendjebbar P., Hainzelin E., Giordano T., Bricas N. (ed.), *Food systems at risk. New trends and challenges*, Rome/Montpellier/ Brussels, FAO/Cirad/European Commission, 75–78.

Global Nutrition Report, 2020. *Action on equity to end malnutrition*, Bristol, Development Initiatives, 172 p.

GRAIN, 2021. *Contrôle numérique: comment les Big Tech se tournent vers l'alimentation et l'agriculture (et ce que cela signifie)*, Barcelona, GRAIN, 18 p.

Griffith C.J., 2006. Food safety: where from and where to? *British Food Journal*, 108(1): 6–15. https://doi.org/10.1108/00070700610637599

Gustavsson J., Cederberg C., Sonesson U., van Otterdijk R., Meybeck A., 2011. *Global food losses and food waste: extent, causes and prevention*, Rome, FAO, 29 p.

Hainzelin E., 2019. Risks of irreversible biodiversity loss, in Dury S., Bendjebbar P., Hainzelin E., Giordano T., Bricas N. (ed.), *Food systems at risk. New trends and challenges*, Rome/Montpellier/Brussels, FAO/Cirad/European Commission, 59–62.

Hermabessiere L., Dehaut A., Paul-Pont I., Lacroix C., Jezequel R., Soudant P., Duflos G., 2017. Occurrence and effects of plastic additives on marine environments and organisms: a review. *Chemosphere*, 182: 781–793. https://doi.org/10.1016/j.chemo sphere.2017.05.096

Internal Displacement Monitoring Centre, 2020. *Global report on internal displacement*, Geneva, Internal Displacement Monitoring Centre, 126 p.

IPBES, 2019. *Summary for policymakers of the global assessment report on biodiversity and ecosystem services*, Bonn, IPBES Secretariat, 56 p. https://doi.org/10.5281 /zenodo.3553579

IPCC, 2013. *AR5 climate change 2013: the physical science basis. Contribution of working group I to the fifth Assessment Report of the Intergovernmental Panel on Climate Change*, Cambridge, Cambridge University Press, 1535 p.

IPES-Food, 2019. *Towards a common food policy for the European Union: the policy reform and realignment that is required to build sustainable food systems in Europe*, Brussels, IPES-Food, 111 p.

IPES-Food, ETC Group, 2021. *A long food movement: transforming food systems by 2045*, Brussels, IPES-Food, 175 p.

Kaza S., Yao L.C., Bhada-Tata P., Van Woerden F., 2018. *What a waste 2.0. A global snapshot of solid waste management to 2050*, Washington, DC, World Bank, 272 p.

Labadarios D., 2005. Malnutrition in the developing world: the triple burden. *South African Journal of Clinical Nutrition*, 18(2): 119–121. https://doi.org/10.1080 /16070658.2005.11734052

Lakner C., Yonzan N., Gerszon Mahler D., Castaneda Aguilar R.A., Wu H., 2021. *Updated estimates of the impact of COVID-19 on global poverty: looking back at 2020 and the outlook for 2021*, World Bank Blogs.

Muncke J., Andersson A.-M., Backhaus T., Boucher J.M., Carney Almroth B., Castillo Castillo A. et al., 2020. Impacts of food contact chemicals on human health: a consensus statement. *Environmental Health*, 19(1): 25. https://doi.org/10.1186/s12940-020-0572-5

Peñuelas J., Poulter B., Sardans J., Ciais P., van der Velde M., Bopp L. et al., 2013. Humaninduced nitrogen-phosphorus imbalances alter natural and managed ecosystems across the globe. *Nature Communications*, 4(1): 10. https://doi.org /10.1038/ncomms3934

Pinay G., Gascuel C., Alain M., Souchon Y., Le Moal M., Levain A. et al., 2018. *L'eutrophisation: manifestations, causes, conséquences et prédictibilité*, Versailles, Quæ, 175 p.

Rastoin J.-L., 2016. L'industrie et l'artisanat agro-alimentaires, fondements potentiels d'une stratégie responsable et durable à ancrage territorial. *Pour*, 229(1): 63–70. https://doi.org/10.3917/pour.229.0063

Soulier G., Moustier P., Lançon F., 2019. Risks of smallholder exclusion from upgrading food chains, in Dury S., Bendjebbar P., Hainzelin E., Giordano T., Bricas N. (ed.),

Food systems at risk. New trends and challenges, Rome/Montpellier/Brussels, FAO/ Cirad/European Commission, 79–82.

Stanziani A., 2005. *Histoire de la qualité alimentaire (XIXe–XXe siècles)*, Paris, Seuil, 440 p.

Tang F.H.M., Lenzen M., McBratney A., Maggi F., 2021. Risk of pesticide pollution at the global scale. *Nature Geoscience*, 14(4): 206–210. https://doi.org/10.1038/s41561 -021-00712-5

Tollefson J., 2020. Why deforestation and extinctions make pandemics more likely. *Nature*, 584(7820): 175–176. https://doi.org/10.1038/d41586-020-02341-1

Vancutsem C., Achard F., Pekel J., Vieilledent G., Carboni S., Simonetti D., Gallego J., Aragão L. E. O. C., Nasi R., 2021. Long-term (1990–2019) monitoring of forest cover changes in the humid tropics. *Science Advances*, 7(10): 21. https://doi.org/10.1126 /sciadv.abe1603

von Grebmer K., Saltzman A., Birol E., Wiesmann D., Prasai N., Yin S. et al., 2014. *2014 global hunger index. The challenge of hidden hunger*, Bonn/Washington, DC/Dublin, Welthungerhilfe/International Food Policy Research Institute/Concern Worldwide, 51 p.

WHO, 2015. *WHO estimates of the global burden of foodborne diseases*, Geneva, WHO, 254 p.

Part Three

Food and ecology

What if the unsustainability of the lifestyles of a part of humanity stemmed from a 'crisis of connection'? The collective imaginary of infinite progress, based on technological advances, maintains the illusion that humans could free themselves from the ecological limits of the planet and disassociate themselves from the fate of the community of living beings to which they nonetheless belong. The individualization of behaviour and the exacerbated pursuit of private interests are contributing to huge economic and social inequalities that are making us lose sight of the idea of common sense and the development of collective well-being.

When it comes to food, the industrialization of food systems is the result of – and contributes to – this 'crisis of connection'. Myriad forms of 'progress' pervade food systems and impact the interdependencies that structure the living world: the disruption of biological cycles, soil degradation, resource depletion and pollution; the unfair distribution of economic value between farmers, on the one hand, and processors and retailers on the other; the emergence of new forms of malnutrition; and so on.

Faced with this situation, we call for adopting an 'ecological' approach to meet the challenges surrounding food systems (Chapter 8), centred on living beings' relationships with themselves, with one another, and with their environment. Thus, the question at stake is no longer just which criteria define a sustainable food system and the conditions to achieve it: this approach also strives to understand the nature of the interactions that we seek to establish around our food habits. Food ecology invites us to adopt a holistic view of food (Chapter 9) and commit to the transformation of food systems (Chapter 10).

8

Why an ecological approach to food?

Marie Walser, Nicolas Bricas and Damien Conaré

Ecology first developed as a scientific discipline and subsequently as a political movement. This points to two arguments for adopting ecology as an analytical framework for thinking about food from a sustainability angle: it constitutes a 'hub science' for the study of relationships and has an inherently political dimension.

This book explores food and associated sustainability issues from an ecological perspective. This choice of words sets a daunting challenge, given that ecology encapsulates a host of imaginaries and expectations, some of which often go unfulfilled. Moreover, in French, the use of the multifaceted word 'alimentation'[1] contributes to this challenge, as it alludes to the sheer complexity of the question of food, though without explicitly describing it. This chapter seeks to explain the rationale behind this conceptual choice.

Ecology, ecological, ecologism . . .

What exactly is an ecological approach? The term 'ecological' may refer to anything environmentally friendly. The expression 'ecological practices' is used in industrialized societies to designate behaviours that seek to limit their environmental impact. Food waste composting and organic farming, for instance, are regularly presented as alternatives – often described as 'sustainable' – to environmentally damaging practices. Given the environmental damage caused by industrialized food system operations (Chapter 7), a transition towards a

---

[1] This complex term can at once refer to food, nutrition, diet, foodways, food dishes, eating practices, foodscapes, food styles and related aspects of culinary life.

more ecological system is an absolute priority. This is a first interpretation of what constitutes an 'ecological approach to food'. However, we use the term 'ecological' here not simply in the strict sense of being environmentally friendly but in its primary sense of 'relating to ecology'.

The word 'ecology' was coined in 1866 by the German biologist Ernst Haeckel. This novel term – derived from the Greek words *oikos* (house) and *logos* (knowledge) – denotes the study of relationships among living organisms and between these organisms and their environment. The term emerged shortly after the publication of *On the Origin of Species* by Charles Darwin, whose theory of evolution by natural selection posits living organisms as a vast, dynamic and transformative system rather than simply a collection of static, independent species. However, ecology was not institutionalized as a scientific discipline until twenty-five years later in the 1890s.

This new field of knowledge was grounded in the biological sciences and had the distinctive feature of being considered a nexus science from the outset – the result of a complex interplay between various disciplines such as biogeography, natural history and physiology. Its pioneers, including the French naturalist Georges-Louis Leclerc de Buffon (1707–88) and the German geographer and explorer Alexander von Humboldt (1769–1859), set out its main principles by seeking to identify, based on their observations, 'the interaction of natural forces'. The unpredictable nature of ecological phenomena proved to be a major challenge for scientific ecology, as the use of conventional scientific criteria – which seek to identify the regularity of a structure or model that can be explained, predicted or quantified – is ill-suited to understanding what eludes the usual representations of order in complex ecosystems. Although ecological processes are governed by the laws of physics, living organisms retain some degree of autonomy, thereby making it impossible to place them within a set of predictive laws. Living systems are therefore both constrained and autonomous, which makes them unique. The distinction between different organizational levels (populations, species, communities, ecosystems) does of course enable scientists to classify living organisms and distinguish between different research topics. But their object of study is still a tangle of trajectories (individual, population etc.), which gives it a dynamic dimension. The latter is shaped by the variability in space and time of living organisms that are continually co-evolving with their environment and other forms of life. By studying sets of nested ecological systems, ecology provides a paradigm that has served as inspiration for the development of conceptual models in several scientific disciplines, including nutrition (Sobal et al., 1998) (Chapter 9).

Ecology has interrogated the role of the human species in the living world from the start, with a long intellectual tradition of attentiveness to and a sensitive relationship with nature (Hepburn, 1967; Kormondy, 1969; Hausman, 1975; Rousseau, 2004). Ecologists are not limited to studying 'pristine' environments that conjure up images of the original lost Eden of the Western Christian tradition but instead focus on the impact of human activities on the environment. In the nineteenth and early twentieth centuries, pioneers such as John Muir (1897), Jean-Baptiste Charcot (Pénard, 1913) and Albert Howard (1940) warned of the effects of destroying nature in pursuit of profit or through war. In 1864, George Perkins Marsh argued that 'the ravages committed by man subvert the relations and destroy the balance which nature had established between her organized and her inorganic creations' (Perkins Marsh, 1864).

After the Second World War, as Western countries embraced a consumer society and developed an unparalleled destructive and exploitative capacity, the impact of human activities on the environment became a growing concern. As early as 1962, in her ground-breaking book *Silent Spring*, Rachel Carson warned of the impact of pesticides on the entire living world: soil, waterways, plants and animals and even human DNA. In the same decade, as the initial images of the earth taken from the moon underscored the fragility of the world's habitability, the first political ecology movements emerged (e.g. Friends of the Earth in the United States in 1969). They highlighted the global nature of ecological issues and called for the protection and even safeguarding of the diversity of living organisms through the project of a society built on a renewed relationship between humans and non-humans.

It was not until the early 1970s that political and public awareness of the looming ecological crisis began to gather momentum. In 1972, the report 'The Limits to Growth' (otherwise known as the 'Meadows Report'), commissioned by the Club of Rome, predicted the collapse of the global system as a result of the pressure exerted by human activities on natural resources. After decades of developing an academic identity, scientific ecology is now in the spotlight and, at the dawn of the twenty-first century, is contributing to the quest for solutions to global issues. To this end, international expert bodies are being set up, such as the Intergovernmental Panel on Climate Change (IPCC) created in 1988 and the Intergovernmental Science-Policy Platform on Biodiversity and Ecosystem Services (IPBES) set up in 2012. There is growing consensus that the lifestyles of some segments of humankind urgently need to be called into question if we are to avoid an ecological crisis. In this respect, social ecology draws the links between ecological and social inequality crises. For instance, as wealth creation in a country becomes increasingly monopolized by a small number of people, the rest of the population has to counterbalance this monopolization through increased economic development, which can be environmentally destructive. The social impact of environmental degradation differs across income classes, thereby generating 'environmental inequality' (Laurent, 2015).

Ecological movements – whether activist, political or social – have long been the main driving force for change that is struggling to become widespread. Note that there are also rifts within the political ecology space which, shaped by different philosophical and ideological roots, is rife with controversy fuelled by the clash between sometimes contradictory value systems (Chansigaud, 2018). This is true for biodiversity conservation, sustainable development and resilience (Lévêque, 2013). Co-viability, which implies the sustainable coexistence of ecological and social systems, could serve as a unifying approach (Barrière et al., 2019). This concept is one of the building blocks of both scientific and political ecology.

Studying food and associated sustainability issues

This historical overview shows that ecology offers a relevant framework for studying food and associated sustainability issues for at least two reasons.

First, as a nexus science of relationships, ecology has an integrative dimension – that is, it is geared towards gaining holistic insight into the phenomena studied, focusing on the links between the different facets of these phenomena and the dynamics produced by their interaction. This approach thus fosters the articulation of complementary viewpoints. While the segmented study of the different facets of a phenomenon is certainly essential to gaining a comprehensive understanding of each facet, relying solely on this approach limits the potential for understanding the overall complexity of a phenomenon, while also running the risk of reducing it to just one of its multiple dimensions. This is illustrated by the parable of the elephant and the blind scholars in the Jaina metaphysical doctrine of Anekāntavāda ('relative reality'), in which six blind Indian scholars try to learn what an elephant is like by studying it from different angles. One studies the trunk, the second the ears, the third the tusks, the fourth the sides, the fifth the tail, and the sixth the legs. Finally, the scholars all interpret the elephant from their own obviously relativistic standpoint and are never able to agree on what an elephant is really like. An integrated approach will not overlook possible conflicts between sometimes antagonistic positions but will instead provide a space to identify these conflicts (Luyckx, 2020) along with the properties that emerge through interaction.

Food is indeed a multidimensional issue that can be interpreted from several perspectives (Figure 8.1). Historically, the different disciplines that have studied food have each been structured around a specific dimension. For instance, nutrition is mainly concerned with the biological aspects of food, psychology and neuroscience with its hedonic aspects and sociology with its social aspects; while anthropology examines the role of culture, economics analyses food as a commodity for consumption, exchange and value creation, agronomy studies the agricultural production system from a technical perspective and so on. This epistemological fragmentation is rooted in the history of science. In the wake of the Age of Enlightenment, the twenty-first century was permeated by a positivist vision of knowledge that could only be gained by gathering facts through experiments and therefore through disciplinary specialization. This

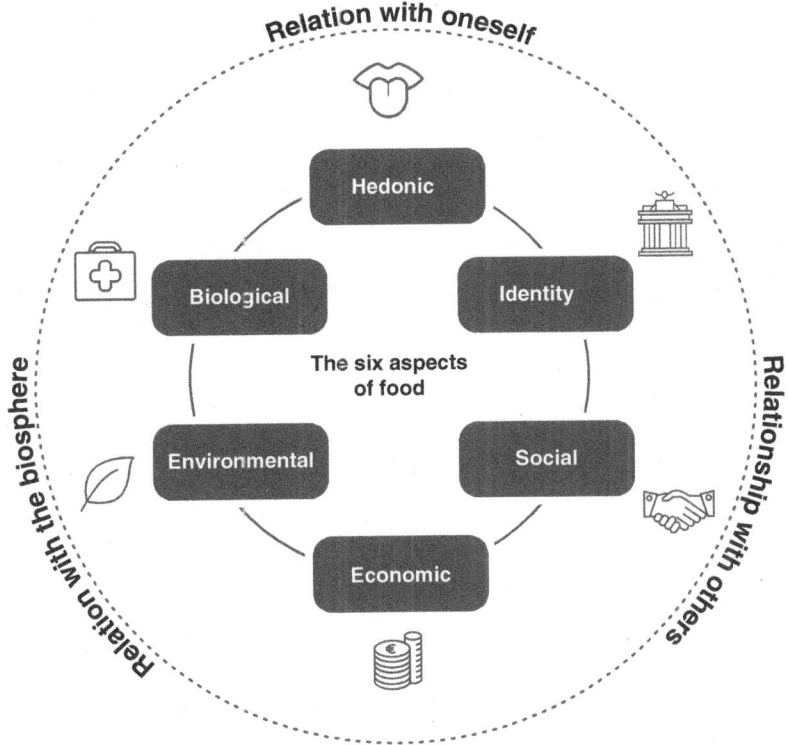

Figure 8.1 The multidimensional nature of food.

means that food research comes with the risk of 'knowledge scattering' (Poulain, 2017), which is extremely detrimental at a time when the social and ecological crisis we face requires a global approach to sustainability issues so as to grasp and leverage interconnections.

In practice, 'food ecology' therefore involves breaking down the barriers of knowledge on food through interdisciplinary dialogue so as to gain an overarching understanding of the sustainability issues that underlie the functioning of food systems (Chapter 9). This articulation of different perspectives on food is guided by a holistic approach that is able to recognize the diverse dimensions of food without presuming any hierarchy, draw links between them and shed light on the dynamics produced by their interactions. This approach seeks to avoid the temptation to investigate food issues while excluding some key aspects from the analysis (looking at health without considering pleasure or culture, looking at environmental and social issues without considering economic aspects etc.). There is also a risk of failing to objectify the contradictions and emerging issues at play along the pathway to sustainability, which may sometimes impede or conversely foster change.

Second, ecology's central focus on the links between living beings gives it an ethical dimension. It urges us to change our relationships in the world and to reconsider ourselves as being 'amongst others' – that is, among other human beings, forms of life and generations before and after us. In essence, ecology champions an exhilarating sense of being part of the living world, with a responsibility to uphold decent living conditions for other humans and non-humans, now and in the future. From this ecological perspective, non-sustainability is viewed as the result of the breakdown of socioecological bonds, thereby undermining the ability to sustain decent living conditions within our collective home (*oikos*).

Contemplating sustainability, especially in terms of food, thus implies rethinking our interactions within socioecological systems in the light of principles such as diversity, resilience, symbiosis, reserves, cycles, free flows and sensitive links. These notions run counter to rationalistic, reductionist, productivist and individualistic views of existence in many contemporary societies. In this respect, intensive, concentrated and uniform industrialized food systems are a far cry from serving as a primary sustainable nurturing source and generally operate at the expense of substantial social and environmental externalities. The main stakeholders in such systems are aware of their vulnerability (Les Greniers d'Abondance, 2020), yet they rely on advanced technology, bolstered by the advent of synthetic biology, nanotechnology and digital technology (IPES-Food and ETC Group, 2021) to ensure that the systems remain firmly entrenched outside the fabric of living relationships and dynamics.

In practice, 'food ecology' thus involves a political commitment to ensuring that food systems contribute to the achievement of present and future socioecological co-viability (Chapter 10). Protesting, advocating and experimenting are some of the pathways pursued by actors engaged in this new relationship with the world, including civil society actors, the private sector, local authorities, politicians and so on. For anyone seeking to get involved in transforming food systems, the key is to be aware of and overcome the unforeseeable factors, technical barriers and political resistance that hinder change.

Conclusion

This proposed 'food ecology' is intended to offer a new way of thinking about food (Figure 8.2). It is a scientific call to connect the different dimensions of food and to commit to transforming food systems.

The purpose of food ecology is to fuel reflection by researchers and students, but it may also inspire anyone involved in food systems or anyone who is aware of and curious about sustainable food issues. Its aim is not to define a normative framework or prescribe good sustainable food practices. We believe that food should be studied within its context in order to act as consistently as

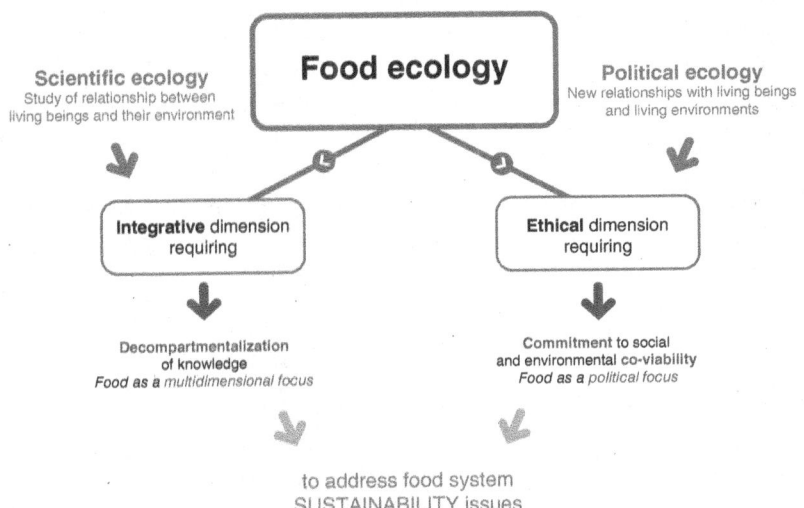

Figure 8.2 Food ecology principles.

possible in relation to the situation at hand. Food ecology is more of a school of thought concerned with the complexity of food and its contemporary issues – this captures the perspective of the UNESCO Chair in World Food Systems, which has matured over several years of science–society dialogue on sustainable food issues. The next two chapters outline the two proposals underlying food ecology: decompartmentalizing knowledge on food and taking a political stand for the transformation of food systems. The practical implications of these two proposals are presented in Parts 4 and 5 of the book.

The authors would like to thank Mathilde Coudray, Vincent Devictor and Jacques Tassin for proofreading this chapter and for their suggested improvements.

References

Barrière O., Behnassi M., David G., Douzal V., Fargette M., Libourel T. et al. (ed.), 2019. *Coviability of social and ecological systems: reconnecting mankind to the biosphere in an era of global change*. Vol. 1: The foundations of a new paradigm, New York, Springer International Publishing, 728 p.

Carson R., 1962. *Silent spring*, Boston, Houghton Mifflin, 368 p.

Chansigaud V., 2018. *Les combats pour la nature: de la protection de la nature au progrès social*, Paris, Éditions Buchet-Chastel, 256 p.

Darwin C., 1859. *On the origin of species by means of natural selection, or, the preservation of favoured races in the struggle for life*, London, J. Murray, 502 p.

Hausman D.B., 1975. What is natural? *Perspectives in Biology and Medicine*, 19(1): 92–100. https://doi.org/10.1353/pbm.1975.0018

Hepburn R., 1967. Contemporary aesthetics and the neglect of natural beauty, in Williams B., Montefiore A. (ed.), *British analytical philosophy*, London, Routledge/Kegan Paul, 285–310.

Howard A., 1940. *An agricultural testament*, London, Oxford University Press, 254 p.

IPES-Food, ETC Group, 2021. *A long food movement: transforming food systems by 2045*, Brussels, IPES-Food, 175 p.

Kormondy E.J., 1969. *Concepts of ecology*, Englewood Cliffs, Prentice-Hall, 232 p.

Laurent É., 2015. La social-écologie: une perspective théorique et empirique. *Revue française des affaires sociales*, 1: 125–143. https://doi.org/10.3917/rfas.151.0125

Les Greniers d'Abondance, 2020. *Vers la résilience alimentaire: faire face aux menaces globales à l'échelle des territoires*, Gap, Yves Michel, 180 p.

Lévêque C., 2013. *L'écologie est-elle encore scientifique ?*, Versailles, Quæ, 144 p.

Luyckx C., 2020. L'écologie intégrale: relier les approches, intégrer les enjeux, tisser une vision. *La pensée écologique*, 6(2): 77–95. https://doi.org/10.3917/lpe.006.0077

Muir J., 1897. The American forests. *Atlantic Monthly*, 80(478): 145–157.

Pénard E., 1913. *Deuxième expédition antarctique française 1908–1910*, commandée par le Dr Jean Charcot. Rhizopodes d'eau douce, Paris, Masson, 16 p.

Perkins Marsh G., 1864. Man and nature: or, physical geography as modified by human action, London, S. Low, Son and Marston, 560 p.

Poulain J.-P., 2017. *The sociology of food: eating and the place of food in society*, London/ New York, Bloomsbury Academic, 238 p. Translation of 'Sociologies de l'alimentation' (2002).

Rousseau J.-J., 2004. *A discourse upon the origin and the foundation of the inequality among mankind*, ebook, Project Gutenberg. Translation of 'Discours sur l'origine et les fondements de l'inégalité parmi les hommes' (1755).

Sobal J., Kettel Khan L., Bisogni C., 1998. A conceptual model of the food and nutrition system. *Social Science & Medicine*, 47(7): 853–863. https://doi.org/10.1016/S0277 -9536(98)00104-X

9

Decompartmentalizing knowledge on food

Jean-Marc Louvin and Marie Walser

Food is a multidimensional issue. Together, the perspectives of different scientific disciplines have converged to achieve a shared understanding of this research topic and its associated issues.

This chapter represents the first step towards an 'ecological approach to food' – the decompartmentalization of knowledge to enable us to grasp the complexity of food and associated sustainability issues. After introducing the concept of holism, the chapter illustrates how three disciplines – nutrition, the humanities and social sciences (HSS) and agronomy – have shifted their respective research lenses to work towards a multidimensional approach to food. The chapter then considers the recent formalization of a new interdisciplinary research topic, 'sustainable food systems', in connection with the advent of the systemic approach and the growing sustainability issues of the late twentieth century. It concludes with a discussion on the vital role of disciplinary interfaces in decompartmentalizing knowledge both within and beyond the boundaries of science and fostering transformative interaction.

Holism

An ecological approach to food calls for a holistic perspective so as to gain an overarching understanding of food without reducing it to any one of its dimensions. While the idea of holism (from the Greek *hólos*: 'whole, entire') can be attributed to the writings of Plato (*Meno*) and Aristotle (*Politics*), the term itself is a neologism first coined by the South African philosopher and statesman Jan Christiaan Smuts in his book *Holism and Evolution* (1926), in which he defined it as a 'fundamental factor operative towards the creation of wholes in the universe'. In other words, holism was initially seen as an entity in itself. This meaning, however, was not the one that attracted the attention of twentieth-century scientists, for whom the concept primarily referred to the idea that the whole is greater than (or at least different from) the sum of its parts. Holism is thus at variance with reductionist theory, which posits the whole as reducible to its constituent parts.

Food is at the crossroads of a range of individual, societal and global issues (Parts 1 and 2) and is a 'total human reality' (Poulain, 2017). It affects all aspects of life and, in turn, can be understood in terms of the material and symbolic features of the context in which it occurs. In academic circles, however, food has long been investigated following a segmented approach, with scientists studying individual aspects of food through the lens of their specific disciplines. At a time when sustainability issues are becoming increasingly globalized and interconnected, it is vital to break down the barriers between different areas of food-related knowledge so as to offer appropriate guidance for food system transformation initiatives. Several scientific disciplines have, each in their own way, taken a chance on decompartmentalization and adopted paths towards a more holistic – and one might even say more ecological – approach to food.

Holistic approaches to nutrition

The origins of nutrition date back to Ancient Greek dietetics. As a science and everyday practice, dietetics placed food within the realm of life (work, physical exercise etc.), with health interpreted as a balance between bodily humours (fluids) and food properties (Montanari, 1993; Shapin, 2014). Following the rise of modern science in the sixteenth century, the qualitative approach to people's state of health gave way to a quantitative approach based on the study of food compounds and their impact on the body. In 1875, with the advent of the chemically biased nutrition paradigm (Hall, 1974), nutrition research became even more focused on the study of the various biochemical components and processes underlying the connection between diet and health. This prompted scientists in the late nineteenth century to identify all macronutrients (proteins, carbohydrates and lipids), followed by micronutrients (vitamins, minerals and trace elements) in the second half of the twentieth century and to distinguish between healthy and less healthy components. The discovery of DNA marked the beginning of nutritionists' interest in how diet influences genetic expression.

In the nineteenth and twentieth centuries, this scientific approach – segmenting humans and their diet into ever smaller components so as to condense the functioning of living organisms into laws – gained momentum with the success of its societal applications,[1] to the extent that nutrition became trapped in a nutritionist paradigm (Scrinis, 2008, 2013). This paradigm was rooted in a biological reductionism that reduced food and health to nutritional compounds and quantifiable physiological processes respectively. Moreover, the many scientific advances in nutrition contributed to the gradual 'nutritionalization of food' (Dixon, 2009) – that is, the adoption by society as a whole of a reductive understanding of food, limited solely to its role as a means of ensuring health. The latter is thus central to the nutritionist paradigm.

This nutritionist ideology (Pollan, 2008; Scrinis, 2008) has been the focus of substantial epistemological, methodological, social and moral criticism while also potentially stalling advances in nutrition research (Burlingame, 2004). This approach is reproached for being unable to propose solutions to meet current challenges (be they health, social or ecological) (Cannon and Leitzmann, 2005) and is claimed to be a source of often ineffective and even counterproductive technological solutions (Dixon et al., 2009). This is exemplified by medicinal foods, with controversy surrounding their effect on people who already have an adequate diet (Poulain, 2017). Finally, from a moral perspective, nutritionism is one of the drivers contributing to excessive responsibility being placed at the feet of eaters (Coveney, 1999; Fischler, 2011) and even to stigmatizing anyone who deviates from the norm, such as people with anorexia, bulimia or obesity (Poulain, 2009).

Nutritionists have developed a range of approaches to overcome these failings. We present them here from the perspective of their holistic dimension. For clarity, we distinguish three different categories: intranutritional approaches – in other words, those which adopt a holistic perspective within the framework of the science of nutrition itself; nutritional approaches, which strive to integrate knowledge from other disciplines to shed light on their object of study; and extra-nutritional approaches, which go so far as to overhaul the conceptual, methodological and axiological foundations of nutrition.

Intranutritional approaches have been applied in research carried out by the nutritionists Colin Campbell and Thomas Campbell (2006) and Colin Campbell and Howard Jacobson (2013) in the United States and Anthony Fardet (2017) in France. These approaches take a fresh look at nutritional analysis by considering

---

[1] For instance, the discovery that food could prevent scurvy.

the whole as an entity that cannot be reduced to its parts (Fardet and Rock, 2014), particularly through the concepts of food synergy (Jacobs and Steffen, 2003; Jacobs et al., 2009) and the food matrix (Fardet et al., 2013; Aguilera, 2019) (see Box 9.1). Unlike nutritionism, which focuses specifically on studying the effects of individual chemical compounds on health in a decontextualized framework, this research highlights the need to study the health effects of interactions between different nutrients at the individual food, meal and even diet level.

Nutritional approaches are distinguished by the fact that they take food dimensions other than purely biological aspects into account. They have a public health orientation, studying food consumption from the perspective of the relationships between biological, psychological, economic and sociological

Box 9.1 Food matrices

Claire Mouquet-Rivier

The food matrix concept goes beyond merely considering nutritional compounds (macro- and micronutrients) and bioactive compounds (polyphenols, phytates, saponins, fibres etc.) together – it captures the complex arrangement of these compounds, which are subject to multiple interactions, thereby forming microstructures. Compound arrangements and interactions in food matrices give foods novel nutritional or organoleptic properties that individual compounds alone cannot provide. The properties of these microstructures are the outcome of physical interactions involving the size, spatial conformation and plasticity of the molecules, as well as chemical interactions involving pH, different energy bonds, oxidation-reduction phenomena and solubility. They may be modified over time in the process of food processing – for example, under the effect of pressure or heat – or during digestion as a result of the action of mastication, digestive fluids, gut microbiota and so on. Food should therefore be understood in kinetic terms, with the availability of matrix components – including nutrients and aromatic compounds, as well as any heavy metals and other compounds with harmful health effects – being shaped by these temporal dynamics. The food matrix thus has a major regulatory impact on intestinal absorption.

Find out more: Aguilera J.M., 2019. The food matrix: implications in processing, nutrition and health. *Critical Reviews in Food Science and Nutrition*, 59(22): 3612–3629.

factors (Fattore and Agostoni, 2016). These approaches incorporate knowledge and methods from other disciplines such as the social sciences and agronomy. The 'sociology of nutrition', for instance, studies the impact of macrosocial forces on eating practices (Glass and McAtee, 2006; Traverso-Yepez and Hunter, 2016); nutritional anthropology focuses on the impact of culture on these practices (Calandre, 2002); and nutrition economics analyses the impact of eaters' economic status on their nutritional well-being (Perignon et al., 2017). Finally, cross-sectoral health and agricultural approaches shed light on how agricultural developments can affect people's nutritional status (Frison et al., 2006; Hawkes and Ruel, 2007; Dury et al., 2014). The journal *Ecology of Food and Nutrition* showcases these cross-cutting perspectives, which shed light on contemporary nutritional issues shaped by a range of challenges.

Lastly, extra-nutritional approaches involve the reorganization of the conceptual framework of nutrition – individual health here encompasses public health, while the health concept incorporates environmental health and social well-being. The French nutritionist Jean Trémolières was one of the first to pave the way for these approaches by fostering dialogue between the so-called hard sciences and the social sciences and humanities with the publication of his Cahiers de nutrition et de diététique in 1965. Recognizing the one-sided bias of the nutritional approach, which 'when it focuses on everyday life [. . .] only sheds light on one aspect of it' (1975), Trémolières proposed approaching food from the more holistic perspective of diaita (dietetics), which also takes into account the social, cultural and hedonic dimensions of food.

Over the last forty years, the rise of sustainability issues has led to a renewal of the science of nutrition. Nutritional ecology, for instance, embraces an interdisciplinary approach that takes into account interactions between physiological, social, cultural and environmental factors (Gussow, 1978; Schneider and Hoffmann, 2011). Cannon and Leitzmann (2005) proposed a new conceptual framework through the New Nutrition Science Project, which led to the signing of the Giessen Declaration.[2] This project brought together scientists from different disciplinary backgrounds with a view to overhauling the foundations and principles of nutrition (Beauman et al., 2005). Guided by a 'philosophy of co-responsibility' towards non-human living beings (Meyer-Abich, 2005), these scientists sought to shed light on the network of real and symbolic relationships that connect humans, non-humans and their biophysical environment.

---

[2] The Giessen Declaration. Public Health Nutrition, 8(6A), pp. 783–6.

More recently, in the wake of the ecological crisis, the scope of nutrition has broadened to include its environmental dimension. Eco-nutrition (Wahlqvist and Specht, 1998) thus incorporates health and environmental issues in the study of diets that contribute to meeting nutritional needs as well as safeguarding biodiversity and the environment (Frison et al., 2006; Marlow et al., 2009; Chappell and Lavalle, 2011; Perignon et al., 2016). In line with this approach, the French nutritionist Christian Rémésy (2020) has drawn up a charter for 'nutriecology' – 'a discipline that aims to fulfil human nutritional needs while preserving the Earth's ecological resources and enhancing its nutritional potential'.

Holistic approaches in the social sciences and humanities

Both in Europe and across the Atlantic, food has struggled to prevail as a research object in its own right in the social sciences and humanities (Montanari, 1993; Poulain, 2017). Food has either been deemed trivial due to its ordinary nature or illegitimate because of its biological dimension and has therefore not been seen as a relevant prism for shedding light on the functioning of societies. In the nineteenth century, sociology was a nascent discipline still carving out a space of its own and considered food solely in terms of its most 'sociologically amenable' aspects, such as the role of meals in family life (Halbwachs, 1912). Up until the mid-1960s, the issue of food was merely considered as a point of entry to investigate other anthropological and sociological issues deemed more important, such as health, family and rural life (Poulain, 2017).

Despite these epistemological roadblocks, interest in food within the social sciences and humanities grew in the second half of the twentieth century. Claude Lévi-Strauss's (1969) structuralist perspective played a key role in consolidating the anthropological status of food and cooking through the identification of structures such as the so-called culinary triangle. This model of relationships between different forms of cuisine based on the way in which food is cooked (raw-roasted, rotted-fermented, cooked-smoked) was believed to reflect how societies function. Moreover, the study of consumption patterns in Europe (Moulin, 1975) and in France (Lambert, 1986; Herpin, 1988) provided sociologists and socio-economists with a gateway to food research.

At the same time, the social sciences and humanities developed a more holistic approach to food. Four different approaches are presented here: interdisciplinarity and food studies, followed by a biocultural approach and finally what we call a multi-scalar approach.

First, the decompartmentalization of perspectives can involve the sharing of knowledge and/or methods specific to several social sciences and humanities disciplines. In France, for example, an interdisciplinary approach to food developed through cross-disciplinary hybridizations such as socio-anthropology (Serra-Mallol, 2010; Tibère, 2013), psychosociology (Barthes, 1961) and even a form of historical sociology of food (Depecker et al., 2013). In the Americas, another type of holistic approach emerged in the 1990s, inspired by cultural studies: food studies, which amounts to a food metadiscipline combining a number of sciences (history, literature, philosophy, sociology, anthropology etc.).

Second, one particular approach transcends the barriers between the hard and social sciences insofar as it focuses on the articulations between the biological, psychological and social facets of food. This so-called biocultural approach, inspired by the complexity approach proposed by Edgar Morin in the 1970s, was exemplified through the collaboration between the nutritionist Elsie May Widdowson and the anthropologist Audrey Richards in a study of Bemba communities in southern Africa (de Garine, 1988). It was promoted thereafter by the anthropologist Igor de Garine (de Garine, 1972, 1979; Froment et al., 1996) and further conceptualized by Claude Fischler in Issue 31 of the journal Communications (1979) and in his book *L'Homnivore* (1990). Fischler acknowledged food as a 'truly transdisciplinary theme' and laid the foundations for a sociology of eaters, taking a holistic approach by exploring disciplinary interfaces. This drive to articulate the natural and the cultural is also found in Jean-Pierre Poulain's theorization of the 'food social space' concept, which allows for thinking about food cultures in terms of an organism's biological limitations as well as environmental constraints in connection with eaters' ways of relating to nature (Poulain, 2017).

Finally, the multi-scalar approach to food – that is, considering food on several levels – offers another way for the social sciences to investigate food from a holistic perspective. This approach, borrowed from geography, articulates different levels of observation (individual, family, social group etc.) to gain a comprehensive understanding of the research object and capture the complexity of reality. In relation to food, this involves the articulation of knowledge produced at the macrosocial, meso-social, micro-social (Germov and Williams, 2016) and biological (Desjeux, 1996) levels to fully grasp all the dimensions of food.

Although this is beyond the scope of this chapter, it is important to note that alongside this focus on eaters, social science studies on topics such as rurality, health, organizations and economic networks also contribute to our understanding of food as an 'all-encompassing human reality'.

Holistic approaches in agronomy

While agronomy largely studies food from the perspective of agricultural production, a number of French researchers – often agronomists and sometimes technologists – have been drawn to a more holistic approach. Within the framework of their discipline, they have gradually developed a passion for their research object, namely a plant or a food product, to the point of ultimately becoming encyclopaedic specialists able to connect its origins, agronomic features, processing methods, uses and symbolic dimensions. Some publications have thus endeavoured to articulate previously fragmented knowledge on products such as yams (Degras, 1993; Dumont and Marti, 1997), oil palm (Jacquemard, 1995), fonio (Cruz et al., 2016) and even beer (Hébert and Griffon, 2010, 2012) in the form of large integrative syntheses.

Given the systemic nature of its subject matter, agronomy is intrinsically multidisciplinary. It encompasses a range of disciplines, including hard sciences – for example, ecophysiology, bioclimatology and soil science – as well as the social sciences and humanities, such as economics, geography, sociology and management science, to investigate production systems from a broader perspective. Scientific knowledge is always articulated with farmers' empirical knowledge, which existed long before the advent of the academic discipline (Perret, 2005). In particular, agroecological knowledge – which aims to leverage biological processes to fulfil both production needs and a range of ecosystem services – initially emerged on the fringes of the scientific sphere.

Agroecology has now been institutionalized as a discipline (Wezel and Soldat, 2009), which posits the agricultural production space as a complex adaptive system encompassing biodiversity, humans, their social structures and their representations (Hubert and Couvet, 2021). Some scientists have broadened the scope of agroecology to encompass the entire food system. Francis and colleagues (2003) thus describe agroecology as 'the integrative study of the ecology of the entire food system' while advocating the need to 'build bridges and connections among and beyond our disciplines in production agriculture, as well as beyond the farm gate into the rural landscape and community'. Stephen Gliessman (2016) describes agroecology as a stepwise approach to transforming food systems, from agricultural production to downstream activities. This understanding of agroecology, which seeks to connect the environmental, economic and social dimensions of the food system with its different stages, provides an integrative approach that is relevant for addressing sustainability issues.

A systems-based approach to food

The systems paradigm emerged in Western scientific thinking in the second half of the twentieth century. It partially eclipsed the analytical rationale of explaining the whole by studying its parts, which had prevailed since the seventeenth century but had struggled to account for the complexity of the world. Systems thinking – based on the work of neurobiologists, mathematicians and cyberneticians – is characterized by a global or holistic approach to complex phenomena, grounded in the study of a 'set of dynamically interacting elements' (Cambien, 2007) that are treated as a system in order to meet a specific research objective. The systems-based approach is therefore an epistemological choice. Given the complex nature of its objects of study, this approach is cross- and interdisciplinary. It strives not to replace conventional disciplines but to foster 'synergy and synthesis between them' (Cambien, 2007).

The systems paradigm has broadened the horizons in many scientific and societal fields, including that of food. The application of this approach to food systems has radically reshaped the way in which food is understood, which was previously fragmented across different disciplinary silos or sectors of activity. In its early definitions (Collins, 1963; Marion, 1986; Malassis, 1994), a food system was understood to refer to all or part of the food chain, 'from land to mouth' (Kneen, 1993), including production, processing, distribution, transport and consumption. The study of the key dimensions of the food system thus became driven by the need to gain a comprehensive understanding of food at a time when there was a vital need to feed a growing population (Béné et al., 2019b). In 1998, Jeffery Sobal and colleagues proposed one of the first integrated models of the 'food and nutrition system', a tool 'depicting the extent of the system and outlining the processes, transformations and interactions involved in food systems'. Since the food system was first recognized as a subject of scientific and societal interest, a number of conceptual models have been proposed to define and explain its functioning. Integrating spatiotemporal scales, disciplines, stakeholders, practices and customs is becoming central to part of the research on agriculture and food (Chevassus-au-Louis et al., 2008).

The rise of environmental and social issues has challenged the prevailing modes of food production and consumption and has markedly altered the purpose of food systems. The primary concern is still guaranteeing food security,[3] but the

---

[3] 'Food security exists when all people, at all times, have physical and economic access to sufficient safe and nutritious food that meets their dietary needs and food preferences for an active and healthy life' (FAO World Food Summit Declaration, 1996).

sustainability of food systems has now been identified as a major challenge (Eakin et al., 2017). A new research area is emerging: 'sustainable food systems' (Blay-Palmer, 2010; Marsden and Morley, 2014; FAO, 2018; Willett et al., 2019). It articulates so-called integrated, systems-based, holistic or multidimensional approaches to study the conditions required for a food system transition that takes into account both the complexity of the system and the multidimensional nature of sustainability[4] (Foran et al., 2014; Moscatelli et al., 2016; Horton et al., 2017; Blay-Palmer et al., 2019). Interdisciplinarity is pivotal to these approaches, since monodisciplinary strategies are unable to cope with the complexity of the issues inherent in food system sustainability (IPES-Food, 2015). The food system is often depicted as 'socio-ecological'. In many fields, this new approach brings together the hard and social sciences (Schoon and van der Leeuw, 2015) and calls for fully taking into account the interdependence between human and natural systems – here in relation to food issues (Ericksen, 2008; Allen and Prosperi, 2016). This approach allows for considering the interdependence of food security, environmental integrity and social well-being and for exploring the concept of food system resilience (Hodbod and Eakin, 2015; Tendall et al., 2015; Schipanski et al., 2016; Doherty et al., 2019).

The food system may be a unified object of study for experts in different disciplines, but perspectives on sustainability issues and the resulting transition scenarios that are proposed can vary widely across diverse knowledge communities (Eakin et al., 2017; Béné et al., 2019a). Thus while there is consensus on the need for a sustainable food system, the proposed pathways to achieve such a system differ. While these divergences reflect how sustainability is narrowed down to only some of its dimensions, they also highlight profound antagonisms surrounding the pathways of transition. Developing a complex approach to food helps (among other things) to make these antagonisms more explicit. By suggesting that the environmental, economic, social, health and political dimensions of diets be considered on an equal footing, the sustainable diets approach developed by Pamela Mason and Tim Lang (2017) offers a tool for the multidimensional food governance.

---

[4] According to Béné and colleagues (2019a), 'sustainability, in its most universal sense, is a multi-dimensional concept that incorporates three fundamental elements: the pursuit of social equity, the creation of human welfare (often presented as an economic dimension), and the maintenance of the environmental integrity of the resource-base on which the economic and social dimensions are built. A fourth dimension is often superimposed on these three, one that involves time and the idea that the sustainability of today should not be achieved at the cost of the sustainability of tomorrow' (Brundtland, 1987).

People as keystones in food ecology

The food ecology approach advocates the dissemination and articulation of the scientific approaches presented above, which to varying extents seek to decompartmentalize perspectives on food so as to address the multidimensional nature of both food and its associated issues. Furthermore, food ecology is also geared towards developing inter- and even transdisciplinary approaches, whereby scientists come together to share their perspectives on food (Chapter 21).

The key idea underpinning this approach is that of a 'return to the subject' in science (Gosselin, 1987) – that is, establishing dialogue between scientists rather than between scientific disciplines, through and beyond their diverse disciplinary horizons. Any discipline, prior to becoming a framework for the production of knowledge, is ultimately a group of men and women who 'play the role of scientists' (Bourdieu, 2000, 2004). This role essentially consists in applying the paradigms, methods and analyses of a given discipline, and all actors must play it with 'full awareness' (Morin, 1982). Insofar as 'all knowledge stems from our worldview' (Hubert et al., 2015), the main challenge with this approach is no longer to produce a highly integrated body of knowledge but rather to encourage actors to become more reflexive as a first step towards grasping the complexity of the subject at hand. While food ecology recognizes the need to maintain disciplinary fields, it also advocates the creation of interfaces – in other words, spaces for dialogue, exchange and experimentation – in which to articulate knowledge, debate controversies, interrogate representations, compare research programmes and collectively recognize the grey areas and antagonisms involved in their articulation. These so-called interface spaces are many and varied and may include anything from symposia and seminars to scientific journals and interdisciplinary research projects. They enable researchers to keep abreast of what is happening in the field of food beyond their specialist area, to question their personal viewpoints and to experience moments of collective awareness regarding food issues.

Food ecology also recognizes the need to transcend the limits of the scientific community and foster 'the cohabitation of disciplinary and generalist knowledge' (Poulain, 2017) or even their interaction as part of an 'ecology of knowledge' (Santos, 2016). Without falling into the trap of relativism, this involves the scientific method not having primacy over other forms of relationship to reality (Mormont, 2015), insofar as knowledge is equally intellectual on the one hand and practical and emotional on the other. Food must be approached as a perceived object and a lived experience, which structures sensitive relationships and practices between individuals, society and the biosphere. Interaction between scientific and non-scientific actors is essential to address sustainability issues in food systems: 'cross-knowledge dialogue' (Santos, 2016) and the co-construction of research problems afford a shared understanding of what transition can involve (Lamine et al., 2019), catalyse change by drawing on the knowledge specific to each actor (IPES-Food, 2015) and allow for the development of improved practices. Transdisciplinary interfaces foster a sense of belonging to a 'community of fate', rallied to build shared values. These shared values in turn inform reflection on, and the organization of, solutions that incorporate the multidimensional nature of food and grasp the complexity of the issues involved.

Conclusion

Food ecology promotes the decompartmentalization of food knowledge and thereby fosters a complex understanding of food (Morin, 2008). It is therefore essential to make explicit the antagonisms (the simultaneous expression of positive and negative effects), feedbacks (an action triggered in response to one's own) and recursiveness (repetition of a fact that induces a consequence which in turn induces the fact) involved in the different dimensions of food (Morin, 1990). Thus, it is clear that although certain watchwords pointing the way to achieving food sustainability have their role to play (Part 4), there are no straightforward answers to the multidimensional challenges raised by our contemporary eating habits.

Articulating focused approaches and openness to interdisciplinarity – in other words 'distinguishing between' and 'connecting' these approaches' different perspectives – better equips food-related sciences to identify relevant pathways for change towards sustainable food systems. Inter- and transdisciplinary approaches – as spaces for interaction and co-construction – not only help strengthen ties between researchers in pursuit of a common goal, but they also anchor the search for solutions in everyday life by linking them to the actors, processes and institutions involved in food systems (Chapter 21). The ecology of food thus calls for dialogue between scientific disciplines and between science and society.

This chapter largely draws on the research of Jean-Marc Louvin during an internship at the UNESCO Chair in World Food Systems on the topic of 'Holistic approaches to food – state of the art' (2017).

The authors would like to thank Mathilde Coudray, Vincent Devictor, Bernard Hubert and Jacques Tassin for proofreading this chapter and for their suggested improvements.

References

Aguilera J.M., 2019. The food matrix: implications in processing, nutrition and health. *Critical Reviews in Food Science and Nutrition*, 59(22): 3612–3629. https://doi.org/10.1080/10408398.2018.1502743

Allen T., Prosperi P., 2016. Modeling sustainable food systems. *Environmental Management*, 57(5): 956–975. https://doi.org/10.1007/s00267-016-0664-8

Barthes R., 1961. Pour une psycho-sociologie de l'alimentation contemporaine. *Annales*, 16(5): 977–986. https://doi.org/10.3406/ahess.1961.420772

Beauman C., Cannon G., Elmadfa I., Glasauer P., Hoffmann I., Keller M. et al., 2005. The principles, definition and dimensions of the new nutrition science. *Public Health Nutrition*, 8: 695–698. https://doi.org/10.1079/PHN2005820

Béné C., Oosterveer P., Lamotte L., Brouwer I.D., de Haan S., Prager S.D. et al., 2019a. When food systems meet sustainability. Current narratives and implications for actions. *World Development*, 113: 116–130. https://doi.org/10.1016/j.worlddev.2018.08.011

Béné C., Prager S., Achicanoy H., Toro P., Lamotte L., Bonilla C., Mapes B., 2019b. Understanding food systems drivers. A critical review of the literature. *Global Food Security*, 23: 149–159. https://doi.org/10.1016/j.gfs.2019.04.009

Blay-Palmer A. (ed.), 2010. *Imagining sustainable food systems: theory and practice*, Aldershot, Ashgate, 246 p.

Blay-Palmer A., Conaré D., Meter K., Di Battista A., Johnston C. (ed.), 2019. *Sustainable food system assessment: lessons from global practice*, London, Routledge, 282 p.

Bourdieu P., 2000. *Pascalian meditations*, Cambridge, Polity Press, 264 p. Translation of 'Méditations pascaliennes' (1997).

Bourdieu P., 2004. *Science of science and reflexivity*, Chicago, University of Chicago Press, 168 p. Translation of 'Science de la science et réflexivité' (2001).

Brundland G.H., 1987. *Our common future: Report of the World Commission on Environment and Development*, Geneva, UN.

Burlingame B., 2004. Holistic and reductionist nutrition. *Journal of Food Composition and Analysis*, 17: 585–586. https://doi.org/10.1016/j.jfca.2004.06.002

Calandre N., 2002. *Alimentation, nutrition et sciences sociales: concepts, méthodes pour l'analyse des représentations et pratiques nutritionnelles des consommateurs*, Mémoire de DEA « Économie et gestion du développement agricole, agroalimentaire et rural », Montpellier, Ensam.

Cambien A., 2007. *Une introduction à l'approche systémique: appréhender la complexité*, Lyon, Centre d'études sur les réseaux, les transports, l'urbanisme et les constructions publiques, 83 p.

Campbell T.C., Campbell T., 2006. *The China study: the most comprehensive study of nutrition ever conducted and the startling implications for diet, weight loss and long-term health*, Dallas, BenBella Books, 417 p.

Campbell T.C., Jacobson H., 2013. *Whole: rethinking the science of nutrition*, Dallas, BenBella Books, 328 p.

Cannon G., Leitzmann C., 2005. The new nutrition science project. *Public Health Nutrition*, 8: 673–695. https://doi.org/10.1079/PHN2005819

Chappell M.J., Lavalle L., 2011. Food security and biodiversity: can we have both? An agroecological analysis. *Agriculture and Human Values*, 28: 3–26. https://doi.org/10.1007/s10460-009-9251-4

Chevassus-au-Louis B., Génard M., Glaszmann J.-C., Habib R., Houllier F., Lancelot R. et al., 2008. L'intégration, art ou science ?, in Kammili T., Brossier J., Hubert B., Tourrand J.-F. (ed.), *Colloque international Inra-Cirad partenariat, innovation, agriculture*, Paris, IFRAI, 130–154.

Collins N.R., 1963. The development of a coordinated food production and distribution system in Western Europe. *Journal of Farm Economics*, 45(2): 263–272. https://doi.org/10.2307/1235973

Coveney J., 1999. *Food, morals and meaning: the pleasure and anxiety of eating*, London, Routledge, 224 p.

Cruz J.-F., Beavogui F., Drame D., Diallo T. A., 2016. *Fonio, an African cereal*, Montpellier, Cirad, 154 p. Translation of 'Le fonio, une céréale africaine' (2011).

De Garine I., 1972. The socio-cultural aspects of nutrition. *Ecology of Food and Nutrition*, 1(2): 143–163. https://doi.org/10.1080/03670244.1972.9990282

De Garine I., 1979. Culture et nutrition. *Communications*, 31(1): 70–92. https://doi.org/10.3406/comm.1979.1470

De Garine I., 1988. Anthropologie de l'alimentation et pluridisciplinarité. *Écologie humaine*, 6(2): 21–40.

Degras L., 1993. *The yam: a tropical root crop*, London/Basingstoke, Macmillan, 408 p. Translation of 'L'igname: plante à tubercule tropicale' (1986).

Depecker T., Lhuissier A., Maurice A. (ed.), 2013. *La juste mesure: une sociologie historique des normes alimentaires*, Rennes, PUR, 398 p.

Desjeux D., 1996. Tiens bon le concept, j'enlève l'échelle. . . . d'observation ! *Utinam*, 20: 15–44.

Dixon J., 2009. From the imperial to the empty calorie: how nutrition relations underpin food regime transitions. *Agriculture and Human Values*, 26(4): 321–333. https://doi.org/10.1007/s10460-009-9217-6

Dixon J.M., Donati K.J., Pike L.L., Hattersley L., 2009. Functional foods and urban agriculture: two responses to climate change-related food insecurity. *New South Wales Public Health Bulletin*, 20(2): 14–18. https://doi.org/10.1071/NB08044

Doherty B., Ensor J., Heron T., Prado P., 2019. Food systems resilience: towards an interdisciplinary research agenda. *Emerald Open Research*, 1(4). https://doi.org/10.12688/emeraldopenres.12850.1

Dumont R., Marti A., 1997. *Panorama sur l'igname*, Montpellier, Cirad, 188 p.

Dury S., Alpha A., Bichard A., 2014. *What risks do agricultural interventions entail for nutrition?*, Working paper MOISA/ACF, Montpellier, Cirad/ACF.

Eakin H., Connors J.P., Wharton C., Bertmann F., Xiong A., Stoltzfus J., 2017. Identifying attributes of food system sustainability: emerging themes and consensus. *Agriculture and Human Values*, 34(3): 757–773. https://doi.org/10.1007/s10460-016-9754-8

Ericksen P.J., 2008. Conceptualizing food systems for global environmental change research. *Global Environmental Change*, 18(1): 234–245. https://doi.org/10.1016/j .gloenvcha.2007.09.002

FAO, 1996. *Rome Declaration on World Food Security and World Food Summit Plan of Action: World Food Summit*, 13–17 November 1996, Rome, FAO, 43 p.

FAO, 2018. *Sustainable food systems. Concept and framework*, Rome, FAO, 8 p.

Fardet A., 2017. L'effet matrice des aliments, un nouveau concept. *Pratiques en nutrition*, 13: 37–40.

Fardet A., Rock E., 2014. Towards a new philosophy of preventive nutrition: from a reductionist to holistic paradigm to improve nutritional recommendations. *Advances in Nutrition*, 5(4): 430–446. https://doi.org/10.3945/an.114.006122

Fardet A., Souchon I., Dupont D. (ed.), 2013. *Structure des aliments et effets nutritionnels*, Versailles, Quæ, 474 p.

Fattore G., Agostoni C., 2016. Health, wellbeing and social sciences. *Critical Reviews in Food Science and Nutrition*, 56(12): 1960–1963. https://doi.org/10.1080/10408398 .2015.1018041

Fischler C., 1979. Présentation du numéro « La nourriture, pour une anthropologie bioculturelle de l'alimentation ». *Communications*, 31: 1–3.

Fischler C., 1990. *L'homnivore*, Paris, Odile Jacob, 448 p.

Fischler C., 2011. The nutritional cacophony may be detrimental to your health. *Progress in Nutrition*, 13: 217–221.

Foran T., Butler J.R.A., Williams L.J., Wanjura W.J., Hall A., Carter L., Carberry P.S., 2014. Taking complexity in food systems seriously: an interdisciplinary analysis. *World Development*, 61: 85–101. https://doi.org/10.1016/j.worlddev.2014.03.023

Francis C., Lieblein G., Gliessman S., 2003. Agroecology: the ecology of food systems. *Journal of Sustainable Agriculture*, 22(3). https://doi.org/10.1300/J064v22n03_10

Frison E., Smith I., Johns T., Cherfas J., Eyzaguirre P., 2006. Agricultural biodiversity, nutrition, and health: making a difference to hunger and nutrition in the developing world. *Food and Nutrition Bulletin*, 271: 67–79. https://doi.org/10.1177/156482650 602700208

Froment A., Garine I. de, Binam Bikoï C., Loung J.F. (ed.), 1996. *Bien manger et bien vivre: anthropologie alimentaire et développement en Afrique intertropicale: du biologique au social*, Paris, L'Harmattan, 520 p.

Germov J., Williams L. (ed.), 2016. *A sociology of food & nutrition: the social appetite* (4th edition), Melbourne, Oxford University Press, 389 p.

Glass T.A., McAtee M.J., 2006. Behavioral science at the crossroads in public health: extending horizons, envisioning the future. *Social Science & Medicine (1982)*, 62(7): 1650–1671. https://doi.org/10.1016/j.socscimed.2005.08.044

Gliessman S., 2016. Transforming food systems with agroecology. *Agroecology and Sustainable Food Systems*, 40(3): 187–189. https://doi.org/10.1080/21683565.2015 .1130765

Gosselin G., 1987. Le retour du sujet et l'éthique de la complexité. *L'Homme et la société*, 84(2): 29–39. https://doi.org/10.3406/homso.1987.2282

Gussow J.D., 1978. *The feeding web. Issues in nutritional ecology*, Palo Alto, Bull Publishing, 496 p.

Halbwachs M., 1912. *La classe ouvrière et les niveaux de vie*, Paris, Félix Alcan, 495 p.

Hall R.H., 1974. *Food for nought: the decline in nutrition*, Hagerstown, Harper & Row.

Hawkes C., Ruel M., 2007. The links between agriculture and health: an intersectoral opportunity to improve the health and livelihoods of the poor. *Bulletin of the World Health Organization*, 84: 984–990. https://doi.org/10.1590/S0042-96862006001200015

Hébert J.-P., Griffon D., 2010. *Toutes les bières moussent-elles ? 80 clés pour comprendre les bières*, Versailles, Quæ, 226 p.

Hébert J.-P., Griffon D., 2012. *Des bières et des hommes*, Versailles, Quæ, 702 p.

Herpin N., 1988. Le repas comme institution. Compte rendu d'une enquête exploratoire. *Revue française de sociologie*, 29(3): 503–521. https://doi.org/10.2307/3321627

Hodbod J., Eakin H., 2015. Adapting a social-ecological resilience framework for food systems. *Journal of Environmental Studies and Sciences*, 5: 474–484. https://doi.org/10.1007/s13412-015-0280-6

Horton P., Banwart S.A., Brockington D., Brown G.W., Bruce R., Cameron D. et al., 2017. An agenda for integrated system-wide interdisciplinary agri-food research. *Food Security*, 9(2): 195–210. https://doi.org/10.1007/s12571-017-0648-4

Hubert B., Aubertin C., Billaud J.-P., 2015. Connaître ? Agir ? Interagir ? *Natures Sciences Sociétés*, 23(2): 95–96. https://doi.org/10.1051/nss/2015032

Hubert B., Couvet D. (ed.), 2021. *La transition agroécologique. Tome 1*, Paris, Presses de l'École des Mines, 260 p.

IPES-Food, 2015. *The new science of sustainable food systems. Overcoming barriers to food systems reform*, Brussels, IPES-Food, 21 p.

Jacobs D.R., Gross M.D., Tapsell L.C., 2009. Food synergy: an operational concept for understanding nutrition. *American Journal of Clinical Nutrition*, 89(5): 1543S–1548S. https://doi.org/10.3945/ajcn.2009.26736B

Jacobs D.R., Steffen L., 2003. Nutrients, foods, and dietary patterns as exposures in research: a framework for food synergy. *American Journal of Clinical Nutrition*, 78(3 suppl.): 508S–513S. https://doi.org/10.1093/ajcn/78.3.508S

Jacquemard J.-C., 1995. *Le palmier à huile*, Paris, Maisonneuve et Larose, 210 p.

Kneen B., 1993. *From land to mouth: understanding the food system*, Toronto, NC Press, 173 p.

Lambert J.-L., 1986. *L'évolution des modèles de consommation alimentaire en France*, thèse de doctorat, spécialité Sciences économiques, Université de Nantes, Nantes, 245 p.

Lamine C., Magda D., Amiot M.-J., 2019. Crossing sociological, ecological and nutritional perspectives on agrifood systems transitions: towards a transdisciplinary territorial approach. *Sustainability*, 11(5): 28. https://doi.org/10.3390/su11051284

Lévi-Strauss C., 1969. *The raw and the cooked. Introduction to a science of mythology*. (Vol. I), New York, Harper & Row; Paris, Plon, 387 p. Translation of 'Mythologiques. Le cru et le cuit' (1964).

Malassis L., 1994. *Nourrir les hommes: un exposé pour comprendre, un essai pour réfléchir*, Paris, Flammarion, 126 p.

Marion B.W., 1986. *The organization and performance of the US food system*, Lanham, Lexington Books, 584 p.

Marlow H., Hayes W., Soret S., Carter R., Schwab E., Sabaté J., 2009. Diet and the environment: does what you eat matter? *American Journal of Clinical Nutrition*, 89: 1699S–1703S. https://doi.org/10.3945/ajcn.2009.26736Z

Marsden T., Morley A. (ed.), 2014. *Sustainable food systems: building a new paradigm*, New York, Routledge, 230 p.

Mason P., Lang T., 2017. *Sustainable diets. How ecological nutrition can transform consumption and the food system*, Oxon, Routledge, 369 p.

Meyer-Abich K.M., 2005. Human health in nature. Towards a holistic philosophy of nutrition. *Public Health Nutrition.* 8(6a): 738–742. https://doi.org/10.1079/PHN2005788

Montanari M., 1993. *La fame e l'abbondanza. Storia dell'alimentazione in Europa*, Bari, Laterza, 262 p.

Morin E., 1982. *Science avec conscience*, Paris, Fayard, 328 p.

Morin E., 1990. *Introduction à la pensée complexe*, Paris, ESF éditeur, 160 p.

Morin E., 2008. *La méthode: coffret en 2 volumes*, Paris, Seuil, 2512 p.

Mormont M., 2015. L'environnement entre science et sens commun. *Natures Sciences Sociétés*, 23(2): 150–153. https://doi.org/10.1051/nss/2015031

Moscatelli S., El Bilali H., Gamboni M., Capone R., 2016. Towards sustainable food systems: a holistic, interdisciplinary and systemic approach. *International Journal AgroFor*, 1: 103–112. https://doi.org/10.7251/AGRENG1601103M

Moulin L., 1975. *L'Europe à table. Introduction à une psychosociologie des pratiques alimentaires*, Paris/Brussels, Elsevier Sequoia, 204 p.

Perignon M., Dubois C., Gazan R., Maillot M., Muller L., Ruffieux B. et al., 2017. Co-construction and evaluation of a prevention program for improving the nutritional quality of food purchases at no additional cost in a socioeconomically disadvantaged population. *Current Developments in Nutrition*, 1(10). https://doi.org/10.3945/cdn.117.001107

Perignon M., Masset G., Ferrari G., Barré T., Vieux F., Maillot M., Darmon N., 2016. How low can dietary greenhouse gas emissions be reduced without impairing nutritional adequacy, affordability and acceptability of the diet? A modelling study to guide sustainable food choices. *Public Health Nutrition*, 19(14): 2662–2674. https://doi.org/10.1017/S1368980016000653

Perret S., 2005. *Quelle agronomie pour le développement durable ? Histoires, concepts, pratiques et perspectives*, dossier d'habilitation à diriger des recherches, spécialité: Sciences agronomiques, Cirad-Tera, Montpellier.

Pollan M., 2008. *In defense of food: an eater's manifesto*, London, Penguin Books, 256 p.

Poulain J.-P., 2009. *Sociologie de l'obésité*, Paris, PUF, 385 p.

Poulain J.-P., 2017. *The sociology of food: eating and the place of food in society*, London/New York, Bloomsbury Academic, 288 p. Translation of 'Sociologies de l'alimentation' (2002).

Rémésy C., 2020. *La nutriécologie. Le seul futur alimentaire possible*, Vergèze, Thierry Souccar, 291 p.

Santos B. de S., 2016. *Epistemologies of the South: justice against epistemicide*, New York, Routledge, 284 p.

Schipanski M.E., MacDonald G.K., Rosenzweig S., Chappell M.J., Bennett E.M., Bezner Kerr R. et al., 2016. Realizing resilient food systems. *BioScience*, 66(7): 600–610. https://doi.org/10.1093/biosci/biw052

Schneider K., Hoffmann I., 2011. Nutrition ecology. A concept for systemic nutrition research and integrative problem solving. *Ecology of food and nutrition*, 50: 1–17. https://doi.org/10.1080/03670244.2010.524101

Schoon M., van der Leeuw S., 2015. The shift toward social-ecological systems perspectives: insights into the human-nature relationship. *Natures Sciences Sociétés*, 23(2): 166–174. https://doi.org/10.1051/nss/2015034

Scrinis G., 2008. On the ideology of Nutritionism. *Gastronomica*, 8(1): 39–48. https://doi.org/10.1525/gfc.2008.8.1.39

Scrinis G., 2013. *Nutritionism: the science and politics of dietary advice*, New York, Columbia University Press, 368 p.

Serra-Mallol C., 2010. *Nourritures, abondance et identité: une socio-anthropologie de l'alimentation à Tahiti*, Papeete, Au vent des îles, 552 p.

Shapin S., 2014. 'You are what you eat': historical changes in ideas about food and identity. *Historical Research*, 87(237): 377–392. https://doi.org/10.1111/1468-2281.12059

Smuts J.C., 1926. *Holism and evolution*, New York, Macmillan, 375 p.

Sobal J., Kettel Khan L., Bisogni C., 1998. A conceptual model of the food and nutrition system. *Social Science & Medicine*, 47(7): 853–863. https://doi.org/10.1016/S0277-9536(98)00104-X

Tendall D.M., Joerin J., Kopainsky B., Edwards P., Shreck A., Le Q.B. et al., 2015. Food system resilience: defining the concept. *Global Food Security*, 6: 17–23. https://doi.org/10.1016/j.gfs.2015.08.001

Tibère L., 2013. Alimentation et vivre-ensemble: le cas de la créolisation. *Anthropologie et Sociétés*, 37(2): 27–43. https://doi.org/10.7202/1017904ar

Traverso-Yepez M., Hunter K., 2016. From 'healthy eating' to a holistic approach to current food environments. *SAGE Open*, 6(3). https://doi.org/10.1177/2158244016665891

Trémolières J., 1975. *Diététique et art de vivre*, Paris, Seghers, 323 p.

Wahlqvist M., Specht R., 1998. Food variety and biodiversity: econutrition. *Asia Pacific Journal of Clinical Nutrition*, 7(3–4): 314–319.

Wezel A., Soldat V., 2009. A quantitative and qualitative historical analysis of the scientific discipline of agroecology. *International Journal of Agricultural Sustainability*, 7(1): 3–18. https://doi.org/10.3763/ijas.2009.0400

Willett W., Rockström J., Loken B., Springmann M., Lang T., Vermeulen S. et al., 2019. Food in the anthropocene: the EAT-Lancet Commission on healthy diets from sustainable food systems. *Lancet*, 393(10170): 447–492. https://doi.org/10.1016/S0140-6736(18)31788-4

10

A commitment to food system transformation

Damien Conaré, Nicolas Bricas and Marie Walser

Food is an inherently political issue. We argue that this means inspired commitment is needed in order to keep faith in the possibilities of the food system transition and that this faith is key to overcoming resistance to change.

This chapter expands on the second meaning that can be attributed to food ecology as a commitment to achieving sustainable food systems. This commitment is driven by awareness of the failure of industrialized modes of food production, processing and distribution and the inadequacy of the associated modes of consumption to address environmental, social and health issues (Chapter 7). This is not a new movement; many different actors have been campaigning for years to partially or even totally transform our food systems. The focus has often been on agricultural production methods or product processing and commercialization. Only recently – as illustrated by the growing use of the term 'food system' – have more downstream segments of the food chain (distribution, consumption, waste management) and governance issues attracted more attention.

Food directly concerns all human beings and is pivotal to the everyday life of citizens, making it an inherently political issue. As Richard Wilk (2006) points out, 'food is both an effective symbol and a concrete entity capable of catalysing political and social movements'. More broadly, for Jeffrey Pratt and Peter Luetchford (2014), 'food has become a focal point for action (and reflection) on contemporary economic processes [. . .] and the most prominent area in which people try to realise an alternative economy'. This chapter considers commitment in the sense of Howard S. Becker (1960), that is, as 'an alignment of convictions and practices' (Rodet, 2018) and discusses the driving forces and principles underpinning the transformation of food systems within the framework of food ecology. We put forward several proposals to guide the actors striving for change, namely building commitment around an inspiring narrative, developing the capacity for action in complex environments and taking a stand in power struggles.

An inspiring narrative

At a time when many countries are experiencing a crisis of political representation, compounded by growing communitarianism and the generalization of cognitive bias as a result of so-called filter bubbles,[1] addressing sustainability issues requires renewing the dominant imaginaries. This includes resituating food – which links humans to themselves, to other humans and to the biosphere – within an inspiring narrative. Why should this narrative, which underpins the commitment discussed here, be inspiring? Contemporary philosophers such as Baptiste Morizot (2022) point out that, from a vantage point like that propounded by Spinoza, commitment subsists over time thanks to the confluence of two seemingly antagonistic feelings – namely injustice and enthusiasm.

Injustice sparks indignation and leads to problems being denounced, thereby imparting an initial, combative dimension to commitment. With regard to food, this indignation, shared by a range of actors, stems from the realization that food systems are primarily geared towards the reproduction of economic stakeholders' capital at the expense of individual health, social justice and environmental conservation (Chapter 7). Exposing the extent of food insecurity (Chapter 15), animal suffering and pesticide impacts on living organisms, for instance, thus galvanizes action against these injustices. It is also often indignation that spurs the adoption of responsible consumption practices (Dubuisson-Quellier, 2009) (Chapter 18). Through these practices, eaters voice their ethical criticism of food production methods (e.g. through vegetarianism or veganism), address human and environmental health concerns (e.g. by supporting organic farming or boycotting certain products) or take action in response to calls for economic justice (e.g. by supporting fair trade; Fischler, 2015; Fouilleux and Michel, 2020).

The growing number of collective grievances surrounding food expressed throughout the twentieth century reflects the emergence of a form of food activism (Siniscalchi, 2014). These different forms of commitment – including activist movements (e.g. Via Campesina or Slow Food), local civil society (e.g. efforts to reform school catering) and networks of actors pursuing economic

---

[1] The information we access online has already been filtered according to our interests identified during earlier browsing sessions, thus fostering forms of intellectual and cultural isolation.

initiatives (e.g. short supply chains or cooperative supermarkets) – challenge the conventional food system, which is deemed unfair and destructive (Nestle, 2009; Siniscalchi, 2015). They also offer alternatives that advocate a different model.

Faced with the sheer magnitude of the task at hand, however, commitment based solely on this sense of injustice can lead to frustration, deepening resentment and rigid radicalization. Hence, commitment must also be fuelled by genuine enthusiasm, or even 'a politicized sense of wonder' (Truong and Morizot, 2020), to enable individual and collective capacity for action to grow exponentially. Commitment itself is inspiring in that it enables us to experiment with new ways of relating to ourselves, others and the world. It is thus not just about taking a stand against a dysfunctional food system: it also involves committing ourselves to developing alternatives that could renew our social and environmental interactions.

Weaving ties with the community of the living

The raison d'être and purpose of the commitment that underpins food ecology are tightly linked: it is to interlace the threads of life, to weave together individuals, societies and the biosphere. This approach does not overlook the conflicts that permeate both socioecological and food systems; in line with the principles of permaculture, it is sometimes necessary to form alliances with certain entities in order to counter others (pests, pathogens etc.) (Centemeri, 2019). Yet we also have to reconsider what we call pests and acknowledge their role as indicators and even regulators. Ecology is therefore a game-changing catalyst that fosters a diverse range of arrangements of living organisms in viable biospheres specific to their respective contexts, rather than a single model geared towards maximizing economic wealth within food systems.

The narrative conveyed by food ecology thus calls for a new social imaginary in which food is a means of redefining the links between the living. It calls for considering food as a means of 'touching down' – that is, of building roots not in the territories where we live but in those on which we depend for our subsistence (Latour, 2018) in order to forge relationships of interdependence, protection and care (between ourselves and other human and non-human organisms). Similarly, Laura Centemeri (2019) approaches permaculture as the 'art of reinhabiting' the shared home (*oikos*). Echoing a vision of food as a common good, this perspective thus posits collective well-being as the raison d'être of food systems. If shaped by a so-called socio-diversity of alternatives, these systems should guarantee access to food that is adequate for and sought by all while promoting the multidimensional nature of food (Vivero Pol et al., 2020). The structure of food systems must therefore now be rethought based on new principles guided by ecology: diversity (in the field, on the plate but also in the forms of organization of food systems), resilience (e.g. to climate change), combinations and symbioses (e.g. with microorganisms, which are present all the way from the soil to the stomach), the maintenance of reserves (in contrast with just-in-time 'efficiency'), cycle-based functioning (seasons, elements), sensory interactions (associated with the proximity between actors, with livestock) and related ecological dynamics.

Food ecology is rooted in the emergence of new relationships in the world, as advocated by certain scientists and philosophers. First, the scientific 'socio-ecological co-viability' paradigm (Barrière et al., 2019) is built on the observation that social and ecological systems are intertwined. Its proposed responses to major global environmental challenges are thus informed by a new 'social contract' between humans and the rest of the biosphere to which they belong and on which they depend. This approach encourages us to move beyond the division between instrumental rationality – according to which the biosphere serves humans – and non-instrumental rationality – which posits that the biosphere exists for reasons other than the simple benefits that human societies reap from it (Mace, 2014). It calls for thinking of individuals, societies and the biosphere as forming part of a single interdependent socioecological unit. Second, from a philosophical perspective, every human being is encouraged to 'get reacquainted' by rethinking their relationship with living beings. This involves becoming aware of oneself as a living being and as belonging to a wider community of living beings but also acknowledging the intrinsic value of other ways of living and constructing territory (Morizot, 2016, 2022; Coccia, 2018; Despret, 2021; Legros and Damasio, 2021). This new relationship with the living stems from a renewed commitment, no longer to defending nature as external to us but to our embodying a 'nature that can defend itself' in interaction with the rest of the living world.

Principles to guide commitment

When fuelled by an inspiring narrative, commitment leads to taking tangible action to transform food systems. Setting such change in motion is particularly complex for several reasons: it is contextual; it is unpredictable over the long term; it can take multiple forms; and it is restricted by the interdependence between the different components of the food system (within and outside this system – energy metabolism, public policies in different areas, international trade rules etc.).

First, the implementation of change is necessarily shaped by the specific features of the context at hand (spatial, cultural, political, economic, social, environmental etc.). There are no one-size-fits-all inherently sound solutions, the suitability of a solution depends on the context, and the interdependencies that underpin alliances among humans and between humans and non-humans are constantly evolving (Centemeri, 2019). Observation, consultation and action must therefore be articulated together from the outset and throughout the process of change. In this respect, participatory methods for identifying impact pathways offer a prime example of a way to take into account the influence of context on the effects of actions deemed transformative (Chapter 20).

Second, the outcomes of actions in complex systems, like food systems, are uncertain (Morin, 1990). These actions are subject to unpredictable events (climatic, political, economic, health related, linked to technological changes etc.), which raise uncertainty regarding their medium- and long-term impacts. Action must therefore be guided by a strategic and targeted approach rather than a rigid plan for a transition whose outcome cannot really be predicted. This allows for making tactical adjustments to initiatives in response to unexpected events and/or to capitalize on new opportunities that may arise.

Third, the quest to transform food systems involves charting a course between highly transformative actions and modest successes. Actors involved in change processes could therefore draw inspiration from one of the permaculture principles put forward by Bill Mollison (1988): 'the extent of the change (to be made) should be inversely proportional to the effect it will have on the system' (Mollison, 1988). This means prioritizing actions that produce transformative effects that are greater than the effort (or investment) required for their implementation. However, to fuel commitment, quick wins achieved through actions that mobilize actors more easily should not be overlooked. Some changes, though not very transformative, may still serve to highlight what is possible and, because they are meaningful, may have substantial galvanizing potential. 'Bricolages' (makeshift arrangements) and tactics (de Certeau, 1984), or even small daily steps, can trigger dynamics of change, provided their proponents view them as stages in a transformative process and not as an actual end goal.

Finally, the transformation of industrialized food systems may also be hampered by the fact that their different sociotechnical dimensions are tightly intermeshed. This includes the food system actors, institutions and policymakers whose interests are closely interlinked – agricultural markets and organizations, rural and urban planning, health safety, scientific research, industrial development and other sectors (IPES-Food, 2015; De Schutter, 2017). It is difficult to transform one component of the system independently of the others, and, likewise, it is futile for a single actor to seek to transform all of these components simultaneously. The transformation of food systems therefore cannot be achieved simply through the cumulative action of isolated stakeholders. Instead, it requires a coordinated combination of diverse forms of commitment at different levels (Part 5). All food system actors – activist movements, civil society, local authorities, the conventional private sector and related social actors – have complementary roles to play. The challenge for these actors is therefore twofold: to make change happen at their own level, 'where they are', and to articulate their strengths with those of others by getting to know their allies so as to flip the balance of power that is significantly hampering efforts to overcome deadlocks within food systems (IPES-Food, 2015).

Stepping into the arena of power struggles

The magnitude of the social and environmental crisis we face today is prompting a change in the very nature of commitment. It is no longer just a matter of informing policymakers or experimenting with alternatives but also of engaging in power struggles with actors who are highly resistant to change. Certainly, the first step in ensuring that environmental and social issues are taken into account in public policies and corporate strategies is to raise awareness. One aspect of this task is indeed to inform decision-makers about the deteriorating situation, to convince them of the seriousness of the risks and to show that alternatives are possible. Scientists and civil society movements have been doing this for several decades, sounding the alarm about the potential impacts of climate change, genetically modified organisms (GMOs), livestock farming conditions and so on.

Informed opposition to the much-needed changes has, however, become apparent since the 1980s (Rowell, 1996). In recent years, Donald Trump in the United States and Jair Bolsonaro in Brazil – to name but two of the most glaring examples – supported by part of the electorate and economic powerhouses in their countries, withdrew from international agreements designed to bring about a food system transformation. They implemented policies that went against the recommendations of scientists and environmental movements. In so doing, they revealed that the challenge is no longer simply to inform, raise awareness and convince but also to engage in power struggles and form political alliances to counter efforts to maintain the status quo. Bruno Latour has proposed what he calls 'compositionism': a political, scientific and aesthetic programme to spark a diplomatic effort to distribute, redistribute and reset 'agencies'. His starting point is that a common world does not exist; everywhere there are multiple ways of doing things, thinking and believing. Within the context of ensuring the sustainability of food systems, this points to the need to reset agencies so as to empower those defending social and ecological co-viability.

Engaging in these power struggles also requires understanding the functioning of the 'systems of actors' involved, investigating the power plays at stake from a political economy perspective. Food systems at all levels are marked by power disparities between actors (often linked to economic inequalities) that influence the governance of these systems and the ways in which food issues are framed. Some powerful actors are able to steer debates, as was the case, for instance, in France within the framework of the États généraux de l'alimentation (French national food conference) or at European level as part of the series of negotiations on the Common Agricultural Policy (Corporate Europe Observatory, 2020). These actors may also seek to disseminate a narrow interpretation of certain food issues, often with a view to legitimizing a vested financial or political interest. This is to some extent the case with regard to food safety (Chapter 11), food fortification practices (Chapter 12) and plant protein consumption (Chapter 13).

Conclusion

Food ecology calls for a commitment to foster a new relationship with the world. Food is an inherently political issue, and the way we organize it defines the world in which we live and the one we want. This commitment, underpinned by individual and collective enthusiasm, should be tailored to specific contexts. It must also be understood as being multifaceted, shaped by external forces and unpredictable over the long term. Taking action is highly complex and also involves engaging in power struggles with actors resisting the changes needed. Tangible examples of different forms of commitment are discussed in Part 5, which analyses the modalities of engagement available to citizens (Chapters 18 and 19), businesses (Chapter 20), academia (Chapter 21) and public authorities (Chapter 22).

The authors would like to thank Mathilde Coudray, Vincent Devictor, Danièle Magda and Jacques Tassin for proofreading this chapter and for their proposed improvements.

References

Barrière O., Behnassi M., David G., Douzal V., Fargette M., Libourel T. et al. (ed.), 2019. *Coviability of social and ecological systems: reconnecting mankind to the biosphere in an era of global change*. Vol. 1: The foundations of a new paradigm, New York, Springer International Publishing, 728 p.

Becker H.S., 1960. Notes on the concept of commitment. *American Journal of Sociology*, 66: 32–40. https://doi.org/10.4000/traces.257

Centemeri L., 2019. *La permaculture ou l'art de réhabiter*, Versailles, Quæ, 152 p.

Certeau M. de, 1984. *The practice of everyday life*. Berkeley, University of California Press, 256 p. Translation of 'L'invention du quotidien. 1. Arts de faire' (1974).

Coccia E., 2018. *The life of plants: a metaphysics of mixture*, Cambridge, Polity Press, 176 p. Translation of 'La vie des plantes. Une métaphysique du mélange' (2017).

Corporate Europe Observatory, 2020. *CAP vs Farm to Fork: will we pay billions to destroy, or to support biodiversity, climate, and farmers?*, Brussels, Corporate Europe Observatory, 25 p.

De Schutter O., 2017. The political economy of food systems reform. *European Review of Agricultural Economics*, 44: 705–731. https://doi.org/10.1093/erae/jbx009

Despret V., 2021. *Living as a bird*, Cambridge, Polity Press, 180 p. Translation of 'Habiter en oiseau' (2019).

Dubuisson-Quellier S., 2009. *La consommation engagée*, Paris, Presses de Sciences Po, 144 p.

Fischler C. (ed.), 2015. *Selective eating: the rise, the meaning and sense of 'personal dietary requirements'*, Paris, Odile Jacob, 272 p. Translation of 'Les alimentations particulières. Mangerons-nous encore ensemble demain ?' (2013).

Fouilleux E., Michel L. (ed.), 2020. *Quand l'alimentation se fait politique(s)*, Rennes, PUR, 349 p.

IPES-Food, 2015. *The new science of sustainable food systems. Overcoming barriers to food systems reform*, Brussels, IPES-Food, 21 p.

Latour B., 2018. *Down to Earth: politics in the new climatic regime*, Cambridge, Polity Press, 140 p. Translation of 'Où atterrir ? Comment s'orienter en politique' (2017).

Legros C., Damasio A., 2021. Alain Damasio, écrivain: « On ne retrouvera l'envie de vivre qu'en renouant les liens au vivant ». *Le Monde.fr*, 4 juin 2021.

Mace G., 2014. Ecology. Whose conservation? *Science*, 345: 1558–1560. https://doi.org/10.1126/science.1254704

Mollison B., 1988. *Permaculture: a designer's manual*, Tyalgum, Tagari Publication, 576 p.

Morin E., 1990. *Introduction à la pensée complexe*, Paris, ESF éditeur, 160 p.

Morizot B., 2016. *Les diplomates. Cohabiter avec les loups sur une autre carte du vivant*, Marseille, Wildproject Editions, 314 p.

Morizot B., 2022. *Ways of being alive*, Cambridge, Polity Press, 290 p. Translation of 'Manières d'être vivant. Enquêtes sur la vie à travers nous' (2020).

Nestle M., 2009. Reading the food social movement. *World Literature Today*, 83(1): 37–39.

Pratt J., Luetchford P., 2014. *Food for change: the politics and values of social movements*, London, Pluto Press/Macmillan, 240 p.

Rodet D., 2018. Engagements militants, professionnalisés ou distanciés: les visages multiples de l'alimentation engagée. *Anthropology of Food.* http://journals.openedition.org/aof /8261 [online].

Rowell A., 1996. *Green backlash: global subversion of the environment movement,* London, Routledge, 504 p.

Siniscalchi V., 2014. La politique dans l'assiette. Restaurants et restaurateurs dans le mouvement Slow Food en Italie. *Ethnologie française*, 44(1): 73–83. https://doi.org /10.3917/ethn.141.0073

Siniscalchi V., 2015. « Food activism » en Europe: changer de pratiques, changer de paradigmes. *Anthropology of Food*, S11. https://doi.org/10.4000/aof.7920

Truong N., Morizot B., 2020. Baptiste Morizot: « Il faut politiser l'émerveillement ». *Le Monde.fr*, 4 août 2020.

Vivero Pol J., Ferrando T., De Schutter O., Mattei U. (éd.), 2020. *Routledge handbook of food as a commons*, London, Routledge, 424 p.

Wilk R., 2006. From wild weeds to artisanal cheese: an introduction to slow and fast food, in Wilk R. (ed.), *Fast food/slow food: the cultural economy of the global food system*, Lanham, AltaMira Press, 13–28.

Part Four

Discussing the watchwords of sustainable food systems

Numerous imperatives have been put forward for the implementation of sustainable food systems: increasing agricultural production to feed the world by 2050 (Chapter 11), fortifying foods to reduce micronutrient malnutrition (Chapter 12), consuming less animal protein (Chapter 13), reducing food waste (Chapter 14), providing food aid to the poorest (Chapter 15), prioritizing homemade food (Chapter 16), eating local food (Chapter 17), making consumers the main actors in the transformation of food systems (Chapter 18) and so on.

These proposals for changing habits or paradigms are well founded and necessary, but they are not 'inherently' solutions that are fundamentally right and should be universally applied. While they can undeniably serve as a lever for the transformation of food systems, these proposals are partly grounded in preconceived ideas or present certain limitations that are often left unaddressed in public debates. It is important to shed light on these preconceived ideas and limitations to avoid the impasse of a sustainable food system that could only partially meet the challenges it faces.

This fourth part discusses some of the watchwords of sustainable food systems. It revisits them through the prism of an ecology of food that recognizes the multidimensionality of food and reveals the set of actors at work behind each of these watchwords. It thus calls for a holistic and political approach to these proposals.

11

Should food production be doubled to feed the world?

Nicolas Bricas and Éric Malézieux

The strategies of the different actors involved in international debates have led to a shift in the concept of food security. In the wake of the 2008 food price crisis, the renewed drive to take a technological quantum leap forward to double food production by 2050 has hindered reflection and discussions on this concept.

The term 'food security' was coined in 1943 at the *Hot Springs Conference* in Virginia, which two years later led to the creation of the Food and Agriculture Organization of the United Nations (FAO). But the term did not truly become widespread until the World Food Conference in Rome in 1974 organized by the UN Economic and Social Council. The definition endorsed by consensus at this summit essentially sought to strike a balance between supply and demand. For any country, food security consists of the 'availability at all times of adequate, nourishing, diverse, balanced and moderate world food supplies of basic foodstuffs to sustain a steady expansion of food consumption and to offset fluctuations in production and prices'.

Food insecurity is primarily an issue of access

This definition, which places emphasis on the availability of food, should be resituated within the political and economic context of its time. Until the late 1970s, food supplies were insufficient to meet the global population's energy needs. These supplies were below the threshold of 2,500 kilocalories per person per day (kcal/capita/d), considered the minimum average to ensure food security for all. In 1974, food prices soared on international markets as a result of the oil crisis and several extreme climate events (droughts, floods) that affected agricultural production in several regions around the world. The population growth rate continued to climb and the stabilization of the global population still seemed like a distant prospect. Malthusian fears of an exponential increase in the world population – and therefore in the food demand despite agricultural production still growing linearly – were thus highly prevalent in debates on the subject.

To balance the equation, it was therefore necessary either to increase the food supply by boosting agricultural production while reducing post-harvest losses or to curb the rise in demand by putting strict limits on births – or both. Markets had to be regulated to mitigate the impacts of fluctuations, particularly by building up security reserves. At an institutional level, after the FAO and the World Food Programme (WFP), Rome became home to a third institution – the International Fund for Agricultural Development (IFAD). This body, which was founded in 1974, implements projects geared towards increasing food production in developing countries.

The 1980s heralded a major shift in the understanding of food security. In 1982, Amartya Sen – future Nobel Prize winner in economics – published *Poverty and Famines: An Essay on Entitlement and Deprivation*. Based on an analysis of famines in Bengal (India), Ethiopia, the Sahel and Bangladesh, he demonstrated that food insecurity is less a matter of food supply than of access. People suffer from hunger because they do not have access to sufficient food production resources (land, inputs) or to food purchasing power. Amartya Sen thus identified poverty as the cause of food insecurity. This explained why some countries that were self-sufficient or even benefited from a cereal surplus, such as Brazil and India, had not yet solved the hunger problem within their own borders. In addition to striving to produce enough, the challenge was thus to ensure that everyone had access to food production and/or consumption resources. This perspective shifted the focus from a purely agricultural question to one of land access, purchasing power and, therefore, poverty and inequality.

As a result, a new definition of food security emerged in 1986 in a report published by the World Bank – the remit of which is specifically to combat poverty (World Bank, 1986). This definition was reiterated and extended at the World Food Summit, which reconvened in Rome in 1996. Food security was defined as being met 'when all people, at all times, have physical and economic access to sufficient safe and nutritious food that meets their dietary needs and food preferences for an active and healthy life'. This definition clearly highlights the issue of access and, of course, still refers to food supply and its regularity. It also introduces the idea of the health and nutritional quality of food and its cultural acceptance. The World Bank definition thus introduced what would come to be known as the four pillars of food security, namely availability, access, utilization and stability.

An intersectoral issue

This definition again reflects the novel context of its time. By the early 1980s, the average global food supply calculated by the FAO had surpassed the 2,500 kcal/capita/day threshold. There were certainly still many countries where this threshold had not been reached, and undernourishment continued to prevail in parts of countries with food surpluses, as was the case again in Brazil and India. Moreover, this new conception of food security proved compatible with the economic liberalization that had begun in the 1980s. Since the focus was now on being able to access food, why should countries try to produce it locally if others could do so more cheaply? All countries could then benefit from the lowest possible food prices.

This definition of food security was, however, criticized for overly focusing on technical issues (increasing access or availability, improving food quality etc.) and for overlooking the political dimension of food. It made no reference to the power dynamics between countries or to the influence and domination of certain countries and private actors. The definition also failed to address the risks of economic and therefore political dependence associated with increased reliance on the international market. In 1980, many African countries came together to draft the so-called Lagos Plan of Action, opposing pressure to liberalize their markets. This plan asserted these countries' desire for greater food self-sufficiency and the freedom to pursue their own development outside the liberal framework advocated by the World Bank and the International Monetary Fund (IMF). This position was later defended by the international farmers' movement Via Campesina at the 1996 World Food Summit. The movement promoted the concept of food sovereignty, which it defined as 'peoples', countries' or state unions' right to define their agricultural and food policy, without any dumping vis-à-vis third countries'.

These statements of refusal to bow to liberal dogma did not prevent the signing of international trade liberalization agreements (General Agreement on Tariffs and Trade, GATT) at the Marrakech Conference in 1994, which set the stage for the creation of the World Trade Organization. It is worth noting that global food markets had been relatively stable since the price surge of 1974. Over the years, many countries turned to these markets as a way of securing their food supplies to supplement their often inadequate domestic production. Many of them thus began to reduce their support for the agricultural sector, encouraged by donor organizations that were increasingly turning their attention to the social, educational and health sectors at the expense of agriculture.

Viewing the issue of food security primarily as a matter of access shifted the focus of action and explains the increased involvement of international institutions such as the World Bank, which were no longer devoted solely to agricultural production but instead to economic development and combating poverty more broadly. The FAO and other agricultural institutions could no longer claim food security as their exclusive remit. It was becoming a cross-sectoral issue involving agriculture, health, economic development, trade and so on. Nevertheless, in practice, food security policies at the national level generally remained the preserve of agriculture ministries. Food security was still largely measured and monitored in terms of food balances, particularly cereal balances – each year, countries would calculate whether food production and imports would be sufficient to feed their people.

At best, in situations where the management of food aid became a significant concern, food security commissions would be set up. However, these commissions seldom mustered sufficient political clout to be able to provide cross-sectoral coordination. Brazil is a noteworthy exception. Under the impetus of President Lula da Silva and inspired by the experience of the city of Belo Horizonte since 1993, the country developed an ambitious policy to eradicate hunger – the so-called Fome Zero project, based on intersectoral coordination (Chapter 22). Food security councils were set up at both regional and national level, bringing together public policy representatives from agriculture, labour, trade, education, health and other sectors as well as civil society representatives.

The 2008 global food price crisis and the return of a productionist vision

By the early 2000s, the overall context had changed considerably compared with the 1970s and 1980s. After a long thirty-year period of stable, low agricultural prices, far fewer countries suffered from chronic food deficits, such that food insecurity was primarily viewed as a poverty issue.

Food surpluses and stocks gradually dwindled as a result of market liberalization. In 2007–8, this decline in stocks was exacerbated by several extreme climate events, combined with occasional slowdowns in the continuous production-growth trend and a rapid rise in demand for cereals and oils to produce biofuel. The global balance of supply and demand was once again thrown off kilter, causing prices to rise. This increase was further fuelled by speculation on agricultural futures markets and export restrictions imposed by some countries. The crisis affected net food-importing countries and – despite policy efforts to curb price rises on domestic markets – hit the most vulnerable people hardest, particularly in urban areas. This food price crisis was one of the factors that sparked the so-called hunger riots in around thirty cities worldwide, raising fears of international instability.

This fear initially galvanized the international community and contributed to putting food security and nutrition back on the political agenda. In June 2008, the FAO convened a major conference in Rome, followed by a series of global and regional initiatives. The international community agreed on the common objective of doubling agricultural production, so as to be able to feed the nine billion people expected to be living on the planet by 2050. The conference's conclusions echoed this objective. This may not have solved the food crisis at hand, but it did firmly put agriculture back in the spotlight. The declaration called for 'immediate support for agricultural production and trade' and, over the longer term, investment in food production.

The 2007–8 crisis thus heralded the return of a productionist vision[1] of food security, narrowly focused on the balance between supply and demand (Bricas and Daviron, 2008). A growing number of forecasts assessed the likelihood of achieving this balance in the future based on a range of assumptions regarding population growth, increased purchasing power, urbanization and changes in agricultural land use and yields. That being said, new forecasts relating to climate change dramatically altered the outlook. Scenarios based on simulations by climatologists introduced another major constraint. Although the findings differed depending on the hypotheses chosen, many forecasts agreed. Those of the International Food Policy Research Institute (von Braun et al., 2005), the Institute of Social Ecology in Vienna (Erb et al., 2009), the French Agricultural Research Centre for International Development (CIRAD), the French National Research Institute for Agriculture, Food and Environment (INRAE) (Paillard et al., 2010), the FAO (2018a) and the World Resources Institute (Searchinger et al., 2018) highlighted the need to reform both the prevailing modes of production to take environmental issues into account

---

[1] Productionism can be understood as a 'philosophy that emerges when production is taken to be the sole norm for evaluating agriculture' (Thomson, 1995).

and consumption practices – particularly by reducing waste and overconsumption of animal products to alleviate pressure on demand (Even and Laisney, 2011).

The call to double (and now increase by 70 per cent) food production by 2050 has been echoed by many agricultural players. Seed companies selling GMOs and chemical manufacturers supplying fertilizers and pesticides view this as a golden opportunity, despite being widely criticized for their negative impacts on the environment (Fouilleux et al., 2021). Agricultural-exporting countries (France, Argentina, Ukraine, Australia, the United States etc.) are also vying to consolidate their positions on a competitive international market, affirming their role in feeding the world. Despite these stances, the situation in some parts of the world continues to be problematic. Faced with still rapid population growth and the risk of major waves of migration, the need to increase food production is clear. This is particularly evident in Africa, where more than a fifth of the population continues to suffer from hunger (FAO, 2018b).

Population growth projections for 2050 remain especially high for sub-Saharan Africa. The climate change outlook further compounds the already alarming prospects for the continent (Lobell et al., 2008). The regions most heavily impacted and where agricultural production will be hit the hardest are often home to the poorest and most vulnerable populations. This area of Africa, which is highly prone to food insecurity, is where the gap between actual and potential crop yields is widest (Licker et al., 2010). Increasing agricultural productivity remains essential to improve food security and enable vulnerable farming communities to escape poverty. It is important to note, however, that the solution to food insecurity cannot simply rely on a technological strategy of intensifying agricultural production in the conventional way using chemical inputs and improved varieties. In the light of past failures and proven environmental impacts, new ways of solving the food equation must be found. These include novel biodiversity-based agricultural practices as well as new forms of organization of the food system that are more favourable to farmers. Recent guidelines proposed by the High Level Panel of Experts on Food Security and Nutrition (HLPE, 2019) and stakeholder discussions on nature-based solutions at the United Nations Food Systems Summit held in 2021 may herald change in the way that future forms of support are devised.

The shroud of productionism

Most studies agree that global agricultural biomass requirements for food and energy should increase by an estimated 50–70 per cent between 2010 and 2050.

The actual increase in these needs will naturally depend on how dietary practices evolve, particularly in terms of the prevalence of meat consumption. However, some actors argue that stressing the need to increase production legitimizes the continued development of the industrial farming techniques which, over the last century, enabled food supplies to grow faster than the population in many parts of the world. It is not so much the absence of technical progress that is holding back production in countries which need to increase it. Instead, it is farmer poverty that hampers access to this 'technical progress' or the fact that these so-called technical advances are not suited to the socio-cultural or environmental characteristics of their farms. Less technology-oriented solutions also exist, based on farmers' knowledge and research, which have proven their effectiveness but are still inaccessible to the poorest farmers: hybrid varieties, crop associations, bunds, anti-insect nets and similar farming innovations (Affholder et al., 2012). One option sometimes proposed is to target the wealthiest farmers, who are in a position to adopt these techniques. Yet this option runs the risk of marginalizing disadvantaged farmers and accelerating millions of farmers' exit from agriculture. Their subsequent outmigration could lead to a swell in urban population numbers, as was the case with the Green Revolution in India (Dorin and Landy, 2009).

Changes to agriculture therefore need to be managed in conjunction with demographic changes and the job market, rather than pursuing a futile technological leap forward. In countries that have yet to complete their demographic transition, such as in sub-Saharan Africa, agriculture will continue to be the main potential source of employment in the years to come (Losch, 2016). But these jobs are also the least attractive to young people. Making them more appealing would require improving living conditions in rural areas and ensuring greater fairness in supply chains in order to ensure better incomes for farmers. New sectors (such as organic farming) could also be sources of innovation, offering new opportunities and boosting the employment chain all the way to consumers. In Africa, given that the people suffering from malnutrition are often peasants, crop diversification and certain agroecological practices could – under the right conditions – increase incomes and improve diets (directly or indirectly) (Bezner Kerr et al., 2021; Temple et al., 2022). The relationship between poverty, agricultural production and food security is nevertheless complex, and there are still many hurdles to overcome.

Productionism has also relegated key environmental issues to the background. There is a need not only to curb the negative environmental impacts of industrial agriculture but also to foster the positive effects of new forms of agriculture stemming from the agroecological transition: biodiversity generation, carbon sequestration, landscape management and resilience to climate change. Broadly speaking, this is a matter of promoting new forms of agriculture that are conducive to healthier ecosystems. Beyond food production methods, this also involves restoring all four functions that agriculture served until the nineteenth century, producing food as well as energy, materials and fertilizers (Chapter 4). Given the need to move away from fossil fuels for reasons pertaining to climate change, the environment (pollution) and resource depletion, agriculture can no longer be reduced to the supply of food. It must (once again) be recognized as a bio-economic issue, that is, as a multifunctional issue that transcends food. The question of biofuels recently sparked this debate. Various studies have highlighted the competition between food and non-food uses of agricultural biomass (Cornelissen et al., 2012; Erb et al., 2012). Most suggest that there is a potential risk of conflict between global food security objectives and climate change mitigation targets. This perspective thus echoes the question raised by Malthus before the Industrial Revolution: how many people can agriculture feed if it has to produce food, energy, materials and fertilizers all at once?

Finally, beyond the issue of production, the key question of consumption patterns is now emerging. The balance between supply and demand can only be achieved by adjusting both sides of the equation. Current consumption patterns in rich countries cannot be replicated worldwide – several planets would be needed to satisfy this appetite. Moreover, these modes of consumption must necessarily be challenged (willingly or by force), or they risk giving rise to unmanageable social inequality. Changing consumption patterns has largely been treated as a matter of consumer goodwill and choice, in connection with a quest to enhance individual well-being. Beyond information and awareness campaigns, public policy on this issue is still scarce (Chapter 18). In terms of governance, the emphasis on the production side of the supply–demand equation inflates the power of agricultural export lobbies in addressing the food issue while minimizing the weight of impoverished food producers and consumers. Eaters themselves, especially the most disadvantaged ones, are most often conspicuously absent from debates on food security. These actors are silently bearing the brunt of food crises – with a notable exception in 2008, when they did make their voices heard through food riots. While civil society actors defending the right to food for all are increasingly well organized, they still have little political clout compared to the powerful lobbies defending the status quo.

Conclusion

While the food crises of 2008 and 2011 pushed the agricultural sector back to the top of the international political agenda for a few years, it has once again been sidelined by other priorities. Environmental and (more recently) health issues have now taken centre stage. The goal of doubling food production has not been forgotten, but the issue has become more complex – rather than just striving to feed the world population 'globally', the challenge is now to ensure food security 'locally', in the most vulnerable areas and for the most disadvantaged populations. Agriculture often remains the main source of livelihood in these circumstances.

The concept of food systems offers new ways of addressing the complex relationships between production and food, and it is central to questions of sustainable development. By articulating the agricultural sector together with the processing, distribution and consumption sectors within the same 'system', it provides fresh perspectives beyond the traditional frameworks of the supply–demand equation. Under this umbrella, all these areas require renewed attention given the environmental and health issues associated with them. But more needs to be done. First, agriculture should not be reduced to its function as a commodity producer – its role (sometimes vital in developing countries) in creating jobs, improving rural people's livelihoods and protecting the environment must also be taken into account. Second, food should not be reduced to its purely material dimension – eating not only nourishes us but also weaves special relationships with ourselves, with others and with the biosphere.

This chapter largely draws on the following publications: Bricas and Daviron (2008), Bricas and Alpha (2018), Malézieux and Corbeels (2019), Malézieux and Dabbadie (2019), and Fouilleux et al. (2021).

The authors would like to thank Damien Conaré, Mathilde Coudray and Marie Walser for proofreading this chapter and for their suggested improvements.

References

Affholder F., Bricas N., Daviron B., Fouilleux E., 2012. La faim dans le monde, alibi pour le développement des OGM. *Libération*, 18 octobre 2012.

Bezner Kerr R., Madsen S., Stüber M., Liebert J., Enloe S., Borghino N. et al., 2021. Can agroecology improve food security and nutrition? A review. *Global Food Security*, 29: 100540.

Bricas N., Alpha A., 2018. Une lecture politique des débats sur la sécurité alimentaire et la nutrition, in Martin-Prével Y., Maire B. (ed.), *La nutrition dans un monde globalisé. Bilan et perspectives à l'heure des ODD*, Paris, Karthala-IRD, 29–48.

Bricas N., Daviron B., 2008. De la hausse des prix au retour du « productionnisme » agricole: les enjeux du sommet sur la sécurité alimentaire de juin 2008 à Rome. *Hérodote*, 131(4): 31–39. https://doi.org/10.3917/her.131.0031

Cornelissen S., Koper M., Deng Y.Y., 2012. The role of bioenergy in a fully sustainable global energy system. *Biomass and Bioenergy*, 41: 21–33. https://doi.org/10.1016/j.biombioe.2011.12.049

Dorin B., Landy F., 2009. *Agriculture and food in India. A half-century review, from independence to globalization*, Inde, Manohar Publishers and Distributors, 280 p.

Erb K.-H., Haberl H., Plutzar C., 2012. Dependency of global primary bioenergy crop potentials in 2050 on food systems, yields, biodiversity conservation and political stability. *Energy Policy*, 47: 260–269. https://doi.org/10.1016/j.enpol.2012.04.066

Erb K.-H., Helmut H., Krausmann F., Lauk C., Plutzar C., Steinberger J.K. et al., 2009. *Eating the planet: feeding and fuelling the world sustainably, fairly and humanely – a scoping study commissioned by Compassion in World Farming and Friends of the Earth UK*, Social Ecology Working Paper, Vienna, Institute of Social Ecology and PIK Potsdam, 132 p.

Even M.-A., Laisney C., 2011. *La demande alimentaire en 2050: chiffres, incertitudes et marges de manœuvre*, Analyse du Centre d'étude et de prospective, Ministère de l'Agriculture, de l'Alimentation, de la Pêche, de la Ruralité et de l'Aménagement du territoire, 4 p.

FAO, 2018a. *The future of food and agriculture. Alternative pathways to 2050*, Rome, FAO, 224 p.

FAO, 2018b. *The state of food insecurity and nutrition in the world*, Rome, FAO, 184 p.

Fouilleux E., Bricas N., Alpha A., 2021. Produire plus pour nourrir le monde. Processus et enjeux politiques de la construction d'un mot d'ordre global, in Bernard de Raymond A., Thivet D. (ed.), *Un monde sans faim ? Gouverner la sécurité alimentaire au 21e siècle*, Paris, Presses de Sciences Po, 129–151.

HLPE. 2019. *Agroecological and other innovative approaches for sustainable agriculture and food systems that enhance food security and nutrition*. A report by the High Level Panel of Experts on Food Security and Nutrition of the Committee on World Food Security, Rome, 163 p.

Licker R., Johnston M., Foley J.A., Barford C., Kucharik C.J., Monfreda C., Ramankutty N., 2010. Mind the gap: how do climate and agricultural management explain the 'yield gap' of croplands around the world? *Global Ecology and Biogeography*, 19(6): 769–782. https://doi.org/10.1111/j.1466-8238.2010.00563.x

Lobell D.B., Burke M.B., Tebaldi C., Mastrandrea M.D., Falcon W.P., Naylor R.L., 2008. Prioritizing climate change adaptation needs for food security in 2030. *Science*, 319(5863): 607–610. https://doi.org/10.1126/science.1152339

Losch B., 2016. Youth Employment: a challenge for the continent, in Pesche D., Losch B., Imbernon J., 2016. *A new emerging rural world: an overview of rural change in Africa*, Montpellier, Cirad-Nepad, 76 p.

Malézieux E., Corbeels M., 2019. Limited food availability, in Dury S., Bendjebbar P., Hainzelin E., Giordano T., Bricas N. (ed.), *Food systems at risk: new trends and challenges*, Rome/Montpellier/Brussels, FAO, Cirad and European Commission, 99–102. https://doi.org/10.19182/agritrop/00080

Malézieux E., Dabbadie L., 2019. Resource overexploitation and running out, in Dury S., Bendjebbar P., Hainzelin E., Giordano T., Bricas N. (ed.), *Food systems at risk: new trends and challenges*, Rome/Montpellier/Brussels, FAO, Cirad and European Commission, 55–58. https://doi.org/10.19182/agritrop/00080

Paillard S., Treyer S., Dorin B. (ed.), 2010. *Agrimonde. Scénarios et défis pour nourrir le monde en 2050*, Versailles, Quæ, 296 p.

Searchinger T., Waite R., Hanson C., Ranganathan J., Dumas P., Matthews E., 2018. *Creating a sustainable food future*, Washington, DC, World Resources Institute, The World Bank, United Nations Environment Program.

Sen A., 1982. *Poverty and famines. An essay on entitlement and deprivation*, Oxford, Oxford University Press, 276 p.

Temple L., Malézieux E., Gauthier D., Aubry C., Pourrias J., Punete Asureros R., de Bon H. 2022. Agroecological innovations, food and nutrition security and food safety for small farmers: Africa-Europe perspectives, in Thomas A., Alpha A., Barcczak A., Zakhia-Rozis N. (ed.), *Sustainable food systems for food security. Need for combination of local and global approaches*, Versailles, éditions Quae, 99–112.

Thomson P.B., 1995. *The spirit of the soil: agriculture and environmental ethics*, London, Routledge, 216 p.

von Braun J., Rosegrant M.W., Pandya-Lorch R., Cohen M.J., Cline S.A., Brown M.A., Bos M.S., 2005. *New risks and opportunities for food security: scenario analyses for 2015 and 2050*, 2020 Vision Discussion Papers, Washington, DC, International Food Policy Research Institute (IFPRI).

World Bank, 1986. *Poverty and hunger. Issues and options for food security in developing countries*, A World Bank Policy Study in Developing Countries, Washington, DC, The World Bank, 69 p.

12

Fortified foods to fight malnutrition?

Sylvie Avallone, Arlène Alpha and Nicolas Bricas

Fighting malnutrition requires diet diversification. This is also a good way to support crop diversity. Yet technical solutions, such as food supplements or (bio)fortification, are still considered more innovative, and these dominate policies tackling the challenges of malnutrition.

The issue of micronutrient deficiencies, particularly in vitamins or minerals such as iron or zinc, was placed on the international agenda in 1992 at the first *International Conference on Nutrition* organized by the FAO and the World Health Organization (WHO). Numerous nutrition studies have shown the effects of these deficiencies ('hidden hunger' or 'silent hunger') on children's growth and health (Golden, 2009). Worldwide, the most common are iron, vitamin A, iodine and zinc deficiencies. According to Allen and colleagues (2006), over two billion people suffer from iron-deficiency anaemia, and one in two pregnant women and about 40 per cent of preschool children in developing countries are anaemic. The authors further estimate that just under two billion people have inadequate iodine intake and that 254 million preschool children are vitamin A deficient (Allen et al., 2006). The FAO and the WHO (1992) identified four main types of strategies to combat micronutrient deficiencies:

- Dietary diversification, through the diversification of crops grown by households for self-consumption or through market mechanisms and the preparation of a broader range of dishes;
- Food fortification, with micronutrients added during processing in the form of additives, an approach promoted by agri-food companies; or, in recent years, biofortification through conventional variety selection or the creation of micronutrient-rich genetically modified organisms – an approach promoted by the seed industries – or through the application of chemical fertilizers, promoted by the fertilizer industries;

- Supplementation, in other words the use of micronutrient-rich medicinal products;
- Infectious or parasitic disease control (vaccination, screening, hygiene, sanitation etc.), contributing to adequate metabolic functioning and nutrient absorption and ensuring good health.

While supplementation and disease control are strategies driven by the healthcare system, diversification and fortification arise directly from the food system. This chapter discusses these two strategies.

Promoting a diversified diet

Dietary diversification has been recognized as an effective strategy for combating malnutrition in both the Global North and the Global South for several decades. A diversified diet particularly helps prevent micronutrient deficiencies and chronic diseases (Hoddinott and Yohannes, 2002; Arimond and Ruel, 2004): the more diverse an individual's diet, the less likely they are to develop a micronutrient deficiency. As the different food groups have complementary nutritional profiles, a diversified diet is the best guarantee of adequate nutrient intake, the required amounts of which are either known or to be determined in the coming years. For instance, eating red meat at a reasonable frequency and in reasonable amounts helps prevent iron, zinc and vitamins A and B deficiencies, while fruit and vegetables provide essential elements such as vitamin C and antioxidants. Dietary diversity scores have therefore been developed and tested to serve as nutritional quality indicators to detect risks of developing nutritional deficiencies (Drescher et al., 2007; Kennedy et al., 2013; FAO, 2021).

Many industrialized countries have strong public policies in place to promote dietary diversity, such as the National Nutrition and Health Programme in France. These policies recommend eating foods from all food groups in moderation and sometimes specify ideal frequencies and portion sizes to better guide consumers. A diversified diet can potentially be achieved across all continents by working with the local products, the preferences of the populations, their identity and their culture. The food diversity strategy does not provide a 'magic bullet'; on the contrary, by encouraging the consumption of foods from all food groups, it tends to support a wide variety of agricultural and food activities and production.

Promoting dietary diversity to combat micronutrient deficiencies thus appears to be compatible with an ecological approach (in the sense of an 'ecology of food') insofar as it encourages biological diversity on the plate, on farms and in territories. It also seems to contribute to strengthening the ecosystem services of food systems and to provide a way to limit populations' dependence on solutions provided by actors that they cannot control.

The success of technical solutions

In countries of the Global South, public authorities nevertheless tend to prefer technical solutions such as supplementation, fortification and biofortification to address the challenges of micronutrient malnutrition. These solutions are heavily promoted by certain private companies and major funders in the field of nutrition, such as GAIN Foundation and the Bill & Melinda Gates Foundation. Perhaps the old adage 'Vary your diet' is not innovative or compelling enough?

Fortification and biofortification raise a number of economic, scientific and political issues. First, these 'targeted' interventions are developed by private actors (in the agri-food, chemical and seed industries) who have a financial interest in promoting their use to combat micronutrient malnutrition. Numerous studies – particularly financed by these companies, which use their results – support the effectiveness of these solutions.

Second, in the scientific world, publication and funding strategies encourage researchers to focus their efforts on technical solutions. Eating a diversified diet is not seen as a 'modern' and innovative strategy. Moreover, while much research has demonstrated the value of dietary diversity in preventing deficiencies, it is often based on statistical correlation studies rather than controlled clinical trials, which are very popular at present. This difference in methodology has led to the gradual marginalization of dietary diversity in the debate on public policies. The scientific evidence supporting technical solutions (fortified foods, biofortified varieties, supplements) tends to saturate the scientific literature and create a smokescreen that overshadows dietary diversity as an effective solution (Delisle, 2004). It is also important to note that studies on dietary diversification receive less backing from the economic actors in the food system, as they tend to emphasize a cross-cutting and comprehensive approach to the ideal diet rather than support for a few supply chains.

Finally, politicians – especially in the Global South – prefer short-term solutions, as these can yield quick results to enhance indicators that are more compatible with their electoral mandate, as well as donors' and international organizations' progress requirements. Technological solutions are especially well perceived, as many actors – whether in the scientific world or among consumers, supply chain operators or decision-makers – associate them with modernity and innovation. Moreover, agricultural policies are generally approached from a sectoral perspective, by supply chain, and are therefore more difficult to tailor to the promotion of a diversified diet.

Taking into account the multidimensionality of food

Evaluating strategies to combat micronutrient deficiencies solely through the prism of nutritional efficiency isolates the issue of nutrition from the other dimensions of food. Yet nutritional deficiencies cannot be tackled independently of everything that food represents for eaters, nor can they be treated as a priority, treating the psychological, social, cultural, economic and political dimensions of food as secondary. At best, nutritional interventions integrate these other dimensions by considering that they can facilitate or hinder the achievement of the overarching health objective.

The first issue to consider in the fight against malnutrition is thus the multidimensional nature of food. Food cannot be reduced to bundles of nutrients: it incorporates the environmental, economic and social conditions of its production, as well as symbolic, cultural and even religious values, which cannot be overlooked. Emphasizing the nutritional dimension of foods by labelling them as fortified can have the perverse effect of discrediting traditional foods that do not have such labelling. It may even lead consumers, especially mothers with very low purchasing power, to feel guilty about not being able to buy such foods, which are promoted as good for their children's health (Kimura, 2013). Aggressively advertising these fortified products can therefore contribute to devaluing traditional food. Beyond the issue of combating micronutrient deficiencies, the nutrition labelling of fortified foods therefore raises questions regarding their guilt-inducing effects. While this system indeed informs consumers and can help them make better-informed choices from a nutritional perspective, it emphasizes the weight of the nutritional dimension of food at the expense of its other dimensions.

How nutritionally beneficial is (bio)fortification?

Another issue surrounding the mode of intervention for combating micronutrient malnutrition is the scale of the intervention. While dietary diversity is guided by the principle that the nutrients provided by one's diet combine over time (Mason and Lang, 2017), fortification uses a food vehicle to target one or more specific nutritional needs. The identification of nutritional or pharmaceutical properties specific to certain foods and their prescription for health reasons is not new. These practices exist in all societies and involve both wild and farmed plants and animals These natural medicinal foods are known, and their properties are identified through knowledge accumulated via traditional practices in particular ecological. health and cultural contexts. This empirical knowledge has been little studied or evaluated and has not informed the development of fortified foods: the latter are the product of a representation of nutrition that reduces it to the satisfaction of independent nutrient needs.

While such a strategy may have some effectiveness, it has several limitations. First, it overlooks the effects of interactions between nutrients within food matrices (Chapter 9). A well-known example is the interaction between iron intake and that of vitamin C or tannin-rich products. While the former facilitates iron uptake, the latter reduces it. Moreover, depending on the way in which fortified products are made and commercialized, there may be a long distance and time lag between their production and their consumption by the target groups. Many products are manufactured in Europe, stored in exporters' storage facilities, shipped to target countries by boat in containers, stored again in ports and only then distributed in the target territories and sold by local retailers. Several studies have shown that the sensitive fraction of fortified foods (polyunsaturated fatty acids, vitamins) may degrade during shipping in these long supply chains (Hemery et al., 2015; Mousties et al., 2019). The nutritional claims made are therefore not always verified.

Furthermore, promoting a fortified food without taking into account the diet of the target population overlooks the possibility of meeting micronutrient needs through the more or less frequent consumption of foods already found in local dishes. For example, researchers have shown that the vitamin A needs of populations deficient in this nutrient can easily be met through a slightly more frequent use of unrefined palm oil, which is rich in ß-carotene and familiar to these populations (Zeba et al., 2005). Finally, dietary diversification involves a more comprehensive approach to the nutritional situation of a population, as it allows for the simultaneous improving of intakes of many nutrients, not just micronutrients.

This diet-based approach, which therefore takes into account the combination of foods in dishes, of dishes in meals, of meals in a day and of daily food consumption over a series of weeks or months, accounts for the effects of interaction between foods over time, factoring in digestion and assimilation speeds. From a nutritional point of view, eating one kilogram of a food per week is not necessarily equivalent to eating 150 grams every day. Pamela Mason and Tim Lang (2017) thus prefer the term 'sustainable diet' to 'sustainable food': rather than seeking a solution based on a single universal food product, the focus here is on dietary diversification, if possible working with local resources or solutions tailored to the local context. There may of course be situations where these resources are lacking locally, which call for sourcing resources from other places or even adopting more 'universal' solutions.

Building on local solutions can also change the way data from food and nutrition surveys are processed. Such surveys generally seek to shed light on the determinants of nutritional situations: they compare rich and poor, male and female, young and old and other social groups in order to identify what determines the nutritional status of individuals. Yet these surveys can be approached in a completely different way by characterizing the practices of subjects with a good nutritional status within a population, including and especially in the category that is on average most at risk. This 'positive deviance' approach (Marsh et al., 2004) focuses on the ways in which individuals or households achieve satisfactory nutritional status in adverse conditions. The solutions are therefore not extraneous; on the contrary, they stem from the practices of the target populations themselves. This approach allows for identifying endogenous resources specific to a given context.

Identifying the risks of dependence

Adopting a more ecological approach to the issue of nutrition calls for taking into account the very modalities of intervention and their effects. The endogenous or exogenous nature of the proposed solutions raises questions of sovereignty and dependence. Using fortified industrial foods or biofortified varieties entails a risk of dependence on the chemical or pharmaceutical industry (for the production of additives) or on seed manufacturers, a risk further compounded by the high concentration of activities in the hands of a few major players. The COVID-19 crisis revealed the challenges surrounding this dependence on a limited number of actors with the resources to tackle urgent problems. While specializing in certain food activities based on comparative advantages reduces costs, it carries risks regarding autonomy in strategic decision-making.

Conclusion

One of the strategies applied by companies to remain competitive and conquer new markets is to add new attributes to their products, relating to taste, sustainability, ethical practices and related product values. Nutrition has not escaped this trend, with the development of the market for medicinal or health foods – either enriched or low-content foods. This strategy has led to a proliferation of products within the same range, resulting in an abundance of choice (Schwartz, 2005). As a consequence, foods tend to be considered merely as a sum of attributes. Certain marketing tools, such as conjoint analysis, thus measure the relative weight of these attributes in purchase decisions (Rao, 2014). But eaters do not necessarily perceive a food item as an assemblage of discernible attributes. On the contrary, it forms an integrated and indivisible whole; only during the preparation of dishes does the combination of ingredients come into play. Through this assembly process in the kitchen, the ingredients eventually fuse or even 'materialize', as the philosopher Gilbert Simondon (1958) theorized regarding the mode of existence of technical objects: through the addition of initially distinct functions – flavour, rheological attributes, colouring and so on – the dish (or the technical object) ultimately incorporates these functions through the interactions between them, making them inseparable. In bread, through fermentation and baking, the mixture of flour, yeast and water generates a holistic product that is more than the sum of its parts. This is where the magical character of cooking lies: going beyond a conception of food reduced to a simple nutritional function.

The authors would like to thank Damien Conaré, Mathilde Coudray and Marie Walser for proofreading this chapter and for their suggested improvements.

References

Allen L., de Benoist B., Dary O., Hurrell R., 2006. *Guidelines on food fortification with micronutrients*, Geneva/Rome, WHO/FAO, 341 p.

Arimond M., Ruel M.T., 2004. Dietary diversity is associated with child nutritional status: evidence from 11 demographic and health surveys. *Journal of Nutrition*, 134(10): 2579–2585. https://doi.org/10.1093/jn/134.10.2579

Delisle H., 2004. Food diversification strategies are neglected in spite of their potential effectiveness: why is it so and what can be done?, in Brouwer I.D., Traoré A.S., Trèche S. (ed.), *Voies alimentaires d'amélioration des situations nutritionnelles en*

Afrique de l'Ouest: le rôle des technologies alimentaires et des nutritionnistes. Actes du 2e atelier international Ouagadougou 23-28/11/2003, Ouagadougou, Presses universitaires de Ouagadougou et IRD, 151–166.

Drescher L.S., Thiele S., Mensink G.B.M., 2007. A new index to measure healthy food diversity better reflects a healthy diet than traditional measures. *Journal of Nutrition*, 137(3): 647–651. https://doi.org/10.1093/jn/137.3.647

FAO, 2021. *Minimum dietary diversity for women. An updated guide to measurement – from collection to action*, Rome, FAO, 158 p.

FAO, WHO, 1992. *International conference on nutrition, Final Report of the Conference*, Rome/Geneva, FAO/WHO, 75 p.

Golden M.H., 2009. Proposed recommended nutrient densities for moderately malnourished children. *Food and Nutrition Bulletin*, 30(3 suppl.): S267–S342. https://doi.org/10.1177/15648265090303S302

Hemery Y.M., Fontan L., Moench-Pfanner R., Laillou A., Berger J., Renaud C., Avallone S., 2015. Influence of light exposure and oxidative status on the stability of vitamins A and D3 during the storage of fortified soybean oil. *Food Chemistry*, 184: 90–98. https://doi.org/10.1016/j.foodchem.2015.03.096

Hoddinott J., Yohannes Y., 2002. *Dietary diversity as a food security indicator*, FCND Discussion Paper, Washington DC, IFPRI, 94 p.

Kennedy, G., Ballard, T., Dop, M.C., 2013. *Guidelines for measuring household and individual dietary diversity*, Rome, Nutrition and Consumer Protection Division, Food and Agriculture Organization of the United Nations, 53 p.

Kimura A.H., 2013. *Hidden hunger. Gender and the politics of smarter foods*, Ithaca/London, Cornell University Press, 226 p.

Marsh D.R., Schroeder D.G., Dearden K.A., Sternin J., Sternin M., 2004. The power of positive deviance. *BMJ*, 329(7475): 1177–1179. https://doi.org/10.1136/bmj.329.7475.1177

Mason P., Lang T., 2017. *Sustainable diets. How ecological nutrition can transform consumption and the food system*, Oxon, Routledge, 369 p.

Moustiès C., Bourlieu C., Baréa B., Servent A., Alter P., Lebrun M. et al., 2019. Lipid composition and state of oxidation of fortified infant flours in low-income countries are not optimal and strongly affected by the time of storage. *European Journal of Lipid Science and Technology*, 121(11): 12. https://doi.org/10.1002/ejlt.201900173

Rao V.R., 2014. *Applied conjoint analysis*, Heidelberg, Springer, 389 p.

Schwartz B., 2005. *The paradox of choice: why more is less*, New York, Harper Perennial, 304 p.

Simondon G., 1958. *Du mode d'existence des objets techniques*, Paris, Aubier, 368 p.

Zeba A.N., Prével Y.M., Somé I.T., Delisle H.F., 2006. The positive impact of red palm oil in school meals on vitamin A status: study in Burkina Faso. *Nutrition Journal*, 5(1): 17. https://doi.org/10.1186/1475-2891-5-17

13

Would you like some more protein?

Olivier Lepiller and Estelle Fourat

The question of proteins is one that has developed over time. Today, it features in a range of public debates relating to important nutritional, economic and environmental issues. The excessive focus on proteins makes us run the risk of paying less attention to the need to reduce food consumption, as well as avoiding alarming issues surrounding the status of particular types of foods and animal-related concerns.

In debates on how to achieve a sustainable food supply that can feed the entire human population, proteins are ubiquitous, particularly in terms of health and environmental impacts. The focus on these macronutrients contrasts with everyday experience, where people mostly refer to the names of foods, that is, complex, cooked combinations of foodstuffs, ingredients or products. At most, proteins are featured as the main component of specific diets, namely medical (severe malnutrition, old age) and performance-oriented (sports, weight loss) diets.

We analyse this disconnect between academic, political and media discourse on the one hand and the everyday experience of food on the other. In so doing, we shed light on the factors that have led to this focus on proteins, which has given the latter such a significant role in our kitchens and cuisines. This focus is exemplified by the use of the term 'protein' to designate all foods of animal origin or 'plant-based protein' to refer to pulses only, often excluding cereals – some of which are nevertheless high in protein. These expressions reduce foods to this component of nutritional interest. Conversely, they reduce proteins to the two main categories of animal-based foods and pulses. As a result, these categories are presented as interchangeable. However, while this substitutability may hold true from a nutritional point of view, it cannot always be applied to culinary practices and eating habits when it comes to cooking pulses or meat. Moreover, basing substitutions between food categories on proteins relegates other nutritional intakes to the background, thus framing protein intake as the most important health challenge. The tendency to reduce foods to just one of their biochemical components conceals other issues associated with their consumption and with contemporary nutrition more generally, which we discuss in this chapter.

A recent history

To understand the focus on proteins, it is useful to look at the history of their discovery. The story of proteins begins in the 1830s, when they were identified by a new discipline – biochemistry. The term itself was proposed in 1838 by a Dutch chemist, Gerardus Johannes Mulder, who demonstrated the presence of these organic molecules in all 'animal substances'. This ultimately led to the term 'protein' being gradually applied to all matter previously described as 'animal substance' (Carpenter, 2003). This historical link between animal substance and proteins fostered the analogical relationship between the two and incidentally led to the term 'protein' being mapped onto symbols associated with meat, a food that conveys strength (Vialles, 2007), wealth and ease (Goody, 1982). The German chemist Justus von Liebig also worked on proteins from the late 1830s. He defended the idea that proteins were not only the primary component of animal bodies (apart from water) but also the fuel for the biochemical reactions responsible for muscle contraction and therefore animals' motor skills. This ultimately led him to present proteins as the only true nutrient, an idea that was later disproved (Carpenter, 2003). This pioneering work in the nineteenth century was followed by an inventory of the different proteins, the identification of their roles in a wide range of functions in living organisms and the discovery of their basic components, peptides and – smaller yet – amino acids. Some amino acids are now called 'essential' in human nutrition, as regular intake is necessary to maintain good health and the human body is not capable of synthesizing them itself.

After the Second World War, proteins found themselves at the centre of nutritional and development research and public health policies. With the challenge of recovering agricultural production, the issue of protein deficiency became the main concern in the fight against undernutrition in the poorest countries. This focus on the world protein 'gap', 'crisis' or 'problem' was denounced by nutritionist Donald S. McLaren (1974) in a landmark article published in *The Lancet*. According to McLaren, whose stance was subsequently confirmed by scientific advances, this focus on protein deficiency was the product of an overgeneralization based on cases of severe undernutrition. Scientists particularly concentrated their attention on the kwashiorkor syndrome observed in young children. This syndrome was initially wrongly attributed to a weaning diet that was too low in protein, neglecting other micronutritional, energy or infectious factors (Brown, 1991).

Following McLaren's article, a critical review within the scientific community showed the role of political and financial interests in the focus on the world protein gap, particularly through the funding of research in nutrition and other scientific fields such as the anthropology of health and development (Diener et al., 1980). With the United States having majorly mobilized its agricultural sector to feed the countries devastated by the war, the surpluses generated by the gradual recovery of Europe's production capacity, particularly in the dairy sector, plunged the country into an agricultural crisis. These surpluses were then valorized as milk powder, a product with a very high protein content, and exported to the least developed countries, thus securing outlets for US dairy production and its protein and oil-protein crop suppliers (Diener, 1984).

At the turn of the twenty-first century, studies investigated the satiating power of proteins in connection with the public health problem of obesity. For the same caloric value, protein-rich foods were found to generate a greater and more sustained feeling of satiety than those containing more fats and carbohydrates (Louis-Sylvestre, 2002). Given the excessive and overly rich food intake fuelling obesity, the protein content of diets and foods thus offers an interesting avenue for research into appetite regulation in a context of food abundance.

This brief history of proteins highlights their foundational, scientific and symbolic link with animals, the exaggeration of their role in certain nutrition-related pathologies and the interest in proteins as a way to address the harmful effects of overabundance.

Let us now turn to the contemporary public debates involving proteins, so as to better understand the food issues with which they are associated.

Proteins in contemporary public debates

The first public debate surrounding proteins concerned the sustainability of food, particularly with regard to human health and the environment. These two issues were popularized from the early 1970s, notably in a book by the American Frances Moore Lappé, *Diet for a Small Planet* (1971). This book already pointed to the negative consequences of excessive meat consumption for both health and the environment, based on the argument of the low efficiency of converting plant-based proteins into animal proteins via livestock farming. This argument, which has become commonplace today, has been revised to consider 'net feed conversion efficiency', which takes into account the share of animal feed that humans would not be able to digest directly themselves, such as oilcake or straw (Laisse et al., 2018). Even in its revised form, this argument still calls into question the consumption of animal-based foods. For example, it sheds light on the relative environmental impacts of equal quantities of plant-based proteins and animal proteins. Over the last two decades, the environmental impacts of excessive 'animal protein' consumption have been widely documented, starting with the FAO's global report *Livestock's Long Shadow* (Steinfeld et al., 2006). In Europe, the report *The Protein Puzzle* (Westhoek et al., 2011) detailed the challenges of rebalancing the share of animal foods in total calorie intake by increasing the share of plant-based foods, using protein quantity as the unit of analysis. It has since become widely accepted in the scientific community that, for both health and environmental reasons, a reduction in per capita consumption of animal-based foods is desirable in the wealthiest countries, where average consumption levels far exceed requirements.[1]

A second public debate, closely linked to the previous one, pertains to the geopolitical issues involving proteins. In 2019, during the negotiations on the new Common Agricultural Policy, the president of France defended Europe's 'protein sovereignty'. In 2021, a 'Plant Protein Plan' was launched by the French Ministry of Agriculture and Food, while the issue of protein autonomy is being addressed at regional or farm level. After the last global conflict, major trade liberalization agreements encouraged an international division of agricultural production. This largely devolved the production of protein-rich animal feed to the American continent, such that European animal production is now largely dependent on imports from the Americas, particularly for soybean (Boucly and Decoret, 2020). With the gradual decrease in per capita consumption of meat and milk, this division of production is now being challenged in Europe, particularly by France, which is seeking to relocalize its production of plant-based protein foods. Proteins are thus becoming a key geostrategic issue, particularly

---

[1] The European Food Safety Authority (EFSA), the Food and Agriculture Organization of the United Nations (FAO) and the WHO recommend a total protein reference intake of 0.83 g/day/kg of body weight, that is, for a person weighing 67 kg (the average weight of French adults), nearly 56 g/day, with a 1:1 ratio of animal proteins to plant-based proteins. In France, the INCA3 food consumption survey shows that adults consume on average 83.2 g/day.

surrounding oil-protein crops – especially soybean, which also provides raw material for biofuels at the same time. The contentious discussions between the French and Brazilian Presidents in 2020 on the topic of deforestation by fire in Brazil attest to the international significance of the issue.

Proteins are at the heart of a third public debate on food-based self-optimization practices. These practices raise questions about the cult of performance as well as moral and health perfectionism (Dalgalarrondo and Fournier, 2019). One example is meal-replacement drinks, products intended as time-saving solutions which present their protein content – often plant based – as the key to their satiating power. Proteins are also central to sports nutrition and weight-loss programmes. Lastly, they feature in discourses on ageing as a necessary ingredient for healthy ageing as a form of performance (beyond the very real and documented issues surrounding the increased protein needs associated with muscle mass loss in very old age).

Proteins are furthermore integral to the rhetoric mobilized in a fourth public debate on the 'de-animalization' of food observed in rich countries such as France (Fourat and Lepiller, 2017). This term refers to the trend towards challenging the centrality of meat and, more broadly, foods of animal origin in eating habits. It has translated into a drop in the consumption of certain foods, such as red meat, and has gone hand in hand with the growing importance of plant-based foods in diets, from the strictest form of veganism to flexitarianism following a 'less but better' approach – eating less food of animal origin but of better quality, guided by greater concern for the dignity of animals. The ability of these diets, especially the more plant-based ones, to meet nutritional protein requirements was long questioned. Recent studies have now shown that the practices observed among vegetarians and vegans satisfy their protein and essential amino acid needs[2] (Mariotti and Gardner, 2020) and that the practices of lacto-ovo vegetarians provide the recommended intakes of macronutrients, including protein (Allès et al., 2017). Public health authorities, as well as dietetics and culinary discourses, now present pulses (peas, lentils, beans, soy etc.) and, to a lesser extent, cereals and nuts as alternative protein sources to meat. The French National Nutrition and Health Program states that 'pulses are naturally high in fibre and contain plant-based proteins. [. . .] They can also replace meat or poultry; in this case, combining them with a cereal product is advised' (PNNS, 2021). In Western countries, where foods of animal origin have pride of place in culinary know-how

---

[2] For purely vegan diets, other nutrients may be a problem. For vitamin B12, for instance, supplementation is necessary.

(unlike in India, for example), the challenge raised by the growing role of plant-based foods in dietary practices is therefore first and foremost the acquisition of culinary skills and nutritional knowledge.

In connection with this trend towards more plant-based diets, proteins fuel a fifth and final debate, pertaining to the emerging markets for meat and dairy substitutes. For some years now, multinational food companies have taken an interest in plant-based 'milks', as illustrated by Danone's acquisition of the leading American organic plant juice company, WhiteWave. More recently, startups specializing in plant-based meat alternatives, such as Impossible Foods or Beyond Meat, have attracted investors from the digital world, and their products are now distributed by international fast-food chains (Porcher, 2019). In vitro meat, or cultured meat, which is based on techniques to grow animal cells in bioreactors, offers new promises of technological means to escape the need to slaughter animals for meat and to reduce the environmental impact of farming. However, these promises, which are highly dependent on the technical skills of large financial actors, still have a long way to go to prove their validity and raise many questions about the autonomy of eaters (Fournier and Lepiller, 2019). The high 'protein' content of plant-based alternatives to meat and dairy is often advertised as a selling point. As for in vitro meat, it is commonly presented primarily as a 'new source of animal protein' (Post and Hocquette, 2017).

The need for frugality as a social and political issue

Finally, we highlight several reasons for maintaining a critical distance from an excessive focus on proteins. First, critical examination of the world protein gap theory has shown that an exclusive focus on proteins is by no means always an adequate explanation for diet-related health problems, including in situations of undernutrition. The focus on proteins appears even less relevant in situations of food abundance, as protein needs are largely met in populations with access to adequate caloric intake provided by a sufficiently diverse diet. Abundance and overeating pose health and environmental problems that primarily call for decreasing total caloric intake, followed by a reduction in the consumption of animal-based foods (Vieux et al., 2012; Perignon et al., 2017).

Second, the focus on proteins in the formulation of public health standards and marketing campaigns is part of a wider process of the medicalization of food (Poulain, 2009). It further entrenches the idea of individual health as the primary, if not sole, purpose of the act of eating, at the expense of its other functions – social, convivial, hedonic or even philosophical and spiritual. This process encourages the subjection of eaters to a biomedical normativity, as well as corollary feelings of guilt. Moreover, medicalization is based on an approach to nutrition that is itself reductive, tending to isolate nutrients while neglecting the way in which they are associated within foods or in culinary practices. This leads to overlooking the nutrient density of foods, the key variable in a health-promoting diet (Brown, 1991; Maillot et al., 2006; Tharrey et al., 2017). Protein-rich foods are therefore interesting to consider but more for their micronutrients (with which proteins are associated within these foods), particularly calcium, iron, zinc, vitamin D, long-chain omega-3 fatty acids and vitamin B12.

Third, the focus on proteins encourages the reduction of animals to their biochemical components and thus to their physical materiality. This can lead to the avoidance of increasingly urgent questions, namely regarding the ethics of breeding and killing animals, as well as the legitimacy of food-driven and working relationships with animals (Porcher, 2011). Reducing the animals that are sources of human food to their materiality also leads to overlooking the diverse range of services they provide (landscape maintenance, biodiversity preservation, soil fertilization, farm work etc.) and the associated human–animal relationships.

Finally, this focus on proteins causes foods that play very different culinary roles to be seen as equivalent. This has its benefits, for instance, in rethinking the place of animal and plant-based foods in food repertoires, though it also involves a process of translation into culinary language. But this focus on proteins and equating them raises questions about the interests they serve. This nutritional category can be instrumentalized to generate political and moral opportunities serving economic interests, as in the case, for example, of ultra-processed plant-based products sold as alternatives to animal-based foods or of in vitro meat.

Conclusion

Critical vigilance is thus required in order to ensure that proteins do not distract us from the real issue: the need, in situations of abundance that allow it, to reinvent food models to be less centred on animal foods. These models must promote a certain frugality, making the consumption of those foods more of an exception, more meaningful and, when they involve killing animals, perhaps more solemn. It is important to remember that in situations of food abundance and when diets are sufficiently diverse, the primary challenge is to reduce total caloric intake. Reducing the consumption of animal proteins does not entail a risk of protein deficiency. It is therefore not necessary to compensate for reduced animal protein intake by increasing plant-based protein intake; on the contrary, meat can be replaced with vegetables.

The authors would like to thank Nicolas Bricas, Damien Conaré, Mathilde Coudray, Nicole Darmon and Marie Walser for proofreading this chapter and for their suggested improvements.

References

Allès B., Baudry J., Méjean C., Touvier M., Péneau S., Hercberg S., Kesse-Guyot E., 2017. Comparison of sociodemographic and nutritional characteristics between self-reported vegetarians, vegans, and meat-eaters from the NutriNet-Santé study. *Nutrients*, 9(9): e1023. https://doi.org/10.3390/nu9091023

Boucly M., Decoret P.-M., 2020. L'Europe agricole au défi de sa souveraineté protéinique. *Annales des Mines – Réalités industrielles*, 2020(2): 83–87. https://doi.org/10.3917/rindu1 .202.0083

Brown K.H., 1991. The importance of dietary quality versus quantity for weanlings in less developed countries: a framework for discussion. *Food and Nutrition Bulletin*, 13(2): 1–9. https://doi.org/10.1177/156482659101300219

Carpenter K.J., 2003. A short history of nutritional science: part 1 (1785–1885). *Journal of Nutrition*, 133(3): 638–645. https://doi.org/10.1093/jn/133.3.638

Dalgalarrondo S., Fournier T., 2019. Introduction. Les morales de l'optimisation ou les routes du soi. *Ethnologie française*, 176: 639–651. https://doi.org/10.3917/ethn.194.0639

Diener P., 1984. Humanism and science in cultural anthropology: the great protein fiasco. *Journal of Social Philosophy*, 15(1): 13–20. https://doi.org/10.1111/j.1467-9833.1984 .tb00683.x

Diener P., Moore K., Mutaw R., 1980. Meat, markets, and mechanical materialism: the great protein fiasco in anthropology. *Dialectical Anthropology*, 5(3): 171–192. https:// doi.org/10.1007/BF00257766

Fourat E., Lepiller O., 2017. Forms of food transition: socio-cultural factors limiting the diets' animalisation in France and India. *Sociologia Ruralis*, 57(1): 41–63. https://doi .org/10.1111/soru.12114

Fournier T., Lepiller O., 2019. Se nourrir de promesses. Enjeux et critiques de l'introduction de deux innovations dans le domaine alimentaire: test nutri-génétique et viande in vitro. Socio. *La nouvelle revue des sciences sociales*, 12: 73–95. https://doi.org/10.4000/socio.4529

Goody J., 1982. *Cooking, cuisine and class: a study in comparative sociology*, New York/ London/Melbourne, Cambridge University Press, 253 p.

Laisse S., Baumont R., Dusart L., Gaudré D., Rouillé B., Benoit M. et al., 2018. L'efficience nette de conversion des aliments par les animaux d'élevage: une nouvelle approche pour évaluer la contribution de l'élevage à l'alimentation humaine. *INRAE Productions Animales*, 31(3): 269–288. https://doi.org/10.20870/productions-animales.2018.31.3.2355

Louis-Sylvestre J., 2002. Toutes les protéines ont-elles le même pouvoir satiétogène ? *Cahiers de nutrition et de diététique*, 37(5): 313–321. https://doi.org/CND-10-2002-37-5-0007-9960-101019-ART4

Maillot M., Darmon N., Drewnowski A., Arnault N., Hercberg S., 2006. Le coût et la qualité nutritionnelle des groupes d'aliments: quelle hiérarchie ? *Cahiers de nutrition et de diététique*, 41(2): 87–96. https://doi.org/10.1016/S0007-9960(06)70612-5

Mariotti F., Gardner C.D., 2020. Adéquation de l'apport en protéines et acides aminés dans les régimes végétariens. *Cahiers de nutrition et de diététique*, 55(2): 66–81. https://doi.org/10.1016/j.cnd.2019.12.002

McLaren D.S., 1974. The great protein fiasco. *Lancet*, 304(7872): 93–96. https://doi.org/10.1016/s0140-6736(74)91649-3

Moore Lappé F., 1971. *Diet for a small planet*, New York, Ballantines Books, 301 p.

Perignon M., Vieux F., Soler L.-G., Masset G., Darmon N., 2017. Improving diet sustainability through evolution of food choices: review of epidemiological studies on the environmental impact of diets. *Nutrition Reviews*, 75(1): 2–17. https://doi.org/10.1093/nutrit/nuw043

PNNS, 2021. Les légumes secs (lentilles, haricots, pois chiches . . .), *Manger Bouger*.

Porcher J., 2011. *Vivre avec les animaux: une utopie pour le XXIe siècle*, Paris, La Découverte, 168 p.

Porcher J., 2019. *Cause animale, cause du capital*, Lormont, Le Bord de l'eau, 115 p.

Post M.J., Hocquette J.-F., 2017. New sources of animal proteins: cultured meat, in Purslow P.P. (ed.), *New Aspects of Meat Quality*, Cambridge, Woodhead Publishing, 425–441.

Poulain J.-P., 2009. *Sociologie de l'obésité*, Paris, PUF, 385 p.

Steinfeld H., Gerber P., Wassenaar T., Castel V., Rosales M., Haan C. de, 2006. *Livestock's long shadow: environmental issues and options*, Rome, FAO, 390 p.

Tharrey M., Maillot M., Azaïs-Braesco V., Darmon N., 2017. From the SAIN, LIM system to the SENS algorithm: a review of a French approach of nutrient profiling. *Proceedings of the Nutrition Society*, 76(3): 237–246. https://doi.org/10.1017/S0029665117000817

Vialles N., 2007. Des invariants du régime carné, in Poulain J.-P. (ed.), *L'homme, le mangeur, l'animal: qui nourrit l'autre ?*, Paris, OCHA, 197–206.

Vieux F., Darmon N., Touazi D., Soler L.G., 2012. Greenhouse gas emissions of self-selected individual diets in France: changing the diet structure or consuming less? *Ecological Economics*, 75: 91–101. https://doi.org/10.1016/j.ecolecon.2012.01.003

Westhoek H., Rood T., van den Berg M., Janse J., Nijdam D., Reudink M. et al., 2011. *The protein puzzle: the consumption and production of meat, dairy and fish in the European Union*, The Hague, PBL Netherlands Environmental Assessment Agency, 218 p.

14

The fight against food waste

Marie Mourad and Nicolas Bricas

Food waste, though it must be fought, also serves social functions. It is important to put into perspective the responsibility of consumers seen as failing to manage their food waste adequately and to recognize that waste is above all the result of overproduction that has ultimately led to food being devalued.

Human societies have often had to save and protect their resources when they were scarce and there was a risk of shortage (Jarrige and Le Roux, 2020). In farming, this has involved preventing 'losses' caused by climate hazards, animals (rodents, insects, birds) and microorganisms that degrade food (such as mould). These losses received considerable international attention in the 1960s and 1970s, as the quantities of food produced did not seem to be, or risked not being, sufficient to meet populations' needs. Much effort thus went into fighting plant diseases and pests as well as reducing post-harvest losses, particularly in countries where increasing food availability was a strategic priority for food security.

A seemingly consensual cause

Since the 1980s, as a result of the industrialization of food systems, global food availability has increased significantly. The world has shifted from a state of relative food scarcity to a situation of overproduction, which has gone hand in hand with a rise in waste. In their report for the FAO, Gustavsson et al. (2011) argued that almost a third of global food production is lost or wasted. In France, a study conducted for the National Agency for Ecological Transition (Ademe) in 2016 estimated that 10 million tonnes of food are diverted from human consumption each year, worth €16 billion. This contributes to climate change, accounting for 3 per cent of national greenhouse gas emissions (Income Consulting and AK2C, 2016).

The definitions of loss and waste do however differ depending on the authors and the scope or nature of the surpluses studied. Based on a comprehensive review of the literature, the HLPE[1] defines food 'loss' as a reduction, at any stage of the food supply chain prior to consumption, in the mass of foodstuffs originally intended for human consumption, irrespective of the cause. The organization defines food 'waste' as food fit for human consumption that is discarded or spoiled at the consumption stage, irrespective of the cause (HLPE, 2014). The FAO (2019), for its part, defines 'losses' as the decrease in the quantity or quality of food resulting from decisions and actions taken by food producers and suppliers, and 'waste' as the product of decisions and actions taken by retailers, food service providers and consumers. In both definitions, losses tend to occur upstream and waste downstream in food supply chains.

While food loss has been less prominent on the political agenda since the 1980s and the topic of waste is still emerging, the two issues have regained prominence since the late 2000s. First, the surges in international prices in 2008 and then 2011 revived the productivist goal of doubling, or greatly increasing, food production to meet the challenge of feeding the world's population, which is set to reach 9 to 10 billion people by 2050 (Bricas and Daviron, 2008). Combating food losses and waste has also been presented as a way to increase food availability. Second, the rise in environmental awareness has contributed to making this problem – which places unnecessary pressure on non-renewable resources and causes environmental degradation (Chapter 7) – a priority on political agendas. Since it supports food security and the reduction of environmental impacts, the fight against food loss and waste is seen as a moral duty (FAO, 2015). In 2020, United Nations Secretary-General António Guterres described food waste as an 'ethical outrage'.[2] This fight is an 'uncontested' cause – one that can only give rise to consensus, which no individual or organization publicly opposes (Juhem, 2001). Therein lies one of the strengths of this issue, which partly explains why it has prevailed on the international agenda.

At a national level, the fight against food loss and waste is also a non-partisan and essentially consensual cause, which political actors can take up to address social concerns (the fight against food insecurity) and environmental commitments (resource preservation, impact reduction) simultaneously. As this cause can easily be linked to sustainable development goals, supporting

---

[1] High Level Panel of Experts on Food Security and Nutrition of the Committee on World Food Security.
[2] According to a tweet by António Guterres on the occasion of the First International Day of Awareness for Food Loss and Waste on 29 September 2020.

it is politically advantageous. In France, this is exemplified by the Garot law of 2016, which required large supermarkets to give any unsold food to non-profit organizations (Chapter 15), and the 2017–20 National Pact against Food Waste, signed by multiple public, private and non-profit actors. As it is currently approached, however, the fight against food waste risks focusing policy and reforms on strategies to address the consequences and symptoms of waste, without eliminating its causes.

The social and cultural function of food

Although human societies save and protect their resources, they also waste some of them, even in situations of relative scarcity. Wastage is a way to create temporary or permanent abundance and consume without (over)monitoring. Festivities and ceremonies are opportunities to stage such abundance: for wedding meals, funerals, and banquets, people prepare more food than necessary. This waste – if it can still be called waste – is not the product of poor management. It is socially accepted, even sought after, as food plays more than a nutritional role; it also serves a social and cultural function.

Wasting is in fact a sign of 'being able to afford' to plan for more than the careful management of our primary needs. François Jarrige and Thomas Le Roux (2020) describe waste as a 'manifestation of freedom and abundance'. Acquiring or accumulating more food than we need to meet our nutritional needs means leaving room for enhanced well-being. It means lightening our mental load by avoiding the need to manage supplies as tightly as possible, having the opportunity to choose between several types of food or to wait until the last minute to decide what to eat, being able to host unexpected guests, trying new foods without being sure they will be liked or protecting ourselves from a health risk. The pursuit of such a 'possibility of consumption' is not specific to food. Over the course of our lives, we acquire or wish to acquire many things that we may not consume, such as clothes that we will rarely, if ever, wear and books that we will never finish.

Being wealthy makes it easier to increase one's possibilities of consumption. Seeking to create a sense of abundance, if only for a moment or a particular event, is a way of freeing oneself from the daily and burdensome constraints of managing scarcity. In particular, this explains the likely disconnect between people in precarious situations and well-meaning volunteers seeking to help them, who find it difficult to understand why these individuals would rather buy a very expensive mobile phone than feed their families better. Acquiring consumer goods is a way to pamper oneself, to boost one's self-esteem or to gain social status. These goods therefore play a fundamental role, as has long been shown by socio-economists, guided by Thorstein Veblen (1899) and his concept of 'conspicuous consumption'.

This perspective questions the prioritization of consumption objects based on the needs they fulfil. According to Abraham Maslow (1943) and the hierarchy of needs he described, any consumption that fulfils secondary or higher needs while basic needs are not fully met constitutes a form of waste. This implies that acquiring works of art, spending time decorating or wearing jewellery amounts to mismanaging resources. Yet all societies, even with modest resources, engage in such activities. This observation has led to criticism and relativization of Maslow's hierarchy of needs. Nevertheless, the latter still significantly informs value judgements about poor people, who often continue to be stigmatized as not knowing how to manage their money properly. With regard to food, this entails considering foods that provide the most important nutrients at the lowest cost as fundamental and those that build bonds of belonging, bring pleasure or allow one to be well regarded by others as secondary. Yet even in situations of hardship, the pursuit of food that fosters social ties, provides recognition and is a source of pleasure for the taste buds and for the eyes is not a superfluous effort that is 'wasted' at the expense of 'basic needs'.

The causes of food waste therefore do not really lie in irrational decision-making by consumers who do not know how to adjust their consumption to their basic needs. The issue is not so much the existence of food waste as its current scale. The drop in food spending as a share of households' budgets (especially wealthier ones), due to food overproduction, has facilitated and generalized wasteful practices that previously remained exceptional, especially in times of lesser abundance. This overproduction exceeds societies' need to protect themselves from the risk of food shortages. It has led to a decline in the economic and symbolic value of food, which has become a mere commodity.

Consumers' responsibility?

The fight against waste has so far largely involved calling on consumers to better manage their purchases and supplies. There has been a proliferation of media articles and awareness campaigns explaining how to avoid waste. Non-profits have organized the collection of unsold goods and shared ways of reusing them. Digital apps have been developed to help consumers manage their food supplies. Putting the onus on consumers in this way aligns with the interests of food industry actors, who keep seeking to increase their sales. They do so using advertising and promotional offers. Consumers end up having to deal with waste at home that was in fact generated by the overabundant supply from the agri-food industry and mass retail. In rich countries, where food consumption is relatively saturated (i.e. supply exceeds demand), the market for 'possibilities of consumption' remains a source of economic growth.

In France, food manufacturing and retail businesses have in the past drawn on quantitative data to push responsibility for waste onto consumers, as a way to avoid criticism. For example, in 2013, the National Association of Agri-Food Industries stated on its website that households accounted for 67 per cent of food waste, while the agri-food industries produced only 2 per cent. Arguing that companies had no economic interest in generating waste in their production or distribution processes, it shifted responsibility to the last link in the chain – the consumer. Yet the responsibility of each actor in the food supply chain cannot simply be measured as the share of total waste that they directly throw away. For example, a retailer – a supply chain actor in a position of strength – that returns an unwanted order to a supplier or that donates its unsold products to non-profit food assistance organizations at the last moment (and receives a tax rebate for it) generates little waste itself but transfers the waste upstream and downstream of its activity.

Are redistribution and recycling real solutions?

In France, the actors involved in the National Pact against Food Waste have institutionalized and formalized a 'hierarchy of uses for surplus food'. This hierarchy is inherited from European regulations on waste and recommends first reducing waste 'at the source' across all stages of the food supply chain and then reusing surpluses. Reuse should prioritize feeding humans (mainly through redistribution to food assistance non-profits), followed by feeding animals and lastly recycling. This implies repurposing surpluses to create organic matter and energy, namely through composting and biogas production. Food industry and distribution companies, as well as non-profits working with vulnerable populations, have linked their actions to combat waste to this hierarchy, which both benefits them financially and enhances their image.

First, industrial actors have worked on optimizing their food production, manufacturing, storage, packaging and transportation processes to minimize the losses as much as possible. Such developments were particularly recommended in countries where the infrastructure made it difficult to always ensure the sanitary quality of products (Gustavsson et al., 2011). In industrialized countries such as France, this form of waste prevention is driven by a 'managerial' approach, seeking economic efficiency throughout the food supply chain. It is based on technical and logistical adaptations, such as 'smart' packaging that incorporates electronic chips to improve flow and temperature management.

Another option to combat food waste is reusing food surpluses to feed vulnerable populations through food assistance. This activity is not new and has evolved since it was first institutionalized (Schneider, 2011). From the creation of the Fund for European Aid to the Most Deprived (FEAD) in 1987, agricultural intervention stocks (bought back from farmers to support prices) were redistributed to food aid non-profits. This mechanism was guided by the idea of a win–win process, matching unused supply with unmet demand: redistributing (over)production stabilizes both the quantities present on national markets and food prices while also contributing to the food security of vulnerable populations. In France, food assistance was thus coupled with agricultural surplus management policies. Non-profits fighting food insecurity also receive donations from food processing and distribution companies, which in return benefit from particularly high tax rebates in France. Even though the benefits for people who use food aid are debatable (Chapter 15), private actors receive not only social recognition but also financial support from the state. This raises a question: if producing surplus food has become morally and financially profitable, how can we encourage the most reasonable management of production and stock?

The bottom level of the surplus food hierarchy of uses is the transformation of human food surpluses and waste into animal feed, compost or energy. The wasted products thus become raw materials for new industries and new markets. Yet feeding uneaten, cooked ready-made meals to animals instead of raw products, for example, is in fact a form of waste. Likewise, uses that involve processing and transporting surpluses across long distances, particularly in the case of large-scale biogas production or composting infrastructure, are more costly environmentally. Furthermore, in order to make such infrastructure profitable and legitimize its existence, the actors developing these solutions have an interest in maintaining food surpluses rather than reducing them at the source.

A problem of overproduction

These different solutions, widely promoted in France by corporate social responsibility (CSR) departments, non-profits fighting food insecurity and new entrepreneurs involved in reuse or recycling, do not allow for the prevention of food waste in the long term. While they manage existing surpluses, very few structurally challenge the power relations, organizations and practices at the root of these surpluses (Mourad, 2016). On the contrary, redistribution and recycling solutions may even be favoured over reduction at the source, since they generate visible, concrete and measurable results (such as tonnes of waste avoided or the number of meals served to disadvantaged populations) to meet public policy objectives or CSR commitments. Prevention mechanisms, on the other hand, struggle to measure 'the absence of something' (Mourad, 2018). Each actor is ultimately free to align its actions against food waste with the recommendations stemming from the hierarchy of uses of food surpluses, and to derive financial, image or legitimacy benefits from them. This comes at the expense of structural change in the functioning of capitalist forms of organization (Boltanski and Chiapello, 2005).

The way in which these food system actors have engaged in multi-stakeholder initiatives to combat waste (such as the National Pact) has influenced the institutionalization of the subject. Through the weight of their interests in negotiations, some actors are able to directly or indirectly block pathways to preventing losses and waste at the source. Such pathways include fighting the overexploitation of natural resources in farming, challenging certain promotional offer practices in retail or even initiating a movement towards decreasing consumption. The fight against food waste in France did of course give rise to welcome (and even necessary) changes in the 2010s: the Garot law, the National Pact against Food Waste and, more recently, the law regulating relationships between food manufacturers, distributors and farmers (Egalim Law). These measures have had tangible results, insofar as the quantities of food thrown away seem to have decreased. However, changes to combat food waste must go further and be integrated into a comprehensive food system reform to avoid food overproduction.

Conclusion

Combating surplus production is a twofold challenge. First, it involves avoiding the unnecessary exploitation of natural resources and reducing the pollution associated with overproduction. Second, it requires a reduction of overconsumption, which leads to health problems and obesity. While better control of one's consumption allows eaters, on an individual level, to take their share of responsibility for reducing waste and to rethink the social and environmental value of food, this in no way means that individuals should be responsible for bringing about major change alone. In this sense, framing the problem in terms of overproduction – of which food waste is a consequence – would allow for a more balanced distribution of responsibilities between the actors (Chapter 18).

This chapter draws heavily on Nicolas Bricas's opinion piece 'Pourquoi faudrait-il lutter contre le gaspillage alimentaire?' (2018), published on the website of the UNESCO Chair in World Food Systems, and Marie Mourad's PhD research, published as 'De la poubelle à l'assiette: contre le gaspillage alimentaire. Dix ans de lutte en France et aux États-Unis' (2022).

The authors would like to thank Marie Walser for the synthesis of their works, which provided the initial framework for this chapter, and Damien Conaré and Mathilde Coudray for proofreading this chapter and for their suggested improvements.

References

Boltanski L., Chiapello È., 2005. *The new spirit of capitalism*, London/New York, Verso, 601 p. Translation of 'Le nouvel esprit du capitalisme' (1999).

Bricas N., 2018. Pourquoi faudrait-il lutter contre le gaspillage alimentaire ? Chaire Unesco Alimentations du monde – Opinions.

Bricas N., Daviron B., 2008. De la hausse des prix au retour du « productionnisme » agricole: les enjeux du Sommet sur la sécurité alimentaire de juin 2008 à Rome. *Hérodote*, 131(4): 31–39. https://doi.org/10.3917/her.131.0031

FAO, 2015. *Regional strategic framework: reducing food losses and waste in the Near East and North Africa Region*, Cairo, FAO, 16 p.

FAO, 2019. *The State of Food and Agriculture 2019, moving forward on food loss and waste reduction*, Rome, FAO, 158 p.

Gustavsson J., Cederberg C., Sonesson U., van Otterdijk R., Meybeck A., 2011. *Global food losses and food waste: extent, causes and prevention*, Rome, FAO, 29 p.

HLPE, 2014. *Food losses and waste in the context of sustainable food systems. A report by the High Level Panel of Experts on Food Security and Nutrition of the Committee on World Food Security*, Rome, HLPE, 117 p.

Income Consulting, AK2C, 2016. *Pertes et gaspillages alimentaires: l'état des lieux et leur gestion par étapes de la chaîne alimentaire*, Ademe, Income Consulting, AK2C, 164 p.

Jarrige F., Le Roux T., 2020. L'invention du gaspillage: métabolisme, déchets et histoire. *Écologie politique*, 60(1): 31–45. https://doi.org/10.3917/ecopo1.060.0031

Juhem P., 2001. La légitimation de la cause humanitaire: un discours sans adversaires. Mots. *Les langages du politique*, 65(1): 9–27. https://doi.org/10.3406/mots.2001.2484

Maslow A.H., 1943. A theory of human motivation. *Psychological Review*, 50(4): 370–396. https://doi.org/10.1037/h0054346

Mourad M., 2016. Recycling, recovering and preventing 'food waste': competing solutions for food systems sustainability in the United States and France. *Journal of Cleaner Production*, 126: 461–477. https://doi.org/10.1016/j.jclepro.2016.03.084

Mourad M., 2018. *La lutte contre le gaspillage alimentaire en France et aux États-Unis: mise en cause, mise en politique et mise en marché des excédents alimentaires*, thèse de doctorat, spécialité Sociologie, Institut d'études politiques de Paris, Paris.

Schneider F., 2011. The history of food wastage, in *Proceedings of the 3rd International Conference on Waste – The Social Context*, Edmonton.

Veblen T., 1899. *The theory of the leisure class: an economic study in the evolution of institutions*, New York, Macmillan, 400 p.

15

Food aid to fight food insecurity?

Pauline Scherer and Nicolas Bricas

While food aid is reserved for emergency situations at international level, in France it has become the main tool to fight food insecurity. Although this aid has an important social function, it has nonetheless been widely criticized for a number of reasons. This has led to experiments with other forms of solidarity based on greater food democracy.

Sharing or giving food to show solidarity with the most disadvantaged is a practice that has been documented since Antiquity. This form of family and neighbourhood solidarity supports people who are unable to meet their own needs: children, the elderly, the sick, the disabled or those in difficult situations. Beyond interpersonal relationships, this solidarity also takes on institutional forms through frameworks involving any or a combination of wealthy citizens, the state, religious groups, civil society organizations and, since the Second World War, international organizations (Clément, 2001). Relief, almsgiving, donations, charity, assistance or even food aid cannot be reduced to practices guided by pure generosity, with nothing in return.

For individuals, and depending on the era and society, giving increases one's social prestige and power, allows one to redeem one's sins or hope for divine support, and gives concrete expression to a desire to show solidarity or to reduce injustice. For private or public institutions, and here again depending on the era and society, organizing food aid can be a way to mitigate risks of uprising or migration that are difficult to manage, as well as a way to integrate beneficiaries into society, but also to dispose of production surpluses or open up new markets. But food aid has always been subject to criticism: the way it is implemented and the forms it takes raise questions about how society treats its poor.

From emergency food aid to budget support

Internationally, food aid developed as a way to address emergency situations: disasters, wars and massive population displacements. It relies on state or private company donations and is managed by humanitarian organizations such as the Red Cross or the United Nations World Food Programme (WFP). It takes on different forms depending on the context, from emergency aid, particularly in refugee camps, to food-for-work programmes.

International food aid has drawn criticism for the disruptive effects that free or subsidized food distribution can have on local markets, as well as the changes it can cause in eating habits, developing demand for foreign products and thereby generating food dependency. These criticisms led to the adoption of an international Food Assistance Convention in 2012 (Cuq, 2014). In particular, this convention encourages the purchase of local products rather than the use of surpluses from donor countries. It formalizes a practice that had been developing for a few years, particularly in the United States with the Supplemental Nutrition Assistance Program (the famous Food Stamp Program), aimed at providing monetary assistance to buy food rather than supplying food that is not always suited to local contexts. The WFP thus distinguishes between its former approach of providing food aid in the form of food donations, now mainly reserved for emergency situations, and its new 'food assistance' approach, which involves more or less conditional budget support for individuals.

This evolution reflects a desire to offer food-insecure people the possibility to choose what they want to eat and not be imposed what they receive. In Europe, and particularly in France, this shift remains very timid, and food aid is still the dominant form of food solidarity.

Rising food insecurity in France

In countries that do not suffer from food shortages, not having access to enough food of sufficient quality is a matter of lack of economic resources at individual level and relates to a problem of poverty (Clément, 2001). In France, in 2018, according to the National Institute of Statistics and Economic Studies (INSEE), 9.3 million people, or 14.8 per cent of the population, were living below the monetary poverty line, defined here as 1,063 euros per month. In April 2020, the country's Directorate General for Social Cohesion estimated that 8 million people lived in households that identified as food insecure for financial reasons.

According to the General Inspectorate for Social Affairs (IGAS), food aid was distributed to 5.5 million people in 2019 (Le Morvan and Wanecq, 2019). This figure only reveals part of the problem, as it does not account for the number of food-insecure people who, for various reasons, do not use food aid. Since 2020 and the COVID-19 crisis, part of the population has seen its income decline. This deteriorating situation has translated into increased demand for food aid, as reported by several non-profit organizations, such as the food banks and the Secours Populaire (CNA, 2021).

Food insecurity is however not limited to a lack of means. Approached through a social lens, it is characterized by processes that cause individuals to feel disaffected (Castel, 1991) and degraded (Paugam, 1991) and can lead to various forms of exclusion. This is evidenced by the difficulties that individuals in vulnerable situations face in accessing the labour market and decent working conditions (job insecurity). Exclusion affects groups of individuals suffering from different forms of economic and social vulnerability, such as single-parent families, large families, students, the elderly, the working poor and refugees, but also the middle classes whose living conditions have deteriorated in recent years. While some situations are accidental and temporary, a significant share of this vulnerability has become structurally embedded in society. French public institutions and actors in the field of social work thus speak of 'food precarity'. This term differs from 'food insecurity' in that it equally encompasses the issue of social ties central to processes of exclusion and that of unequal access to food (Paturel, 2018).

A social support function

Food aid was initially managed by the public authorities (through municipal distribution points or free meals in restaurants). In the twentieth century, however, civil society gradually became involved (Retière and Le Crom, 2018). Since the mid-1980s and the explosion of unemployment in France, civil society organizations have taken over from the state – which has struggled to tackle the root causes of precariousness – by distributing meal parcels, vouchers, unprepared foodstuffs and meals to the most disadvantaged (Clément, 2001). The effectiveness of food aid, owed to its strong institutional roots and dense national coverage, means that it can rapidly benefit a large number of vulnerable people and thus meet an obvious moral imperative: 'to give food to all those who are hungry', to quote an expression attributed to the famous French comedian

Coluche. Moreover, through their commitment to the most disadvantaged, the volunteers of non-profits play an important role in maintaining social ties. During food distributions, they meet the 'beneficiaries', chat with them and help them with their non-food needs, providing them with various types of information, assisting them in administrative procedures or simply listening. According to Philippe Sassier (1990), giving is a form of attention to others that creates social ties and therefore differs from the aid provided by the state. With the COVID-19 crisis, this social function of aid was jeopardised, as volunteers found themselves overwhelmed by distributions and struggled to provide other forms of support.

Food aid thus appears to constitute an essential mechanism for meeting the food needs of individuals with limited economic resources, especially in times of crisis. Nevertheless, this system has been called into question, insofar as it does not address the root causes of precariousness – it was not initially intended to do so – and its operating methods can steer towards forms of aid that are degrading for the beneficiaries.

An adjustment variable of the industrialized food system?

In Europe, food aid became institutionalized from 1987, with the European Union Food Distribution Programme for the Most Deprived Persons (MDP). Backed by the Common Agricultural Policy (CAP), this programme made agricultural raw materials from EU intervention stocks (cereals, milk powder, sugar etc.) available to Member States. Agricultural surpluses, which until then had been stored or destroyed to support prices and ensure adequate income for farmers, could be bought through a public intervention process. This provided a response to the growing challenges of food insecurity while maintaining the stability required on agricultural markets, which had become internationalized.

It is important to note that products from European intervention stocks were not redistributed as such. In France, raw materials were traded for finished products through public tenders with food manufacturers. The foodstuffs collected were then distributed to those in need. Thus, although the social goal of food aid was evident, it was initially organized as an adjustment variable for agricultural (over)production and the agri-food industry. On an international level, emergency food aid served the commercial interests of agricultural-exporting countries by providing a 'gateway' to new markets, sometimes leading to dumping by creating competition between emergency food aid and local production (Pinaud, 2016).

Due to the decrease in European intervention stocks, in 2014 the MDP was replaced with the Fund for European Aid to the Most Deprived (FEAD), on which food aid funding now partly relies. In France, the main vehicle for public support to fight food insecurity is the set of tax breaks available to companies and individuals for donations made to non-profit food aid organizations (Le Morvan and Wanecq, 2019). These financial incentives to donate, which have existed since the 1980s, were reinforced in the 2000s. Since 2010, due to the coupling of the fight against food insecurity and food waste within the framework of the food aid system,[1] food donations have further increased, particularly with the introduction of the Garot law (2016) and, subsequently, the ordinance of 21 October 2019 (in application of Article 15 of the Egalim Law). These laws require companies to sign agreements with authorized non-profit organizations to distribute their unsold food and thus reduce food waste.

This coupling anchors food aid in an industry 'that does not speak its name' and that relies on the long supply chains of the agroindustrial system to source agri-food products, with several consequences that are worth highlighting. First, food aid tends to encourage the exploitation of surpluses rather than their reduction (Chapter 14). It even facilitates their management, since products that are nearing their use-by date are now given to food aid non-profits, which thus become responsible for managing the food that can no longer be distributed because it has expired. Not only do supermarkets no longer have to manage unsold products, but they also benefit from tax breaks as a result.

Second, food aid fails to establish territorial cohesion between local producers' supply and the demand of eaters in vulnerable situations, and instead favours long supply chains which, on the surface, are cheaper and have better-organized logistics:[2] logistical constraints drive non-profits to turn to the largest organizations rather than multiple smaller ones. The system thus tends to favour the largest players.

Finally, the tax break is not targeted based on the products supplied: this leads to an imbalance in the range of products received, with a prevalence of long-life processed foods at the expense of fresh products. As a result of these constraints, food aid is often deemed to be of insufficient nutritional quality (Darmon et al., 2020), which can worsen health situations already made fragile by recipients' living conditions.

---

[1] In 2016, the website of the Ministry of Agriculture, Food and Forestry stated that 'food aid both addresses social justice issues and contributes to the fight against food waste'.
[2] Ibid.

A degrading and moralizing framework?

For the past thirty years, French political discourse has tended to emphasize the individual responsibility of those in precarious situations. So-called welfare approaches are often denounced as being too costly and unable to sufficiently motivate individuals to take action to improve their situation (Chemin, 2017). From this individualizing perspective, people in precarious situations are considered in terms of deficits: of means, of skills, of will and so on. Such social representations weigh on these individuals and conceal the multiple steps they take to fight food insecurity (including resorting to food aid but not only): restricting consumption (particularly in the case of mothers prioritizing their children), establishing a hierarchy of spending, fragmenting purchases to avoid having stocks at home that are difficult to control, choosing products that are primarily filling and cutting out 'treats', identifying special offers requiring high mobility, choosing specific (discount) shops, preparing food at home and turning down invitations and avoiding restaurants (Masullo and Dupuy, 2012).

Although taking up food aid appears to be indispensable when the tactics implemented are no longer enough, it is generally not experienced positively. Many accounts reveal the degrading feeling that comes from resorting to food aid (Ramel et al., 2016). Moreover, the food aid received is not always enough or suited to the recipients' needs. When the products come from individual donations, collected at the doors of supermarkets, for example, they are often the cheapest products, of poor culinary or taste quality; donors implicitly consider that quantity should be prioritized over quality. The products may also simply not meet the customs (e.g. cultural practices) or preferences (e.g. tastes) of the beneficiaries.

Thus, individuals in precarious situations are not entirely free to use the aid they receive as they wish, at the risk of exposing themselves to a form of moral judgement. First, they are expected to take 'what there is' or, rather, 'what is left'. Second, what they receive 'belongs' to society, which intends to define its proper use (Colombi, 2020). There is claimed to be a hierarchy of needs to follow (Maslow, 1943), according to which biological needs, the most vital, must first be met before attending to those deemed less fundamental, such as the need for belonging, esteem or self-actualization. Thus, beneficiaries are expected to use food first and foremost to address their health needs, which are considered a priority precisely because they are more fragile, even if the food offered does not suit their habits or tastes. This primary focus on the health of the poor is also reflected in the dissemination of top–down information on nutritional quality and how to prepare products, the relevance of which has been challenged given its potentially infantilizing nature (Le Morvan and Wanecq, 2019).

The 'horse lasagne' case offers a good illustration in this regard. After these lasagnes were withdrawn from the market for misleading consumers (they were sold as beef lasagnes), they were offered to food aid organizations on the grounds that they presented no health or nutritional risk, that no one had noticed a difference in taste and that it was important not to waste. If the product became unworthy of consumption by anyone, it could still be consumed by the poor, thus denying their right to eat like everyone else and depriving them of their dignity.

In summary, critics of food aid stress its consequences on health (deficiencies, malnutrition), socialization and self-esteem (loss of dignity, parental guilt). In fact, once minimum nutritional needs are met and hunger is quelled, other needs, especially the need for belonging and social interaction, become crucial. As a Senegalese proverb says, 'the poor are not those who have nothing, but those who have no one'. Eating like everyone else, that is, what everyone else eats, is fundamental, even if not all nutritional needs are met, as shown in refugee camps (Reed and Habbicht, 1998) and, more broadly, in the case of food aid in severely food-insecure countries (Barrett and Maxwell, 2007).

It is important to note that the strong sectorization of aid through places and frameworks 'dedicated to the poor' further exacerbates the stigmatization of 'beneficiaries'. Likewise, the mode of functioning and the training of volunteers in food aid organizations have also been challenged. This is not to stigmatize these individuals in turn, nor to question their generosity and willingness to help, but to highlight the social relations and the relations of domination at work in society that inevitably play out in these spaces, and which can further contribute to recipients feeling degraded.

Towards new forms of food solidarity

As it stands, food aid does not generally promote people's dignity, citizenship and autonomy. It would thus benefit from shifting towards a more horizontal way of operating, capable of implementing forms of 'food justice' (Gottlieb and Joshi, 2010). Beyond the transformation of food aid, fighting food insecurity therefore involves developing new forms of solidarity. In France, these are enshrined in the *Code de l'action sociale et des familles* (Social Action and Family Code), which emphasizes emancipation, autonomy, social change, citizenship and the involvement of the persons concerned. Food solidarity can be rethought in light of these principles, in line with currents promoting social intervention in the collective interest to escape the biases of individualization (which is now largely prevalent in social work). If these are collective problems, the solutions must also be collective and inclusive in order to restore or foster individuals' agency. Based on this perspective, alternative ways of fighting food insecurity are multiplying in France, particularly within certain civil society networks, as well as among more activist and self-managed initiatives.

The fight against food insecurity must place the issue of the right to food at the centre to its thinking. This right, recognized by international law, is the right of every human being to feed themselves with dignity, whether by producing their own food or by buying it. Olivier De Schutter, the United Nations Special Rapporteur on the right to food from 2008 to 2014, defines this right as 'the right to have regular, permanent and unrestricted access, either directly or by means of financial purchases, to quantitatively and qualitatively adequate and sufficient food corresponding to the cultural traditions of the people to which the consumer belongs, and which ensure a physical and mental, individual and collective, fulfilling and dignified life free of fear'. Although citizens' demands and initiatives surrounding food are multiplying as part of a movement known as 'food democracy' (Paturel and Ndiaye, 2020), research has shown the difficulty of articulating these emancipation movements with social justice issues, thereby sidelining the most economically fragile populations to the benefit of those with high social capital. The question of democracy therefore appears to be crucial for reflecting on access to food for people in precarious situations (Paturel and Ramel, 2017) but also for thinking about and promoting equal access to sustainable food for all, upstream of food aid.

Since the law for balanced trade relations in the agricultural and food sector and healthy, sustainable food accessible to all, known as the 'Egalim Law' (2018), the subject has started to be addressed politically through bodies, programmes and frameworks dedicated to the fight against food insecurity, with a view to ensuring access to quality food. However, these frameworks are often limited to food aid modernization processes (Paturel and Bricas, 2019). They are certainly necessary but not sufficient. Changing the way we respond to the problem of food insecurity is a necessity and is one of the levers likely to influence the evolution of food systems, economic models, modes of social intervention and social protection mechanisms.

Conclusion

Inequalities in access to food and the food insecurity to which they give rise thus appear to be a complex problem, which ought to be approached in connection with various issues: the right to food, the evolution of the food system towards greater sustainability, the reduction of inequalities and access to income, modes of social intervention and social protection frameworks and citizens' participation and democracy. Fighting food insecurity therefore involves mechanisms to restore people's freedom to choose, in socially mixed settings that do not stigmatize them and reintegrate them into the life of neighbourhoods or villages, where food is approached as a medium for relationships and not just as a source of nutrients. For example, community food centres are emerging in Canada and France. They are managed by local residents and combine various group purchasing, grocery and catering facilities with easy and solidaristic access to food chosen collectively. They also allow people to learn food-related trades, gardening and cooking. Food social security, a credit system for all allowing access to democratically chosen products financed through social contributions (Chapter 22), is also an avenue under consideration for the implementation of a true right to sustainable food (Paturel and Ndiaye, 2020). These new forms of solidarity could lead to food aid becoming a marginal supplement reserved for emergency situations only.

The authors would like to thank Damien Conaré, Mathilde Coudray and Marie Walser for proofreading this chapter and for their suggested improvements.

References

Barrett C.B., Maxwell D., 2007. *Food aid after fifty years: recasting its role*, London, Routledge, 337 p.

Castel R., 1991. De l'indigence à l'exclusion, la désaffiliation, in Donzelot J. (éd.), *Face à l'exclusion, le modèle français*, Paris, éditions Esprit, 137–168.

Chemin A., 2017. Le « cancer » de l'assistanat: origine d'un préjugé. *Le Monde*, 26 octobre 2017.

Clément A., 2001. De l'évergétisme antique aux Restos du cœur: État et associations dans l'histoire du secours alimentaire. *RECMA*, 279(1): 26–43. https://doi.org/10.7202/1023752ar

CNA, 2021. *Retour d'expérience de la crise Covid-19. Période du premier confinement national*, Paris, Conseil national de l'alimentation, 113 p.

Colombi D., 2020. *Où va l'argent des pauvres: fantasmes politiques, réalités sociologiques*, Paris, Payot, 348 p.

Cuq M., 2014. La Convention de 2012 relative à l'assistance alimentaire: une avancée pour l'aide et le développement en faveur d'un accès à une alimentation adéquate ?, in Collard-Dutilleul F., Bréger T. (ed.), *Penser une démocratie alimentaire*, San José, INIDA, 413–421.

Darmon N., Gomy C., Saïdi-Kabeche D., 2020. La crise du Covid-19 met en lumière la nécessaire remise en cause de l'aide alimentaire. *The Conversation.*

Gottlieb R., Joshi A., 2010. *Food justice*, Cambridge/London, MIT Press, 304 p.

Le Morvan F., Wanecq T., 2019. *La lutte contre la précarité alimentaire. Évolution du soutien public à une politique sociale, agricole et de santé publique*, Paris, Inspection générale des affaires sociales, 142 p.

Maslow A.H., 1943. A theory of human motivation. *Psychological Review*, 50(4): 370–396. https://doi.org/10.1037/h0054346

Masullo A., Dupuy A., 2012. *Représentations et stratégies alimentaires des personnes en situation de précarité* (lettre scientifique n° 4, conférence du 14 février 2012), FFAS.

Paturel D., 2018. Insécurité alimentaire et/ou précarité alimentaire, démocratie alimentaire . . . de quoi parle-t-on ? *Journal Resolis*, 19: 13–14.

Paturel D., Bricas N., 2019. Rethinking our food solidarity commitments. *So What? A collection of the Unesco Chair in World Food Systems*, (9): 4 p.

Paturel D., Ndiaye P. (ed.), 2020. *Le droit à l'alimentation durable en démocratie*, Nîmes, Champ social éditions, 238 p.

Paturel D., Ramel M., 2017. Éthique du *care* et démocratie alimentaire: les enjeux du droit à une alimentation durable. *Revue française d'éthique appliquée*, 4(2): 49–60. https://doi.org/10.3917/rfeap.004.0049

Paugam S., 1991. *La disqualification sociale: essai sur la nouvelle pauvreté*, Paris, PUF, 254 p.

Pinaud S., 2020. Genèse et fragilité de l'aide alimentaire, in Naulin S., Steiner P. (ed.), *La solidarité à distance: quand le don passe par les organisations*, Toulouse, PUM, 49–81.

Ramel M., Boissonnat Pelsy H., Sibué-De Caigny C., Zimmer M.-F., 2016. *Se nourrir lorsqu'on est pauvre. Analyse et ressenti de personnes en situation de précarité*, Montreuil, ATD Quart Monde, 187 p.

Reed B.A., Habicht J.-P., 1998. Sales of food aid as sign of distress, not excess. *Lancet*, 351(9096): 128–130. https://doi.org/10.1016/S0140-6736(97)06329-0

Retière J.-N., Le Crom J.-P., 2018. *Une solidarité en miettes. Socio-histoire de l'aide alimentaire des années 1930 à nos jours*, Rennes, PUR, 313 p.

Sassier P., 1990. *Du bon usage des pauvres. Histoire d'un thème politique: XVIe–XXe siècles*, Paris, Éditions Fayard, 450 p.

16

Should we return to cooking and 'homemade' food?

Anindita Dasgupta, Hayat Zirari, Nicolas Bricas,
Marie Walser and Audrey Soula

Home cooking has many cultural and health benefits. Nevertheless, it remains a relatively undervalued daily task that is largely shouldered by women. The commercialization of 'homemade' dishes presents interesting opportunities in this regard.

Around the world, the development of the agri-food industry and mass retailing has led to the growing use of processed products in everyday food practices. Despite the benefits of these products, which last longer and make cooking easier, some have been severely criticized, particularly for nutritional reasons. Processed foods often have higher sugar, fat and salt content and are lower in fibre and micronutrients. They may also contain various flavouring, colouring, preservative and texture additives that are suspected of being harmful to health. This is particularly the case with so-called ultra-processed foods – in other words, foods produced through a series of industrial processes (Monteiro et al., 2019; Chapters 6 and 7) – which are thought to contribute to the rise in obesity and non-communicable diseases such as type 2 diabetes or cardiovascular disease (Monteiro et al., 2010; Lawrence and Baker, 2019). The giant agri-food companies that distribute standardized industrial products worldwide (breakfast cereals, powdered milk, refined oils and sugar, biscuits, crisps, hamburgers, flavour cubes, sodas etc.) have been accused of homogenizing food (Ritzer's 'McDonaldization', 1992) and threatening the diversity of artisanal or local products. The 'artificial' nature of processed foods in turn raises the question of the 'naturalness' of food items (Lepiller, 2012). The increasing use of food packaging and overwrap involves energy consumption and generates plastic pollution in particular (Ritchie and Roser, 2018). This critique is not limited to academic circles. It has been widely conveyed by the media and taken up by local actors challenging the power and opacity of large agri-food companies more generally, including in countries where industrialization is still recent, such as Morocco (Zirari, 2020).

The return of homemade food?

In several parts of the world, this rejection of industrial food products has resulted in a new cooking craze driven by a desire to consume freshly prepared dishes made from raw or minimally processed foods. Domestic cooking (or 'homemade' food), which can be perceived very differently depending on the context (Mazzonetto et al., 2020), is embedded in a positive imaginary that holds it in particularly high regard (Daniels et al., 2012). First, homemade food is considered to be of better nutritional and taste quality than industrial preparations (Mathé and Hébel, 2015). Being able to control the nature and origin of ingredients, along with the naturalness associated with the preparation process, helps soothe the anxieties inherent in food intake (Fischler, 1990). Moreover, various studies in the field of nutrition suggest a positive influence of home cooking on health (Larson et al., 2006; Reicks et al., 2014; Mills et al., 2017; Wolfson et al., 2020).

Homemade food also serves a cultural function for eaters. Through culinary work, family or community traditions are passed on and reinvented. In Morocco, 'handmade' food made 'at home' immediately anchors eaters in their food and culinary tradition (Soula and Zirari, 2023). Similarly, in multi-ethnic societies such as Malaysia, homemade food gives expression to the traditional culinary repertoire and allows for regularly reaffirming one's cultural roots in a rapidly urbanizing society. Taste plays a role in this process of identity, grounding eaters in a family, local or national culture. From a social point of view, cooking provides a way of connecting with others and showing them care (Mazzonetto et al., 2020). It is also a cement of family life in shared imaginaries (Plumauzille and Rossigneux-Méheust, 2019). In the United States, for example, homemade food is central to the idealized moment of sharing a family dinner (Bowen et al., 2019). For the cook, the work involved can be a source of satisfaction – the satisfaction of taking care of oneself, of others and of one's health and well-being – and can give them the pleasure of 'doing it yourself'. Finally, home cooking may be popular for economic reasons: it is common to hear that it is cheaper to cook at home than to buy pre-prepared food in shops or restaurants. This argument, which especially held true in the past when families were often large, is still valid today and may particularly resonate with lower- or middle-class families.

Tedious work

There are therefore many benefits associated with home cooking, linked to the different dimensions of food. However, one question often remains unaddressed: How do we organize ourselves to cook? As a domestic task, cooking consists of a long series of more or less planned steps that are carried out almost daily: stocktaking, food shopping, meal planning, food preparation, serving meals, clearing up and doing the dishes. Cooking at home involves managing resources according to multiple and sometimes contradictory constraints such as the household budget, time availability, guests' preferences and available ingredients. Moreover, this work requires skills that confer social recognition. In Morocco, for example, the cook is valued for her manual dexterity, which endows her with recognized expertise. Likewise, in Malaysia, sourcing and cooking fresh local produce from the *pasar malam* (night market) or the *pasar tani* (farmers' market), avoiding waste and maintaining a certain frugality are qualities valued by the family.

Approaching home cooking through the prism of domestic work, however, reveals two things. First, the economic cost of home cooking is often overlooked. If homemade food were given a financial value, taking the cost of labour into account, it could become more beneficial to buy industrial products than to cook oneself (Tharrey et al., 2018). It is worth noting that on a global scale, the economic value of all domestic activities (including cooking) is estimated to reach 13 per cent of the planet's GDP (McKinsey Global Institute, 2015). Most importantly, this domestic work still largely falls on women. In patriarchal societies, the norm of a gendered division of roles continues to assign women a reproductive and nurturing role and makes them responsible for cooking-related tasks. In 2010 in France, 82 per cent of women reported cooking on a daily basis compared with 47 per cent of men (Ricroch, 2012). And in 2011 in Morocco, the national 'Time Use' survey revealed that cooking is an activity neglected by men: across all socio-professional categories, men in urban areas spend only five minutes a day on cooking (three minutes in rural areas), compared with two hours and twenty-six minutes for women (three hours and five minutes in rural areas) (Haut-Commissariat au Plan, 2019).

The kitchen as a prism through which to analyse gender relations

Domestic cooking is generally seen as an intergenerational female activity involving mothers, daughters and grandmothers, while the supply of ingredients can be carried out by men following the women's instructions. But the actual daily preparation of meals is managed by the women of the household, possibly with the help of other women (from their family network or neighbourhood or under their employ). In fact, socially, women used to be – and to some extent still are – judged on their cooking skills, with their ability to manage meals and please their husbands deemed to reflect their value as 'model women'. While men may also decide to cook on their own initiative, this is usually for exceptional occasions in collective and community life.

As the ones in charge of cooking, women shoulder a heavy mental load, which they often carry alone. Cooking is not just about what happens in the kitchen (Counihan, 1999; Dupuy, 2017; Haicault, 1984); it involves thinking, planning, managing the supply and stocks of food as well as cooking energy and utensils, setting the table, serving the food, clearing the table, cleaning up and managing waste. When repeated daily, these tasks can be experienced as a strain. Domestic cooking, which is centred on caring for others (mainly children, husbands and the elderly), forces women to make trade-offs between what they should do and what they aspire to be. They are torn between the responsibility of having to cook at home according to the preferences and needs of different family members, and the desire to relieve themselves of this routine duty. In Morocco, while men living alone learn to cook for themselves, once they are married, they often relegate this task to their wives, who tend to be perceived as the guardians of a culinary tradition to which they are attached. They thus sustain an idealized image of the cuisine of the past, home cooking and their mother's cooking (Zirari, 2020).

At present, women are seeking to highlight the mental load they carry. Some are also striving to free themselves from the nurturing role they have been assigned, while others are seeking greater equity through the reconfiguration of this role. The last few decades have witnessed significant changes in social structures, forms of family organization and the distribution of gendered attributes in many countries around the world. Urbanization in particular has increased women's access to paid work and has enabled them to gain economic and financial autonomy. Likewise, young girls are increasingly attending school. In urban households, women are therefore generally less available and willing to take on cooking activities in addition to the other domestic tasks for which they are responsible. This is especially the case given that, while eating at home is often still the norm, the growing range of places where food is prepared and served in cities offers new options that families are integrating into their food practices. In order to alleviate the daily burden of managing the cooking, women are taking advantage of changing social norms to renegotiate responsibility for cooking in two ways.

The first is through the redistribution of cooking work: in the home, couples increasingly share this work (though not always equitably). While women are still responsible for cooking, men are more willing to help out, and some show a moderate but explicit interest in cooking – for the pleasure of it, to discover, create, innovate with or try out recipes (Zirari et al., forthcoming). It is also a way of gaining recognition, of presenting oneself as a 'modern' man in keeping with the times as cooking has come to be held in such high regard in the media.

Second, women are renegotiating responsibility for the management of meals by minimizing the amount of cooking work involved: in industrialized societies, cooking work can be reduced or even outsourced, particularly owing to the various opportunities afforded by urban life. This burden can be lightened by introducing changes in the management of meals – for instance, simplifying meals, freezing leftovers for later use or hiring help. It is important to note that delegating cooking to domestic workers or young girls from the countryside – who are housed and fed in the city in exchange for their domestic work – reflects a shift in inequalities. It is often still women, possibly from lower social classes, who remain in charge of cooking. This work can also be outsourced to canteens, street food vendors or restaurants. As the standard of living in cities has risen, a wide range of restaurants has developed, providing access to a variety of foods that cater to many diets, are often inexpensive and are perceived as quality foods. It should be noted that for women, eating at friends' homes or with family – whether at restaurants or from street vendors – provides temporary or occasional respite from cooking duties.

While cooking practices and gender relations are evolving, these changes remain slow. The forced return to domestic cooking caused by the lockdowns and restaurant closures due to the COVID-19 pandemic does not seem to have led to a real redefinition of the gendered division of labour. In Morocco, although gender relations remained largely unchanged during the periods of lockdown, with the majority of women still forced to take care of all the food and meal preparation, new male practices surrounding cooking nevertheless emerged, particularly disseminated through social media (Zirari et al., 2022). Conversely, Malaysian women who had enjoyed a certain degree of freedom from cooking activities were once again called upon to become the guardians of the domestic space (Dasgupta and Mognard, 2020). Homemade food remains highly valued in Malaysian society, even though, according to the Malaysian Food Barometer published in 2014, the country has perhaps one of the world's highest rates of food consumption outside the home, closely associated with urbanization (Poulain et al., 2015, 2020).

Turning cooking work into an activity with economic value

Strikingly, messages encouraging people to prioritize cooking over processed foods often implicitly refer to domestic cooking, in both senses of the term: as home cooking and as a form of non-market work. Certainly, some may see the entry of meal preparation into the market sphere as a victory for the commodification of the world. Catering has indeed become a new sector of interest to investors, particularly with the development of digital tools. As internet access and smartphones have become widespread, especially in cities, remote ordering has become easier. Delivery companies and some restaurant chains are now investing in activities limited to the preparation of dishes made to order, with micro-kitchens in containers or basements dedicated to the production of a single speciality, known as 'dark', 'virtual', 'cloud' or 'ghost' kitchens.

This commodification of cooking, however, also takes on other, less 'industrial' forms. Of interest here is the commodification of domestic cooking to change gender relations surrounding cooking activities. In some African cities, for example, practices involving the sale of additional servings prepared as part of family meals have existed for decades: women who cook at home sell portions of surplus food to 'subscribers' (single people, rural people who have come to the city for a few months etc.). People 'subscribe' for a fixed period of time to receive a 'family' dish every day. They can either collect and take away the dish, have it delivered by a child of the family or come and eat it on the spot, often with other subscribers. This practice enables families to reduce the cost of their food and gives consumers access to family-style cooking at a very reasonable price. This practice also exists in Brazil and is developing thanks to social media. The dishes offered by families are listed on websites where they can be ordered in advance for collection. The families buy the ingredients semi-wholesale and therefore at lower prices and save energy by cooking in relatively large quantities. Customers are freed from the mental burden of having to organize and cook meals, and they are able to access varied dishes, which can include regional culinary specialities or cater to nutritional or environmental concerns (light, meat-free, organic etc.). The prices are also attractive, as the meals cost the same as self-prepared ones or are even cheaper.

In Asia, the sale of homemade food available for pre-order online is on the rise. This trend is driven not by a strategy of selling 'surplus' food but by home-based microenterprises that promote themselves on social media. However, in the absence of formal hygiene regulations and independent checks, these informal arrangements can be suspected of being unsafe – an argument often used by industrial companies and consumer groups. Confidence in the quality of the food in fact relies on interpersonal relationships and the reputation of the cooks, whether recommended by word of mouth or through satisfaction ratings on social media.

The women behind these microenterprises delegate the cooking to domestic workers whom they house and feed or pay, to friends or relatives who have spare time and whom they remunerate, or to reputable restaurants in the neighbourhood. Alternatively, they may also sell additional servings cooked as part of their family meals. In all cases, this indeed constitutes a commodification of domestic cooking. The recognition of the know-how, mental workload and labour involved is no longer merely social and symbolic; it becomes economic. As a result, it changes gender relations. First, it contributes to increasing women's economic and financial autonomy and, through the income generated, gives recognition to work that was previously invisible (Abarca, 2007). Second, as the activity becomes lucrative and moves beyond the purely domestic sphere, this commodification can potentially help redefine the gendered boundaries of economic spaces. Men are entering the catering business, just as they did with the mechanization and motorization of other household tasks traditionally performed by women, such as husking and grinding grains and pressing oils. Conversely, some women are becoming involved in cooking activities previously dominated by men, such as grilling meat (Boubakar-Akali, 2020). When commodified cooking moves out of the home to become a commercial activity, women's behaviour can resemble that previously 'symbolically' associated with men, to the point that these small traders are referred to as 'male women', as in Abidjan, Côte d'Ivoire (Egnankou, 2020).

Conclusion

By providing access to dishes that not only promote food cultures but also offer an alternative to industrial food, which is not always healthy, and to potentially expensive catered food, the commodification of domestic cooking produces interesting effects. Furthermore, this commodification enables the women who engage in it to derive benefits from their cooking, especially financial ones. However, it is important to bear in mind that by remaining assigned to culinary work, women remain tied to functions that are given little value, taken for granted and still largely invisible. Therefore, beyond the opportunities offered by the commodification of domestic cooking, challenging this assignment of roles remains a priority.

This chapter partly draws on the three symposia on the theme of 'Eating in the City' organized by CIRAD and the UNESCO Chair in World Food Systems.

The authors would like to thank Damien Conaré, Mathilde Coudray and Tristan Fournier for proofreading this chapter and for their suggested improvements.

References

Abarca M.E., 2007. Charlas culinarias: Mexican women speak from their public kitchens. *Food and Foodways*, 15(3–4): 183–212. https://doi.org/10.1080/07409710701620094

Boubacar-Akali H., 2020. Hommes et femmes dans la transformation de la viande à Niamey: une activité traditionnellement masculine contestée par les femmes, in Symposium international « Manger dans les villes d'Afrique, d'Amérique latine et d'Asie », 3e édition « Genre et alimentation à l'épreuve de la vie urbaine », 30/09 et 01/10/2020, Paris, Cirad, MoISA/Chaire Unesco Alimentations du monde.

Bowen S., Brenton J., Elliott S., 2019. *Pressure cooker: why home cooking won't solve our problems and what we can do about it*, New York, Oxford University Press, 353 p.

Counihan C., 1999. *The anthropology of food and body: gender, meaning, and power*, New York/London, Routledge, 256 p.

Daniels S., Glorieux I., Minnen J., van Tienoven T.P., 2012. More than preparing a meal? Concerning the meanings of home cooking. *Appetite*, 58(3): 1050–1056. https://doi.org/10.1016/j.appet.2012.02.040

Dasgupta A., Mognard E., 2020. Mother can try new recipes for their families: COVID-19 lockdown in Malaysia, a lens on the changing gender relations within food ways, in Symposium international « Manger dans les villes d'Afrique, d'Amérique latine et d'Asie », 3e édition « Genre et alimentation à l'épreuve de la vie urbaine », 30/09 et 01/10/2020, Paris, Cirad, MoISA/Chaire Unesco Alimentations du monde.

Dupuy A., 2017. La division sexuelle du travail alimentaire: qu'est-ce qui change ?, in Dubet F. (ed.), *Que manger ? Normes et pratiques alimentaires*, Paris, La Découverte, 164–179.

Egnankou A.P., 2020. Femmes-mâles et jeux de pouvoir par l'alimentation à Abidjan, in Symposium international « Manger dans les villes d'Afrique, d'Amérique latine et d'Asie », 3e édition « Genre et alimentation à l'épreuve de la vie urbaine », 30/09 et 01/10/2020, Paris, Cirad, MoISA/Chaire Unesco Alimentations du monde.

Fischler C., 1990. *L'homnivore*, Paris, Odile Jacob, 448 p.

Haicault M., 1984. La gestion ordinaire de la vie en deux. *Sociologie du travail*, 26(3): 268–277. https://doi.org/10.3406/sotra.1984.2072

Haut-Commissariat au Plan, 2019. *Enquête nationale sur l'emploi du temps des Marocains 2012*. Tableaux statistiques, Rabat, 59 p.

Larson N.I., Perry C.L., Story M., Neumark-Sztainer D., 2006. Food preparation by young adults is associated with better diet quality. *Journal of the American Dietetic Association*, 106(12): 2001–2007. https://doi.org/10.1016/j.jada.2006.09.008

Lawrence M.A., Baker P.I., 2019. Ultra-processed food and adverse health outcomes. *BMJ* 365: l2289. https://doi.org/10.1136/bmj.l2289

Lepiller O., 2012. *Critiques de l'alimentation industrielle et valorisations du naturel: sociologie historique d'une « digestion » difficile (1968–2010)*, thèse de doctorat, spécialité Sociologie, Université de Toulouse II-Le Mirail, Toulouse, 713 p.

Mathé T., Hebel P., 2015. *Le plaisir du cuisiné maison: pour le goût et la qualité*, Paris, Credoc, 4 p. https://doi.org/10.13140/RG.2.1.4439.7929

Mazzonetto A.C., Dean M., Fiates G.M.R., 2020. Perceptions about home cooking: an integrative review of qualitative studies. *Ciencia & Saúde Coletiva*, 25(11): 4559–4571. https://doi.org/10.1590/1413-812320202511.01352019

McKinsey Global Institute, 2015. *The power of parity: how advancing women's equality can add $12 trillion to global growth*, McKinsey Global Institute, 156 p.

Mills S., Brown H., Wrieden W., White M., Adams J., 2017. Frequency of eating home cooked meals and potential benefits for diet and health: cross-sectional analysis of a population based cohort study. *International Journal of Behavioral Nutrition and Physical Activity*, 14(1): 109. https://doi.org/10.1186/s12966-017-0567-y

Monteiro C.A., Cannon G., Levy R.B., Moubarac J.-C., Louzada M.L., Rauber F. et al., 2019. Ultraprocessed foods: what they are and how to identify them. *Public Health Nutrition*, 22(5): 936–941. https://doi.org/10.1017/S1368980018003762

Monteiro C.A., Levy R.B., Claro R.M., Castro I.R.R., de, Cannon G., 2010. Increasing consumption of ultra-processed foods and likely impact on human health: evidence from Brazil. *Public Health Nutrition*, 14(1): 5–13. https://doi.org/10.1017/S1368980010003241

Plumauzille C., Rossigneux-Méheust M., 2019. Le *care*, une « voix différente » pour l'histoire du genre. Clio. *Femmes, Genre, Histoire*, 49: 7–22. https://doi.org/10.4000/clio.16058

Poulain J.P., Laporte C., Tibere L., Mognard E., Ari Ragavan N., Zadeh A., Ismail M., 2020. Malaysian Food Barometer (MFB): a study of the impact of compressed modernisation on food habits. *Malaysian Journal of Nutrition*, 26: 1–17. https://doi.org/10.31246/mjn-2019-0042

Poulain J.-P., Smith W., Laporte C., Tibère L., Ismail M.N., Mognard E. et al., 2015. Studying the consequences of modernization on ethnic food patterns: development of the Malaysian Food Barometer (MFB), *Anthropology of Food*. https://doi.org /10.4000/aof.7735

Reicks M., Trofholz A.C., Stang J.S., Laska M.N., 2014. Impact of cooking and home food preparation interventions among adults: outcomes and implications for future programs. *Journal of Nutrition Education and Behavior*, 46(4): 259–276. https://doi .org/10.1016/j.jneb.2014.02.001

Ricroch L., 2012. *En 25 ans, moins de tâches domestiques pour les femmes, l'écart de situation avec les hommes se réduit*, Paris, Insee, 67–80 p.

Ritchie H., Roser M., 2018. *Plastic pollution, Our World in Data*. [online].

Ritzer G., 1992. *The McDonaldization of society*, Newbury Park, Pine Forge Press, 221 p.

Soula A., Zirari H., 2023. Le goût des origines. Discours et pratiques face à l'industrialisation et à la "tradition culinaire" en milieu urbain marocain. *Anthropology of Food*, 17. https:// doi.org/10.4000/aof.14322

Tharrey M., Godin O., Dubois C., Drogue S., Perignon M., Privet L., Darmon N., 2018. La cuisine maison coûte-t-elle moins cher ? *Alimentation, santé et petit budget*, 77: 1.

Wolfson J.A., Leung C.W., Richardson C.R., 2020. More frequent cooking at home is associated with higher Healthy Eating Index-2015 score. *Public Health Nutrition*, 23(13): 2384–2394. https://doi.org/10.1017/S1368980019003549

Zirari H., 2020. Entre alimentation (*makla*) et nutrition (*taghdia*): arbitrages et réinvention au quotidien des pratiques alimentaires en contexte urbain. *Hespéris-Tamuda*, 55(4): 385–407.

Zirari H., Soula A., El Alami H., 2022. « As-tu vu l'homme en train de pétrir le pain ? ». Alimentation, genre et réseaux sociaux en période de confinement au Maroc. *Anthropology of Food*, S17. https://doi.org/10.4000/aof.13054

17

Taking a step back from local production

Damien Conaré and Nicolas Bricas

The relocalization of our food restores trust between producers and consumers, often broken by the industrialization and globalization of food supply chains. However, it is entirely possible to recreate locally the same dysfunctions observed at larger scales or to simply promote a narrow-minded localism. This points to the need for a cosmopolitan localism.

The last few years have witnessed the rise of a local food craze widely platformed by the media. This trend, driven by economic actors, non-profit organizations, consumers and public authorities, seeks to reconnect eaters and farmers. It has translated into the re-territorialization of food systems, that is, the affirmation of the territorial anchoring of food growing and processing activities; the relocalization of food systems, in other words, the reduction of the geographical distance between places of production and consumption; and the development of short supply chains – forms of commercialization with few or no intermediaries (Wallet et al., 2017; Chiffoleau, 2019).

As new ways of building proximity proliferate, localness in particular is emerging as a new attribute that seems to have it all. But we should beware of the 'local trap', which tends to posit this scale of activity as inherently virtuous.

Demand for proximity

A trend towards the institutionalization and massification of local consumption, similar to that observed with organic products, indeed appears to be underway, with the establishment of farmers on urban land by local authorities, the promotion of urban agriculture, the development of 'vertical farms' in cities, the publication of catalogues of local product suppliers, the opening of farm shops or farm drive-throughs, the development of local supply in collective catering and the development of local offerings in mass retail.

This movement has a long history and is growing around the world. In Japan, direct farm food purchasing groups, *teikei* (提携), developed in the late 1960s. They emerged under the impetus of young urban women who were eager to source organic products (milk in particular) for their children, against the backdrop of numerous food poisoning incidents linked to the excessive use of chemical inputs (Amemiya, 2011).

In the United States and Canada, the Community Supported Agriculture (CSA) movement, which emerged in the 1980s and was inspired by a model developed in Switzerland, allows consumers to reserve a portion of a farm's future harvest in advance. These local solidarity partnerships, which are still limited in scope, generally share a commitment to preserving small farms using environmentally friendly farming methods (Pouzenc, 2020).

In Italy, from the 1980s, the Slow Food movement was quick to promote the beneficial effects of eating local, quality food. In Brazil, in 1993, the city of Belo Horizonte (2.4 million inhabitants at the time) launched a public food security policy based on the promotion of food grown by small peri-urban family farmers through subsidized prices at popular restaurants, farmers' markets in the city, food banks and a law requiring 30 per cent local purchases in public tenders for school catering (Rocha, 2001).

On the African continent, local production has been promoted in response to changes in eating habits (Touré, 1982), the increase in food imports and the economic dependence they generate. For example, in the Sahel, the Regional Programme for the Promotion of Local Cereals (Procelos, *Programme régional de promotion des céréales locales*) was implemented across the region from 1987 for nearly ten years to encourage the resurgence of African millet, sorghum, maize, rice and fonio in domestic markets (CTA, 1989). Furthermore, following the food price crises on international markets in 2008 and 2011, a French network of NGOs, the CFSI (Comité français pour la solidarité internationale), launched 'the battles for local consumption in West Africa' (Eloy et al., 2019). Localness here refers to the national or even regional space – in contrast with international markets – rather than to a more restricted territorial area.

In France, the early 2000s witnessed the development of a network of non-profit organizations for the maintenance of peasant farming, AMAP (*Associations pour le maintien d'une agriculture paysanne*). This network is partly inspired by the North American CSA model: consumers subscribe to receive food baskets supplied by local farmers. In addition, beyond the long-standing practices of direct sales by farmers at markets or on farms, a wide range of initiatives has emerged to encourage the sourcing of local products by households and catering establishments (Dedinger et al., 2021). These initiatives, which often started out as a way to challenge conventional farming and its commercialization through mass retail, are now supported by public authorities and are also being imitated by the private sector, which sees opportunities in this new market segment. Supermarkets are thus promoting local farmers on their shelves – this is particularly the case within independent chains where each owner is free to choose the products they supply. Urban agriculture is also attracting interest from many companies. The Lufa urban farms in Montreal, for example, are inspiring cities and supermarkets that are starting to set up farms on their roofs (Pouyat, 2018).

The 'local' promise

There is no official definition of what constitutes a local product. The 'reasonable' geographical distance between the place of production and the place of consumption varies depending on the location and the products concerned. In France, for example, this distance ranges from a few kilometres to less than 150 km for 'proximity supply chains', as defined by the French Agency for Ecological Transition (Ademe, 2017). In Africa, the concept of 'local' extends to national production or even to neighbouring countries. In industrialized countries, relocalization initiatives are most often presented as alternatives to the conventional model based on their forms of production, processing and organization and/or on their desire for transformation, which some authors describe as a 'promise of difference' (Le Velly, 2017). The promoters of these initiatives generally consider that they contribute to

- restoring economic and social ties of trust between consumers and farmers, offering the latter remuneration deemed more equitable by charging a 'fair price' (Chiffoleau, 2019);
- giving new meaning to both farming activity and the act of consumption, thus restoring the value of food;
- promoting the product attributes of freshness and seasonality;
- reducing packaging;
- minimizing losses and waste along the supply chain by reducing the number of intermediaries and valourizing products that do not meet the criteria set for long supply chains;

- maintaining agricultural and processing activities, thus contributing to local economic development and employment;
- raising consumers' awareness of how their food is produced;
- restoring the balance of power between the actors in the food chain to the benefit of farmers and consumers;
- reducing environmental impacts in terms of energy consumption and greenhouse gas (GHG) emissions.

Analyses generally posit localism as a response to the social, economic and environmental failures of a 'dominant', 'conventional', 'intensive', 'agro-industrial' or 'productivist' food system (Renting et al., 2003; Deverre and Lamine, 2010). This food system, also considered 'global', produces food that is removed from the places and conditions of its production. It is deterritorialized food, that is, 'food from nowhere', as opposed to food anchored in its social and cultural context – 'food from somewhere' (Fonte and Papadopoulos, 2010). The global scale has been that of the petro-chemicalization of farming, the commodification of seeds, the globalization of transport, the development of large distribution channels and the financialization of agricultural markets. The rise of local food thus appears as a counterpart to the critique of global food, a locus of resistance to a global approach deemed anomic (DuPuis and Goodman, 2005; Paddeu, 2017).

The relocalization of food can also be seen as a response to the various forms of distancing (geographical, economic, political, cognitive and sensory) between eaters and their food (Chapter 6). This distancing was already noted by Walter P. Hedden (head of the Port of New York trade office) in his book *How Great Cities Are Fed*, published in 1929. In this book, he showed how New York City, which depended on distant food supplies (lettuce from California, lemons from Italy, butter from Denmark etc.) and was losing its surrounding farmland to urban sprawl, would be threatened by any interruption to this supply (Cohen, 2010; McCabe, 2010). Hedden was the first to use the concept of a 'foodshed' (drawing an analogy with watersheds) to denote the whole geographical area from which food reaches a group of eaters. It includes the farmland, processing and distribution facilities, transport systems, wholesalers and retailers involved. He noted that fruit and vegetables travelled an average of nearly 2,500 km from farm to New Yorkers' tables. He thus explained that 'the widening gap in physical distance between the point of production and the point of consumption has its counterpart in the attenuation of the contact and mutual understanding between producers and consumers' (Hedden, 1929). This was almost a hundred years ago.

The term 'foodshed' was revisited much later by permaculturist Arthur Getz (1991) to ask the question: 'Where does our food come from and how does it reach us?' Beyond the metaphor, this concept reveals that consumers are often so far removed from the source of their food that they cannot grasp the consequences of their purchasing habits (Kloppenburg et al., 1996). Recognizing their food catchment area can give a person a sense of anchorage in biological and social realities but also a sense of responsibility towards that territory.

The COVID-19 crisis, with the border closures and restrictions on movement it caused, was an opportunity for many countries to reflect on their degree of food dependence on other nations. In France, food sovereignty[1] – which the peasant organization La Via Campesina had long called for in response to the liberalization of international markets in the 1990s – emerged as a theme of public debate. Fears of shortages even led some actors to promote forms of food autonomy[2] (Rouillay and Becker, 2020).

Beware of the local trap

Some of the arguments in support of relocalization must however be put into perspective. First, it is important to remember that, historically, cities have not always developed in the heart of foodsheds with the capacity to feed them – far from it. Some cities were built by the sea or on rivers and, as Braudel (1993) has shown, they relied heavily on distant trade, which multiplied as inexpensive means of transport developed from the time of the Industrial Revolution (Chapter 5). Moreover, local production is not possible everywhere. Even if all industrial wastelands and urban interstices were converted into farmland and building roofs were used to grow food, urban agriculture could only make a marginal contribution to cities' food supplies. For example, by increasing Paris's agricultural surface area tenfold to 33 hectares, the city could hope to produce 500 tonnes of food per year or 0.26 per cent of what it consumes (Leray, 2018).

Relocalizing agricultural production as close as possible to consumption areas would require a complete reconfiguration of agricultural production, as well as

---

[1] According to La Via Campesina, food sovereignty is 'the right of peoples to healthy and culturally appropriate food produced through ecologically sound and sustainable methods, and their right to define their own food and agriculture systems'.

[2] The degree of food autonomy of a territory refers to its capacity to produce locally, with local agricultural resources, the food (raw, prepared, processed or cooked) consumed by its inhabitants. According to a study by the consultancy Utopies (2017), the average degree of food autonomy of the hundred largest urban areas in France is of 2 per cent.

giving up regional specialities to some extent. Yet many countries have policies in place to promote and protect the typicity of products and the associated know-how in the face of food standardization. Thus, a compromise is needed between two seemingly contradictory trends: diversifying to reduce the negative effects of specialization and specializing to capitalize on the characteristics of a territory.

Relocalization is often seen as environmentally beneficial because it reduces the distances travelled. For this reason, the display on food products of the food miles calculation method, proposed by Tim Lang and formalized by Angela Paxton (1994), was initially promoted by some as a way to help consumers reduce their carbon footprint. Since then, life cycle assessment calculations regarding food systems have revealed the ultimately limited share of emissions associated with transport. In France, for example, transport accounts for less than 14 per cent of the food system's GHG emissions, whereas agricultural production accounts for about two-thirds (Barbier et al., 2019). Reducing supply distances therefore has little impact on a food system's carbon footprint. Thus, food that is produced locally but out of season in a heated greenhouse may consume more energy and emit more GHGs than an imported product grown outdoors, even when transport is included. Moreover, logistics is crucial: large volumes transported efficiently over long distances can emit less GHGs per tonne than small volumes transported over short distances in under-filled or returning-empty vans (Ademe, 2017). Food's environmental impact is also strongly linked to the distances travelled by consumers: increasing the number of trips made to purchase supplies from different farmers who are not necessarily grouped together can prove very costly from an environmental point of view.

Moreover, direct sales by local farmers can place the burden of the cost and know-how associated with distribution work (order fulfilment etc.) on them, when they are not necessarily equipped for this additional (and mental) workload. A study on the functioning of the AMAP in the Rhône-Alpes region (France) also highlighted the fear expressed by some farmers of feeling dependent on consumers (Mundler, 2007). This fear points to the relationship of domination that could develop between consumers who generally have a high level of social and cultural capital and a farmer, should their income come to depend on the strength of these same consumers' commitment. In practice, the solidarity that develops may thus be top–down, from consumers to the producer. However, we should note that farmers generally combine several distribution channels, which affords them a certain amount of leeway (Maréchal, 2008).

Like all other scales, the local scale is not an independent entity with inherent qualities. The scale itself is not a given; it is a social construct, dependent on the actors involved and the agenda they have set for themselves. It is the content of that agenda that will produce sustainability or social justice objectives, not the scale at which that agenda is implemented (Born and Purcell, 2006). Thus, a relocalized food system is just as likely to be more or less sustainable or more or less fair as a food system at another scale (Stein and Santini, 2021). Local food is not inherently 'good'. Geographical proximity does not guarantee the non-use of large quantities of pesticides (especially on peri-urban land, where the price of land encourages more intensive farming) or the non-use of exploited foreign labour. Nor does it guarantee a better food supply in terms of health, taste or nutrition.

Finally, while relocalization undeniably creates opportunities for the inclusion and participation of new actors, the local scale remains dependent on the dominant political economy and existing social privilege can therefore be reproduced at this scale by serving the interests of a small 'local elite' withdrawn into its 'protected' food territory (Allen, 2010; DuPuis and Goodman, 2015).

Localness also has a dark side, with an identity focus characterized by withdrawal and the rejection of otherness, pandering to a sense of specificity and authenticity. A fairly widespread discourse, echoed by far-right parties, promotes a defensive version of 'localism' (Hinrichs, 2003; Winter, 2003; Charbonnier, 2018) that is traditionalist and narrow. It also risks fomenting competition between territories that succeed in managing local food systems (owing to social, economic, geographical or political attributes) and those that do not (Allen and Guthman, 2006; Feagan, 2007). The activation of localness may also contradict the goal of territorial integration in countries seeking above all to appease risks of internal conflicts and to build national unity.

Ultimately, where the local scale proves particularly interesting is undoubtedly in the mobilization of stakeholders – farmers, citizens, consumers, politicians – and the development of new forms of governance to regain sovereignty over food systems. The growing number of territorial food projects, particularly in France, is evidence of this. These projects generally emphasize the principles and values associated with sustainability and equity. Even as they work towards these goals, they need to make trade-offs between benefits to farmers and accessibility for low-income consumers, and to strike the right policy balance between reform at the local level and the pursuit of systemic change on broader scales (Feenstra and Campbell, 2014). In short, it is important to ensure that local initiatives do not distract from the macroeconomic policies and structures that organize our agriculture and food, such as the EU Common Agricultural Policy. The challenge is to ensure that these local governance frameworks are gradually able to federate into networks and form real political forces that can have an impact on national or international food system governance bodies (Chapter 22).

For a cosmopolitan localism

We eat our way through the world from breakfast-time, drinking our tea, coffee or cocoa, possibly with sugar (Grataloup, 2017). By its very nature, food connects us to other territories (Chapters 2 and 5). For example, according to a study by the International Center for Tropical Agriculture, two-thirds of the food we eat historically originated from other parts of the world, irrespective of where we find ourselves (Khoury et al., 2016). It seems that the whole world is indeed nestled on our plates – the outcome of a long history of the spread of food production, human migrations, conquests, great discoveries and trade.

Bruno Latour (2021) proposes the concept of 'subsistence territories': 'Tell me what you live off and I'll tell you how far your living space extends.' This concept seeks to shift from a cartographic and administrative definition of territory (seen from above), with a clear demarcation between inside and outside, to a more horizontal understanding of dependencies and interactions with other territories, however distant. It captures the difference between the territory within which we are situated ('the world in which we are') and the distant territories on which we depend or even from which we profit ('the world in which we live'): when it comes to food, some territories are subject to the domination of others. Historically, this is clearly exemplified by the spice trade or the slave plantation system. But even today, we still, for example, consume bananas grown on land 'elsewhere' in the French Caribbean, which has been knowingly polluted with a pesticide that is banned in mainland France, chlordecone (Ferdinand, 2022).

If we recognize that we are linked across food territories, let us commit to a 'cosmopolitan localism' that 'cherishes a particular place, yet at the same time knows about the relativity of all places' (Sachs, 1992): a localism embedded in a global dynamic where communities are not isolated from one another but interconnected in a world of circulations (Manzini, 2007). With regard to food, fair trade and products with a quality and origin label (protected geographical indications, registered designations of origin etc.) perfectly illustrate this solidarity between territories and the possibility of translocalism (Ho, 2020), transporting a product with a territorial origin from one place to another. Even if they come from regions far from where consumers live, terroir products, which are 'localized' (their origin or even their conditions of production are known), allow for this cognitive connection (Bazzani and Canavari, 2017). Similarly, some cities support agriculture that guarantees access to quality products in the territories that supply them by establishing solidarity contracts, as the city of Hanoi in Vietnam does with the provinces that supply it or as exemplified by the collective in Rennes that runs the 'Terres de source' project (Zeggoud, 2021).

Conclusion

Herein lies the value of processes of hybridization between local and more distant supplies, allowing for territorial anchoring without being locked into a local space. These processes are defined by some as 'food systems of the middle': they have intermediate configurations in terms of size, and they are hybrid in terms of their actors, their organization and the values they hold (Chazoule et al., 2015). Local food is thus valued beyond the confines of a specific space. After all, we are always consuming someone else's local food.

The authors would like to thank Mathilde Coudray, Ronan Le Velly and Coline Perrin for proofreading this chapter and for their suggested improvements.

References

Ademe, 2017. *Alimentation – Les circuits courts de proximité*, Paris, Ademe, 8 p.

Allen P., 2010. Realizing justice in local food systems. *Cambridge Journal of Regions, Economy and Society*, 3(2): 295–308. https://doi.org/10.1093/cjres/rsq015

Allen P., Guthman J., 2006. From 'old school' to 'farm-to-school': neoliberalization from the ground up. *Agriculture and Human Values*, 23(4): 401–415. https://doi.org /10.1007/s10460-006-9019-z

Amemiya H., 2011. *Du Teikei aux Amap, le renouveau de la vente directe de produits fermiers locaux*, Rennes, PUR, 350 p.

Barbier C., Couturier C., Pourouchottamin P., Cayla J.-M., Silvestre M., Pharabod I., 2019. *L'empreinte énergétique et carbone de l'alimentation en France*, Paris, Club Ingénierie Prospective Énergie et Environnement, 24 p.

Bazzani C., Canavari M., 2017. Is local a matter of food miles or food traditions? *Italian Journal of Food Science*, 29: 505–517. https://doi.org/10.14674/IJFS-733

Born B., Purcell M., 2006. Avoiding the local trap: scale and food systems in planning research. *Journal of Planning Education and Research*, 26(2): 195–207. https://doi.org /10.1177/0739456X06291389

Braudel F., 1993. *Civilisation, économie et capitalisme, XVe–XVIIIe siècle, tome 3: Le temps du monde*, Paris, Livre de Poche, 922 p.

Charbonnier P., 2018. Quand les réactionnaires se mettent au vert. *AOC*.

Chazoule C., Fleury P., Brives H., 2015. Systèmes alimentaires du milieu et création de chaînes de valeurs: concepts et études de cas dans la région Rhône-Alpes. *Économies et Sociétés*, 37(8): 1203–1219.

Chiffoleau Y., 2019. *Les circuits courts alimentaires: entre marché et innovation sociale*, Paris, Érès, 176 p.

Cohen N., 2010. How great cities are fed revisited: ten municipal policies to support the New York City foodshed. *Fordham Environmental Law Review*, 22(3): 691–710.

CTA, 1989. *Procelos: priorité aux céréales locales*, Spore 19, CTA, Wageningen.

Dedinger P., Parant M.-F., Ory X., 2021. *Les produits locaux*, Paris, DGAAER, 75 p.

Deverre C., Lamine C., 2010. Les systèmes agroalimentaires alternatifs. Une revue de travaux anglophones en sciences sociales. *Économie rurale. Agricultures, alimentations, territoires*, 317: 57–73. https://doi.org/10.4000/economierurale.2676

DuPuis E.M., Goodman D., 2005. Should we go 'home' to eat?: toward a reflexive politics of localism. *Journal of Rural Studies*, 21(3): 359–371. https://doi.org/10.1016/j.jrurstud.2005.05.011

Eloy D., Basquin-Fané H., Diagne D., CFSI, 2019. *Les batailles du consommer local en Afrique de l'Ouest*, Paris, Fondation de France/CFSI, 128 p.

Feagan R., 2007. The place of food: mapping out the 'local' in local food systems. *Progress in Human Geography*, 31(1): 23–42. https://doi.org/10.1177/0309132507073527

Feenstra G., Campbell D., 2014. Local and regional food systems, in Thompson P.B., Kaplan D.M. (éd.), *Encyclopedia of food and agricultural ethics*, Dordrecht, Springer, 1345–1352.

Ferdinand M., 2022. *Decolonial ecology – thinking from the Caribbean World*, Cambridge/Medford, Polity Press, 300 p.

Fonte M., Papadopoulos A.G., 2010. *Naming food after places: food relocalisation and knowledge dynamics in rural development*, London, Routledge, 306 p.

Getz A., 1991. Urban foodsheds. *Permaculture Activist*, 7(3): 26–27.

Grataloup C., 2017. *Le monde dans nos tasses. Trois siècles de petit-déjeuner*, Paris, Armand Colin, 272 p.

Hedden W.P., 1929. *How great cities are fed*, Boston/New York, Heath and Co., 302 p.

Hinrichs C.C., 2003. The practice and politics of food system localization. *Journal of Rural Studies*, 19(1): 33–45. https://doi.org/10.1016/S0743-0167(02)00040-2

Ho H.-T., 2020. Cosmopolitan locavorism: global local-food movements in postcolonial Hong Kong. *Food, Culture & Society*, 23(2): 137–154. https://doi.org/10.1080/15528014.2019.1682886

Khoury C.K., Achicanoy H.A., Bjorkman A.D., Navarro-Racines C., Guarino L., Flores-Palacios X. et al., 2016. Origins of food crops connect countries worldwide. *Proceedings of the Royal Society B: Biological Sciences*, 283(1832): 20160792. https://doi.org/10.1098/rspb.2016.0792

Kloppenburg J., Hendrickson J., Stevenson G.W., 1996. Coming into the foodshed. *Agriculture and Human Values*, 13(3): 33–42. https://doi.org/10.1007/BF01538225

Latour B., 2021. *Où suis-je ? Leçons du confinement à l'usage des terrestres*, Paris, Les empêcheurs de penser en rond, 192 p.

Leray C., 2018. Pour en finir avec l'agriculture urbaine à Paris (et ailleurs). *Chroniques d'architecture.*

Le Velly R., 2017. *Sociologie des systèmes alimentaires alternatifs. Une promesse de différence*, Paris, Presses des Mines, 203 p.

Manzini E., 2007. Design research for sustainable social innovation, in Michel R. (éd.), *Design research now: essays and selected projects*, Basel, Birkhäuser, 233–245.

Maréchal G., 2008. *Les circuits courts alimentaires. Bien manger dans les territoires*, Dijon, Éducagri éditions, 214 p.

McCabe M., 2010. Foodshed foundations: law's role in shaping our food system's future. *Fordham Environmental Law Review*, 22(3): 563–598.

Mundler P., 2007. Les Associations pour le maintien de l'agriculture paysanne (AMAP) en Rhône-Alpes, entre marché et solidarité. Ruralia. *Sciences sociales et mondes ruraux contemporains*, 20. https://doi.org/10.3917/pour.201.0155

Paddeu F., 2017. Manger local. Leurres et promesses. *Vacarme*, 81(4): 40–45. https://doi.org/10.3917/vaca.081.0040

Paxton A., 1994. *Food miles report*, London, SAFE Alliance, 62 p.

Pouyat A., 2018. La grande distribution mise sur l'agriculture urbaine. *WE Demain.*

Pouzenc M., 2020. Articuler un « penser global » et un « agir local »: la territorialisation des « Community Supported Agriculture ». Développement durable et territoires. *Économie, géographie, politique, droit, sociologie*, 11(1). https://doi.org/10.4000/developpementdurable.16922

Renting H., Marsden T.K., Banks J., 2003. Understanding alternative food networks: exploring the role of short food supply chains in rural development. *Environment and Planning A: Economy and Space*, 35(3): 393–411. https://doi.org/10.1068/a3510

Rocha C., 2001. Urban food security policy: the case of Belo Horizonte, Brazil. *Journal for the Study of Food and Society*, 5(1): 36–47. https://doi.org/10.2752/152897901786732735

Rouillay F., Becker S., 2020. En route pour l'autonomie alimentaire. Guide pratique à l'usage des familles, villes et territoires, Mens, éditions Terre Vivante, 207 p.

Sachs W., 1992. *The development dictionary: a guide to knowledge as power*, London, Zed Books, 332 p.

Stein A.J., Santini F., 2021. The sustainability of 'local' food: a review for policy-makers. *Review of Agricultural, Food and Environmental Studies*, 103: 77–89. https://doi.org/10.1007/s41130-021-00148-w

Touré A., 1982. *La civilisation quotidienne en Côte-d'Ivoire: procès d'occidentalisation*, Paris, Karthala, 280 p.

Utopies, 2017. *Autonomie alimentaire des villes. État des lieux et enjeux pour la filière agroalimentaire française.* Note de position n°12.

Wallet F., Philipon P., Chiffoleau Y., 2017. *Et si on mangeait local ? Ce que les circuits courts vont changer dans mon quotidien*, Versailles, Quæ, 170 p.

Winter M., 2003. Embeddedness, the new food economy and defensive localism. *Journal of Rural Studies*, 19(1): 23–32. https://doi.org/10.1016/S0743-0167(02)00053-0

Zeggoud A., 2021. Terres de Sources, de la ville à la campagne. Accompagner la transition agroécologique au-delà de son territoire grâce à la protection de l'eau, in Albert S., Bricas N., Conaré D., Coudray M., Fournier S., Moity-Maïzi P., Razes M. (ed.), *Actes de la Journée des innovations pour une alimentation durable*, JIPAD 2020, Montpellier, Montpellier SupAgro/Chaire Unesco Alimentations du monde/Cirad, 51–57.

18

Active consumers as drivers of change?

Nicolas Bricas

Despite some individuals' conviction that they are playing their part by leveraging their purchasing power, their responsibility in the transition to sustainable food systems is limited. Their consumption behaviour is ultimately constrained by a material, social and political environment, and they cannot be the sole drivers of change.

Individual behaviour has an impact on the sustainability of food systems. The quantities one consumes, the composition of one's diet – with more or fewer animal or processed products – and the choice of foods based on the way they were produced, as well as product purchasing, cooking and waste management practices, all influence one's health, the environment and social equity. Industrialized societies, where the food supply increased and became more diverse over the course of the twentieth century (Chapter 5), have reached levels and styles of consumption that cannot be generalized to the global population at the risk of far exceeding all 'planetary boundaries', several of which have already been crossed (Chapter 7).

In response to this situation, the United Nations' (2021) sustainable development goal 12, 'Sustainable Consumption and Production', calls for the adoption of consumption practices that support a 'more sustainable future' by 'doing more and better with less'. This chapter discusses different levers for influencing individual consumption and behaviour. It particularly addresses the common idea that consumers are a powerful driver – if not the main driver for some – of these necessary changes.

Consumer responsibility

The sovereignty or responsibility of consumers or 'active consumers', responsible or activist consumption (Dubuisson-Quellier, 2009), boycott and buycott

(Friedman, 1996) and political consumerism (Micheletti et al., 2004) have become watchwords for the transition to sustainable food systems. This can be seen as a neoliberal approach to change, which advocates reducing the scope of state intervention and defends individual freedom on the grounds that each person is the best judge of their own well-being. From this perspective, one's economic choices are deemed effective in satisfying one's own interests through consumption. The sovereignty of consumers in their purchasing practices underlies a form of democracy in which individuals are freed from the constraints and limits of their social and class affiliations, internalized in the form of habitus (Bourdieu, 1984). This approach regards training, raising awareness and educating consumers, while leaving them free to make informed choices, as preferable to entrusting the state with defining what is good for society. For companies, consumer choices are signals that they can use to steer their innovations and offerings. They use marketing tools to identify 'consumer expectations' and then measure them as 'willingness to pay' for new attributes. This means of action has the benefit of being inexpensive for the state: it is limited to setting a general framework and informing consumers. It is therefore not very restrictive for companies, which are to some extent free to act 'in response to demand'. This avoids the need for states to impose rules on them and then have to enforce these rules, which always carries the risk that they will be circumvented.

Encouraging individual action also enables citizens to take action for change in a context where they have lost confidence in political action. Rather than despair over political paralysis, we may as well start 'doing our bit' to contribute to a more sustainable world, even in a very small way, by changing our behaviour.

Political consumerism practices

Individual activism can take different, more or less restrictive forms. Most commonly, it involves choosing products based on their quality and the way in which they were produced and traded in particular – products certified as organic, palm oil–free or fair trade, products displaying a nutritional assessment, products of a specified geographical origin and so on. Food labelling relating to various dimensions of sustainability has developed considerably and allows companies to sell environmental, social or nutritional value added. These products are often sold at a higher price than 'conventional' products. Activist consumer choices can also relate to certain types of distribution and purchasing methods – for example, opting for short circuits, shopping in cooperative supermarkets or boycotting large supermarkets. Other forms of action can be more restrictive. They can involve a reorganization of food practices that is costly in terms of money, time, travel or information gathering, and they can differentiate a consumer from the social norm, for instance, when bulk buying, growing one's own food, becoming vegetarian or vegan, or eating homemade food as much as possible (Chapter 16).

Some individual actions do not involve consumption per se – they do not play out in the market space – but rather changes in domestic practices, such as gardening for personal consumption, using shopping lists to best tailor purchases to the meals one has planned, cooking for the week, reducing the quantities consumed and sorting waste (Daniel and Sirieix, 2012).

All these individual actions constitute tactics to navigate constraints, both on the demand side – getting by with limited purchasing power – and on the supply side – making do with what is on offer. They allow people to take ownership of their diet by regaining control over their consumption. Tips and tricks to 'make do with what you have' are multiplying on social media. For example, 'grocery haul' videos and *Gestion budgétaire, entraide et minimalisme* (GBEM, 'budgeting, mutual aid and minimalism') groups bear witness to these everyday practices and acts of cultural poaching (de Certeau, 1984; de Certeau et al., 1998).

The limits of individual responsibility

The idea that the food system can be changed through individual practices alone has its limits. The first relates to the illusion of perfect consumer information and the need to recognize consumers' cognitive limits. Not all food consumption is informed by well-thought-out choices on the part of eaters. It is partly guided by emotional processes, particularly pleasure (Jacquier et al., 2012). Food consumption is also shaped by routines that are not consciously thought out; they can of course be interrogated but nonetheless facilitate purchasing behaviour. For example, these routines minimize the number of choices that eaters have to make, even if they know that these are not necessarily optimal routines (Dubuisson-Quellier, 2006). Furthermore, food-consumption practices can result from addictions. While there is still controversy surrounding this topic, certain food compounds such as sugar, salt and fat, along with ultra-processed products, are strongly suspected of causing physiological and behavioural addictions (Gordon et al., 2018). Similarly, portion sizes are a discrete incentive that determines the quantities consumed (Wansink, 1996) through the cognitive biases they generate (Chandon et al., 2017).

Some of the effects of consumption escape consumers' awareness. For example, the presence of pesticides, drug residues or microplastics in food is invisible. Likewise, the environmental impact of the food production pathway is still very poorly measured and not reported to consumers due to the difficulty of doing so. The health or environmental effects of certain products (e.g. GMOs) are still uncertain. Should these effects be made visible to enable consumers to make informed choices? Or should states legislate to protect eaters from the risks associated with the consumption of these products? Other effects are better known but still controversial, sometimes due to campaigns to disparage scientific results that are inconvenient for certain actors; this is the case of GMOs, pesticides, glyphosate herbicide and ultra-processed products, for example. The proliferation of contradictory messaging ends up sowing doubt in the minds of consumers and making the choices they have to make more difficult, especially since consumers do not necessarily have the technical knowledge to understand what is at stake and to sift through this information. This is what Claude Fischler (1990) calls 'dietary hubbub' and the 'food cacophony'. More broadly, the multiplication of food products on offer, which is supposed to increase freedom of choice, generates a perverse effect that has been described as the 'paradox of choice': frustration grows when faced with too much choice, which makes it difficult to compare the different options and leaves the consumer convinced that they have probably not found the optimal product (Schwartz, 2005). Today, digital applications designed to assist individuals in making choices are proliferating. These applications rate products according to various sustainability criteria. But these criteria can be controversial, and their selection escapes arbitration by public authorities (Soutjis, 2020). The private nature of these technical devices thus raises questions about their legitimacy and governance.

A second limitation of changing the food system through individual practices is the resulting exclusion of a portion of consumers. Because sustainable products are often more expensive or require more knowledge to be assessed as sustainable, they remain the preserve of a fringe of the population with enough economic or cultural capital. When it comes to 'voting with their wallets', the more capital consumers have, the more power they possess to shape the food system; this is called plutocracy (from the Greek *ploutos*, god of wealth, and *kratos*, power). In her book *The Sum of Small Things*, Elizabeth Currid-Halkett (2017) shows how this sum of small, discreet things – for example, buying organic vegetables and fair-trade products or cooking vegetarian dishes – practised by young New York graduates and Hollywood stars signals more than an economic position: it conveys a moral superiority. The discourse of this elite and the visibility of their practices in gentrified neighbourhoods or in the media place guilt on all those who cannot afford to adopt these practices due to a lack of money, time, space and knowledge of the subject. Their inaccessibility gives rise to cognitive dissonance: individuals know what they should be doing to adopt a virtuous purchasing behaviour but cannot do so. The result is either frustration or a sense of injustice or a rejection of the values held by the elites. Scepticism ensues regarding the reality of environmental problems, seen as fads of these elites.

A third limitation is that household consumption accounts for only a small share of the environmental or health impacts of the entire food system. For example, adopting frugal consumption practices in a wealthy country like France contributes only to a part of the effort required to reach the target set by the Paris Agreement to limit global warming (see Box 18.1) and should not distract from the necessary resource savings required in industrial production processes.

A fourth limitation of individual responsibility is the unequal 'ease' of access to the food supply. This may relate to physical factors: it is easier to acquire products found locally than to make the effort to travel a longer distance. Food deserts (Cummins and Macintyre, 1999) refer to poor neighbourhoods with no local shops selling healthy food and food swamps to neighbourhoods with a high concentration of shops selling nutritionally unhealthy food. Both of these food environments, especially the latter, are suspected of contributing to the overconsumption of products high in fat, sugar and salt, which is detrimental to balanced nutrition (Cooksey-Stowers et al., 2017). If we approach price not as the result of an equilibrium between independent supply and demand but as a factor shaping demand, accessibility also has an economic dimension. Choosing an option that is desirable but requires significant cognitive, physical or economic effort and brings only limited moral satisfaction – because its desirable attribute is non-observable (as in the case of long-term environmental or health benefits) – quickly diminishes motivation. This may explain why concern for the fairness of trade or respect for the environment is satisfied with just a few products: coffee in the case of fair trade and intermittent consumption in the case of environmentally friendly food (Lamine, 2008).

A final limit surrounding individual responsibility concerns conformity to social norms. Food is consumed not just to satisfy an individual need but also to demonstrate one's belonging to a social group or, at the risk of being marginalized, one's uniqueness (Chapter 1). Vegetarianism and veganism are examples of

Box 18.1 Simulation of the carbon impact of frugal food consumption

The French Agency for Ecological Transition (Ademe) provides a calculator to simulate the effect of changes in consumption on one's carbon impact. As a reminder, the carbon footprint of a French person's consumption is approximately 9.8 tonnes of CO_2e*/person/year (including 2.8 tonnes for food, 2.8 tonnes for transport and 2.1 tonnes for housing). The target to stay within the limit that keeps global warming below 2°C by 2100 is a footprint of about 2 tonnes of CO_2e/person/year, which would imply a reduction of about 8 tonnes. Table 18.1 shows the effects of changes in diet and food practices on a person's carbon footprint.

Table 18.1 Effects of a change in diet and dietary practices on a person's carbon footprint

	Current average diet		Frugal diet	
	Frequency	kg CO_2e	Frequency	kg CO_2e
Breakfast	7×/week	135	7×/week	135
Meal with red meat	4×/week	1,310	1×/week	330
Meal with white meat or cheese	4×/week	280	2×/week	140
Vegetarian meal	4×/week	105	8×/week	210
Vegan meal	2×/week	40	3×/week	60
Sugary drinks	2 L/week	120	1 L/week	60
Beer, wine	1 L/week	100	0.5 L/week	50
Hot drinks	–	20	–	20
Zero waste	No	710	Yes	210
Total		**2,800**		**1,215**

Adopting a diet that can be described as frugal can more than halve the carbon footprint of one's food consumption, reducing it by about 1.6 tonnes CO_2e/person/year – this accounts for 20 per cent of the footprint reduction needed to stay below a maximum of 2°C global warming. Significantly reducing one's car travel (filling the car with an average of two people, compared with 1.2 at present, and reducing the distance travelled from 10,000 to 2,000 km/year) would further save 1.1 tonnes/person/year, and lowering one's home temperature in winter by 1°C would save 0.2 tonnes/person/year. This would afford total savings of 2.9 tonnes/person/year. While other, more marginal savings can be made, this simple simulation shows that a significant effort to reduce the carbon footprint of household consumption would hardly save more than 4 tonnes/person/year of CO_2e – that is, a third of the effort required. The other half can only be achieved by improving the environmental performance of agricultural, industrial and service processes.

These average consumption figures should not conceal the major differences in emissions depending on households' standard of living. While there is little difference in the carbon footprint of food by income level, the differences for transport and housing are significant: the carbon footprint of two round trips per year by plane to a destination 2,000 km away is estimated at 1.2 tonnes, and owning an SUV compared with an average car also increases the carbon footprint associated with one's travel by 1.2 tonnes. For example, Kartha et al. (2020) estimate that the wealthiest 10 per cent of households worldwide, or 630 million people, emit 52 per cent of greenhouse gases, while the poorest 50 per cent emit only 7 per cent.

* CO_2e stands for 'CO_2 equivalent', a unit of measurement used to compare emissions of various greenhouse gases according to their warming potential.

practices that are starting to be recognized as normal but are still difficult to uphold in certain cultures, particularly in situations where conforming to social norms is important (family meals and banquets, for example). Conforming to what others around oneself are doing, and thereby avoiding the burden of having to make choices, is also a way of reducing one's mental load.

Determinants of individual behaviour

In recent years, two disciplinary fields have seen the convergence of new frameworks for analysing the determinants of individual behaviour that challenge the standard economic model of utility maximization. Informed by a new approach to health, formalized by the World Health Organization (WHO, 1986) with the Ottawa Charter for Health Promotion, the role of food environments in eating behaviour is increasingly recognized in the field of nutrition. This approach typically distinguishes between social environments, which define behavioural patterns and social norms; physical environments in living areas, which determine the conditions of access to food; and macro-environments, made up of the policies, legislation, strategies and practices of the actors involved in the food supply. This model of representation has recently gained recognition, particularly from the High Level Panel of Experts on Food Security and Nutrition (HLPE) in its report on 'Nutrition and Food Systems' (HLPE, 2017).

In the field of psychosociology, several decades of research, synthesized in particular in Saadi Lahlou's installation theory (2018), have led to a similar model. This model posits that the freedom of individual choice is structured by three types of installations: mental, physical and social installations.

Such models identify consumer education, information and awareness-raising as indeed necessary but insufficient to change behaviour. The example of cycling illustrates this well: explaining to individuals that cycling is good for their health and the environment (mental installation) is not enough to get them to use this mode of transport. Almost everyone is likely already convinced. Protected cycle lanes or cycle parks must be built (physical installations) and cycling must become the social norm, with driving a car the exception if not an anomaly (social installation).

These models thus no longer place responsibility for changing individual practices on individuals alone: this responsibility must be shared with the actors who organize the food supply. Public policies that regulate food quality or incentivize companies to improve it can influence prices to encourage or discourage the consumption of certain products, regulate advertising and combat food deserts or food swamps. They therefore remain indispensable in shaping individual behaviour. We can also question the risks associated with the development of digital tools wielded by big data multinationals for the 'conduct of conduct', to use Michel Foucault's expression – in other words, to organize individuals' self-discipline no longer through 'external and corrective constraint applied to bodies but through desire internalized by way of suggestion, prevention and manipulation' (Le Texier, 2011).

Conclusion

Is the sum of individual behaviours enough to change the system? The example of the boycott of Nestlé products in the late 1970s to protest against the promotion of bottle-fed infant formula as a substitute for breastfeeding (Sasson, 2016) is interesting: it was organized and platformed by a political movement that was able to influence the balance of power and led to the adoption of the International Code of Marketing of Breast-Milk Substitutes. This example points to the possible risk of depoliticizing individual activism if it is not given political expression (Michel et al., 2020).

'Voting with one's wallet', thus sending a signal to companies and politicians, is not the only way for citizens to voice their concerns. This form of action ultimately operates only in response to suppliers' offerings – by buying into or rejecting them – but in no way through negotiation allowing for the co-construction of positions. Should the governance of food systems be rethought to enable citizens to take part in defining the food they want? This can be done through spaces such as citizens' conventions, community food centres or even frameworks for agreeing on the products of a food social security system yet to be imagined. These are spaces where, through dialogue, citizen proposals negotiated with public and private actors can be developed to orient food supply, build foodscapes, define solidarity policies and establish transition pathways towards sustainable systems (see Part 5).

Part of this chapter draws on Figuié and Bricas (2009) and on discussions within the IPES-Food panel on consumer sovereignty. The author would like to thank Mathilde Coudray for proofreading this chapter and for her suggested improvements.

References

Bourdieu P., 1984. *Distinction: a social critique of the judgement of taste*, Cambridge, MA, Harvard University Press, 613 p. Translation of 'La distinction: critique sociale du jugement' (1979).

Certeau M. de, 1984. *The practice of everydayl life*. Berkeley, University of California Press, 256 p. Translation of 'L'invention du quotidien. 1. Arts de faire' (1974).

Certeau M. de, Giard L., Mayol P., 1998. *The practice of everyday life*. Vol. 2: Living and cooking, Minneapolis/London, University of Minnesota Press, 292 p. Translation of 'L'invention du quotidien. 2. Habiter, cuisiner' (1994).

Chandon P., Touati N., Ordabayeva N., 2017. Les biais de perception des tailles des portions. *Pratiques en nutrition*, 52: 41–46. https://doi.org/10.1016/j.pranut.2017.09.010

Cooksey-Stowers K., Schwartz M.B., Brownell K.D., 2017. Food swamps predict obesity rates better than food deserts in the United States. *International Journal of Environmental Research and Public Health*, 14(11): 1366. https://doi.org/10.3390/ijerph14111366

Cummins S., Macintyre S., 1999. The location of food stores in urban areas: a case study in Glasgow. *British Food Journal*, 101(7): 545–553. https://doi.org/10.1108/00070709910279027

Currid-Halkett E., 2017. *The sum of small things: a theory of the aspirational class*, Princeton, Princeton University Press, 267 p.

Daniel M., Sirieix L., 2012. Les pratiques durables. Une forme de résistance ordinaire. *Décisions Marketing*, 68: 11–24.

Dubuisson-Quellier S., 2006. De la routine à la délibération. *Réseaux*, 135–136(1–2): 253–284.

Dubuisson-Quellier S., 2009. *La consommation engagée*, Paris, Presses de Sciences Po, 144 p.

Figuié M., Bricas N., 2009. Équité internationale. La surresponsabilisation des consommateurs. *Courrier de la planète*, 87: 41.

Fischler C., 1990. *L'homnivore*, Paris, Odile Jacob, 448 p.

Friedman M., 1996. A positive approach to organized consumer action: the 'buycott' as an alternative to the boycott. *Journal of Consumer Policy*, 19(4): 439–451. https://doi .org/10.1007/BF00411502

Gordon E.L., Ariel-Donges A.H., Bauman V., Merlo L.J., 2018. What is the evidence for 'food addiction?' A systematic review. *Nutrients*, 10(4): 477. https://doi.org/10.3390 /nu10040477

HLPE, 2017. *Nutrition and food systems. A report by the High Level Panel of Experts on Food Security and Nutrition of the Committee on World Food Security*, Rome, Committee on World Food Security, 151 p.

Jacquier C., Bonthoux F., Baciu M., Ruffieux B., 2012. Improving the effectiveness of nutritional information policies: assessment of unconscious pleasure mechanisms involved in food-choice decisions. *Nutrition Reviews*, 70(2): 118–131. https://doi .org/10.1111/j.1753-4887.2011.00447.x

Kartha S., Kemp-Benedict E., Ghosh E., Nazareth A., 2020. *The carbon inequality era. An assessment of the global distribution of consumption emissions among individuals from 1990 to 2015 and beyond*, Oxford, Stockholm Environment Institute and Oxfam International, 50 p.

Lahlou S., 2018. *Installation theory: the societal construction and regulation of behaviour*, Cambridge, Cambridge University Press, 512 p.

Lamine C., 2008. *Les intermittents du bio. Pour une sociologie pragmatique des choix alimentaires émergents*, Paris, Maison des sciences de l'homme, 341 p.

Le Texier T., 2011. Foucault, le pouvoir et l'entreprise: pour une théorie de la gouvernementalité managériale. *Revue de philosophie économique*, 12(2): 53–85. https://doi.org/10.3917/rpec.122.0053

Michel L., Fouilleux E., Bricas N., 2020. Conclusion. Politiser pour ne rien changer ? L'alimentation entre critiques et canalisation de la critique, in Fouilleux E., Michel L. (ed.), *Quand l'alimentation se fait politique(s)*, Rennes, PUR, 329–344.

Micheletti M., Follesdal A., Stolle D. (ed.), 2004. *Politics, products and markets: exploring political consumerism past and present*, New Brunswick/London, Transaction Publishers, 346 p.

Sasson T., 2016. Milking the third world? Humanitarianism, capitalism and the moral economy of the Nestlé boycott. *American Historical Review*, 121(4): 1196–1224. https://doi.org/10.1093/ahr/121.4.1196

Schwartz B., 2005. *The paradox of choice: why more is less*, New York, Harper Perennial, 304 p.

Soutjis B., 2020. Gouverner la qualité alimentaire par les applications. *Sociologies pratiques*, 41(2): 81–94. https://doi.org/10.3917/sopr.041.0081

United Nations, 2021. *Sustainable development goals. Goal 12: ensure sustainable consumption and production patterns*, Brussels, United Nations.

Wansink B., 1996. Can package size accelerate usage volume? *Journal of Marketing*, 60(3): 1–14. https://doi.org/10.1177/002224299606000301

WHO, 1986. *The Ottawa Charter for Health Promotion*, Copenhagen, WHO.

Part Five

An ecology of food to transform food systems

Addressing the sustainability issues facing many food systems is a major challenge for the present and the future of humanity. It also provides an opportunity to establish a new relationship with living beings, both human and non-human.

This requires a different form of organization of food production and consumption, based on a renewed value system shared by all actors. This final part of the book calls for mobilizing citizens (Chapter 19), businesses (Chapter 20), education and research (Chapter 21) and public authorities (Chapter 22) – all actors with a role to play and the power to invent new possibilities together.

This part of the book seeks to spark inspiration and enthusiasm. It presents the pathways of change that some actors are already pursuing. There are of course obstacles to contend with and no single pathway can bring about change alone. Be that as it may, we look at the opportunities, the cooperation, the attempts and the successes that prove that there are many actors calling for change and many levers for action. It is the strength of the ties fuelling this drive for change that is making transformation happen.

Based on shared experience from the last ten years of the Chair's existence, we present initiatives by various actors working towards the transformation of food systems and make a few proposals guided by an ecological approach to food.

19

Citizen initiatives and how to scale them

Nicolas Bricas and Mathilde Douillet

The world of tomorrow is already being experimented with today through a proliferation of citizen initiatives that are inventing new ways of organizing food systems. We explore several ways for these initiatives to expand and enable the necessary transformation of food systems.

During the first lockdown due to the COVID-19 pandemic, references to the 'world that comes after' proliferated in France. It would be reached through the transformative phase of the crisis and would resemble the world that collapsologists have been calling for: one that is respectful of the environment, less thirsty for non-renewable resources, where the health of humans, non-humans and the planet is safeguarded, allowing for a liveable climate; a world that is more equitable, inclusive, democratic and characterized by shared well-being (Lancement and Lévêque, 2019). The great uprising seemed to have finally arrived, and many eyes turned to the citizens who were already trying to invent and experiment with this world beyond new consumption practices (Chapter 18) with new ways of producing, trading, managing and governing.

Does the 'world that comes after' already exist?

This 'world that comes after' seems to have been in the making for years now, under the impetus of citizens and entrepreneurs – for instance, through the movements initiated by the pioneers of organic farming and fair trade. There has been a proliferation of diverse initiatives seeking to build alternative agricultural and food systems, founded on principles such as renewable resource use, relocalization (Chapter 17), the reduction of the number of intermediaries in supply chains, solidarity between producers and consumers, inclusive participation, cooperative purchasing groups and similar initiatives. In France, various studies and surveys have investigated this profusion of initiatives.[1] Among others, the Daniel and Nina Carasso Foundation has supported many such initiatives in France and Spain, considering that these 'daring men and women' are bringing forth solutions that society must take up (Fondation Daniel et Nina Carasso, 2019). Worldwide, but especially in industrialized countries, these initiatives are supported by philanthropic actors concerned with sustainable food systems.[2]

The initiatives are led by a diverse range of actors, all of whom share civic participation as their starting point. Their status varies greatly depending on national legislation, public funding opportunities and the possibilities for volunteer involvement. In France, these actors all fall under the umbrella of the social solidarity economy (SSE), which is taking increasingly diverse forms, particularly with social enterprises, some of which choose to engage in the capitalist market economy (Chapter 20). What these actors have in common is their desire to address one or more of the environmental, social, health and governance concerns that they feel are insufficiently taken into account in dominant models. They strive to invent and experiment with alternatives, often explicitly seeking to challenge industrialized food systems, even if some of them are partly based on this model. Virtually all these initiatives operate on a local scale – that of a farm, a workshop, a neighbourhood or even a small town – and they often involve only a few dozen to a few thousand people.

These initiatives have given rise to abundant scientific literature, which has detailed their characteristics and investigated their role in the transformation of food systems. Many authors have described these initiatives as social innovations spanning a wider range of action than citizen initiatives. These innovations provide new answers to social needs that are inadequately or insufficiently met. Many of them ascribe to an agroecological approach that is at once technical, social and political (Gliessman, 2007). In the English-speaking world, they are often analysed as 'alternative food networks' (Roep and Wiskerke, 2012).

It is important to note that several of these initiatives originated in countries with a rather liberal political philosophy, where individuals or communities are encouraged to address environmental or social issues themselves: permaculture

---

[1] See, for example, the RESOLIS observatory or the Transiscope, the collection of testimonials by the civil society organization 'On passe à l'acte' and the video 'Ça bouge pour l'alimentation' (https://vimeo.com/251774302), and the case studies by students of the Advanced M.Sc' in 'Innovations and Policies for Sustainable Food' (*Mastère spécialisé Innovations et politiques pour une alimentation durable*) (Conaré et al., 2015; Albert et al., 2016, 2017,2018, 2019,2020, 2021,2022).

[2] For example, the Global Alliance for the Future of Food highlights these initiatives in its 'Beacons of Hope' programme (Biovision Foundation for Ecological Development and Global Alliance for the Future of Food, 2019; Global Alliance for the Future of Food, 2021).

was theorized in Australia; the French 'AMAP' (Associations pour le Maintien de l'Agriculture Paysanne) networks are based on the US principle of Community Supported Agriculture; and agricultural and food 'third places' are partly inspired by Community Food Centres in Canada. In France, where the state is more interventionist, interest in these initiatives is more recent. In the agricultural and food sectors, they were long ignored by public authorities, academic research, professional training programmes or advisory and funding institutions. However, the development of the SSE did provide a foothold for them (Bardot, 2020).

These initiatives are based on a set of principles of action: respect for all knowledge, inclusive participation, emancipation and the empowerment of vulnerable persons (Chiffoleau and Paturel, 2016). They invent new possibilities and experiment with alternatives to prove their feasibility and effectiveness (Lutz and Schachinger, 2013). But to what extent do these initiatives have a transformative effect? (see Box 19.1). How can they move beyond the stage of local and confined experiments to account for a greater share of the volumes produced and consumed so as to have a truly massive and positive influence on the environment, health, social equity and governance?

Box 19.1 Social innovations in countries of the Global South

Opposition to industrial agriculture is also emerging in countries of the Global South, led in particular by peasant organizations inspired by the Via Campesina movement that originated in Brazil. Agroecology is championed by numerous civil society organizations that are experimenting with its implementation (IPES-Food, 2018; HLFE, 2019), with the growing support from research actors, for instance, as part of the Transformative Partnership Platform on Agroecology.[3] These movements are still relatively marginal in the face of strong pressure from dominant actors seeking to spread their production and consumption models to countries that are witnessing the emergence of a middle class (allegedly) drawn to the consumer society.

In countries of the Global South, certain non-industrialized agricultural practices can be considered 'sustainable' in the sense that they do not (yet) follow the technological paths of chemical agriculture, which is now being challenged in places where it is dominant. Farmers have been innovating for decades in the fields of soil fertility management, biodiversity and plant and

[3] https://www.agroecologytpp.org.

animal diseases specific to their environments. All this knowledge is a source of inspiration for finding alternatives to conventional farming. How to label these practices remains an issue, as shown in the case of food production in Uganda, a country that is highly involved in organic farming for export markets. Describing them as 'traditional' fails to account for the ways in which they evolve and the farmers' ability to innovate, and risks framing them as rejecting modernity. Calling them 'organic farming practices by default', since no chemicals are used, is problematic as it likens them to organic farming, which is regulated by specifications and certification. As chemical farming has only recently begun to develop in this country, labelling them as 'conventional farming practices' risks conflating them with those of conventional farming in industrialized countries. The women who practise this form of farming speak of *agriganda*, short for 'agriculture' and 'Uganda', referring to a practice that could be described as 'terroir agriculture' (Bendjebbar, 2018).

The same trend can be observed in food processing and retail. Artisanal food makers, street vendors and neighbourhood markets are facing competition from the largest international industries and supermarkets. This industrialization has been criticized for jeopardizing jobs but also more recently for its negative effects on the environment, health and the governance of food systems. From this perspective, 'informal' artisans and retail thus appear as a model that should be supported.

In both cases, it is difficult to describe these initiatives as alternatives, in the sense that they do not aim to replace a dominant model. However, many authors have recognized their ability to approach economic activities as being inextricably linked to social and/or environmental issues (Leloup, 2018). Rather than considering this sector as 'informal', thereby defining it in relation to a formal sector, Jacques Bugnicourt and the teams of Enda Third World have described it as the 'popular economy' (Bugnicourt, 1973; Ndione, 2015). However, the recognition and legitimization of these activities are still controversial: while some see them as constituting a creative sector for sustainable farming or a social solidarity economy (Nyssens, 1999), others regard them as a sign of poverty to be eradicated as part of the modernization process (Maloney, 2003).

Three conceptual frameworks to grasp transformation

Most scientific analyses and many programmes supporting these initiatives assume that, as they multiply, the initiatives are bound to form a system – that is, to interact and synergize with one another to bring about sweeping transformations of the existing conventional food system. Three major conceptual frameworks are articulated to grasp the transformation of food systems:

- The most widely used concept is that of sociotechnical transitions, popularized in particular by Frank Geels (2002). This concept stems from evolutionary economics and science and technology studies. Transitions result from interactions between a sociotechnical landscape, a regulatory regime and innovation niches. Innovation niches are the home ground of citizen initiatives and other social innovations that seize the opportunities created by challenges to, and the destabilization of, the regulatory regime to ultimately change it and bring about a new ecological and social regime.
- Food regime theory (Friedmann and McMichael, 1989), which stems from political economy, places greater emphasis on the power dynamics at play in challenging the dominant regime. Social innovations represent a critical force that seeks to delegitimize it. The dominant regime responds to this challenge by offering products with new environmental and social attributes through product certification and labelling, without any real structural change occurring. As with the sociotechnical transitions approach, this theory is articulated at a societal scale within the framework of critical and rather descriptive analysis and says nothing about the potential for changing the scale of alternative initiatives.
- Pragmatic sociology combines the actor–network theory of Bruno Latour and Michel Callon with the sociology of criticism based on the works of Luc Boltanski, Laurent Thévenot and Francis Chateauraynaud. It is more concerned with grasping the multiple forms of action of 'agents' and the detailed changes underway, through the analysis of ordinary practices and controversies among actors.

Drawing on these three conceptual frameworks, Lamine et al. (2015) consider the initiatives through the prism of a new question: Do they embody a real paradigm shift or are they business as usual?

Alternative or reform pathways

The development of these initiatives can be split into two categories: alternative pathways and reform pathways. Alternative pathways seek to build a system – generally local – based on radically different values that depart from the dominant capitalist or even market model. They propose answers to the various environmental, social, health, cultural and governance issues surrounding food systems through multidimensional initiatives. Permaculture exemplifies this type of alternative. In his book *Permaculture: Principles and Pathways Beyond Sustainability*, David Holmgren (2002) contrasts the principles of industrial farming with those of sustainable farming and considers that there is no possible compromise between the two: sustainable farming can only come about after the inevitable decline of industrial agriculture, following a chaotic postmodern climax. This in turn points to the need to experiment with alternative solutions, to prepare them today for the 'world that comes after' and, as he puts it, to 'use small and slow solutions'. In her study on sustainable food and the SSE, Florence Bardot (2020) notes that the leaders of multidimensional initiatives are mainly concerned with developing and stabilizing their project in its specific context and that they need more time to do so than projects tackling just one issue. Hence why they sometimes struggle to 'capitalize on' their experience and to define key principles to facilitate the latter's application elsewhere. For these actors, the question of changing the scale of the initiatives does not necessarily arise, as it is not a priority. Some may even be reluctant to do so for fear of losing control of the process and of the values they uphold being corrupted as the innovations become institutionalized.

Reform pathways, on the other hand, focus on developing new market niches by forming alliances or compromising with the actors of the dominant system. The leaders of projects that follow such pathways can be simple opportunists who see these initiatives and the interest they spark as signs of possible market demand that they can exploit, without seeking to truly transform the system. This includes, in part, social business and many of the innovations denounced as greenwashing or fairwashing. In their book *The New Spirit of Capitalism*, Luc Boltanski and Ève Chiapello (2005) clearly showed the dominant system's ability to be sensitive to the criticisms levelled at it – even the most radical ones – and to use them as sources of inspiration to commodify the answers to these criticisms, with products labelled as respectful of the environment, fair and socially responsible. This is what makes capitalism so resilient, so capable of overcoming the criticisms it receives by absorbing them without ever being called into question.

Other actors are convinced that this alliance with the dominant system gives rise to reforms that are conducive to the development of sustainable food systems. The 'fair trade' label, for instance, has taken the issue of equity in international trade beyond the confines of activist circles and raised awareness among the general public. The institutionalization of organic farming has increased its importance and offers the hope of large-scale environmental impact. These reformers claim to be pragmatic: they recognize the might of the dominant system and the impossibility of replacing it in the short term and seek instead to reform it from within. In both cases, the innovations driven by these actors often pertain to one, or perhaps two, dimensions of sustainability: the environment or social equity, or at best both – for instance, with the 'organic and fair trade' label. Integrating all environmental, social, health and governance issues is very complicated.

Behind this distinction between reform pathways and alternative pathways lies a complex reality, of course, and there are also intermediate pathways that evolve over time. Ronan Le Velly (2018) shows that certain so-called alternative approaches are not always so alternative. Often, they are hybridized with elements of the dominant system. For example, many of these alternative initiatives make extensive use of the digital tools of GAFAM (Google, Apple, Facebook, Amazon, Microsoft). They can also define themselves in relation to the system they are challenging, as in the case of fair trade, which establishes a fairness premium for farmers based on conventional market prices. A collective research programme coordinated by Pierre Gasselin et al. (2023), which analysed these initiatives' relationships with dominant systems, called into question evolutionary visions that consider the various food systems as stages – from domestic to artisanal and then to industrial systems – towards new sustainable models in the future. While such approaches have the merit of defining simple models and their 'modernist' narrative can be appealing, they struggle to account for grey and hybrid areas – those of dynamic coexistence between artisanal, industrial or alternative systems where complementarities can be leveraged, affording resilience.

Changing scale

Expanding the scale of these initiatives is generally seen as the main driver of the transformation of conventional agri-food systems. What the initiatives' critics denounce is, indeed, their lack of impact 'at scale'. Michele-Lee Moore et al. (2015) distinguish between three types of scale change:

- Scaling out consists of increasing the number of people or organizations impacted. This can be done by replicating the initiative in other territories (multiplying the number of social and solidarity grocery shops or community gardens) or through cross-pollination – that is, the dissemination of principles or know-how, particularly through specifications or labels (certified fair trade, for example). The actors of alternative initiatives often endeavour to scale out their innovations through swarming and multiplication. To state one of the principles of permaculture: 'Think globally, act locally'.

- Scaling up consists in institutionalizing the initiative, which translates into it becoming embedded in public policies or regulations, at the risk of simplifying and weakening its initial principles. Organic farming, for example, is in the process of being scaled up.
- Scaling deep consists in profoundly changing the cultural values and beliefs that become entrenched in a society. The importance given to 'local' food, which is on track to become a widely shared norm in France, could illustrate this process (Chapter 17).

There is a fourth type of change of scale to consider: diversification. This approach is central to the multidimensional alternative initiatives described above and is exemplified by the Canadian food hubs that are developing in France. It consists in integrating a new activity focused on a new dimension of sustainability to enrich an initiative's model (adding social objectives to activities that were initially geared mainly towards environmental goals, for example). It can also involve collective cooperation dynamics, as is often observed in alternative projects that are firmly anchored in their territories (such as partnerships between social actors and agricultural producers for solidarity boxes). These different types of scaling up are diverse, and in practice they are combined or carried out successively over time, based on how the initiative evolves (Avise, 2021).

A key question that has received little attention in the literature concerns the role of public funding in supporting the growth of citizen-led innovations in sustainable food systems, their changes in scale and their ability to survive in the current market economy. The public funding cuts witnessed around the world are inextricably linked to the rise of a liberal ideology inspired by Anglosphere countries, which advocates only short-term support for the development of these innovations and modest support for scaling them up, and mainly prioritizes social entrepreneurs seeking profitability through a commercial model. However, some initiatives, which provide a public service, cannot be remunerated by the current market and need long-term public support. Scaling up of what citizen initiatives are inventing in order to accelerate the transformation of food systems requires public policies to create environments that foster access to financial services, training, research and so on. Philanthropy can play a role in supporting precursors and innovation, but it cannot replace public support in the long term.

Conclusion

Discussions with the actors involved in 'alternative' initiatives clearly show that most of them are so preoccupied with implementing their projects that they do not necessarily have the time or the skills to define their contribution to the changes that they want to see in food systems. Nor is it necessarily their role. Therein should lie the purpose of public support for these initiatives and of the policies they fuel: they should support the learning and scaling of actions beyond confined initiatives. For example, a municipal school catering initiative to reduce waste, improve nutrition and provide access to a balanced meal for the most disadvantaged demands considerable energy. But it is important to remember that school catering accounts for no more than 2 per cent of the meals eaten by a city's entire population. The challenge is therefore not only to improve this catering, which is limited in scope, but also to develop its ripple effect on the rest of the food system. Public research has an important role to play in this reflection and support (Chapter 21).

It is also important to bear in mind the 'counterfactual' context in which these initiatives are developing: an industrialized food system that feeds the population on a large scale at low economic cost (made possible by very high hidden environmental and social costs). Alternative solutions often go hand in hand with economic and social conditions of access as well as particular discourses that make true social inclusion difficult. As we heard during our fieldwork, 'the best place for social diversity in the city is the supermarket'. The difficulty of spreading initiatives to a whole population and particularly to the large mass of people with little money, time or space to spare, already well documented in the context of projects in developing countries (Chambers, 1983), can also be observed in various sustainable food initiatives. Despite the conviction of their promoters, who are often highly educated and aware, getting the whole population to embrace their views is in no way straightforward. Breaking out of social enclaves and ensuring social inclusion (which needs to be developed from the outset of a project) is a crucial challenge when changing the scale of an initiative (Lepiller and Valette, 2021).

Finally, even if initiatives can be recognized as providing solutions, they disrupt the existing set of actors in place and implicitly or explicitly challenge some of them. As long as they remain marginal, there is little pushback. When they become truly influential, however, they can sometimes be openly challenged.[4] Being able to stand their ground in negotiation spaces requires a

---

[4] See American trade unionist Nicholas Klein's statement to garment workers in 1918 or Gandhi's statement in his *Young India* journal of 9 March 1921: 'First they ignore you, then they laugh at you, then they fight you, then you win' (Refalo, 2019).

political strength that scattered actors lack. Although various networks exist to connect the actors working in the sustainable food space, they are often dedicated to organizing best practice and sharing experiences. They have only recently begun to form a political force capable of negotiating like the dominant players. This undoubtedly provides a path towards a real transformation of future food systems.

The authors would like to thank Damien Conaré, Mathilde Coudray and Marie Walser for proofreading this chapter and for their suggested improvements.

References

Albert S., Bricas N., Conaré D., Coudray M., Fournier S., Moity-Maïzi P., Razes M. (ed.), 2019. *Actes de la journée des innovations pour une alimentation durable. JIPAD 2019*, Montpellier, Montpellier SupAgro/Cirad/Chaire Unesco Alimentations du monde, 127 p.

Albert S., Bricas N., Conaré D., Coudray M., Fournier S., Moity-Maïzi P., Razes M. (ed.), 2020. *Actes de la journée des innovations pour une alimentation durable. JIPAD 2020*, Montpellier, Montpellier SupAgro/Cirad/Chaire Unesco Alimentations du monde, 119 p.

Albert S., Bricas N., Conaré D., Coudray M., Fournier S., Moity-Maïzi P., Razes M. (ed.), 2021. *Actes de la journée des innovations pour une alimentation durable. JIPAD 2021*, Montpellier, Montpellier SupAgro/Cirad/Chaire Unesco Alimentations du monde.

Albert S., Bricas N., Conaré D., Coudray M., Fournier S., Moity-Maïzi P., Razes M. (ed.), 2022. *Actes de la journée des innovations pour une alimentation durable. JIPAD 2022*, Montpellier, Montpellier SupAgro/Cirad/Chaire Unesco Alimentations du monde.

Albert S., Bricas N., Conaré D., Debru J., Fournier S., Misrahi A., Moity-Maïzi P. (ed.), 2016. *Actes de la journée des innovations pour une alimentation durable. JIPAD 2016*, Montpellier, Montpellier SupAgro/Cirad/Chaire Unesco Alimentations du monde, 117 p.

Albert S., Bricas N., Conaré D., Fages R., Fournier S., Misrahi A., Moity-Maïzi P. (ed.), 2017. *Actes de la journée des innovations pour une alimentation durable. JIPAD 2017*, Montpellier, Montpellier SupAgro/Cirad/Chaire Unesco Alimentations du monde, 165 p.

Albert S., Bricas N., Conaré D., Fages R., Fournier S., Misrahi A., Moity-Maïzi P. (ed.), 2018. *Actes de la journée des innovations pour une alimentation durable. JIPAD 2018*, Montpellier, Montpellier SupAgro/Cirad/Chaire Unesco Alimentations du monde, 213 p.

Avise, 2021. *Stratégies pour changer d'échelle. Le guide des entreprises de l'économie sociale et solidaire qui veulent maximiser leur impact social*, Paris, Avise, 56 p.

Bardot F., 2020. *Alimentation durable et économie sociale et solidaire: les liaisons fertiles*, Paris, Fondation Daniel et Nina Carasso, 34 p.

Bendjebbar P., 2018. *Vers un modèle bio africain ? Trajectoires comparées d'institutionnalisation de l'agriculture biologique au Bénin et en Ouganda*, thèse de doctorat, spécialité Sciences politiques, Université Paris-Est, Paris, 424 p.

Biovision Foundation for Ecological Development, Global Alliance for the Future of Food, 2019. *Beacons of hope: accelerating transformations to sustainable food systems*, Zurich, Biovision Foundation for Ecological Development/Global Alliance for the Future of Food, 80 p.

Boltanski L., Chiapello È., 2005. *The new spirit of capitalism*, London/New York, Verso, 601 p. Translation of 'Le nouvel esprit du capitalisme' (1999).

Bugnicourt J., 1973. *Économie infra-urbaine et marginaux. Quelques éléments pour une controverse*, Dakar, IDEP, 30 p.

Chambers R., 1983. *Rural Development: Putting the Last First*, London, Longman, 246 p.

Chiffoleau Y., Paturel D., 2015. Les circuits courts alimentaires « pour tous », outils d'analyse de l'innovation sociale. *Innovations*, 50(2): 191–210. https://doi.org/10.3917/inno.050.0191

Conaré D., Haon L., Bricas N., Fournier S., Chamussy G. (ed.), 2015. *Actes de la journée des innovations pour une alimentation durable. JIPAD 2015*, Montpellier, Montpellier SupAgro/Cirad/Chaire Unesco Alimentations du monde, 215 p.

Fondation Daniel et Nina Carasso, 2019. *La transition en actions. Des initiatives inspirantes pour une agriculture et une alimentation plus durables*, Paris, Fondation Daniel et Nina Carasso, 43 p.

Friedmann H., McMichael P.. 1989. Agriculture and the State System: the rise and decline of national agricultures, 1370 to the present. *Sociologia Ruralis*, 29(2): 93–117. https://doi.org/10.1111/j.1467-9523.1989.tb00360.x

Gasselin P., Lardon S., Cerdan C., Loudiyi S., Sautier D., (ed.), 2023. *Coexistence and confrontation of agricultural and food models: a new paradigm of territorial development?*, Dordrecht, Springer, 315 p. Translation of 'Coexistence et confrontation des modèles agricoles et alimentaires. Un nouveau paradigme du développement territorial ?' (2023). https://doi.org/10.1007/978-94-024-2178-1

Geels F.W., 2002. Technological transitions as evolutionary reconfiguration processes: a multi-level perspective and a case-study. *Research Policy*, 31(8–9): 1257–1274. https://doi.org/10.1016/S0048-7333(02)00062-8

Gliessman S.R., 2007. *Agroécology: the ecology of sustainable food systems*, Boca Raton, CRC Press, 384 p.

Global Alliance for the Future of Food, 2021. *Beacons of hope: stories of food systems transformation during COVID-19*, Toronto, Global Alliance for the Future of Food, 37 p.

HLPE, 2019. *Agroecological and other innovative approaches for sustainable agriculture and food systems that enhance food security and nutrition. A report by The High Level Panel of Experts on Food Security and Nutrition of the Committee on World Food Security*, Rome, Committee on World Food Security.

Holmgren D., 2002. *Permaculture: principles and pathways beyond sustainability*, Hepburn, Holmgren Design Services, 286 p.

IPES-Food, 2018. *Breaking away from industrial food and farming systems: seven case studies of agroecological transition*, Brussels, IPES-Food, 112 p.

Lamine C., Bui S., Ollivier G., 2015. *Pour une approche systémique et pragmatique de la transition écologique des systèmes agri-alimentaires*. Cahiers de recherche sociologique, 58: 95–117. https://doi.org/10.7202/1036208ar

Lancement K., Lévêque S., 2019. *Théma – L'action citoyenne – Accélératrice de transitions vers des modes de vie plus durables*, Paris, Commissariat général au développement durable, 73 p.

Leloup F., 2018. Introduction au numéro « Économie populaire et développement réel dans les Suds: un état des lieux des savoirs ». *Mondes en développement*, 181(1): 7–10. https://doi.org/10.3917/med.181.0007

Lepiller O., Valette E., 2021. Urban food innovations – scaling and social inclusion issues. *So What? A collection of the Unesco Chair in World Food Systems* (14), 4 p.

Le Velly R., 2018. Is it relevant to talk about 'alternative' agrifood networks? *So What? A collection of the Unesco Chair in World Food Systems* (8), 4 p.

Lutz J., Schachinger J., 2013. Do local food networks foster socio-ecological transitions towards food sovereignty? Learning from real place experiences. *Sustainability*, 5(11): 4778–4796. https://doi.org/10.3390/su5114778

Maloney W.F., 2003. Informal self-employment: poverty trap or decent alternative?, in Fields G.S., Pfeffermann G. (ed.), *Pathways out of poverty: private firms and economic mobility in developing countries*, Dordrecht, Springer, 65–82.

Moore M.-L., Riddell D., Vocisano D., 2015. Scaling out, scaling up, scaling deep: strategies of non-profits in advancing systemic social innovation. *Journal of Corporate Citizenship*, 58: 67–84. https://doi.org/10.9774/GLEAF.4700.2015.ju.00009

Ndione E.S., 2015. *Le don et le recours, ressorts de l'économie urbaine*, Dakar, Enda Graf Sahel, 274 p.

Nyssens M., 1999. L'économie populaire: creuset de pratiques d'économie solidaire ?, in Fonteneau B., Fall A. (ed.), *L'économie sociale au Nord et au Sud*, Bruxelles, De Boeck, 159–178.

Refalo A., 2019. About a quote falsely attributed to Gandhi: « First they ignore you. Then they laugh at you. Then they attack you. Then you win ». *Nonviolence, Écologie et Résistances*.

Roep D., Wiskerke J.S.C., 2012. Reshaping the foodscape: the role of alternative food networks, in Spaargaren G., Oosterveer P., Loeber A. (ed.), *Food practices in transition: changing food consumption, retail and production in the age of reflexive modernity*, New York, Routledge, 207–228.

20

Towards new company models?

Myriam Kessari, Magalie Marais, Maryline Meyer,
Florence Palpacuer, Leïla Temri and Marie Walser

*There are two forms of corporate commitment within the food system: the
Social and Solidarity Economy (SSE) and Corporate Social Responsibility
(CSR). While these two movements have developed independently of each
other, at present both are contributing to the transformation of food systems.*

Among the many actors able to influence the sustainability of food systems,
businesses have a key role to play. Their ways of doing so are as diverse as the
companies themselves, which differ in both their functions (production,
processing, distribution, services etc.) and their profiles (status, size, mission,
geographical location, mode of governance etc.). The question then becomes
how much room for manoeuvre these companies have, what their motivations
are and which concomitant forms of commitment to food system sustainability
exist (Marais, 2014). The economic, social and environmental responsibility
approaches of companies operating in the food system follow two main routes:
the social solidarity economy (SSE) and corporate social responsibility (CSR).
This chapter looks at the benefits and limitations of these two frameworks and
discusses the opportunities afforded by their articulation.

The SSE: Solidarity as an anchor point

The SSE has its roots in the Industrial Revolution in Europe (Nicolas, 1988). The
emergence of a working class in the late nineteenth century saw the formation of
the first trade unions and the first consumer cooperatives, with the emblematic case
of the Rochdale Society of Equitable Pioneers in the United Kingdom established
in 1866: weavers came together to make joint bulk purchases and thus benefit

from better prices. A few years earlier (1834), in the city of Lyon, France, Michel-Marie Derrion followed in the footsteps of Charles Fourier's socialist utopia and experimented with the very first consumer cooperatives (grocery shops, bakeries, clothing stores etc.) within the framework of a 'true and social commerce'. But the cooperative movement really gained momentum at the very beginning of the twentieth century with the creation of large consumer cooperatives such as La Bellevilloise, La Prolétarienne, L'Union and La Ménagère (Gautier, 2012). Similar organizations also developed in other European countries, particularly in Italy. Agricultural cooperatives emerged during the same wave: farmers pooled their production, then processed and sold it themselves without the help of merchants. The first wine cooperative, created in the Hérault region of France in 1901 under the name 'Vignerons libres de Maraussan' (Draperi and Touzard, 2003), sold its wine directly to La Bellevilloise in Paris. Over the course of the twentieth century, cooperatives gradually secured their place in the European and global economy. In 2021, the International Cooperative Alliance reported more than three million cooperatives in existence worldwide, mainly in the agricultural sector but also in the finance and insurance industries.

In France, SSE enterprises were historically defined by their status. They could be non-profit organizations, mutual benefit societies, cooperatives or foundations, which abided by the same ethical principles of shared governance, non-remuneration of capital and member satisfaction. Since the 2014 law on the SSE, this definition has become inclusive: social enterprises are not-for-profit private organizations providing goods or services directly related to their explicit aim of benefiting the community. They rely on a collective dynamic involving various types of stakeholders in their governing bodies, place a high value on their autonomy and bear the economic risks linked to their activity (Defourny and Nyssens, 2008). This change means that so-called traditional companies that commit to SSE principles can also be considered SSE enterprises. In France, a wide variety of forms of collective organization and legal statuses exist for agricultural and food activities.

The actions carried out by SSE organizations in the field of food and agriculture tend to have a strong collective and cooperative dimension, where joint reflection and planning are essential. In the agricultural and food sectors, cooperatives remain emblematic of this collective dimension, even if their precise actions and societal impacts seem difficult to define. Biocoop (distributor) and Ethiquable (importer, processor) are two examples of cooperatives committed to supporting organic farming or fair trade, which relies on producer groupings upstream (cooperatives or associations).

SSE enterprises are generally anchored in 'the local' and are 'at the service of' and 'connected to' their communities. According to Jérôme Blanc (2008), there is a form of sustainability inherent in the territorial anchoring of SSE enterprises that makes it difficult, for example, to imagine 'employee-members voting to relocate an activity that sustains them'. The boundary that can exist in traditional companies between external stakeholders (users, suppliers, customers) and internal stakeholders (employees, owners) partly disappears in SSE companies, which removes many obstacles to the development of sustainable initiatives (Akhabbar and Swaton, 2011).

Through its very principles, the SSE provides an avenue for the development of economic models geared towards serving the general interest. Many citizen initiatives developing in the sustainable agriculture and sustainable food spaces are rooted in SSE principles (Chapter 19). These initiatives may support professional integration, the development of the circular economy, fair trade and the development of more solidaristic and cooperative modes of production, processing and supply as well as other inclusive economic practices.[1] Their main objective is not the reproduction of capital but social utility. While SSE enterprises are ahead of the game regarding democratic governance, they sometimes fall short in environmental areas (Nyssens and Petrella, 2015). They are now being encouraged to better formalize their responsible initiatives, to improve the implementation of their founding principles (Bidet et al., 2019) and to measure their societal and environmental impacts in concrete terms.

Through its activist foundations and the specificities of its forms of organization, the SSE offers a promising way to co-build new shared narratives on the scale of territories and a new social contract on a national scale (Bernon and Morvan, 2021). At the same time, this is also forcing so-called traditional companies in the food system to change, especially the food processing and distribution giants.

CSR: When 'traditional' companies take responsibility for their impacts

CSR originated in large companies which, from the late nineteenth century, concentrated capital, production tools and human resources, particularly in the United States. Spurred by a religious impetus inspired by Protestantism – or by Catholicism in France – and initially by philanthropic goals, the heads of these

---

[1] For an illustration, see the report *Alimentation durable et économie sociale et solidaire: les liaisons fertiles* (Bardot, 2020).

companies contemplated their responsibility towards society and the communities in which they operated. This was also partly about restoring their legitimacy, which was being challenged by various waves of social movements. The concept of CSR entered academia in the mid-twentieth century with the work of Howard Bowen (1953), who argued that the purpose of this approach for a company is to endow it with a mission that complements and is distinct from its profit motive. In the English-speaking world, this ambition was formalized in the 1970s through the concept of corporate purpose. For example, the Ben & Jerry's ice cream parlour chain, founded in 1978, broke ground by declaring from its early years that it was pursuing a 'triple mission' guided by economic, social and product goals (Utopias, 2021).

In the 1980s, corporate social responsibility became part of the 'sustainable development' movement. The Brundtland Report (Brundtland, 1987) greatly contributed to popularizing this concept. Consulting firms (such as SustainAbility, from 1994) facilitated the articulation of CSR and sustainable development within companies. In 1995, the world's major companies formed the World Business Council for Sustainable Development (WBCSD). The European Union, for its part, adopted CSR in the 2000s, particularly with the publication of a Green Paper (European Commission, 2001) that provided a reference definition of CSR as 'a concept whereby companies integrate social and environmental concerns in their business operations and in their interaction with their stakeholders on a voluntary basis'. Since then, the definition has evolved and places more emphasis on impacts rather than on voluntary integration alone. It now refers to 'the responsibility of enterprises for their impacts on society' (European Commission, 2011).

Different degrees of CSR implementation exist, depending on the level of commitment of a company's leadership and the associated market outlook. These range from avoiding CSR or simply publishing indicators, in cases where the issue is peripheral to the company's activity, to placing transformation at the very heart of the company's business model (Abdirahman and Sauvée, 2014). Companies' CSR approach can be motivated by criticism levelled at them: as the industrial food system is criticized for the risks it presents (economic, health, environmental etc.; see Chapter 7) and for the opacity maintained by certain multinationals, it in turn feeds on this criticism and responds to it through its innovations (Boltanski and Chiapello, 2005; Lepiller and Yount-André, 2019).

In their most opportunistic forms, CSR approaches are rather inconsistent and mostly involve commercial niches (which ought to be distinguished from greenwashing – marketing practices that aim to give an illusion of environmental responsibility). Some companies thus invest in new markets initially considered as niches but with strong development potential, such as fair trade, organic farming or plant-based protein. Investment in these new commercial areas is most often associated with compliance with specifications and certification procedures to guarantee the sustainability of products (Alphandery et al., 2012).

Some companies develop their CSR approach after being 'shaken' by stakeholders demanding that they commit to more responsible behaviour. These stakeholders can be within the company itself (employees, shareholders etc.) cr in the value chain (suppliers, customers, consumers), or they may be service providers and subcontractors, economic partners (banks etc.), public authorities, media outlets, trade unions or even NGOs, communities of citizens or inhabitants. Some NGOs' documented publications on companies' practices can have a strong impact on their trajectory. Examples include the Oxfam report[2] *Behind the Brands* (Hoffmann, 2013), which assessed the social and environmental policies of ten of the world's most powerful food and beverage companies in 2013,[3] and the *Soy Scorecard* report (WWF, 2016), which examined several major corporations' commitments and actions surrounding soy use in 2016. By mobilizing citizen power and public opinion, such organizations can exert pressure on food processing giants to change their practices positively in order to avoid coming under fire. This is what Weaver (1986) calls the 'politics of blame avoidance'. In the era of impact investing, reports such as that of the Food Foundation (which rates British supermarkets and restaurants) are playing a growing role among investors and shareholders who are increasingly eager to support responsible companies.

The effective implementation of CSR involves a large number of frameworks drawn up by different organizations. At the international level, these include the United Nations Global Compact (2000) and the Organisation for Economic Co-operation and Development (OECD) Guidelines for Multinational Enterprises, with a version tailored to 'responsible agricultural supply chains' released in 2016. It is also worth mentioning the reporting standards of the Global Reporting Initiative, an independent international organization founded in 1997 following the Exxon environmental disaster, and the Food and Agriculture Benchmark of the World Benchmarking Alliance. Finally, the ISO 26000 standard is the result of cooperation among more than 400 representatives from 99 ISO member countries (including sixty-nine developing countries) and forty-two public- and private-sector organizations. This standard offers guidance only; it is not certifiable. It was tailored to the food chain in 2019 with the ISO/TS 26030

---

[2] An international development organization that strives to mobilize citizen power to fight poverty.
[3] Associated British Foods (ABF), Coca-Cola, Danone, General Mills, Kellogg, Mars, Mondelez International (formerly Kraft Foods), Nestlé, PepsiCo and Unilever.

standard. It is important to note that the UN Guiding Principles on Business and Human Rights declared in 2011 also provide a framework for CSR based on respect for human rights, particularly within a company's supply chain or 'sphere of influence'.

One of the most emblematic private initiatives at the international level is the private label 'B Corp', which certifies companies that can demonstrate real impact in five major areas: governance, the environment, community, workers and customers. The ambition of the international community of B Corp–certified companies is to generate an ecosystem of businesses striving to improve their societal and environmental impact beyond their economic performance and to spread their 'best practices' to their suppliers, partners or customers.

The food processing giant Danone offers an example of a company that has explicitly stated its intent to make CSR issues central to its mission. The company's twofold founding project of pursuing economic performance hand in hand with social progress, which was undermined from the 1990s by the growing influence of financial rationales, gave rise to numerous initiatives over the following decade to restore its social legitimacy. For example, the company launched the Danone Communities solidarity fund[4] as well as a partnership with small farmers to guarantee them a 'decent standard of living'. By becoming Danone's first B Corp subsidiary, the company Les prés rient bio (Les 2 Vaches), which is developing a sustainable organic dairy industry in Normandy (using conversion subsidies and innovative contracts with partner dairy farmers), shows that a multinational can commit to preserving the interests of its stakeholders, even the least powerful ones.

Despite the transformations that large shareholding companies have introduced in their governance or management, driven by a desire to commit to strong sustainability, they remain subject to the capitalist imperatives of immediate economic profitability and shareholder remuneration, which can weaken their societal and environmental commitments. As for SSE companies, which are underpinned by a commitment to 'social responsibility', the reality of their practices also confronts them with their own set of tensions.

Towards a convergence of models?

Although SSE and CSR are two distinct forms of commitment that have each followed their own path, some areas of convergence can now be observed. Some SSE enterprises have chosen to follow a 'traditional' CSR labelling route in

---

[4] Social investment fund created in partnership with Nobel Peace Prize laureate Muhammad Yunus.

order to strengthen their legitimacy and meet market requirements: there is growing demand from customers, traders and distributors in the food industry for companies to address new societal and environmental issues. This reflects the increased watchfulness – of consumers in particular – over the industry's practices. In 2017, a small group of cooperative wineries (SSE organizations) thus created the non-profit organization Vignerons engagés to initiate a collective CSR process. Their objective is to support the actions of winemakers within the framework of a global approach to sustainable development, enabling them to capitalize on their differentiation and bring new added value to their production. Beyond commercial considerations, this collective approach strengthens the entities' cooperative identity by professionalizing their practices through the implementation of a structured CSR process. It allows the cooperatives to 'reconnect' with their stakeholders, mainly the cooperative members. The commitment to new environmental requirements strengthens cooperative solidarity, thereby giving new meaning to this organizational model (Meyer et al., 2017). The cooperatives are thus striving to play a political role and demonstrate that, beyond the proliferation of labels in the agri-food industry – intended above all to send signals to the market – an authentic approach to responsible farming that is both federating and transformative can exist.

The proliferation of labels and certifications (Alliot et al., 2021) does however raise questions insofar as it allows any company, irrespective of its actual commitments, to display a 'green', 'local' or 'social' label on food products. This exacerbated commodification of CSR, which casts doubt on the transformative capacity of 'traditional' companies' voluntary initiatives, is paralleled by other potential limitations of SSE enterprises when these tend to prioritize growth, for example, thereby undermining their founding values in the process. Thus, the specific statutes of cooperatives, mutual benefit societies or non-profit organizations can appear as necessary but insufficient conditions to ensure the ESS's effective contribution to more sustainable food systems. Rather, the most promising potential lies in the combination of a strong political project led by organizations committed to a transition and a form of governance that guarantees the prioritization of social and environmental goals over economic rationales (considering these as means, not ends).

In parallel, CSR frameworks are shifting towards recognizing companies' social and environmental functions. In France, for example, the 2019 PACTE law introduced the status of *entreprise à mission* ('mission-based company'), which allows companies to state their raison d'être in the form of several social and environmental objectives beyond their solely economic mission, to which they were previously limited (Segrestin et al., 2021). In line with its twofold economic and societal project initiated in 1972 by Antoine Riboud, in 2020 Danone was the first French CAC 40 company to adopt this status, followed by other food processing companies such as the agricultural cooperative group InVivo. Mission-based companies feature a committee comprised of different stakeholders tasked with monitoring the fulfilment of the company's mission, and the implementation of the commitments is evaluated by an independent body. The creation of this status seems to bring CSR closer to the SSE, but a difference between the two approaches remains. In the case of CSR and even mission-based companies, profit is still the company's primary purpose. What this status recognizes is the ability to exhibit what one might describe as complementary environmental and social functions. Unlike the SSE, the mission-based company status does not impose any constraints surrounding the redistribution of dividends or wage policy. And there is still a risk that the continued prioritization of financial returns will sideline social and environmental objectives and prevent genuine societal impact (Marais et al., 2020). Nevertheless, this law signals a shift towards the recognition of corporate social and environmental responsibility, even if the conditions of its implementation and its real impact are still in question (Morteo and Tchotourian, 2019).

Another development worth mentioning is the involvement of companies in territorial processes such as territorial food projects (*projets alimentaires territoriaux*, PAT) or territorial business clusters for economic cooperation (*pôles territoriaux de coopération économique*, PTCEs). In the food production and distribution space, these projects or clusters are informed by network-based models which, by replacing a linear form of organization of agriculture, encourage sharing or even pooling logistical resources and skills, designing new services, leveraging the strengths of the circular economy and involving consumers (Bernon and Morvan, 2021). These initiatives hinge on SSE organizations collaborating with traditional companies.

Conclusion

The business world appears to be grasping the need to transform food systems in the face of sustainability challenges. The SSE and CSR – two frameworks contributing to this transformation – have been met with a certain enthusiasm. In several regions of the world, these forms of action have been legally institutionalized, with the recognition of a specific status for companies that set themselves a purpose other than profit alone: the Benefit Corporation in the

United States, the *Società Benefit* in Italy, the *Sociedades de Beneficio e Interés Colectivo* in Colombia, the *Sociétés à mission* in France and so on (Utopies, 2021). The pressure from the market, with the demand for food that guarantees its conditions of production and trade, as well as the political pressure exerted by NGOs denouncing certain companies' practices, has largely contributed to the interest in these forms of commitment.

For a company to truly play a role in the transition to sustainable food systems, lessons from past experience show that it needs to combine a strong political commitment with a suitable form of participatory and broad-based internal governance. These two factors can ensure the long-term preservation of the company's social and environmental functions. Both a strong project and the instruments to implement it are needed.

On this last point, there is still progress to be made to transform the environment in which companies operate. Finance is one of the crucial parameters of this environment. Even if a form of social and environmental responsibility is slowly developing among investors and shareholders, they are not the real drivers of change towards social responsibility within businesses. In the financial management of companies, the development of green accounting – which makes it possible to measure not only financial but also environmental results – is showing the way (Rambaud and Richard, 2015).

The authors would like to thank Nicolas Bricas, Damien Conaré, Mathilde Coudray and Mathilde Douillet for proofreading this chapter and for their suggested improvements.

References

Abdirahman Z.-Z., Sauvée L., 2014. Agro-alimentaire. La responsabilité sociétale des entreprises, levier d'une dynamique créatrice de valeur ? *Le Demeter*, 2014: 24–72.

Akhabbar A., Swaton S., 2011. *Économie du développement durable et économie sociale et solidaire: des relations complexes pour des enjeux majeurs*, Munich Personal RePEc Archive, Munich, University Library of Munich, 25 p.

Alliot C., Feige-Muller M., McAdams-Marin D., Alice G., Benoit G., Segré H. et al., 2021. *Étude de démarches de durabilité dans le domaine alimentaire*. Rapport d'analyse transverse, Paris, Basic/WWF/Greenpeace, 54 p.

Alphandéry P., Djama M., Fortier A., Fouilleux E., 2012. *Normaliser au nom du développement durable*, Versailles, Quæ, 198 p.

Bardot F., 2020. *Alimentation durable et économie sociale et solidaire: les liaisons fertiles*, Paris, Fondation Daniel & Nina Carasso, 34 p.

Bernon F., Morvan M., 2021. Pour une dynamique de coopération des acteurs sur les territoires: la contribution du Labo de l'ESS. *Marché et organisations*, 40(1): 53–70. https://doi.org/10.3917/maorg.040.0053

Bidet É., Filippi M., Richez-Battesti N., 2019. Repenser l'entreprise de l'ESS à l'aune de la RSE et de la loi Pacte. *RECMA*, 353(3): 124–137. https://doi.org/10.3917/recma.353.0124

Blanc J., 2008. Responsabilité sociale des entreprises et économie sociale et solidaire: des relations complexes. *Économies et Sociétés*, XLII(1): 55–82.

Boltanski L., Chiapello È., 2005. *The new spirit of capitalism*, London/New York, Verso, 601 p. Translation of 'Le nouvel esprit du capitalisme' (1999).

Bowen H.R., 1953. *Social responsibilities of the businessman*, New York, Harper & Row, 276 p.

Brundtland G.H., 1987. *Our common future: report of the World Commission on Environment and Developement*, New York, UN.

Defourny, J., Nyssens, M., 2008. *Conceptions of social entreprises in Europe and the United States: convergences and divergences*. Leuven, Katholieke Universiteit Leuven.

Draperi J.-F., Touzard J.-M., 2003. De Maraussan 1901 à Maraussan 2001: coopératives, territoires et mondialisation, in Touzard J.-M., Draperi J.-F. (ed.), *Les coopératives entre territoires et mondialisation*, Paris, L'Harmattan, 77–90.

European Commission, 2011. *Communication from the Commission to the European Parliament, the Council, the European Economic and Social Committee and the Committee of the Regions: a renewed EU strategy 2011–14 for Corporate Social Responsibility*, Brussels, European Commission, 15 p.

European Commission, Directorate-General for Employment, Social Affairs and Inclusion, 2001. *Green paper – promoting a European framework for corporate social responsibility*. Luxembourg, Office for Official Publications of the European Communities, 32 p.

Gautier R., 2012. *La Prolétarienne, L'Union, La Ménagère . . . , Les coopératives ouvrières de consommation dans la Basse-Loire (1880–1980)*, Nantes, éditions du Centre d'histoire du travail, 176 p.

Hoffman B., 2013. *Behind the Brands. Food justice and the 'Big 10' food and beverage companies*, Oxford, Oxfam, 58 p.

Lepiller O., Yount-André C., 2019. La politisation de l'alimentation ordinaire par le marché. *Revue des sciences sociales*, 61: 26–35. https://doi.org/10.4000/revss.3901

Marais M., 2014. Quelle marge de manœuvre pour l'engagement socialement responsable des dirigeants ? Enjeux et perspectives du gouvernement d'entreprise. *M@n@gement*, 17(4): 237–265. https://doi.org/10.3917/mana.174.0237

Marais M., Reynaud E., Vilanova L., 2020. CSR dynamics in the midst of competing injunctions: the case of Danone. *European Management Review*, 17(1): 19–39. https://doi.org/10.1111/emre.12305

Meyer M., Narjoud S., Granata J., 2017. When collective action drives corporate social responsibility implementation in small and medium-sized enterprises: the case of a network of French winemaking cooperatives. *International Journal of Entrepreneurship and Small Business*, 32(1–2): 7–27. https://doi.org/10.1504/IJESB.2017.086002

Morteo M., Tchotourian I., 2020. Nouvelles entreprises, progrès ou statu quo ? *Entreprise et Société*, 1(5): 85–111. https://doi.org/10.15122/isbn.978-2-406-10178-9.p.0085

Nicolas P., 1988. Émergence, développement et rôle des coopératives agricoles en France. Aperçus sur une histoire séculaire. *Économie rurale*, 184(1): 116–122. https://doi.org/10.3406/ecoru.1988.3900

Nyssens M., Petrella F., 2015. ESS et ressources communes: vers la reconnaissance d'une diversité institutionnelle. *Revue française de socio-économie*, 15(1): 117–134. https://doi.org/10.3917/rfse.015.0117

Rambaud A., Richard J., 2015. Towards a finance that CARES: from today's Fisherian-(Falsified) Hicksian perspective to a genuine sustainable financial model, designed through accounting principles. Présenté à *Social and Sustainable Finance and Impact Investing Conference*, Oxford, p. 64.

Segrestin B., Hatchuel A., Levillain K., 2021. When the law distinguishes between the enterprise and the corporation: the case of the new French law on corporate purpose. *Journal of Business Ethics*, 171(1): 1–13. https://doi.org/10.1007/s10551-020-04439-y

Utopies, 2021. *Loi Pacte: une opportunité stratégique pour accélérer la transformation de votre entreprise*. Note de position n° 21.

Weaver R.K., 1986. The politics of blame avoidance. *Journal of Public Policy*, 6(4): 371–398. https://doi.org/10.1017/S0143814X00004219

WWF, 2016. *Soy Scorecard. Assessing the use of responsible soy for animal feed*, Gland, WWF, 47 p.

21

The roles of training and research

Nicolas Bricas, Stéphane Fournier, Olivier Lepiller
and Élodie Valette

*Embracing an ecology of food has implications for the worlds of training
and research. Changes are already under way, in terms of both the subjects
addressed and the way in which this is done. We share a few avenues for
reflection on these changes.*

The food systems of tomorrow will be built and governed by the students of today.
While much reflection and many initiatives are emerging around sustainability
training, there is a pressing demand for this trend to accelerate, particularly from
students themselves (Lebard, 2021). The challenge is twofold: to provide training
in the resolution of sustainability problems and to train differently, since resolving
these problems requires approaches different from those that have prevailed until
now. In this sense, we can say that there is a need for a training transformation
and therefore a need to transform training for transformation.

Towards a transformation of training
for sustainable food systems

Several studies have recently investigated the issue of training for transition –
in the broad sense of an ecological and social transition – in higher education.
The Transition Campus, created in 2018 by a collective of lecturer-researchers,
entrepreneurs and students, is a training centre as well as a research laboratory
working 'on new pedagogical practices for teaching complex thinking and
processes of systemic change'. Following the commissioning of a study by the
French Ministry of Higher Education and Research in 2019, this laboratory
coordinated a group to 'carry out interdisciplinary work to develop a shared

knowledge and skill base to which all undergraduate students should have access'. The result of this work (Renouard et al., 2020) establishes a 'pathway' involving different 'points of entry' available to private citizens, individual students or teaching programmes: 'acquiring a systemic view in order to inhabit a common world (*oikos*); discernment and decision-making for collective life (*ethos*); measuring, regulating and governing (*nomos*); interpreting, critiquing and imagining (*logos*); collectively rising to the challenges at stake (*praxis*); and reconnecting with oneself, with others and with nature (*dynamis*)'.

Even more recently, at the request of the same ministry, Jean Jouzel and Luc Abadie (2020) submitted a report detailing the measures to be taken to 'ensure that, within a short space of time, 100% of students who complete an undergraduate degree will have received training on the challenges, pathways and tools of the ecological transition'. This will also involve establishing a skills matrix – which is currently being defined – in consultation with higher education institutions.

What challenges must courses dedicated to the transformation of food systems tackle? The Advanced M.Sc° in 'Innovation and Policies for Sustainable Food' (MS IPAD)[1] can serve as an example. It was created in 2011 by L'Institut Agro Montpellier and the French Agricultural Research Centre for International Development (*Centre de coopération internationale en recherche agronomique pour le développement*, CIRAD) in close collaboration with the UNESCO Chair in World Food Systems. As a 'post-master' or 'post-engineering degree' course, it aims to train senior managers who will go on to work in companies, non-profits, consulting firms, support organizations, local authorities, ministries or international organizations to transform food systems. To this end, several choices have shaped this training course:

– Since its creation, it has been open to students and professionals with diverse backgrounds and experience who are not necessarily from agronomic fields, so as to maintain the interdisciplinary and intersectoral dialogue necessary for the food transition throughout the course. Graduates must be able to act as innovation pilots by facilitating and coordinating heterogeneous systems of actors.
– It constantly seeks to articulate scales from the local to the global, from territorialized citizen initiatives to international coordination efforts, including local food policies and especially urban food policies.

[1]   https://www.institut-agro-montpellier.fr/ipad

- It emphasizes the need for a detailed understanding of context (at different scales) and for appropriating impact assessment methods (by seeking to aggregate the different dimensions of sustainability).
- Finally, it leaves as much room as possible for group work, participation and debate among peers and with the lecturers, as well as within the alumni community, and for acquiring communication skills.

In parallel, since 2011, the UNESCO Chair in World Food Systems has been running an annual seminar on contemporary food issues open to all students. This seminar was created at the request of the course convenors of the Montpellier Master's programmes to provide highly specialized students with a general framework regarding food system sustainability and to give meaning to their training. The seminar is now attended by students from about ten different master's programmes in agronomy, economics, political and social sciences, genetics, food technology, architecture and urban planning and related disciplines.

Towards connective research

Just as training is evolving, so, too, is research, both in its aims and in its working methods. Recent reflection on how to build a 'science of sustainability' provides interesting insights to grasp this evolution. Based on an analysis of 1,129 publications that claim to belong to the discipline, Julien Blanco and Clémence Moreau (2021) identify three founding pillars of sustainability science: understanding socio-ecosystems and their dynamics; co-constructing knowledge across disciplines and with stakeholders; and achieving transformation by embracing sustainability science's inherent commitment to transforming the relationship between humans and their environment. In their defence of a science of sustainability, four researchers and directors from the Research Institute for Development (*Institut de recherche pour le développement*, IRD) also set out ways of 'researching differently' (Verdier et al., 2020). Based on these perspectives and linking them with proposals for an ecology of food systems, we suggest the term 'connective research' to capture current developments in the world of research.

As part of the drive to contribute to the transformation of food systems, research programmes geared towards solving problems are multiplying. This is what institutions such as CIRAD call 'targeted research'. While these programmes recognize the value of more fundamental research, they differ from the exploration of scientific disciplines. However, some projects targeted at resolving specific problems still struggle to obtain funding if they cannot guarantee to enhance the international competitiveness of the teams proposing them, a competitiveness that mainly hinges on progress on academic scientific fronts. Building and running targeted research programmes means embracing advocacy research (Chapter 10), the aim of which is no longer simply to grow knowledge for its own sake but to solve a problem. The broad issue of interest to the science of sustainability, as proposed by Olivier Dangles at the IRD, is the development of societies within a circular band delimited by 'planetary boundaries' (Rockström et al., 2009) on one side and the social floor 'made up of the basic needs and minimum determinants of well-being that should enable all to lead a dignified life' on the other. These two boundaries define the doughnut-shaped 'safe and just space' within which humanity could flourish (Raworth, 2012).

Such a targeted research perspective requires connecting researchers with other actors (Chapter 9). The complexity of the problems to be solved and the need to take into account the effects of possible solutions on different dimensions of sustainability call for the mobilization of different disciplines. This is what the 'Urbal' method, which identifies the effects of food innovations on the different dimensions of sustainability, strives to do (see Box 21.1). While pluridisciplinarity often provides a starting point, articulating the results from different disciplines paves the way for interdisciplinarity (see Box 21.2 below on pluridisciplinarity,

---

Box 21.1 Pluridisciplinarity, multidisciplinarity, interdisciplinarity and transdisciplinarity

Pluridisciplinarity and multidisciplinarity: equivalent concepts that denote the juxtaposition of disciplinary approaches without any particular drive to foster interaction between these approaches. Many research projects that are split into work packages – each of which is specific to a particular discipline – are pluridisciplinary or multidisciplinary projects: each project team publishes in its own discipline's journals. In fact, this is what is required by the research evaluation institutions that determine which journals are legitimate in each discipline.

Interdisciplinarity: interaction between disciplines. It requires methodological and conceptual dialogue between disciplines in order to strive to develop an original perspective on reality. Physical chemistry, socio-economics and agro-economics are examples of interdisciplinary fields.

Transdisciplinarity: an approach that goes beyond disciplines and attempts to develop a new form of analysis with its own methods.

Box 21.2 Example of an interdisciplinary and participatory approach: The Urbal method

Urbal, which has been developing since 2018, is a participatory method for monitoring and evaluating the impacts of food innovations on all dimensions of sustainability. It was designed by a pluridisciplinary team involving CIRAD and the UNESCO Chair in World Food Systems in Montpellier, the Està think tank in Milan and Wilfrid Laurier University in Waterloo, Canada. It is inspired by both the causal model approach to nutritional problems (Beghin, 2002) and the ImpresS method developed by CIRAD (Barret et al., 2017). This method was initially tested on fifteen food innovations in ten countries around the world, all in urban areas, which provide fertile ground for social innovations given the concentration of sustainability issues in cities.

The purpose of Urbal is to help the bearers of innovations, as well as the policymakers and donors in a position to support them, to better understand, anticipate and evaluate the innovations' impacts – in other words, their relatively long-term effects. Urbal is based on an evaluation framework that is designed to require minimal resources (human, time and financial resources). It is built on the concept of 'impact pathways'. It is qualitative in the sense that its objective is not to quantify impacts but to identify impact pathways and develop cognitive maps to represent these pathways – namely the causal chains linking activities (what the innovations do in concrete terms) to their consequences. It is necessary to distinguish between direct effects (products or outputs), medium-term effects (results or outcomes) and longer-term effects (impacts) and to identify the conditions for the transition between each stage. The necessary and facilitating conditions for success, as well as obstacles and hindrances, can then be identified. The final impacts relate to the different dimensions of sustainability. Urbal considers five of these dimensions: economic, environmental, socio-cultural, nutritional health and food security, and governance.

The method is organized in three stages. The first draws on interviews, the analysis of available documentation and a review of the scientific literature. It consists of describing the innovation by retracing its history, mapping its stakeholders and precisely identifying its innovative activities that produce change. The next stage is dedicated to running a multi-actor participatory workshop to collectively identify the main impacts and their pathways. This is followed by an analysis of the data collected to refine and elaborate on them. In the third stage, a new participatory workshop or meeting is run to present, validate and discuss the identified impact pathways. This third stage may place more or less emphasis on a particular key function of Urbal – namely informing the strategy of the innovation, promoting it, networking it, sharing the experience associated with it, informing decision-making regarding support for the innovation or preparing a quantified evaluation of its impacts. In fact, this last key function constitutes a fourth possible step: the use of Urbal as a basis for a quantitative evaluation, using the method to select indicators among the large number of existing options or to develop specific ones.

Urbal is therefore presented as an alternative to quantitative evaluation methods. It is easily implementable by social innovators who often have limited resources at their disposal. The knowledge produced is collective. The general idea is that the diversity of stakeholder views and experiences, as well as their comparison, makes it possible to grasp the full range of impacts. By resituating these diverse impacts in relation to the different dimensions of sustainability, the method sheds light on the synergies between different dimensions or, on the contrary, the conflicts between them, thereby revealing the necessary trade-offs or prioritizations of the different activities. The participatory dimension of Urbal also ensures the evaluation's social relevance, giving it a political dimension: it allows for collective decision-making surrounding the production of knowledge on impacts, and the knowledge produced is shared within a collective brought together through the implementation of Urbal and within a wider community of practice through the open-access sharing of the results (under a Creative Commons licence). By encouraging the sharing of experiences across innovations and the construction of shared knowledge, Urbal is useful for scaling up innovations (Chapter 19). It also facilitates this process by informing decision-making regarding political support (local authorities) or financial support (donors, investors) for innovations (Valette et al., 2020).

multidisciplinarity, interdisciplinarity and transdisciplinarity). The latter fosters dialogue from the very conception of a research programme in order to achieve a cross-pollination of disciplines or, even further, a transdisciplinarity that would attempt to transcend the disciplines. Interdisciplinary spaces surrounding research on food systems vary from one country to the next. Anglosphere countries are developing food studies based on the model of cultural studies, whereas the French have prioritized perspectives that are open to interdisciplinarity but still anchored in a discipline, for example, socio-anthropology (Poulain, 2017).

Practising interdisciplinarity is easier said than done. The research evaluation environment tends to give greater value to academic excellence arising from the exploration of research areas within one's own discipline than from dialogue between disciplines. Since 2011, the UNESCO Chair in World Food Systems has been striving to organize spaces to facilitate such exchange. To this end, it sets up research projects involving several disciplines (e.g. the Foodscapes project) and encourages their interaction on various occasions such as during discussions on research results or the drafting of documents to translate these results into recommended actions (see the 'So What?' policy brief series). Knowledge is also articulated through events – such as the one organized every year on a theme relating to contemporary food issues – which bring together scientific voices from several disciplines along with professional and artistic perspectives. The Chair is also careful to ensure that researchers who are less visible in the scientific community have a voice. These are scientists working with fewer resources or with less access to funding, networks or publications. In this respect, the symposia organized on the theme of 'eating in the city' ('*Manger en ville*') have given African, Latin American and Asian researchers the opportunity to develop a 'Global South' perspective on the issue of food acculturation linked to urbanization (Soula et al., 2020).

Targeted research also faces the challenge of articulating scientific and professional knowledge. Research projects are increasingly conducted in partnership with food system actors such as politicians, NGOs or companies. Such partnerships not only provide a space to discuss the relevance of particular questions or hypotheses together but also allow for staying on track and responding together to unexpected situations over the course of the project. This involves creating long-term partnerships between scientists and stakeholders that are not limited to the duration of a research project. This allows for the scientific analysis of professional or citizen knowledge and makes room for stakeholders' and citizens' critical feedback on the scientific work carried out. This relationship is organized through think tanks such as the International Panel of Experts on Sustainable Food Systems (IPES-Food) or the Institute for Sustainable Development and International Relations (*Institut du développement durable et des relations internationales*, IDDRI), which synthesize expert knowledge to strengthen the argumentation and advocacy skills of actors working to accelerate the transformation of food systems.

Science–society dialogue also involves the relationship between researchers and citizens. Many initiatives to share scientific results with the public exist. The diversification of communication channels has facilitated this dissemination while also enabling the proliferation of false information, which contributes to confusing the issue and discrediting scientific knowledge. But dialogue between the science world and the public can also be fostered by involving citizens in scientific production. The term 'citizen science' encompasses this practice along with a range of other methods (Silva et al., 2017). The approach followed to analyse the data from studies of a specific population can also play a role in legitimizing citizen knowledge. For example, positive deviance analyses, which are beginning to be used in nutrition, consist in identifying the behaviour of 'deviant' individuals within a category of population with similar characteristics who have been able to find solutions to a given problem better than others (Marsh et al., 2004). Research no longer has a monopoly on solutions, and those implemented by citizens become models.

From a targeted research perspective, scientific actors seeking to contribute to the transformation of food systems demonstrate a certain degree of political commitment. Thus, whenever they move beyond the framework of producing research results to provide expertise or share opinions, researchers must be able to demonstrate sufficient reflexivity to maintain the right distance between their research activity and their political positions. A researcher's choice of object of study or methodology is not just informed by a desire to advance knowledge. It also reflects implicit values and societal sensitivities. The social sciences place particular emphasis on critically examining these values and sensitivities so as to ensure objectivity and neutrality of interpretation and to acknowledge the limits of the researcher's position (Grignon, 2015). This reflexivity allows scientists to avoid the influence of intellectual trends and instrumentalization as much as possible.

Lastly, on the point of reflexivity, responsible science must be accountable not only for the usefulness of the knowledge it produces but also for the way in which it produces it. Research can have an environmental cost if we consider the health risks it can impose on societies through the application of its innovations without hindsight and without debate. But it can also have a social cost if we consider the precarious status of young laboratory workers and the misguided academic establishment practices that still exist. Here, too, new practices are developing within universities, schools and laboratories to reconcile the substance and form of teaching and research.

Conclusion

Whether in training or research, many actors are now mobilizing to both tackle the challenges of sustainable food systems and do so differently. Various philosophical or epistemological approaches provide avenues for thinking about these necessary changes. For example, the sustainability sciences seek to articulate knowledge to transform systems and complex approaches (Morin, 1992) and to study arrangements and combinations. The concept of 'rhizome' (Deleuze and Guattari, 1976, 2004) proposes a model to represent organization without subordination between elements. It constitutes a form of resistance to hierarchical models, which the authors consider oppressive. All these approaches show that changing the ways of representing the world is already a way to start changing the world itself.

The authors would like to thank Damien Conaré, Mathilde Coudray and Marie Walser for proofreading this chapter and for their suggested improvements.

References

Barret D., Blundo Canto G., Dabat M.-H., Devaux-Spartakis A., Faure G., Hainzelin E. et al., 2017. *Guide méthodologique ImpresS: évaluation ex post des impacts de la recherche agronomique dans les pays du Sud*, Montpellier, Cirad, 96 p.

Beghin I., 2002. Le modèle causal dans la surveillance nutritionnelle. *Options méditerranéennes*, 41: 29–37.

Blanco J., Moreau C., 2021. Comprendre, co-construire, transformer: un tryptique en mal de sciences sociales ? *IRD – Sciences de la durabilité*, 5: 2.

Deleuze G., Guattari F., 1976. *Rhizome, introduction*, Paris, Les éditions de Minuit, 74 p.

Deleuze G., Guattari F., 2004. *A thousand plateaus*, Vol. 2 of capitalism and schizophrenia. 2 vols. 1972–1980. London/New York, Continuum. Translation of 'Mille Plateaux' (1980).

Grignon C., 2015. *Une sociologie des normes diététiques est-elle possible ?*, La Vie des idées.

Jouzel J., Abbadie L., 2020. *Rapport du groupe de travail « Enseigner la transition écologique dans le supérieur »*, Paris, Ministère de l'Enseignement supérieur, de la Recherche et de l'Innovation, 15 p.

Lebard J., 2021. Dans les écoles d'agronomie, une nouvelle génération d'ingénieurs. *Le Monde.fr*, 28 février 2021.

Marsh D.R., Schroeder D.G., Dearden K.A., Sternin J., Sternin M., 2004. The power of positive deviance. *BMJ*, 329(7475): 1177–1179. https://doi.org/10.1136/bmj.s177

Morin E., 1992. From the concept of system to the paradigm of complexity. *Journal of Social and Evolutionary Systems*, 15(4), 371–385.

Poulain J.-P., 2017. Socio-anthropologie du « fait alimentaire » ou Food Studies. Les deux chemins d'une thématisation scientifique. *L'Année sociologique*, 67(1): 23–46. https://doi.org/10.3917/anso.171.0023

Raworth K., 2012. *A safe and just space for humanity: can we live within the doughnut?*, Oxford, Oxfam, 22 p.

Renouard C., Beau R., Goupil C., Koenig C. (ed.), 2020. *Manuel de la grande transition. Former pour transformer*, Paris, Les Liens qui libèrent, 448 p.

Rockström J., Steffen W., Noone K., Persson Å., Chapin F.S., Lambin E. et al., 2009. Planetary boundaries: exploring the safe operating space for humanity. *Ecology and Society*, 14(2): 32. https://doi.org/10.5751/ES-03180-140232

Silva P.D. da, Heaton L., Millerand F., 2017. Une revue de littérature sur la « science citoyenne »: la production de connaissances naturalistes à l'ère numérique. *Natures Sciences Sociétés*, 25(4): 370–380. https://doi.org/10.1051/nss/2018004

Soula A., Yount-André C., Lepiller O., Bricas N. (ed.), 2021. *Eating in the city: socioanthropological perspectives from Africa, Latin America and Asia*, Versailles, Quæ, 158 p. Translation of 'Manger en ville: Regards socioanthropologiques d'Afrique, d'Amérique latine et d'Asie' (2020).

Valette E., Schreiber K., Conaré D., Bonomelli V., Blay-Palmer A., Bricas N., 2020. An emerging user-led participatory methodology: mapping impact pathways of urban food system sustainability innovations, in Blay-Palmer A., Conaré D., Meter K., Di Battista A. (ed.), *Sustainable food system assessment: lessons from global practice*, Abington, Routledge, 19–41.

Verdier V., Dangles O., Charvis P., Cury P., 2020. Et si on cherchait autrement ? Plaidoyer pour une science de la durabilité. *The Conversation*.

22

Food in politics

Damien Conaré and Nicolas Bricas

The public food policies adopted in Brazil, Canada and France – at both national and local levels – offer valuable insights. There is a proliferation of initiatives encouraging new civil society stakeholders to engage in food systems and thus address emerging issues. The challenges of intersectorality and participation remain to be addressed, and new power dynamics need to be imposed.

Consumer practices (Chapter 18), citizen initiatives (Chapter 19) and corporate social and environmental responsibility (Chapter 20) all contribute to the transformation of food systems, but they are not enough; they must be coupled with public policies that enable structural change.

Historically, public policy has focused on two main concerns surrounding food: first, making sure that there are sufficient food supplies to feed the population. This has involved either agricultural policies to increase food production with a view to achieving self-sufficiency or trade policies to resort to cheap food imports from international markets. The second concern has been ensuring the safety and nutritional quality of foods to protect consumers' health.

The other dimensions of food – social, cultural, ethical and environmental – have been relatively absent from public policy debates and agendas but seem to have become legitimate themes again (Fouilleux and Michel, 2022). New food policies that give greater importance to sustainability issues are now being implemented at different scales. They enable the inclusion of new actors striving for change and thus contribute to disrupting often long-standing power dynamics. The challenge is both to pursue cross-cutting policies – breaking with sectoral approaches to food (governed in a rather compartmentalized way by departments or ministries respectively in charge of agriculture, the environment, health, education, the economy, social affairs, culture etc.) – and to ensure complementarity and interaction between the different political scales.

From the scale of urban regions . . .

The end of the twentieth century saw metropolises around the world regain social, political and economic power. Beyond the demographic weight of these metropolises, this rise in power is partly due to states' financial disengagement from urban planning and the transformation of production systems in a globalized world (Brand et al., 2017): globalization has disconnected the largest cities from their national economies and even removed them from their territorial roots. As a result, the food sector represents a tremendous opportunity for cities to re-establish ties – sometimes lost – with their productive and food-supplying environment. But it also offers a chance to reconnect with their past as 'organic cities' prior to the Industrial Revolution, when cities were still literally shaped by food (Steel, 2008). Since the early 1990s, cities have become increasingly interested in how to meet the expectations of city dwellers and improve their food supply. At the territorial level, this trend has involved a proliferation of food relocalization initiatives (Chapter 17).

This profusion of innovations is beginning to be incorporated into food strategies developed by urban local governments (cities, conurbations, metropolises etc.), which have a number of levers for action at their disposal: calls for tenders for collective catering procurement (school canteens, hospitals and other public institutions), the protection of farmland, commercial urban planning and infrastructure management, the establishment of governance frameworks such as local food policy councils, actions in solidarity with the most disadvantaged and similar community-focused measures (Deakin et al., 2016; Dansero et al., 2017; Battersby and Watson, 2018; Cabannes and Marocchino, 2018; Tefft et al., 2020).

The city of Belo Horizonte in Brazil (2.5 million inhabitants) is often considered a pioneer for having developed an integrated policy to fight food insecurity as early as 1993. This strategy, coordinated by a Municipal Secretariat for Food Security and Nutrition, has stood out for its framework for action (spanning from production to consumption), the flexibility of its measures, its attention to urban-rural links and its social justice objective (Rocha and Lessa, 2009). The city has implemented various measures that have subsequently inspired many other municipalities, such as funding subsidized prices at 'people's restaurants' that serve up to 20,000 meals per day, running school canteen programmes in more than 200 schools, supporting grocery shops to sell fruit and vegetables at reduced prices, establishing peasant markets in the city for peri-urban farmers and running food education programmes. This policy, which very quickly achieved results in the fight against food insecurity, owes its success to several factors: the political will to launch a far-reaching programme; the competence and motivation of a municipal team eager to prove that a public policy to fight poverty could be effective; and last but not least, all this at an estimated cost of 1–2 per cent of the total municipal budget for a target population estimated at nearly 800,000 inhabitants every day (Rocha, 2001).

Urban areas in North America have also been experimenting with food policies – or rather strategies – since the early 1990s (Neuner et al., 2011). The Canadian metropolis of Toronto is particularly emblematic in this regard (Blay-Palmer, 2009). In 1992, it initiated a Food Policy Council as an instrument to promote 'food democratization', comprising community activists, politicians, academics, trade unions and agricultural and business representatives (Welsh and MacRae, 1998). These local food councils have since become more widespread and have stimulated local democratic processes (Guthman, 2008; Lang et al., 2009; Starr, 2009). More broadly, urban food policies have also multiplied around the world, including in Mexico City, Medellín (Colombia), Rosario (Argentina), Gampaha (Sri Lanka), Nairobi (Kenya) and Accra (Ghana), among many other examples.

In 2015, the Milan Urban Food Policy Pact was signed. It now counts 211 signatory municipalities around the world, which have voluntarily committed 'to develop[ing] sustainable food systems [...] that provide healthy and affordable food to all people', through the adoption of actions in the areas of governance, social equity, support for food production, food procurement, the fight against waste and related sustainability initiatives. This international networking of urban food movements opens up opportunities for exchange and, above all, strengthens the legitimacy of these actions at the local level.

The urban food policies implemented, however, are often still fragmented and address only one of the multiple facets of food systems or do not seek to explicitly impact the food system at other scales (Hodgson, 2012). Food-related activities present a challenge for urban governments, as they need to include representatives from different segments of society (citizens, businesses, academia, public authorities), different levels of governance (from local to international) and different public policy sectors (agriculture, social affairs, health, education, environmental affairs, urban planning etc.). What is more, national or regional policies may limit or even conflict with a municipal authority's actions. For example, in late 2020, the French Council of State refused mayors the right to issue 'anti-pesticide' decrees. Effective mechanisms to ensure the engagement of multiple sectors and actors are also often lacking (De Cunto et al., 2017).

More specifically, the comparative analysis of a large number of urban food policy documents reveals several points (Sonnino et al., 2019; Candel, 2020):

– The objectives set are highly similar, with a few particular themes appearing most often: farming and local production, education and economic development. Crucially missing is climate change mitigation.
– There is little use of regulatory instruments and a lack of clear implementation targets with deadlines.
– There is a 'missing middle', that is, a lack of objectives surrounding processing and distribution and of integration of the actors from these sectors. Activities are mostly regulated at the regional, national and international levels.

This last point shows that there is little integration, in cities' food strategies, of the spaces outside the territories that feed them. This can cause cities to lose sight of broader systemic issues and reveals that, through their strategies, they are in fact acting only on a small part of their food system. Hence, investing in a better understanding of the food flows that intersect in cities allows the latter to grasp how they fit into a wider food system, the issues this raises and what they can do to address them (Gaspard, 2020).

Finally, regarding governance, a comparative analysis of food policy dynamics in Toronto and Brussels has highlighted the need for the actors involved to demonstrate reflexivity (Manganelli, 2020), that is, the capacity to readjust over time, reinvent themselves or reformulate objectives and revise actions in order to adapt to inevitable changes in the local socio-economic and institutional environment (elections, administrative changes etc.). It also seems important to document successes and not to take the legitimacy of local food action for granted.

. . . to the national and regional scales

The case of Brazil is emblematic of a national food policy that has drawn on local experiences and has fuelled them in turn. The longevity of the aforementioned food security programmes carried out in Belo Horizonte was significantly aided by a factor that played out at the national level. When President Lula da Silva was elected in 2003, he immediately made the main objective of his presidency to eliminate hunger in Brazil and, to this end, to form a National Council for Food and Nutrition Security (CONSEA) bringing together different stakeholders of the food systems. This operation was a success: in 2014, the UN Food and Agriculture Organization (FAO) declared that Brazil was no longer on the 'Hunger Map', with less than 5 per cent of the population considered undernourished.

The national 'Zero Hunger' strategy developed under the Lula government in 2004 replicated many of the programmes developed in Belo Horizonte ten years earlier and allocated resources to local food security initiatives. In turn, the Zero Hunger strategy played a very important role in the continuation and growth of the programmes in Belo Horizonte: after 2004, in partnership with the federal government, the city was able to increase the number of 'people's restaurants', expand its food bank and improve its school meal programme. Thanks to the federal Food Acquisition Programme (PAA), the city was also incentivized to buy produce for its restaurants and food bank directly from small family farmers. Finally, the legislation passed as part of the National School Feeding Programme (PNAE) required that 30 per cent of federal funds be earmarked for the purchase of food produced by family farms (Rocha et al., 2012).

Similarly, in Canada, metropolitan-level initiatives launched from the 1990s onwards ultimately stimulated a national drive to establish a 'Food Policy for Canada'. The overarching vision of this policy, adopted in 2019 with a five-year investment budget of CAD134 million, is that 'all people in Canada are able to access a sufficient amount of safe, nutritious, and culturally diverse food and that Canada's food system is resilient and innovative, sustains [the country's] environment and supports [its] economy'. Priority areas for action include support for local authorities, the 'Buy Canadian Promotion Campaign', food security in First Nations, Inuit and Métis communities and combating food waste. This policy was particularly informed by public consultations conducted in 2017 with many stakeholders in the Canadian food system and is supported by a Canadian Food Policy Advisory Council (Levkoe and Wilson, 2019).

In France, the 2014 Law for the Future of Agriculture promoted the launch of territorial food projects (*projets alimentaires territoriaux*, PAT) to develop the 'joint assessment of local agricultural production and food needs in a living or consumption area'. In practice, the vast majority of PAT are led by urban local authorities. This impetus from the state, without dedicated funding, initiated a vast movement of local farming and food initiatives. It has been reinforced by the 2018 Egalim Law's target for sustainable and quality products to account for 50 per cent of state procurement – with organic products to make up 20 per cent of school catering supply – along with relatively significant funding dedicated to PAT as part of France's 2020–1 National Recovery and Resilience Plan.

Admittedly, these innovations – which are mainly focused on promoting better market gardening practices, developing short supply chains, preserving farmland and supplying collective catering or food solidarity initiatives with local food – account for only a small part of our daily diet. As such, they do not fully challenge conventional food systems. Nevertheless, PAT open up the possibility of new types of food-based partnerships within a territory between actors that previously did not typically work together or did not have the opportunity to do so, for instance, between chambers of agriculture, urban local authorities and actors involved in social work. These relationships proved particularly valuable and effective for responding to emergency situations of high food insecurity during the periods of lockdown associated with the COVID-19 epidemic (France Urbaine, 2020).

In France, this decentralization of food policies contrasts with more centralized public policies developed in silos. From the early twentieth century, food policies focused on regulating food safety, labelling and other signs of food product quality. The core concern was building confidence in the food being sold, purchased and consumed. From the 2000s, successive National Nutrition and Health Programs (*Programmes nationaux nutrition santé*, PNNS) were then set up, steered by the Ministry of Health. These marked the advent of the 'nutritionalization' of food policies (Chapter 9). Meanwhile, the Ministry of Agriculture and Food retained control of a National Food Plan (*Plan national pour l'alimentation*, PNA), itself linked to the PNNS (Fouilleux and Michel, 2022). Finally, the COVID-19 crisis and the ensuing rise in poverty have accelerated the review of food insecurity policy, with the establishment of a National Coordination Committee for the Fight against Food Precarity (*Comité national de coordination de la lutte contre la précarité alimentaire*, Cocolupa) and a new roadmap signalling a move away from a response exclusively based on food aid, and to recognize that food has a social and cultural dimension and is not limited to meeting nutritional needs (Chapter 15).

At the European level, national agricultural policies are primarily dictated by the Common Agricultural Policy (CAP), which has an annual budget of almost €60 billion and aims to help farmers weather the risks of agricultural commodity markets and stabilize their income. The CAP ensures the regional coherence of the European internal market and protects it from potential social and environmental dumping by international competition. Successive reforms to 'green' the CAP – that is, to make aid to farmers conditional on more environmentally friendly agricultural practices – have always been disappointing. The CAP, which is highly focused on production and trade, largely escapes public debate as private citizens tend to be unfamiliar with this highly complex technical policy. It is governed by forms of regulation or decision-making processes in which industry representatives carry considerable weight and defend the status quo to avoid losing the financial support that their industries have enjoyed for many years, namely the 'agricultural profession' – through its majority unions – the upstream agricultural industries (suppliers of inputs such as seeds, agricultural equipment and phytosanitary products) and food processing players (Fouilleux and Michel, 2022). This situation contributes to locking in and, in a way, institutionalizing the different sociotechnical dimensions of an agroindustrialized food system (De Schutter, 2017).

Food policy as a combat sport

To make food a political object that can be appropriated by citizens on a European scale, a number of civil society actors (NGOs, think tanks, trade unions, research bodies, consumer associations etc.) have joined forces and formed the EU Food Policy Coalition (EUFPC). This coalition advocates an integrated European food policy to replace the CAP, taking various concerns into account: food sovereignty, climate change, environmental protection, social justice and international solidarity, and animal welfare. The coalition carries out lobbying and advocacy work in Brussels to put new issues on the agenda of CAP negotiations and to ensure that proposals arising from the European Parliament are properly addressed in the decision-making process. The coalition's positions are particularly informed by a report from the International Panel of Experts on Sustainable Food Systems (IPES-Food, 2019), *Towards a Common Food Policy for the European Union: The policy Reform and Realignment That Is Required to Build Sustainable Food Systems in Europe*. Territorial and especially urban food policies – which make far more room for consumer concerns than agricultural policies – inspired the proposals for this European policy.

Another way to change the balance of power between food system stakeholders would be to foster the rise of local and regional authorities' influence on the decision-making processes that affect them (such as those surrounding the CAP), but in which they still have little to no representation. In this respect, it is interesting to observe the evolution of national and international networks of local authorities such as Terres en ville, France Urbaine, Organic Cities Network Europe, the signatory cities of the Milan Pact, the members of the Local Governments for Sustainability network (ICLEI) and the network of cities committed to climate action (C40). These collectives, which initially very much focused on sharing experiences, are beginning to develop advocacy work in order to carry more weight in national or international bodies, where policies that exceed the scale of the territories but greatly impact them are discussed and developed.

A 2045 food system transformation forecast scenario calls on civil society to 'take up the torch' to prevent a 'business as usual' scenario (IPES-Food and ETC Group, 2021). To do so, civil society, organized as a 'visionary movement', must develop deeper, broader and more effective collaborations than ever before. This scenario involves four interdependent paths:

- Rooting food systems in diversity, agroecology and human rights;
- Transforming governance structures;
- Shifting financial flows (redirecting R&D and technical budget lines, reforming major commodity subsidies, levying junk food and taxing corporations fairly); and
- Rethinking the modalities of civil society collaboration.

The report, however, highlights certain difficulties involved in establishing such a 'visionary movement': the victories achieved risk being only temporary or potentially being reappropriated by other actors or insufficient in the face of the key challenges ahead (climate change, loss of biodiversity, decline in soil fertility).

On a perhaps less ambitious scale, civil society or citizens themselves are already taking action by experimenting with or inventing new processes. In France, the National Food Conferences (*États généraux de l'alimentation*, EGA), launched in 2000 by Prime Minister Lionel Jospin and then in 2017 by President Emmanuel Macron, have brought together all stakeholders concerned with agricultural and food issues and given citizens a voice through public consultations. At the territorial level, participatory workshops open to citizens and digital consultations have also been organized to contribute to the development of territorial food policies. For example, the Occitanie region launched its first digital consultation in 2018, with the participation of 55,000 inhabitants and the organization of fourteen public meetings in different locations to identify actions to be taken. The analysis of this consultation helped to build the '*Pacte régional pour une alimentation durable en Occitanie*' (regional pact for sustainable food in Occitanie), the main lines of which were put to a vote through a second digital consultation that received 45,000 submissions.

While such consultations do involve citizens in the reflection process, most of the people who take part are 'informed' citizens. In order to better take into account everyone's opinions, the citizens' conventions model, based on random selection, was implemented on a national scale in 2019 for a climate consultation and in 2020 for the national strategic plan for the future Common Agricultural Policy (*Plan stratégique national de la future politique agricole commune*, PSN-PAC) (CNDP, 2021). The latter debate reached over 1.8 million people and gave rise to over 1,000 proposals. Such conventions have also been carried out at territorial level, for instance, in Paris in 2021, to develop the city's sustainable food policy. These consultations have clearly revealed the discrepancy between the proposals made by citizens and the policies implemented to date (Cholet, 2021). Furthermore, some of the policies that have resulted from these conventions, such as the Egalim Law following the EGAs, the Climate and Resilience Law based on the Citizens' Climate Convention, and the PSN-PAC, have been deemed disappointing by civil society, revealing the considerable influence of lobbies in maintaining the status quo or pushing for a slow transition in spite of environmental emergencies.

These new forms of citizen expression have nevertheless legitimized the general population's desire for a rapid and ambitious transformation of food systems. One can posit that the dominant players in these systems will not be able to remain indifferent to this aspiration for very long. These forms of expression have helped to pave the way for new forms of food democracy which could lead to the implementation, for example, of a food social security system (see Box 22.1).

Box 22.1 For a food social security system

Dominique Paturel

Guided by the concept of 'food democracy' (Paturel and Ndiaye, 2020), one can note the gross inequality in access to freely chosen food and to healthier food. The characteristics of these inequalities of access are trivialized in mainstream discourse and conceal class dynamics. They become visible if we take a step aside and adopt the perspective of 'eaters', a position that we all share. Furthermore, social and health policies generalize these inequalities by designating a population as 'vulnerable' and providing targeted assistance. The approach is underpinned by a liberal conception of solidarity based on a neo-paternalistic approach.

A response based on the social protection model offers an interesting avenue to enable all inhabitants of France to regain control of the food system(s) and to be in a position to do so. The answer cannot come from 'informed' or activist citizens alone. The model of a general social security system (for health) appears to provide the right framework for a way forward.

Food social security is founded on two pillars:

- Effective social democracy, of which the right to sustainable food is the cornerstone. A form of organization based on the deployment of local sustainable food funds must be considered as part of the re-examination of traditional forms of democracy (particularly representative democracy);
- An economic democracy in which social contributions and agreements with food system actors play a central role. This calls for mobilizing all existing public policy tools relating to food access (collective catering, the various government food plans, the creation of an allowance for the entire population to access fresh produce based on the family allowance model etc.) as part of this systemic policy approach.

Food social security must therefore draw on all these variables to establish its legitimacy. This will allow it to become a major tool for activating the food transition and transformation and for reducing the contribution of food to climate change issues.

Conclusion

The challenge, to transform food systems, is no longer to raise awareness and convince people that the situation is getting worse. Climate change, the collapse of biodiversity, rising poverty and food insecurity, the explosion of inequalities and the monopolization of wealth by an ever smaller fringe of the population are all glaringly obvious. The system that has produced this situation is in the hands of actors who have built their wealth and power on it and are keen to maintain their positions, as demonstrated by the successive failures of debates on agricultural policies, particularly the CAP. This is therefore now well and truly a matter of restoring a balance of power.

Many citizen initiatives, corporate strategies and policy measures to accelerate the transformation of food systems are currently being identified and tested. The associated demands are largely driven by civil society organizations as well as by 'informed' and activist citizens. The results of the Citizens' Conventions show that, provided citizens can inform themselves and engage in debate, their proposals also call for ambitious change. Local authorities tackling these issues are likewise allies. Food has once again become an eminently political issue. Just as well.

This chapter partly draws on the books *Designing Urban Food Policies* (Brand et al., 2019) and *Quand l'alimentation se fait politique(s)* (Fouilleux and Michel, 2022). The authors would like to thank Mathilde Coudray and Mathilde Douillet for proofreading this chapter and for their suggested improvements.

References

Battersby J., Watson V. (ed.), 2018. *Urban food systems governance and poverty in African cities*, London, Taylor & Francis, 290 p.

Blay-Palmer A., 2009. The Canadian pioneer: the genesis of urban food policy in Toronto. *International Planning Studies*, 14: 401–416. https://doi.org/10.1080/13563471003642837

Brand C., Bricas N., Conaré D., Daviron B., Debru J., Michel L., Soulard C.-T. (ed.), 2017. *Construire des politiques alimentaires urbaines. Concepts et démarches*, Versailles, Quæ, 160 p.

Brand C., Bricas N., Conaré D., Daviron B., Debru J., Michel L., Soulard C.-T., 2019. *Designing urban food policies: concepts and approaches*. Springer, Cham, 142 p.

Cabannes Y., Marocchino C. (ed.), 2018. *Integrating food into urban planning*, London, UCL Press, 376 p.

Candel J.J.L., 2020. What's on the menu? A global assessment of MUFPP signatory cities' food strategies. *Agroecology and Sustainable Food Systems*, 44(7): 919–946. https://doi.org/10.1080/21683565.2019.1648357

Cholet C., 2021. La parole citoyenne face aux enjeux agroalimentaires et environnementaux étude sémiotique des États généraux de l'alimentation. Essais. *Revue interdisciplinaire d'Humanités*, Hors-série 6: 65–77. https://doi.org/10.4000/essais.7403

CNDP, 2021. *Compte-rendu du débat public sur le plan stratégique national de la politique agricole commune*, Paris, Commission nationale du débat public, 224 p.

Dansero E., Pettenati G., Toldo A., 2017. A renewed reading of the food-city relationship: towards urban food policies. *Bollettino della societa geografica italiana*, X(1–2): 167.

Deakin M., Borrelli N., Diamantini D. (ed.), 2016. *The governance of city food systems: case studies from around the world*, Milan, Fondazione Giangiacomo Feltrinelli, 154 p.

De Cunto A., Tegoni C., Sonnino R., Michel C., 2017. *Food in cities: study on innovation for a sustainable and healthy production, delivery, and consumption of food in cities*, Brussels, European Commission, 30 p.

De Schutter O., 2017. The political economy of food systems reform. *European Review of Agricultural Economics*, 44: 705–731. https://doi.org/10.1093/erae/jbx009

Fouilleux E., Michel L. (ed.), 2022. *Quand l'alimentation se fait politique(s)*, Rennes, PUR, 349 p.

France Urbaine, Resolis, Terres en Ville, 2020. *Villes et alimentation en période de pandémie. Expériences françaises*, France urbaine, Resolis, Terres en Ville, 38 p.

Gaspard A., 2020. *Ce que le document d'orientation de votre politique alimentaire dit de vous*, Urban Food Futures.

Guthman J., 2008. Bringing good food to others: investigating the subjects of alternative food practice. *Cultural Geographies*, 15(4): 431–447. https://doi.org/10.1177/1474474008094315

Hodgson K., 2012. *Planning for food access and community-based food systems: a national scan and evaluation of local comprehensive and sustainability plans*, Chicago, American Planning Association, 175 p.

IPES-Food, 2019. *Towards a common food policy for the European Union: the policy reform and realignment that is required to build sustainable food systems in Europe*, Brussels, IPES-Food, 111 p.

IPES-Food, ETC Group, 2021. *A long food movement: transforming food systems by 2045*, Brussels, IPES-Food, 175 p.

Lang T., Barling D., Caraher M., 2009. *Food policy: integrating health, environment and society*, Oxford, Oxford University Press, 282 p.

Levkoe C.Z., Wilson A., 2019. Policy engagement as prefiguration: experiments in food policy governance through the national food policy dialogue in Canada, in Andrée P., Clark J.K., Levkoe C., Lowitt K. (ed.), *Civil society and social movements in food system governance*, London, Routledge, 101–123.

Manganelli A., 2020. Realising local food policies: a comparison between Toronto and the Brussels-Capital region's stories through the lenses of reflexivity and co-learning. *Journal of Environmental Policy & Planning*, 22(3): 366–380. https://doi.org/10.1080/1523908X.2020.1740657

Neuner K., Kelly S., Raja S., 2011. *Planning to eat: innovative local government plans and policies to build healthy food systems in the United States*, Buffalo, Food Systems Planning and Healthy Communities Lab University at Buffalo/The State University of New York, 39 p. https://doi.org/10.13140/RG.2.1.3371.1769

Paturel D., Ndiaye P. (ed.), 2020. *Le droit à l'alimentation durable en démocratie*, Nîmes, Champ social éditions, 238 p.

Rocha C., 2001. Urban food security policy: the case of Belo Horizonte, Brazil. *Journal for the Study of Food and Society*, 5(1): 36–47. https://doi.org/10.2752/152897901786732735

Rocha C., Burlandy L., Maluf R., 2012. Small farms and sustainable rural development for food security: the Brazilian experience. *Development Southern Africa*, 29(4): 519–529. https://doi.org/10.1080/0376835X.2012.715438

Rocha C., Lessa I., 2009. Urban governance for food security: the alternative food system in Belo Horizonte, Brazil. *International Planning Studies*, 14(4): 389–400. https://doi.org/10.1080/13563471003642787

Sonnino R., Tegoni C.L.S., De Cunto A., 2019. The challenge of systemic food change: insights from cities. *Cities*, 85: 110–116. https://doi.org/10.1016/j.cities.2018.08.008

Starr A., 2010. Local food: a social movement? *Cultural Studies - Critical Methodologies*, 10(6): 479–490. https://doi.org/10.1177/1532708610372769

Steel C., 2008. *Hungry city: how food shapes our lives*, London, Chatto and Windus, 383 p.

Tefft J., Jonasova M., Zhang F., Zhang Y., 2020. *Urban food systems governance – current context and future opportunities*, Rome, FAO/World Bank, 212 p.

Welsh J., MacRae R., 1998. Food citizenship and community food security: lessons from Toronto, Canada. *Canadian Journal of Development Studies/Revue canadienne d'études du développement*, 19(4): 237–255. https://doi.org/10.1080/02255189.1998.9669786

Conclusion

Food is an encounter with the world . . . the entire world

Nicolas Bricas, Damien Conaré and Marie Walser

As we have seen, food is a formidable part of the relationships and interactions within the living world, as well as a very particular vector of political commitment: food affects everyone in their daily lives and is relevant to many fields, whether relating to the environment, health, education, solidarity, pleasure, or personal and cultural identities. Food is also connected to the large number of economic activities on which it depends. It is not a closed field operating in a vacuum. It is shaped by external factors and, in turn, shapes the world in which we live. Rather than defending a specific status for food, the 'ecology of food' – given the diverse range of relationships it encompasses – proposes to use it as an entry point to rethink our world. This is a world in crisis, a world crying out to invent and experiment with other relationships. Food, a 'total human fact', can provide the ground for this new human adventure. Let us imagine, then, an adventure we can call a 'world banquet', a tale to rekindle our enthusiasm in these troubled times.

The world on our plates . . .

Under the cool shade of tall trees on this hot summer morning, about thirty people are busy setting up large round tables and chairs, spreading tablecloths, and placing cutlery, food and flowers on the tables. A real ballet plays out between a large old building and the immense area under the canopy, where nearly two hundred guests have been invited to feast. The plates, all identical, were made specially for the occasion. They feature the patterns that male puffer fish draw on the sand of the sea floor in Japan to seduce their females – a sort of sculpted, perfectly geometrical mandala, proving that art is not the preserve of humans. This art reveals a 'relational aesthetic', to quote the curator and art historian Nicolas Bourriaud, for whom 'art is a state of encounter'.[1] On the glasses, also sculpted for the occasion, are drawings taken from Neolithic pottery – for human art may well have begun with the decoration of household utensils. The tables are set, and a light breeze has risen.

The large building is as busy as an anthill. Sacks of onions, rice, potatoes, yams and cassava roots are piled up. There are bottles of various oils, tomatoes, eggs, fish and shellfish on ice. Men and women of all origins are cooking on dozens of stoves. At large tables, we peel, we cut, we pour, we stir, we taste, all in an incredible blend of fragrances. Virtually all the languages of the world can be heard here: there are at least 100 different nationalities from all continents, each with its own people and landscapes. Groups have been formed: about thirty people are each cooking a dish from their own country with the help of other participants from other countries. The next day, other groups will be cooking other dishes. A decision had to be made on the basic ingredients that would be shared by all the cuisines. They were bought from farmers who came to deliver them in person, curious as they were to see this gathering so widely covered in the media. Each cook has also brought from home ingredients specific to their cuisine: seeds, nuts, spices, fruits, vegetables and so on. An Indonesian man gives a taste of galanga, a Senegalese woman lets others smell the yet, a Burkinabé man the soumbala, an Amazonian woman the cupuacu and a Greek man his oregano, while a Mexican woman compares chilli peppers.

The air is filled with laughter and expressions of curiosity and pleasure. Amazement lights up faces. Everyone has also brought kitchen utensils – knives, large spoons, sieves, graters, chopsticks, pestles and similar cooking tools. Everyone has their own habits and dietary beliefs. A Japanese man explains how his gastronomy, which is tied to the seasons and natural tastes, sparks emotions linked to representations of nature. There is also a West African Peul woman who states that what makes one 'human' is not the act of eating in itself (cattle eat as well) but that of sharing, which allows us to build ties with others, with nature and with the spirits. These same spirits, adds a Korean woman, guide the seemingly magical and uncontrolled processes of fermentation in the preparation of kimchi (fermented cabbage). Evidently, all these food identities hybridize and recombine as they come into contact with one another. Discussing

---

[1] Nicolas Bourriaud, *Esthétique relationnelle*, Éditions Les presses du réel, 1998.

ancient African beliefs, the historian and philosopher Achille Mbembe inspires our guests:

> There was no identity except in a fragmented, scattered and shattered form. Besides, what mattered was not the self as such, but the way in which it was composed and recomposed, each time in relation to other living entities. In other words, there was no identity but in the becoming, in the web of relationships of which each was the living sum. Identity, in this sense [. . .], was what was entrusted to the care of others, in the experience of the encounter and the relationship, which always involved trial and error, movement and, above all, the unexpected, the surprise that one had to learn to welcome. For in the unexpected and the surprise lay the event.[2]

Our event is, indeed, the culmination of a process that began over two years ago. It came on the heels of the repeated crises that the planet has experienced since 2020. Various health crises have affected humans, animals and plants. Extreme weather events have become more frequent and severe. The collapse of biodiversity and the depletion of soil and water resources have led to a dramatic drop in agricultural yields. Mass migrations caused by these crises have created great social tensions. In 2040, after months of negotiations and under pressure from hundreds of increasingly powerful citizen movements, governments came – with great difficulty – to an agreement to launch a participatory, grass-roots reconstruction process to transform food systems. Hundreds of collectives were formed around the world to imagine tomorrow's often dreamt of and desired food system.

Thousands of citizens, whether volunteers or randomly selected representatives, together with professionals, experts and locally elected government officials, were involved in building new food systems. The hundreds of proposals developed by these collectives were compiled, analysed and synthesized. The result, beyond specificities, differences and even contradictions, was a broad consensus to invent sustainable food systems guided by a very different direction to the one which many countries had followed until then. This path steered clear of the biotechnological rush proposed by some in the 2020s to embrace industrial food production based on seaweed, bacteria or fungi in order to abandon an agriculture that was deemed predatory and mortiferous. The consensus, on the contrary, was to invent an agroecology based on negotiating the relationships between all living beings, both human and non-human.

---

[2] Excerpt from the column 'Les métaphysiques africaines permettent de penser l'identité en mouvement', published in the newspaper *Le Monde* on 15 December 2019.

The political movement thus formed by these thousands of contributors then went on to draw up a 'Universal Declaration of the Rights of the Living' – emphasizing no longer just humans but all living beings, both human and non-human.

Two bodies were then created. One was comprised of representatives randomly selected from among the thousands of contributors to the respective food projects of specific territories. The other was made up of representatives of animals, forests, waterways, plants and other aspects of nature, who, to become these beings' spokespersons, studied them and endeavoured to communicate with them – with some surprising successes – proving that it was right and just to recognize non-human Earthlings as 'intelligent' beings. Above all, they sought to implement an 'ecology of the sentient', dear to the ecologist Jacques Tassin, for whom 'the sentient escapes theorization; it is a reserve of the invisible where fundamental links are forged in the interweaving through which every living being moves: the sentient connects us to each other. [. . .] not to speak of harmony with Nature but rather to seek to regain a place within this living matrix'.[3]

These representatives decided to redesign the world, starting with the one thing that everyone, without exception, does every day: eat, and in order to do so, gather and produce, process, cook and serve food. The way we eat (and organize ourselves to do so) defines the world in which we live. Hence the starting point: What do we want to eat tomorrow? How do we want this food to be produced? What consequences and uncertainties are acceptable to us and our descendants? For this was not about reverting to ancient ways or freezing ourselves in the present time but about collectively defining which changes we wished to undertake in order not to jeopardize future generations.

Gathered in one village, these representatives have now come from all four corners of the earth for a few weeks to cook and eat together and to discuss the 'Universal Declaration'. As the many dishes are brought to the table, the guests take their seats. In the distance, two magpies perched in a tree enjoy the show and comment on the guests' colourful outfits. The day before, one of the participants cooked a dish to which she added a magical ingredient that gives those who eat it the gift of Tita, a character from the novel and film *Como agua para chocolate* – namely the gift of being able to experience through the food one eats the feelings of the person who cooked it. As a result, when the guests start to eat, they suddenly feel overcome with friendliness, benevolence, generosity and

---

[3]   Jacques Tassin, *Pour une écologie du sensible*, Éditions Odile Jacob, 2020.

humour, brimming with laughter, sensual love and poetry. Such were the feelings that prevailed during the preparation of the meal. As the musicians start to play, some participants get up to dance, cheered on by the others. The trees rustle with pleasure, and the birds accompany the music with their songs.

. . . with everyone

Back to reality, in 2020, the Occitanie Region in France organized a citizens' convention to come up with proposals to improve individual and collective well-being, reduce social and territorial divides and restore trust in society and its institutions. One hundred randomly selected citizens discussed their concerns, and it soon became apparent that the issue of food, although not initially mentioned, was taking up a large part of the discussions. Food, which is part of everyone's daily reality several times a day, was increasingly at the centre of questions surrounding health and environmental risks and of the watchwords conveyed in the media. Although all the participants felt both concerned and qualified to talk about food based on their daily practices, they also admitted to being somewhat lost in the maze of discourses and contradictory information. Who should they believe today? How could something as simple as eating have become so complicated? Many of the proposals discussed during this democratic exercise thus implicitly related to food.

This experience taught us two important lessons. The first is that food is a galvanizing topic for rethinking society. Of course, this is undoubtedly particularly true in France, a country so enamoured with the topic of food. But the fact that, in daily life, everyone applies their own set of principles to try to eat well is far more galvanizing for citizens than a more theoretical reflection on the management of natural resources, for example. Food therefore constitutes a good starting point to rethink our relationships with ourselves, with others and with the environment.

The second lesson, as the actual substance of the discussions revealed time and again, is that there is a gap between two completely separate worlds. On the one hand, we have the scholarly discourses of experts warning of risks, activists proposing new standards of conduct and affluent consumers with sufficient financial and cognitive resources to experiment with new food practices. On the other hand, we have the vast majority of the population with limited means – those with little money, space or time to spare to invest in a more sustainable food supply and for whom 'committed' discourse can come across as out of touch with their daily realities. These are precisely the people one meets during these citizens' conventions. Some of them are no longer represented in opinion polls, which are increasingly conducted online and involve long questionnaires. This segment of the population is partly unaccounted for due to its precarious situation, being unable or unwilling to seek emergency food aid. These citizens are growing increasingly resentful of certain stigmatizing discourses, and they are frustrated with not being able to implement dietary and environmental recommendations for lack of resources. Some may even challenge the new standards proposed as a way of turning a blind eye to the gap between what they should do and what they can actually do. This 'Parliament of the Invisible', as historian and sociologist Pierre Rosanvallon put it, feels misunderstood, forgotten and not taken into account.[4] Hence the crucial importance, in the transformation of food systems, of creating inclusive spaces for dialogue and developing proposals that take into account multiple social, generational and cultural realities.

This is the direction that the UNESCO Chair in World Food Systems wishes to pursue in the years to come, approaching food as a formidable daily opportunity to awaken to the diversity and beauty of the world and to eat it . . . with everyone.

---

[4] Pierre Rosanvallon, *Le Parlement des invisibles*, Seuil, 2014.

Index

Note: Page numbers in *italics* refer to Illustrations.